OPERATION MARKET GARDEN

THE LEGEND OF THE WAAL CROSSING

TIM LYNCH

SPELLMOUNT

A great deal has been written and said about *Operation Market Garden* and there are many experts out there. I have been fortunate enough to be able to draw on both their work and their generosity. In particular I would like to thank Jan Bos for his kindness in providing photographs and material that I would otherwise have missed and which help to fill out the story. Readers with an interest in the subject will recognise the debt owed to Robin Neillands, whose 'myth busting' approach to history sparked my own interest in the myths that have emerged from the campaign in Europe in 1944-45. Thanks also to Jon Cooksey, who first suggested I write about the crossing and to Shaun Barrington and the team at Spellmount who took up the idea.

As always, a special thank you to my wife Jacqueline and to Beth and Josh. They held the high ground so that ultimately I crossed the bridge and got the job done.

Author Tim Lynch served with the Army Air Corps in the Falklands and Northern Ireland, after which he returned to university. His studies led to his work in the development of responses to combat-related psychological readjustment problems among veterans. He is the author of numerous articles for magazines such as *Military Illustrated, Armourer* and *Skirmish* and the books *Battlefield Archaeology* (2007), *Silent Skies* (2008) and *Dunkirk 1940: Whereabouts Unknown* (2010).

First published in 2011 by Spellmount,
an imprint of
The History Press
The Mill, Brimscombe Port
Stroud, Gloucestershire, GL5 2QG
www.thehistorypress.co.uk

© Tim Lynch, 2011

British Library Cataloguing in Publication Data.
A catalogue record for this book is available from the British Library.

ISBN 978 0 7524 5825 0

Typesetting and origination by The History Press
Printed in Great Britain

Contents

	Preface	4
Introduction	'A Storm in a Teacup'	8
Chapter One	Over There	15
Chapter Two	From Breaking Out to Breaking Down	30
Chapter Three	From *Comet* to *Market Garden*	57
Chapter Four	Classless Killers and Yard Long Pedigrees	77
Chapter Five	The Operation: 'Best Possible Speed'	98
Chapter Six	A Change of Plan	119
Chapter Seven	'A Very Iffy Situation'	125
Chapter Eight	'Hail Mary, Full of Grace …'	132
Chapter Nine	A Legend is Born	148
Chapter Ten	Aftermath	160
Chapter Eleven	Stories and Histories	168
Chapter Twelve	The Myth of False Gods	174
	Bibliography	183
	Index	189

Preface

In the September 2009 edition of the US magazine *World War II*, an angry reader wrote to complain about its recent review of a ten-volume history of Germany's role in the Second World War. 'I have not read the 12,000 pages,' he admitted, 'but I am guessing they did not even come close to the truth. I am guessing they left out the part where ...' before going on to list various atrocities and concluding 'I am tired of people trying to rewrite history the way they see it.' With a patience and diplomacy one can only admire, the reviewer pointed out that it was 'unnecessary to guess about its contents. The review includes several specific references to volumes in the series that present the Reich's atrocities in context and in detail.' There are, unfortunately, many people out there searching for a reason to take offence. This book will be a critical goldmine for those readers who enjoy being upset when long cherished 'facts' are challenged and who would rather assume a knowledge of history than acquire one.

History is a commodity like any other to be sold in books, documentaries and films to an audience who want to hear a story they can relate to. Fifty years after the end of the Second World War and at a time when America's use of military might to enforce its foreign policy cast it on more questionable moral ground in the eyes of the international community, harking back to a time when it had fought a 'good' war against an identifiably 'evil' regime was a comfort. In an exchange in Brecht's play *The Life of Galileo,* the character of Andrea claims, 'Unhappy the land that has no heroes', to which Galileo replies, 'No, unhappy the land that needs heroes.' Whether America at that time needed heroes is a debate to be conducted elsewhere but whatever the truth, broadcast journalist Tom Brokaw provided a new form of hero worship when he coined the term *The Greatest Generation* (1998) to describe

> America's citizen heroes and heroines who came of age during the Great Depression and the Second World War and went on to build modern America. This generation was united not only by a common purpose, but also by common values – duty, honor, economy, courage, service, love of family and country, and, above all, responsibility for oneself ... At a time in their lives when their days and nights should have been filled with innocent adventure, love, and the lessons of the workaday world, they were fighting in the most primitive conditions possible across the bloodied landscape of France, Belgium, Italy, Austria, and the coral islands of the Pacific. They answered the call to save the world from the two most powerful and ruthless military machines ever assembled, instruments of conquest in the hands of fascist maniacs. They faced great odds and a late start, but they did not protest. They succeeded on every front. They won the war; they saved the world.[1]

Modestly proclaiming this group of Americans to be 'the greatest generation any society has ever produced,' Brokaw's approach proved immensely popular and celebrated a nostalgia for a time when national self esteem was high and the world was divided more easily into good and bad. His view of the isolationist stance many of that generation favoured and their reluctance to oppose the Nazi regime, or of the hundreds of thousands of American men who were investigated for dodging the draft is less clear but the popularity of the notion of the greatest generation quickly caught on. The book was followed almost immediately by Gerald Astor's *The Greatest War: Americans in Combat, 1941–1945* (1999) and an outpouring of veteran memoirs which escalated still further with the success of Steven Spielberg's television series *Band of Brothers* (2001). Based on Stephen Ambrose's book of the same name, the series triggered an entire industry devoted to the memory of the 101st Airborne Division. Although never quite reaching the same mass audience, veterans of the 82nd Airborne followed suit. Soon, the paradigm spawned a mass market for military history aimed at the general reader that is now heavily slanted towards hagiographies lacking the will to question or analyse wisdom passed down from the exalted position of veteran status. In doing so, the war has become mythologized into a great moral crusade. As historian Michael C.C. Adams puts it:

> All societies to some degree reinvent their pasts … Sometimes we conjure up the past in such a way that it appears better than it really was. We forget ugly things we did and magnify the good things. This is wishful thinking, the desire to retell our past not as it was but as we would like it to have been. If the past is remoulded too drastically, it ceases to be real history … Then, through repetition, people come to believe that this partial portrait is the whole landscape of history, and what is forgotten will be thought never to have existed. Such a process happened with World War II, which has been converted over time from a complex, problematic event, full of nuance and debatable meaning, to a simple, shining legend of the Good War. For many, including a majority of survivors from the era, the war years have become America's golden age, a peak in the life of society when everything worked out and the good guys definitely got a happy ending. It was a great war. For Americans it was the best war ever.[2]

It is not, of course, a uniquely American phenomenon; Britain too is guilty of sanitising its past. Peter Fleming, writing about the events of 1940, speaks of how, in terms of the way the British view that time,

> legend plays a large part in their memories of that tense and strangely exhilarating summer, and their experiences, like those of early childhood, are sharply rather than accurately etched upon their minds. The stories they tell of the period have become better, but not more veracious, with the passage of time. Rumours are remembered as facts, and … the sequence of events is blurred.

Excluded from the decision making process and denied access to detailed information,

> the average citizen knew less than usual about what was happening and why it happened. Like a child who is excluded from the confidence of the grown-ups, he accepted the existence of a sphere of knowledge into which he could not be admitted, even though within it his own destinies were being decided; and like a child he tended afterwards to remember events without a full understanding of their significance.[3]

As one veteran put it, his view of the war was limited to 'what I could see through my rifle sights' and anyone who has experienced frontline service is all too aware that the world of the combat soldier is a very small one bounded by his immediate vicinity and governed by the dictum that a sensible soldier should believe nothing of what he hears and only half of what he sees. Few in the frontlines either know or care what the grand strategy might be, nor do they have the time or opportunity to record details. Yet over time, some come to believe that they, and only they, really know what happened in their battle based on their own small part of it. Those not in their direct sight are always suspect. Those further behind the lines are always slackers. Their memories, often recorded decades later, reflect what they have come to believe about their experiences as much as what actually happened.

For a mass market audience, seeking only an exciting story, the 'greatest generation' paradigm is not necessarily a problem. For the serious student of military history, it becomes a significant barrier to understanding. In keeping with the 'greatest generation' myth Phil Nordyke, for example, opens his finely researched and detailed 776-page account of the experiences of the 82nd Airborne Division during the war with the unequivocal assertion that

> The World War II 82nd Airborne Division has legendary status in the honoured fraternity of great American military units … The veterans of the World War II 82nd Airborne Division are held in awe not only by other members of the airborne fraternity, but by countless others in the US and British armies who fought beside them; the citizens of Sicily, Italy, France, Holland and Belgium who were liberated by them; and the German soldiers who fought against them. Having the 82nd fighting alongside of your unit instilled confidence … It is through the words of these veterans that the reader will come to know incredible bravery under fire, an undying devotion to duty and comrades, and some of the most incredible feats of arms ever achieved by any military unit.[4]

Unsurprisingly he finds nothing to fault in any aspect of the 82nd's behaviour during the war – although to his great credit, in memoirs published shortly after the war 82nd veteran Ross Carter freely admitted that whilst their performance in combat was highly efficient, out of action and in dealings with people outside the unit the paratroopers of the 82nd could be arrogant and boorish to a degree he found hard to justify.

As we shall see, the belief that the US servicemen were an elite lay at the very heart of the problems that emerged between the Allies in the European campaign of 1944–45. Over the years the unquestioning acceptance of the notion of the 'greatest generation' has created the impression that US units were universally excellent and filled with highly motivated and skilled soldiers who were needed to balance the ineptitude and timidity of the British in order to free the world. In 1985, for example, US historian Colonel Trevor Dupuy published a study of the relative fighting capabilities of Allied and German troops in which British performance scored badly. However, as Professor David French has shown, Dupuy's criticism of the poor performance by the British 7th and 50th Infantry Divisions is perhaps best explained by the fact that the 7th existed only on paper as part of a deception campaign whilst the 50th's reported poor performance at the Battle of Monte Grande on 16/17 October was affected by their never having landed in Italy and being in transit back to the UK at the time.[5]

Any attempt to challenge received wisdom will inevitably be criticised by some as 'rewriting history', although those who condemn 'revisionist' history seem at a loss to explain why history must be carved in stone and why new information should be ignored.

In going against the idolising of the 'greatest generation', no doubt this book will also be condemned as 'anti-American' by those who use the term as a synonym for 'wrong'. It is not my intent to be anti-American – a term which, in itself is frequently criticised as being the product of a totalitarian mindset and the antithesis of the American value of free speech – but I do challenge some of the more offensive attitudes and behaviour of people who happen to be American. Those two things are very different. The more astute reader will recognise that no attempt is made to spare the blushes of my own countrymen in describing their often equally petty and self-serving actions.

Although I do not subscribe to the belief that we should idolise the 'greatest generation', this does not mean that I do not hold their achievements in the highest regard. I would argue that by creating a myth that the Second World War generation were somehow more noble, courageous and patriotic than those who followed after, their achievements are actually diminished. They achieved great things, we might say, because they were more capable of great things than their children or grandchildren's generation. For a generation of John Wayne-style heroes, storming the Normandy beaches might be all in a day's work. For an ordinary young man, terrified to the point of soiling himself but going ahead anyway because he was determined to do his duty, it was – and is – an awe-inspiring accomplishment. Perhaps, as Max Hastings has suggested, we should consider them more appropriately as the generation to whom the greatest things happened.

I am very much aware, as I sit in my safe, warm office, that we owe a great deal to that generation. Having experienced war on a small scale, I thank God daily that I was never called upon to experience what the soldiers I am writing about endured. My aim in writing this book is not to pass judgement or to score political points. It is to explain, not excuse, the factors that contributed to the failure of Operation *Market Garden* and the decisions made by ordinary human beings, no matter what uniform they wore.

Tim Lynch

Notes
1 Brokaw, T. *The Greatest Generation* (New York: Random House 1998)
2 Adams, M.C.C. 'Postwar Mythmaking About World War II' in Stoler and Gustafson, ed. *Major Problems in the History of World War II* (Cengage Learning 2002) p.432, pp.428–437
3 Fleming, P. *Invasion 1940* (London: Rupert Hart Davies 1957) pp.9–10
4 Nordyke, P. *All American, All the Way* (Zenith Press 2005) pp.1-2
5 Dupuy, T.N. *Numbers, Predictions and War: The use of history to evaluate and predict the outcome of armed conflict* (Fairfax VA:1985) quoted in French, D. *Raising Churchill's Army* (Oxford University Press 2000) pp.8–9

Introduction:
'A Storm in a Teacup'

No American veteran's account of his experiences in Europe during the Second World War seems complete without reference to the fact that his British allies drank tea. Almost invariably at some point in the narrative the author will encounter a group of British soldiers serenely brewing a cuppa – sometimes using china cups and serving freshly toasted crumpets no matter how remote the position – as all around them chaos reigns. Whilst some might regard the ability to hold a tea party under fire as an example of admirable *sang froid,* the reactions described by their American counterparts many years after the event still range from bemused tolerance of British eccentricity to, more commonly, outright hostility. The overwhelming impression one is left with is that the average American GI was annoyed that the British just weren't taking the war seriously enough.

Bud Warneke, a soldier of the 508th Parachute Infantry Regiment of the US 82nd Airborne Division, was typical. Fifty years later he would recall his first time working with British troops; 'They were good soldiers, but compared to us I thought they had a nonchalant attitude about the war. They would stop whatever they were doing, brew some tea with crumpets but then again I did not work with them much.'[1] By the standards of many veteran memoirs, Warnecke's implied criticism of the British attitude is mild; wildly exaggerated stories of British troops breaking off fire fights to toast crumpets are not unknown.[2] By contrast, it was this same casual approach that so impressed Warnecke's commander, General James Gavin. Gavin was to write that these British troops were 'the best soldiers that I saw on either side in the war – not only because of their soldierly qualities, but because of their nonchalance and style; they seemed to enjoy what they were doing, and I shall always remember some of the teas they gave after things had quietened down.'[3]

American soldiers, of course, preferred coffee. Although adequate supplies could be sent from the United States pre-prepared in sealed tins, 32 US Army mobile trailer-mounted coffee roasting and grinding units attached to field bakeries and each operated by six specially trained men began operations in France on 25 July 1944, to ensure a theatre-wide supply of freshly ground coffee. Together with another 37 such units based in the UK, throughout the campaign in northwest Europe the units produced around 90,000lbs per day, every day.[4] Clearly, the Americans were not averse to hot beverages themselves, so why the preoccupation with tea?

Throughout the war in Europe the US generals, or so the story goes, took risks and suffered enormous casualties to get the job done but the British response was slower, more hesitant and timid almost to the point of cowardice. In short, it was left to American boys to save the world at enormous cost to themselves whilst their 'allies' sat back. The image of British troops on their tea break came to symbolise this belief. The more objective US commanders recognised the simple economics of it all. America could still afford casualties,

Britain could not. From its 1939 population of 46 million, the UK had mobilised 4,758,000 men and 559,390 women totalling just under one in nine of Britons serving in the military. Of these, 264,443 were killed – more than 1 in 20 of those mobilised.[5] The United States mobilised 16,112,566 of its 142,164,569 population (about the same proportion as Britain) of whom 405,399 or about 1 in 40 were killed. During the Second World War, the US Navy suffered a total of 36,950 battle deaths, the US Marine Corps some 19,733. By contrast, British *civilian* casualties alone reached 67,073 – over 60,000 of them by the time the first US troops entered Britain.[6] Having fought the war alone for two years and suffered heavily in doing so, it was perhaps not surprising that British forces were becoming war weary.

British leaders were also aware of the economic cost. Every ship, tank, jeep and bullet supplied by the US would have to be paid for once the war was over – and Britain was almost bankrupt. As the US Army tripled in size yet still retained huge reserves, the British were forced to disband some units to provide reinforcements for others. Montgomery had no reserves to replace his losses. Every casualty weakened his army, every loss had to count. The response was a slower, more measured approach. US commanders, aware that any losses could easily be replaced, could afford to take chances. To the average American, however, the story that the British were sitting back, drinking tea and letting them do all the work was attractive. 'In my mind', wrote Lieutenant 'Maggie' Magellas of the US 82nd Airborne Division, 'tea and the deliberate British approach in combat became synonymous.'[7] Almost 70 years on, the legend of US troops fighting heroically whilst their British counterparts brought out their teapots has evolved into accepted fact, nowhere more so than in the story of the failure of the British attempt in September 1944 to race armoured forces over an 'airborne carpet' across the Dutch countryside to cross the Rhine into Germany at the bridge of Arnhem – Operation *Market Garden*.

On 20 September 1944, as part of that operation, men of the 504th Parachute Infantry Regiment of the US 82nd Airborne Division made a bold and valiant daylight crossing of the river Waal in flimsy boats under heavy fire to secure the Nijmegen bridge and open the route to the besieged British 1st Airborne Division at Arnhem. Once the paratroopers had established control of the northern end of the bridge, tanks of the Guards Armoured Brigade dashed over the span from the south – fully expecting the bridge to be blown beneath them and with no room to even attempt to evade the heavy fire directed at them all the way across.

After their link up with the paratroopers, the British tanks pushed forward, only to be stopped on the single narrow route open to them by anti-tank fire from a German roadblock north of Lent. Without infantry support to neutralise the hidden gun, they pulled back. According to Captain T. Moffatt Burriss, an American company commander of the 504th, 'That's when the British tank crews brought out their teapots. I was furious.' In a dramatic, colourful and vehemently anti-British memoir, he describes meeting a tank commander:

> 'I can't go on without orders,' he said. 'OK,' I said, 'I'm giving you orders.' He was a British captain. I was an American captain. He wasn't about to recognise my authority. 'No,' he said, 'I have to have orders from my British commander ...' I looked him straight in the eye. 'You yellow-bellied son of a bitch. I've just sacrificed half my company in the face of dozens of guns, and you won't move because of one gun.' Then I cocked my tommy gun, put it to his head, and said, 'You get this tank moving, or I'll blow your damn head off.'[8]

In the mythology of American veterans who took part in the campaign, this was the moment that doomed *Market Garden* to failure and proved that the US alone had the drive,

A British tank crewman, kettle in hand, struggles through the mud to find water for tea.

professionalism and courage to win the war. Even today, there remains a widely held belief that where Montgomery failed, Patton would surely have succeeded and, if evidence is needed, the memories of veterans of the Waal crossing are invoked as irrefutable evidence of British incompetence and timidity holding back their allies. But how true is the legend of the Waal?

The story of Operation *Market Garden* has been told and retold many times by writers with far greater tactical experience than this author. It has also, thanks to the internet, received the attention of a great many individuals with no tactical knowledge whatsoever (or often, it seems, even a passing acquaintance to factual information about the subject). With what Gregory Blaxland once termed 'the fraudulent benefit of hindsight' and the wealth of information now in the public domain that was not available to decision makers at the time, pointing the finger of blame has become a popular pastime. The debate usually takes the lines of highly partisan arguments fuelled by national pride and/or inter-service rivalry between British and US armies and air forces and, perhaps most of all, between airborne and ground troops. Arguments rage as to whether it was a British defeat caused by incompetence or a German victory brought about by a superbly improvised and rapid response or whether Patton would, as one overexcited contributor to an internet forum claimed 'have been stood in Arnhem watching the British land and asking what had kept them.' In such forums one quickly gains the impression that Patton would not have needed the bridges but could simply walked over the various waterways, parting the waves behind him for his unstoppable tanks to follow. In discussing *Market Garden*, emotions run high and it will be some considerable time before objective discussions become the norm. In the meantime, whatever the reader's preferred conclusion, ample evidence exists to support it. It is not the intention of this book to tread that well worn path by rehashing the decisions made at command level using the benefit of hindsight to show how failure was inevitable.

Instead, this book adopts an approach first put forward 140 years ago by the French officer and military theorist Charles Jean Jacques Joseph Ardant du Picq. Until his death at the Battle of Metz on 15 August 1870, du Picq studied closely the 'moral and psychological' aspects of battle at the small unit level and his ideas would prove highly influential for the generation who fought the First World War. Essentially, his argument was that whatever technological or tactical advances might be made, human nature remains the same and that an understanding of psychology was vital to the successful management of troops in battle. In *Battle Studies*, published posthumously in 1870, du Picq claimed that

> The smallest detail taken from an actual incident in war is more instructive to me, a soldier, than all the Thiers and Jominis in the world. They speak for the heads of states and armies, but they never show me what I wish to know – a battalion, company or platoon in action … The man is the first weapon of battle. Let us study the soldier for it is he who brings reality to it.[9]

Military histories have tended to describe how objective X was taken by Y Battalion. As a description of events it is a valid approach but in reality, the objective was not taken by an anonymous, homogenous mass called Y Battalion, rather it was taken by the men serving in it – by Tom, Dick and Harry. In contrast, Bill, Fred and George in Z Battalion might have failed. In a series of lectures on military psychology delivered a century ago, Captain LeRoy Eltinge observed that 'on successive days, even, the same body of men will break the first day with a loss of 5 per cent and the next, fight its way to victory, in spite of a loss of 40 per cent' and concluded that 'A leader's knowledge of war is incomplete, if in addition to his skill in conceiving technical combinations he does not possess a knowledge of the human heart, if he have not the power of gauging the momentary temper of his own troops.'[10]

This book, then, explores the reality of the Waal crossing, the myths that have grown around it and what the two between them tell us about the wider war in Europe in 1944–5. To paraphrase Epictetus, history is defined not by events, but by the view people take of them. By applying a forensic examination to the 'smallest details' of the testimonies of those who took part in the Waal crossing, we gain an insight into factors that become so very telling. Why, for example, did Captain Burris immediately assume that cowardice was the only reason for the tanks to fall back? Why did he assume he had any authority over a man of equal rank? Why do two of the most outspoken US veterans of the crossing complain of British delays repeatedly stalling the crossing from an original start at 0800hrs when another veteran, Captain Kappel, reports that the warning order was not issued until 0900hrs for a crossing 'that afternoon' or indeed when the after action report of the engineers assigned to operate the boats notes that they were specifically briefed at 0600hrs to be ready for a crossing at 1400hrs? Why is much made of the difficulties faced by the US troopers in handling the unfamiliar craft when Gavin himself had refused an offer to supply experienced British engineers to operate them? Was this a failure of the British to meet their obligations as the legend claims, or was it a problem amongst the men of the 504th?

The term 'elite' is widely used in military history but rarely defined. In examining the story of the Waal crossing, we will see that both the British and US units involved were considered, not least by themselves, to be elites, but by very different definitions of the term. Regardless of the (usually self-selected) criteria for defining oneself as part of an elite, the effect is the same. Outsiders are automatically inferior. In the following account we will explore the very different cultures that had developed in the two armies and how this influenced their attitudes to each other and the operation.

To do that, however, we need to first understand the wider context, not just of Operation *Market Garden*, but of the political and military climate in which the entire campaign took place. Both armies fought on behalf of democratic countries and political interference in military decision making was commonplace – indeed many of Britain's early setbacks in the war can be traced to Churchill's enthusiastic if incompetent directions to the General Staff. So, too, it is argued, Eisenhower's contention that 'public opinion wins wars' created a situation in which journalists became, in his words, 'quasi-staff officers'. By extension, editors of American newspapers came to heavily influence, if not directly determine, military strategy in what was a US election year.

Compounding the problem was the cult of personality surrounding the leading Allied generals and a competition for personal glory, whatever the cost to the men under their command. The intense loathing and rivalry between Montgomery and Patton was a decisive factor in the failure of *Market Garden*. Patton's powerful influence on his senior, Bradley, and their boasting about actively having sabotaged at least one airborne operation, as we shall see, highlights their vested interest in an airborne failure in order to divert resources to their own ends. Patton's drive for personal glory openly rewarded his men for stealing supplies from other American units to ensure that his army stayed ahead of the rest – even at the cost of leaving their countrymen at risk. Although the behaviour of the two men forms part of this account, the wider implications of their respective personalities have been discussed in far greater detail elsewhere than space permits here. It is important to recognise that Montgomery was a master of the logistical battle and a competent all-round general but was sometimes slow to exploit success. Patton was a superb cavalry leader but, like Rommel before him, was essentially a 'one-trick pony', good in pursuit warfare but, as the experience at Metz amply demonstrates, totally unable to cope with organised resistance. Both Patton and Rommel placed the taking of ground over the need to maintain lines of communication and both tank experts ultimately failed because each outran his supply chain – Rommel in North Africa, Patton in France.

Between them, Montgomery and Patton could have made a formidable team but whatever their individual abilities, both men actively sought to create celebrity status and exploited it to the maximum in order to get their own way in often childish displays, throwing tantrums and using national politics to browbeat the Supreme Commander, Eisenhower. Forced by his subordinates into a diplomatic rather than military command, Eisenhower's strategy was determined primarily to appease the US media and became so reliant on finding compromises that it almost certainly prolonged the war by several months.

The crossing of the Waal during Operation *Market Garden* is rightly seen as a magnificent feat of arms but it was far from unprecedented. At the start of the war German assault pioneers had crossed the Albert Canal under the guns of Eben Emael in daylight on rafts improvised from doors and tables salvaged from nearby houses, with results every bit as spectacular as those achieved at Nijmegen. Like so many gallant actions throughout history, the crossing itself may have been a professional affair, but it was made necessary by earlier mistakes and was very probably avoidable. The vehemence with which British ground performance on Operation *Market Garden* is criticised by the stories of the 82nd Airborne and by many historians serves perfectly to deflect attention away from the simple fact that the plan called for the bridges to be taken 'with thunderclap surprise'. The two Nijmegen bridges weren't. On D-Day, 17 September, only one reinforced platoon was sent – over six hours after the landings were completed – to probe the area around the road bridge. No effort at all was made to capture the nearby rail bridge until D+3 (three days after the landings).

In his own account, General Gavin admits that his plan was, in effect, to leave the armoured force to take it themselves whilst his men remained in position around their own drop zones. It is telling that much is made in histories of the US airborne of the visit by General Dempsey of the British Second Army to the 82nd's commander General James Gavin after the battle at Nijmegen. 'He greeted me warmly,' Gavin recalled, 'with the statement, "I'm proud to meet the Commanding General of the finest division in the world today."' A staff officer nearby overheard the remark and it quickly became part of the 82nd's mythology. Gavin, however, was not so sure. To his credit, in a tacit acknowledgement that the battle had been mishandled he continues; 'I accepted it with reservations, believing that he was being too kind.'[11] Gavin is widely viewed as a superb combat leader and his many admirers have chosen to interpret his remark as the modesty of a great man. His performance during the battle on the ground does him great credit but, as we shall see, Gavin's reservations were not the product of false modesty. It is not too great an exaggeration to say that his confused orders to the 508th concerning the bridges lost the 82nd the element of surprise and thereby the opportunity for a quick and easy victory. If any one decision can be claimed to have fatally undermined Operation *Market Garden*, it was Gavin's decision not to prioritise the crucial bridges at Nijmegen on D-Day.

As du Picq claimed, an analysis of the seemingly trivial details that emerge from the story of a military action tells us more about the men involved than any amount of tactical description ever could. The angry abuse heaped by veterans of the 82nd on their allies, understandable enough at the time, is less so repeated over half a century later. But by exploring the political, military and social context in which the operation took place we will see how the story of an American force let down by Montgomery's men suited the mythology that had developed within the alliance and allowed his arch-rival Patton to enhance his own reputation accordingly.

From the outset it was not in US interests for Operation *Market Garden* to succeed. If it had, Montgomery would be proved right and Patton et al would have been forced to suffer supply shortages that would have effectively brought them to a halt. That was a scenario totally unacceptable to them or to the American public so it is interesting to speculate on how a success might have been received at SHAEF and whether the will really existed to follow up a British-led entry into Germany. Certainly historian Major-General Julian Thompson has questioned whether, had Patton been assigned the northerly route instead of Montgomery, Operation *Market Garden* might have turned out very differently – not because of greater generalship but because the will to halt the secondary advance in order to pour resources into one strong thrust would have been far more evident if it had been for an American-led offensive. As it was, resources were not fully diverted to Montgomery because the Supreme Commander wanted to appease Patton. As a result, the planned advances by VIII and XII Corps on either flank of XXX Corps were limited expeditions unable to provide the protection that might have allowed the main thrust to concentrate on reaching Arnhem rather than fighting one battle to keep its supply lines open, another to take the Nijmegen bridges and a third to complete its primary task.

There is, of course, no evidence to suggest that the plan was deliberately sabotaged – it hardly needed to be. There were a great many factors that could go wrong and most of them did. Responsibility lies with the British for the failure of the operation. But if one mistake alone can be said to have doomed the entire operation, it was the failure to capture the Waal bridges when the opportunity arose on D-Day. Given the powerfully anti-British sentiments expressed in their memoirs, the question is: did the men of the 82nd assume that British failure was a foregone conclusion and plan their own defensive battle accordingly?

The disastrous outcome for Montgomery's men served another purpose. Then, as now, the heavy losses at Arnhem drew attention away from Patton's own mismanagement of operations around Metz. Although the fortifications could have been sidestepped, Patton's openly stated belief that he was the reincarnation of a long line of expert warriors blinded him to any other course of action than to be the first in 1000 years to reduce the fortifications and to take Metz by force – the fact that in 1944 the French forts were filled with Germans suggests that a frontal assault using brute force and ignorance was not the only way to take them but that does not seem to have been considered. Claiming the need to 'blood' his new reinforcements, Patton pushed his men into a largely pointless battle that served primarily to delay the US advance and allow the Germans time to build up forces in preparation for the counter blow that would fall in the Ardennes that winter. With attention firmly focused on the British failure at Arnhem, no-one in the outside world noticed.

'Years later,' wrote Gavin, 'when new cadet barracks were built at the United States Military Academy at West Point, American victories in World War II were commemorated by having granite sally ports through the barracks named after them. The name of the battle was etched above the passageway. Strangely, Arnhem was one of those selected, thus perpetuating the myth that Arnhem was a great victory, but this time an American victory.'[12] Who could regard Arnhem as a victory?

However many times the logistical and tactical problems of the operation are re-examined, the outcome can never be changed. What is perhaps more important to an understanding of why things went wrong comes in an understanding of the attitudes, beliefs and motivation of the men taking part. In a new age of coalition warfare, the way we choose to interpret the events of the past and apply the lessons they teach today assumes a vital significance.

Notes

1 Astor, G. *The Greatest War: Americans in Combat, 1941–1945* (Novato, CA: Presidio Press 1999) p.681

2 From US accounts we could conclude that British soldiers seem remarkably resourceful in finding crumpets in the front line and there may be an element of jealousy as no GI appears to have carried a stock of doughnuts in his kit.

3 Horrocks, Gen Sir B. *Corps Commander* (London: Magnum Books 1977) p.102

4 US War Department. Operational Study No.17 Bakery and Coffee Roasting Operations. (1 November 1945)

5 Corrigan, G. *Blood, Sweat and Arrogance and the Myths of Churchill's War* (London: Phoenix 2007) p.472

6 US Statistics based on 'American War and Military Operations Casualties: Lists and Statistics' prepared by Ann Leland and MJ Oboroceanu of the Congressional Research Service on 26 February 2010. Figures for total numbers of British forces are difficult to obtain since they could include Commonwealth and attached forces. Those given here are taken from official statistics quoted in Howlett, P. *Fighting with Figures: A Statistical Digest of the Second World War* (London: HMSO 1995). Civilian casualty figures from the Commonwealth War Graves Commission. The figure of 60,000 civilian casualties is taken from 'Instructions for US Servicemen in Britain' issued by the War Department, Washington 1942

7 Magellas, J. *All the Way to Berlin* (New York: Ballantyne Books 2003) p.198

8 Burriss, T.M. *Strike and Hold* (Dulles: Brassey's 2000) pp.123–4

9 du Picq, Colonel A. *Battle Studies: Ancient and Modern Battle* translated from the 8th Edition by Colonel JN. Greeley and Major R.C. Cotton, US Army 1921. Accessed via Project Gutenburg at: http://onlinebooks.library.upenn.edu/webbin/gutbook/lookup?num=7294

10 Eltinge, Captain LeRoy. *Psychology of War* Department of Military Art. The Army Service Schools Fort Leavenworth, Kansas 1911

11 Gavin, J. *On to Berlin* (New York: Bantam 1979) p.204

12 Ibid p207

Chapter One

Over There

'We won't be over till it's over over there.'
Sheet music by Earl Watters and Ken Bradshaw, Bloomington Illinois 1940

When Britain went to war with Germany in August 1914, the US declared its neutrality. There was little else President Woodrow Wilson could have done at the time but follow the long-established isolationist foreign policy set out by George Washington in 1796:

> The great rule of conduct for us in regard to foreign nations is in extending our commercial relations, to have with them as little political connection as possible. So far as we have already formed engagements, let them be fulfilled with perfect good faith. Here let us stop. Europe has a set of primary interests which to us have none; or a very remote relation ... Our detached and distant situation invites and enables us to pursue a different course. If we remain one people under an efficient government the period is not far off when we may defy material injury from external annoyance; when we may take such an attitude as will cause the neutrality we may at any time resolve upon to be scrupulously respected; when belligerent nations, under the impossibility of making acquisitions upon us, will not lightly hazard the giving us provocation; when we may choose peace or war, as our interest, guided by justice, shall counsel. Why forego the advantages of so peculiar a situation? Why quit our own to stand upon foreign ground? Why, by interweaving our destiny with that of any part of Europe, entangle our peace and prosperity in the toils of European ambition, rivalship, interest, humor or caprice? It is our true policy to steer clear of permanent alliances with any portion of the foreign world.[1]

The belief that the US stood apart from the problems of the old world was reinforced in 1823 by what became known as the Monroe Doctrine – President James Monroe's declaration that America had no need to become part of any European war or to enter into alliances with the European powers. Its geographical position, it was argued, protected it from the threat of invasion and its immigrant population should owe no particular allegiance to their former homelands. 'The position of the Americans is therefore quite exceptional,' wrote the French political theorist Alexis de Tocqueville in 1831,

> ... and it may be believed that no democratic people will ever be placed in a similar one. Their strictly Puritanical origin, their exclusively commercial habits, even the country they inhabit, which seems to divert their minds from the pursuit of science, literature, and the arts, the proximity of Europe, which allows them to neglect these pursuits without relapsing into barbarism, a thousand special causes, of which I have only been able to point out the most

important, have singularly concurred to fix the mind of the American upon purely practical objects. His passions, his wants, his education, and everything about him seem to unite in drawing the native of the United States earthward; his religion alone bids him turn, from time to time, a transient and distracted glance to heaven. Let us cease, then, to view all democratic nations under the example of the American people.[2]

In establishing itself as the model for world democracy, de Tocqueville argued, the ordinary people of the US had been given too much power to be prepared to defer to others and had chosen the acquisition of wealth over the development of talent and ability as the driving force behind their political actions. Their culture promoted equality, he claimed, but the same mores and opinions that ensured such equality also promoted what he termed a 'middling mediocrity'. True power lay not in the hands of those best prepared for it, but rather decisions were made in the interests of the individual, not those of the greater society. Despite its criticism of democracy as practised in the US, de Tocqueville's work firmly established the concept of 'American exceptionalism' and with it the belief still held that the United States were, and are, qualitatively different from other countries and therefore cannot be judged by the same standards as those applied elsewhere.

Alongside this notion of exceptionalism, in 1845 journalist John L. O'Sullivan coined the phrase 'manifest destiny' to describe what he saw as the divine right of the American people to occupy the whole of the North American continent, used as justification for the annexation of Texas. Later, it became the ideology behind the incorporations of California, Nevada, Utah, Arizona, New Mexico, Colorado and Wyoming from Mexico and for a series of boundary disputes with Canada. Having spread from sea to shining sea, America began to look overseas and by then, 'manifest destiny' had created 'an almost mystical sense that America had a mission to spread freedom and democracy everywhere.'[3] With an influx of immigration from Europe, establishing a national identity would be difficult. Instead, Americans came to define themselves by what they were not. They were not British.

In a letter to John Banister in 1778, Washington stated that the 'injuries we have received from the British nation were so unprovoked, and have been so great and so many, that they can never be forgotten'. Later, another President, Thomas Jefferson, would claim 'I considered the British as our natural enemies, and as the only nation on earth who wished us ill from the bottom of their souls. And I am satisfied that were our continent to be swallowed up by the ocean, Great Britain would be in a bonfire from one end to the other.'[4] As the American sense of national identity became established, the tyranny of Britain and its empire became the yardstick by which foreign policy was judged. Whilst the British empire was exploitative and wrong, US expansion overseas in the late nineteenth century was openly portrayed as part of its divinely inspired 'manifest destiny', with President McKinley expressly using the term to justify the annexation of Hawaii in 1898 and claiming the territory to be even more important to the US than California had been. It also served to underline the need to intervene in the Philippines, which was explained in terms of needing to 'protect' Filipinos from exploitation by the colonial powers. The empires of the old world, it was argued, were 'justified as a benevolent "white man's burden". And in the United States, empire does not even exist; "we" are merely protecting the causes of freedom, democracy, and justice worldwide.'[5] (Ironically, the inherent racism of the 'white man's burden' takes its name from a poem satirising American imperialism by British poet Rudyard Kipling and was written about the US intervention in the Philippines.) Throughout their shared history Anglo-American relations have been defined by antipathy toward Britain's overseas empire. The declaration of war in 1914 offered a chance to finally bring it down.

At the start of the twentieth century, the United States had developed two distinct markets. Geographically, the east coast of America is closer to Europe than it is to its own west coast and many fortunes were based on trade and commerce with the old world. For centuries, the Royal Navy had dominated the seas, using blockades of shipping as its main weapon in times of war. The Atlantic was a gigantic moat isolating the US from the threat of invasion, but it was also British turf. If the Royal Navy chose to interfere with trade to virtually any nation, it could use its considerable strength to do so. For those in the west, China and the Far East offered the greater market and, as a result a rivalry sprang up between the US and Japan. Aware of the potential for Russian influence in the Pacific, Britain was concerned about the risks to its interests in Hong Kong and the Chinese markets and even to Singapore. In 1905, in the wake of the war between Russia and Japan, it signed a mutual protection treaty with the Japanese and renewed it in 1911. This relieved the pressure on the Royal Navy to maintain a presence in the Far East and in return Japanese ships were built in British yards and their officers trained with the Royal Navy.

The geographic isolation that meant the US did not have to rely on alliances with foreign powers also meant that its trade routes were now vulnerable. Worse still, according to H. W. Wilson, the presence of strategic British territories in Canada, the Caribbean and the Falkland Islands 'interfered with the political plan of the plutocracy of the United States. That plan, as was explained by President Polk, Secretary Fish, Secretary Olney and other developers of the Monroe Doctrine, aimed at the absorption of both Northern and Southern America by the United States.' As a result of comments made in 1895 by Robert Olney, the 'ABC League' was formed by three South American countries (Argentina, Brazil and Chile) specifically to unite against possible aggression by the United States. The three sought support from Britain and France in return for concessions on oil in their countries and their fears of a possible attack were raised further by the American intervention in Mexico. War was avoided by President Wilson's refusal to allow the situation to escalate but still, many in the US military – particularly the navy – had their sights on complete domination of the western hemisphere and this meant challenging the Royal Navy. The underlying principle of US foreign policy in the first half of the twentieth century therefore became inextricably linked with the aim of destroying Britain's naval dominance.

When war broke out in 1914, the problems of Europe were remote and of little interest to Americans on the West Coast. The Midwest had been settled by large numbers of German immigrants fleeing the Junker regime in Prussia in the 1850s followed by a second wave of southern Germans in the 1870s. By 1907, the National German-American Alliance, according to an article in the *New York Times* of 2 March 1918, was

> … working to awaken a sense of unity among the people of German origin in America; to 'centralize' their powers for the 'energetic defense of such justified wishes and interests' as are not contrary to the rights and duties of good citizens; to defend its class against 'nativistic encroachments'; to 'foster and assure good, friendly relations of America to the old German fatherland.

By then it had received a Federal charter and boasted a membership of around three million members.[6]

In the states where the alliance was most active, popular support for Germany was such that as late as January 1916, when America seemed likely to be drawn into the conflict, Republican Homer Mann from Missouri openly told Congress that if the United States went to war at all, it should be against Britain, not Germany.[7]

After German raiders shelled towns on the North Sea coast of Britain, Americans on the East Coast realised that whilst the Atlantic might be a barrier, modern ships could reach US waters easily enough and the problems of Europe seemed suddenly less remote. Here, the British and French were generally regarded positively as democratic powers against the German autocratic system exemplified by the rule of the Junkers that had seen so many Germans emigrate. Support, however, was far from universal. Media coverage in a country so vast was parochial and heavily influenced by the attitudes of the newspaper barons who controlled local media outlets and by the advertisers who provided their main source of income. The Hearst press empire, for example, was so strongly pro-German that at least one of its journalists, Albert A Sander, was actually a paid German agent working on behalf of German intelligence.[8]

What concerned everyone, however, was the effect of the war on trade. As always when Britain went to war, the Royal Navy had immediately put in place a blockade to prevent the importation of war materiel to Germany. During the American Civil War, the US Navy had blockaded Confederate ports and seized the cargoes of neutral ships as contraband if they suspected that the goods might be forwarded to the Confederate states. Amongst the goods classified as contraband was cotton on the sole basis that it formed the foundation of the Confederate economy. The impact on the Lancashire cotton industry was catastrophic for British workers and the national economy but, having expressed sympathy with the abolition of slavery, the British government did little to contest the practice. When the British now used a similar tactic against Germany, it provoked a storm of outrage from US industrialists unable to reach the German market. 'The general opinion in Britain and in France,' one British observer wrote, 'was that the American wanted it both ways, with a special law for himself when he was at war, and a very different law for belligerents when he was a trading neutral.'[9]

Although Americans protested the blockade, it was legal under international law. Despite it, the US continued to trade with both sides but the blockade and the growing dependence of the Allies on the US for supplies of food, ammunition and weapons meant that by 1916, most of its dealings were with Britain and France. It was a very healthy trade, too. As Britain's gold reserves fell by £42 million between 1914 and 1918, America's grew by £278.5 million in the same period.[10] However, trading with a belligerent is not the same as siding with them. During 1915 anecdotal stories began to circulate along the western front of American-made shells filled with sand and of men systematically weeding out US-made ammunition to prevent machine-gun stoppages caused by inferior charges. Irish militants and German-Americans were suspected of actively sabotaging the British war effort.

Throughout the blockade the British did not sink merchant ships or kill their crews, but increasingly German U-boats did both. From February 1915, the submarine war began in earnest with the start of unrestricted warfare against shipping crossing the Atlantic. Protests from the US brought it to a halt in September but it began again in 1916. Finally, in 1917, a telegram was intercepted by British intelligence from the German Foreign Minister, Zimmerman, to their embassy in Washington which described how attempts should be made to keep America neutral but to make approaches to Mexico to discuss a German-supported attack should President Wilson decide to enter the war. In return, Mexico would be given back its lost territory in Texas and Arizona. In March, a copy of the telegram was passed to the US ambassador in London and a political storm broke across America. Whilst many on the East Coast reacted with shock, Hearst-owned newspapers immediately declared it a British fake and Congress, choosing to believe the newspapers, refused to pass a bill to arm merchant ships for self defence against U-boats. Incredibly, soon afterwards at a press conference in Berlin, Zimmerman freely admitted that it was genuine. It was an open threat that could not be ignored. (For the remarkable story of the Zimmerman telegram see *'Blinker' Hall: Spymaster* by David Ramsay.) By 1917, Britain and France were heavily in debt to US businesses. It was obvious that, should they fall, the chances of those debts being repaid were slim. Industrialists needed a return on their investment and the Zimmerman telegram clinched the deal. America would need to be in at the kill so that it could emerge as a world power but also so it could profit from the credit it had extended to the Allies. On 6 April 1917, America declared war on Germany.

At the time of its declaring war, the US Army was small. 'Our army,' one American observer noted, 'was less than Field-Marshal French's first seven divisions, and the sole powder plant owned by the War Department had a daily capacity of 11,000lbs – not enough to last the guns of New York harbor for one minute of firing.'[11] As the army rapidly expanded, it was clear that it would lack trained and experienced leaders and it was proposed by the British that raw American battalions should be seconded to their brigades to gain combat experience. Next, these now combat-ready battalions could form a brigade within a British division. Eventually, American divisions would be formed under British Corps and so on until finally a separate, fully formed and battle-ready US Army would be put into the field. It was a sensible military suggestion endorsed by the US commander, General John 'Black Jack' Pershing, who could see the logic in having his men gain from the hard won experience of the British. It was, however, wholly unacceptable to American politicians. They were, they insisted, not an 'Ally' of the British and French, but 'an associate power' – a distinction that meant they would be in a position to broker a separate peace deal when the enemy finally collapsed. Pershing was disappointed and secretly did what he could to ensure that his troops had the opportunity to work alongside British and French units but later wrote that had the request for the commitment of American troops to the Third Battle of Ypres been accepted, it could have ended the war in 1917.[12]

As it was, American troops would now learn the hard way as they were pushed forward across open fields in extended line, just as the British had at the Somme and with the same disastrous results. Of the 43 US divisions sent to France in 1918, the 1st and 2nd Divisions suffered most with each losing over 20,000 dead and wounded. Next came the 93rd Division with 591 killed following its arrival in March. In June, the 92nd Division became active and lost 182 men. Ten divisions, though – almost one in four of those committed – lost not a single man to enemy action. The greatest contribution of the United States was not in the field but in the threat to Germany posed by the potential arrival of up to 100 fresh new US divisions. It was not what America brought to the war, but what it *could* bring that forced Germany's hand.

By entering the war as an associate power, President Wilson was in a position to broker a separate peace deal with Germany, and in January 1918 he laid out his famous 'fourteen points' which would form the basis of peace negotiations. These were prepared without reference to Britain or France and seemed reasonable enough to the American public – and especially so to the US Navy. Amongst the points was the demand for 'Absolute freedom of navigation upon the seas' which, at a stroke, would destroy Britain's chief weapon of blockade and seriously undermine Britain's naval power. It was the only point that Britain refused to consider. Had Germany accepted the proposals at that point, the British and French would have been left in a very difficult situation. Instead, the war dragged on.

When Germany surrendered, President Wilson was keen to extricate the US from Europe as quickly as possible and to resume trade links with Germany. As a result, he sought leniency for the Germans and regarded many of the demands made by France and Britain

A British tank parades through the centre of New York as part of a War Loans drive, 1917.

for reparations as being unduly harsh, although by comparison with those drawn up earlier in the war by Germany to impose on the allies, it was remarkably restrained. Amongst those present, Marshal Foch of France argued for a much more robust and punitive plan declaring, with chilling accuracy, 'This is not Peace. It is an Armistice for 20 years.'[13] Reverting to a policy of isolationism, the US refused to ratify the Treaty of Versailles and thereby fatally undermined the effectiveness of the planned League of Nations despite Wilson's warning that he could 'predict with absolute certainty that within another generation there will be another world war if the nations of the world do not concert the method by which to prevent it'.[14] In doing so, the US government reverted to its belief in its own exceptionalism. The other countries of the world needed to work together to sort out their problems, it argued, but America stood apart.

The US was the only major participant to emerge from the war having made a profit and consequently usurped Britain's position as the world's chief creditor nation whilst Britain itself was in severe financial difficulties. Its Italian allies could not repay war loans made to them whilst its Russian allies blankly refused to, yet Britain in turn was in debt to the US and could not avoid its obligations. Cost cutting measures were needed across the board. By August 1919, the Royal Navy had scrapped some 400 vessels of various types whilst defence chiefs planned a 33 battleship Royal Navy at an annual cost of £171 million. They got £84.5 million and the imposition of a rule that defence spending would be based on an assumption of no major war for the next ten years. America now grabbed its chance to destroy Britain as a naval power.

Realising the economic problems Britain faced, the US Navy started an expansion programme, knowing that if Britain attempted to keep pace she would be bankrupted but if she failed, she would have to concede control of the sea to America. As an island nation with an overseas empire, Britain could not sit back and allow itself to be overtaken. A new ship building programme got under way. Then, in 1922, the US invited the major naval powers – Britain, France, Italy and Japan – to a conference in Washington to discuss limitations to naval armament. The conference decided there should be parity between the British and

American navies but set a lower quota of battleships for the Japanese, French and Italian navies along with a ten-year moratorium on the building of warships. It also set down the maximum size of battleships, cruisers and aircraft carriers and limited the size of the gun armament on existing ships. For Britain, dependent on maintaining its naval power in order to protect its overseas trade, the decision was a potentially dangerous one, but based on the belief that further conferences would address air and land forces it was deemed an acceptable risk and an economic necessity. For the first time in history, Britain was forced to accept parity rather than superiority in determining its defence needs, but it was parity on paper only. The Americans then proposed to reduce fleet sizes by setting limits to overall tonnage. It was a clever trap. America and Japan could do so by cutting back on ships ordered but not built. Britain, however, would have to scrap existing ships and would not be in a position to modernise what was left because of the moratorium. At any other time, it would have been rejected out of hand but Britain simply could not afford to challenge it. By manipulating the negotiations, the US delegates had been able to convince the Japanese that the British had let them down by agreeing a much smaller limit in ship numbers than Japan had expected. With the Anglo-Japanese treaty broken and the Royal Navy rendered almost toothless, Anglophobes in the US Navy had achieved their goal.

In 1930 the London Naval Conference extended the terms of the Washington conference to last until 1936 and Britain, now hit by the effects of the worldwide economic slump, agreed to reduce its fleet of cruisers to 50 – much against the wishes of the Admiralty who pointed out that cutbacks had already had a serious impact on the economy with the shipbuilding, steel and engineering industries and specialist manufacturers of guns, ammunition and naval equipment all being badly hit. The following year, the First Sea Lord, Sir Frederick Field, claimed in a report to the Committee of Imperial Defence that the Royal Navy had declined not only in relative strength compared to other Great Powers but that 'owing to the operation of the 'ten-year-decision' and the claimant need for economy, our absolute strength also has ... been so diminished as to render the fleet incapable, in the event of war, of efficiently affording protection to our trade.'[15] Field also claimed that the navy was below the standard required for keeping open Britain's sea communications during wartime; that if the navy moved to the East to protect the Empire there would not be enough ships to protect the British Isles and its trade from attack; and that no port in the entire British Empire was 'adequately defended'.

A few months after Field's report, Lieutenant-Colonel Ishiwara Kanji, commander of the Japanese garrison at Kwantung in Southern Manchuria, was instrumental in manufacturing the 'Mukden Incident' of 18 September by sabotaging the South Manchurian Railway. Having provoked a confrontation with the Chinese, the Kwantung force used the incident as a pretext for an invasion. In London, Prime Minister Ramsay MacDonald quickly recognised the potential threat to Britain's empire in the Far East and tried to have the Ten Year Rule abolished because he thought the international situation meant it was no longer justified. This was bitterly opposed by Foreign Secretary Arthur Henderson who succeeded in keeping the rule in place for the time being.[16]

Hitler's rise to power in Germany in January 1933 gave the Chiefs of Staff still more reason to press for a strong defence policy. On 14 October, they produced their annual review prepared, as usual, with assistance from the Foreign Office and in it warned that Germany would surely rearm to the point where, in a few years, it could start a war in Europe. Two days later, almost as if in response, Germany withdrew from both the League of Nations and the ongoing Geneva Disarmament Conference. Hitler's unilateral blow to ventures in which Britain had invested heavily forced the government to agree in November

1933, some 20 months after having abandoned the Ten Year Rule, to establish the Defence Requirements Committee to examine the country's defences with the aim not of preparing for war, but rather to 'prepare a programme for meeting our worst deficiencies' and basing its recommendations for the time being on prioritising 'the defence of our possessions and interests in the Far East; European commitments; the defence of India.' Furthermore, 'no expenditure should for the present be incurred on measures of defence required to provide exclusively against attack by the United States, France or Italy.'[17] Simply put, the British needed to consider the strategic threats posed by Germany and Japan but could not afford to contemplate any other hypothetical dangers.

Now, as the situation in Europe and the Far East deteriorated, the US began to consider how it would respond to any future war. Increasingly America had cut herself off from the European economy with the Johnson Act of 1934 prohibiting any further loans to states that had not fully repaid war debts, thereby cutting off credit to every European state except Finland so that American investment in Canada alone was 50 per cent higher than in the whole of Europe combined.[18] In March of that year, *Fortune* magazine published 'Arms and Man', a bitter attack on the armaments moguls whose motto, the article suggested, was: 'When there are wars, prolong them; when there is peace, disturb it.' Gerald Nye, the populist Senator from North Dakota, introduced a resolution for a full inquiry into the 'Merchants of Death', and on 4 September 1934, a series of public hearings started before the Munitions Investigating Committee to investigate the role of arms manufacturers in forcing America into the First World War. The reports published by the committee claimed that there was a strong link between the US government's decision to enter the war and the lobbying of the munitions industry and were also highly critical of the nation's bankers. The war, it concluded, 'had been driven by bankers and munitions traders with business interests in Europe. These findings fuelled a growing "isolationist" movement that argued the United States should steer clear of future wars and remain neutral by avoiding financial deals with countries at war.'[19] Abroad, crippling war debts had transformed 'Uncle Sam' into 'Uncle Shylock' in the minds of many and the admission that US business interests had potentially prolonged the war was greeted with anger. Why, it was argued, should Britain pay America for its profiteering from the war whilst at the same time presenting itself as the saviour of Europe when, in fact, Britain and France had suffered so much apparently for the benefit of US business interests?

From a position of economic strength and moral indignation, the United States held itself aloof from foreign affairs. When Roosevelt suggested in January 1935 that the United States should join the World Court at The Hague he came in for bitter attacks claiming that he was trying to use it as a means of joining the League of Nations. In a heated debate, Senator Homer T. Bone spoke for many Americans when he rejected the idea of any dealings with 'the poisonous European mess'. Senator Thomas D. Schall was even more forthright: 'To Hell with Europe and with the rest of those nations.'[20] On 31 August, Congress passed the first Neutrality Act prohibiting the export of 'arms, ammunition, and implements of war' from the United States to foreign nations at war and requiring arms manufacturers in the United States to apply for an export licence. Although President Franklin D. Roosevelt originally opposed the legislation, he relented in the face of strong congressional and public opinion and on 29 February 1936, Congress renewed the Act until May 1937 and prohibited Americans from extending any loans to belligerent nations. The outbreak of the Spanish Civil War in 1936 and the rising tide of fascism in Europe meant that a new revised Act was passed that included a mandatory arms embargo in the event of any foreign war; a ban on all financial loans to belligerents; a Control Board for American weapons manufacturers to prevent them selling arms; and the right for the President to enforce an embargo on non–

military goods destined for warring powers. The Act was intended to make it clear at home and abroad that whatever happened, America would not interfere.

The Neutrality Act of 1937 did, however, contain one important concession to Roosevelt: belligerent nations were allowed, at the discretion of the President, to acquire any items except arms from the United States, so long as they immediately paid for such items and carried them on non-American ships – the so-called 'cash-and-carry' provision. Since vital raw materials such as oil were not considered 'implements of war'; the 'cash-and-carry' clause would be quite valuable to whatever nation could make use of it. Roosevelt had engineered its inclusion as a deliberate way to assist Britain and France in any war against the Axis Powers because he realised that they were the only countries that had both the hard currency and ships to make use of it. Unlike the rest of the Act, which was permanent, this provision was set to expire after two years.

As arguments about US foreign policy raged, Roosevelt came to believe, like many, that good sense and goodwill could be enough to establish a moral world order that would end war. In 1936–7 he began to explore his idea seriously, hoping that Britain would take the initiative on his behalf. In January 1938 a firm proposal was sent to British Prime Minister Chamberlain for a great summit meeting of world leaders. The British Foreign Office found the proposal 'mysterious and meaningless' whilst Chamberlain himself dismissed it as 'preposterous'. Roosevelt's proposals for universal disarmament and arms limitations to a level needed for 'reasonable self–defence' were met with the same incredulity. Many Europeans regarded Roosevelt's thinking as the product of American insularity and the view in Britain was that Roosevelt's conception of foreign policy was aimed not at any serious attempt to work for world peace but for the consumption of an American audience safe from the threat posed by growing militarism in Germany and Japan. Roosevelt, in turn, was disillusioned in dealing with a Europe in which no one cared 'a continental damn what the United States thinks or does'.[21]

Throughout the 1930s the US traded as openly with Germany and Japan as with any other power and later critics often attacked the shipping of American war supplies, claiming that Roosevelt had hypocritically refused to invoke the neutrality acts when profits were at stake. 'We have,' commented Congressman August H. Andresen in February 1941, 'supplied Japan with enough scrap iron during the past four years to build 50 warships.'[22] By the end of that year, America would be under attack by these same ships.

Elsewhere, American investment in Germany increased by 40 per cent between 1936 and 1940 and gave Germany access to markets and new technologies essential for her war preparations. In 1939, defending investment in Opel, the General Motors subsidiary in Germany, chairman Alfred Sloan Jr stated his belief that 'an international business operating throughout the world should conduct its operations in strictly business terms, without regard to the political beliefs of the country in which it is operating.'[23] The real concern of American business was not the rights or wrongs of trading with fascist states, but the fear that British and French rivals might be able to reach separate agreements with either Japan or Germany that could exclude American goods from Europe and Asia altogether. American businesses abroad demanded that the White House kept American foreign policy away from contentious issues likely to damage America's long–term economic interests, and it was only when Japanese involvement in China and Germany's links with Latin America began to encroach seriously on American trading and investment interests that the business community, as well as the politicians, started to consider which side to back.

The American Nazi Party had proved so unmanageable that Hitler had disowned it in 1937 but two years later it was strong enough to draw 22,000 members to a rally in

New York. Hitler himself, however, regarded Americans as inconsequential and frivolous. Convinced that the Neutrality Acts opened the doors for his conquest of Europe, he privately stated that once he controlled the Atlantic, he would bring the US to its knees. Submarine warfare would block any outside trade and a new generation of long range bombers would strike at US cities at will. With a powerful Jewish lobby protesting Nazi ideology and the brutal Kristallnacht attacks, American preference was for democracy, making Britain and France the natural choice for the majority of the voting public over the more oppressive fascism, but it wasn't that easy. Since 1918, Britain had been the major trading rival and US forces had based their annual defence manoeuvres on the possibility of a British invasion of the United States through Canada.[24] Neither government trusted the other with British politicians regarding America as spouting big ideas but doing nothing, whilst Americans still resented having had to 'bail the British out' in 1917–18 despite having contributed relatively little and gained a great deal from doing so. Although British leaders were very much aware that the cuts to the military left the country dangerously reliant on overseas help, they also knew that America would demand a high price for any support it gave. Nevertheless, trade agreements were made and war materiel began to reach Britain in 1938.

Following Germany's occupation of Czechoslovakia in March of 1939, Roosevelt suffered a humiliating defeat when Congress rebuffed his attempt to renew 'cash-and-carry' and expand it to include arms sales, but as the situation in Europe deteriorated, a fierce debate in Congress led, in November of 1939, to a final Neutrality Act being passed. This Act lifted the arms embargo and put all trade with belligerent nations under the terms of 'cash-and-carry'. The ban on loans remained in effect, and American ships were barred from transporting goods to belligerent ports.

In 1939, Roosevelt attempted to repeal the mandatory arms embargo and to introduce a cash-and-carry policy for all military equipment. This favoured Britain and France, since their naval power could prevent German traffic across the Atlantic and Britain had, as usual, immediately blockaded Germany to prevent just such a trade. After months of lobbying individual senators, however, Roosevelt's proposals were defeated in the Senate by a hostile coalition of isolationists and anti-New Dealers.

When he revived the proposal after war had broken out in September, the White House was deluged with one million letters in three days protesting by a margin of a 100 to 1 against lifting the embargo. As Congressman George A. Dondero commented, 'If two men are fighting in the street and you are standing nearby and give one of them a knife, are you neutral?'[25] With an election due in 1940, even his political friends were anxious about the proposals in case they weakened the chances of re-electing a Democrat. By November, however, things had changed. The Nazis had signed a non-aggression pact with the Soviets. Now, for the first time, Americans could see that the outcome of the war in Europe could have a direct impact on the United States. 'We are not seeking to make a loan to Great Britain,' said Secretary of War Stimson. 'We are really seeking to purchase her aid to our defence. We are buying – not lending. We are buying our own security while we prepare.' It was a strong argument. The embargo was lifted and by the summer of 1940, American arms manufacturers had full order books as they supplied tanks, aircraft and ammunition to Britain, who paid in gold.

By late May 1940, Chamberlain had been replaced as Prime Minister by Churchill and relations with the US President improved. The battle for France was almost over and it was clear Britain would have to stand alone. To do it she needed ships. With many in the US government convinced that the defeat of France and Britain was imminent, the

United States sent a proposal to Britain through the British Ambassador, the Marquess of Lothian, for an American lease of airfields on Trinidad, Bermuda and Newfoundland[26] but Churchill rejected the offer on 27 May unless Britain received something immediate in return. On 1 June, Roosevelt bypassed the Neutrality Act by declaring millions of rounds of American ammunition and weapons as surplus and authorising their shipment to Britain. But Roosevelt, still influenced by the American need to undermine Britain's sea power, refused Churchill's pleas for destroyers for the Royal Navy.

By August, the US Ambassador to London, Joseph P. Kennedy, reported that a British surrender was inevitable. Seeking to persuade Roosevelt to send the destroyers, Churchill warned Roosevelt ominously that if Britain were vanquished, its colonial islands close to US shores could become a direct threat to America if they fell into German hands. At the same time, isolationists in the US Senate called for hemispheric domination. While Senator Roben Rice Reynolds led one crusade, that of permitting the British to cancel their war debts in return for United States ownership of their Caribbean possessions, supporters of the aim of domination of North and South America were voicing concerns about French territories in the area such as Martinique, Guadeloupe and French Guinea. The press was unequivocal; writing of the discussion, the *New York Daily News* demanded that the US 'Quit stalling – just take them.'[27]

Instead, a deal was struck. In return for 50 obsolete US destroyers, Britain would lease US naval and air bases in Newfoundland, Bermuda, the Bahamas, Jamaica, St Lucia, Antigua, Trinidad and British Guiana rent free for a period of 99 years. It was recognised as a cynical move to remove British influence in the Americas but Churchill was in no position to bargain. By 1941, British assets in the US had been liquidated. The price of American assistance, as Chamberlain had said, was high. It became clear that the cash-and-carry option could not last.

On the basis that supplying arms to Britain and the Commonwealth would mean that the war would be kept away from the US, in March 1941 the first Act Further to Promote the Defense of the United States was passed, albeit with a Republican Party amendment slipped in whilst the Democrats were at lunch to ensure that the Presidential powers conferred were time limited. Selling the idea to the American public, Roosevelt used the analogy of lending a garden hose to a neighbour whose house was on fire. 'You don't,' he argued, 'quibble about the price as long as you get your hose back or it is replaced after use.' Some amongst the British might be forgiven for suggesting that if your neighbour's house is on fire, you don't wait for him to come begging before you hand him a hose, negotiate terms and then leave him to sort it out, you take it yourself and help him put out the fire. That, the American public refused to consider.

The 'Lend-Lease' act now put an end to any pretence of true neutrality. During 1941 there were isolated incidents in which US navy ships protecting merchant ships had exchanged fire with German U-boats and in May, the SS *Robin Moor*, a US merchant ship, had been sunk off the coast of West Africa by a U-boat captain who claimed – wrongly – that it was carrying war supplies. Meanwhile, Japanese actions in French Indochina and China had caused the United States to finally impose sanctions, including an oil and scrap metal embargo. The oil embargo, not enforced until June 1941, threatened to force the Japanese military operations to a halt and so alternative plans were drawn up in Tokyo to take control of the oilfields of Malaya and the East Indies – referred to simply as the 'Southern Resource Area'. Believing that war with the United States was inevitable at some point as both countries strived for dominance in the Pacific, the Japanese decided to take pre-emptive action against the United States Pacific Fleet to prevent any attempt to block

Lord Cunliffe (far left) watches as William G. McAdoo, United States Secretary to the Treasury, signs the Treasury Warrant for the first loan of £40,000,000 to Great Britain. It was, in part, fear that a defeated Britain would not be able to repay such loans that added weight to the argument that the US should enter the war against Germany. British blockades of German ports had made trade with the Central European Powers so difficult that most American trade was with Britain and France, thus US businesses stood to lose financially if the Allies were beaten.

their plans. Aware of the threat of Japanese expansionism, Roosevelt had ordered the transfer of the fleet from San Diego to Pearl Harbor on Hawaii in order to present a deterrent. On the morning of 7 December 1941, the Japanese attacked.

Although Germany and Japan had an agreement that if either were attacked, the other would consult to see what help could be given, the Japanese had been the attackers and had not told Germany about their plans. As a result there was no need for Hitler to do anything, but on 11 December, possibly deciding that conflict was inevitable, Hitler declared war on the United States.

Forced now into action,

> Isolationist and pacifist opponents of American entry agreed on one basic premise: participation in war would weaken the United States and indeed place her survival as a free republic in jeopardy. Conservatives saw the capitalist economic system in peril, as full-scale mobilisation was bound to bring in its wake inflation, price and wage controls, compulsory unionisation, and – in practicality -a wartime socialism that would remain after the conflict ended. Colonel Charles A. Lindbergh was even more apprehensive: 'God knows what will happen here before we finish it – race riots, revolution, destruction.'[28]

Almost immediately upon hearing news of the Japanese attack, Churchill made plans for a trip to Washington to meet face to face with President Roosevelt, who told him 'We are all in the same boat now.' To relieve the pressure on Britain, Churchill's primary goal was of gaining solid support for a 'Germany first' military strategy. This, he argued, would free the democratic nations of Europe and allow Britain to join with the US in the destruction of Japan. For Churchill and Britain, the ultimate goal was not only to defeat the Nazis but also to assure arrangements in post-war Europe that prevented Germany from again attacking its neighbours as had now happened three times in the past 70 years. Churchill also believed it essential for Britain to re-establish its worldwide empire, which had allowed it to prosper and stand as one of the world's great powers. Since the 1880s, the empire had been governed with an eye to eventual independence and, despite its chequered history, British imperialism had never been based on openly and oppressively exploitative policies in the same way as those of other European powers. Although it would come to an end, Churchill thought that it could come to a negotiated end that would maintain Britain as a world power through a Commonwealth. For the United States, the greatest good that could result from a second Great War would be the destruction of totalitarian regimes in Germany, Italy and Japan and the rise of American-led democracy everywhere, as President Woodrow Wilson had promised during the First World War. To Roosevelt, the United States' conversion from traditional isolationism to internationalism would be the key to America's future role as a world power.

The declaration of war by Hitler had passed almost unnoticed in the furore over the attack on Pearl Harbor. Americans wanted revenge on the Japanese – and only the Japanese. As Congressman Dewey Short commented earlier in the year, 'Why enter a war in Europe exposing our west coast to a rear attack from Japan?'[29] and the argument held true. Roosevelt, however, agreed with Churchill. It would be 'Germany First'. Now assured that the entry of the United States into the war would guarantee Britain the tools to finish the job, Churchill reportedly observed that 'one can always count on America to do the right thing – after it has exhausted all other possibilities.'

In January 1942 the first US troops arrived in Britain. Having been drawn into the war against their wishes, the US government was now keen to get things over with as quickly as possible and began immediately pressing for an invasion of Europe. In the late 1930s, the US Army was ranked seventeenth in the world, fielding an army only marginally larger (at 160,000 men) than the 147,000 men of the 'contemptible little army' sent by the British to France in 1914. Although rapidly expanding, it was still inexperienced and there was a real danger of over-enthusiasm and national pride repeating the damage done to 1st and 2nd Divisions in 1918. Early showing at the Kasserine Pass in North Africa had highlighted severe failings in American weapons, tactics and training and was already causing friction. Amongst the Allies, there was a clear distinction between the perception of the quality of Rommel's Afrika Korps measured against the larger Italian Army he served under. After Kasserine, British soldiers began referring to Americans as 'our Italians'.

The most senior US commander, Dwight Eisenhower, had spent the First World War at training camps in Texas and Georgia. The man appointed to lead US troops into Normandy, Omar Bradley, had been policing copper mines in Butte, Montana. Matthew Ridgway, a contender for the command of allied airborne forces, had also failed to reach France before the end of hostilities. George Patton, soon to be acclaimed as the leading proponent of armoured warfare, was perhaps amongst the most experienced US battlefield commanders and is credited by a variety of American sources as having effectively created tank warfare. As one source puts it, 'Along with the British tankers, he and his men achieved victory at

Cambrai, France, during the world's first major tank battle in 1917.'[30] A truly remarkable achievement for a man who would not take delivery of his first tank until March 1918. In fact, Patton had spent two weeks as an observer with a French tank unit during the British offensive at Cambrai, admitting that 'I like the French much better than the British, possibly because they do not drink tea.'[31] He had, however, led tanks into action in September 1918 and had some weeks of experience in the front lines including two days of actual battlefield command in combat near St Mihiel followed a fortnight later by one day near Cheppy on the Meuse-Argonne front before being shot in the buttocks. He was, according to the US press, 'The Hero of the Tanks'[32] and lapped up the coverage.

By contrast, British generals like Montgomery had spent nine of the past 30 years fighting the Germans and all had frontline combat command experience. Unfortunately, human nature is such that this often translated into a condescending attitude towards the newcomers that soured relations from the outset. It is sometimes argued that a teacher with 30 years experience has, in fact, just one year that has been repeated 30 times. Although vastly more experienced in their command roles, the British generals had learned their craft in largely static, defensive warfare and were only marginally ahead in terms of fighting the new, highly mobile battles they were encountering.

What Americans regarded as British hesitation in taking the battle to the enemy through an invasion of Europe in 1942 was, instead, the result of hard lessons learned during the First World War about the build up vital to the successful breaching of a strongly prepared defence line. Given the need to make ready, to train and to stockpile the stores and equipment needed to successfully invade Europe, it was simply not possible at that stage and it was not until the disastrous Dieppe raid in August that pressure from the Americans and Russians (by now fighting the German invasion themselves) to open the 'Second Front' eased. In fact, it might be argued that the outcome of the raid was a foregone conclusion but that the sacrifice of the raiding force was necessary to forestall criticism that Britain was holding back.[33] Even so, from the outset, the American approach was impatient and focused on finishing the war in Europe and going home as quickly as possible.

For the British, there was no quick fix. The job needed to be done properly if Germany was to be finally defeated. This was, after all, only the second half of what some historians have come to call the Great European Civil War of 1914–1945. The high price of American support meant there was little sympathy for a nation regarded by the British (even if unfairly) as having dodged its responsibilities until the last minute. The war was costing Britain everything it had and, they believed, they had earned the right to assume that he who pays the piper calls the tune.

Notes

1 Washington's farewell address to Congress XX September 1796. Transcript accessed at the Avalon Project of the Lillian Goldman Law Library, Yale University Law School: http://avalon.law.yale. edu/18th_century/washing.asp

2 de Tocqueville, Alexis, *Democracy in America* (Vintage Books, 1945). See also Foreword on 'American Exceptionalism: Symposium on Treaties, Enforcement, and US Sovereignty' *Stanford Law Review* 1 May 2003 p.1479

3 Steele, J.L. 'Time Essay: How real is Neo-Isolationism? *Time* magazine 31 May 1971

4 Letter to William Carmichael, 15 December 1787. See Ford, P.L. (ed) *The Works of Thomas Jefferson, Federal Edition* (New York and London, G.P. Putnam's Sons, 1904–5) Vol. 5

5 Foster, J.B. 'After the Attack: The War on Terrorism.' *Monthly Review* 53 (6): 7. November 2001

6 Jones, J.P. & Hollister, P.M. *The German Secret Service in America 1914–1918* (Boston: Small, Maynard & Co. 1918) p.241

7 Wilson, H.W. & Hammerton, J.A. (eds) *The Great War* Vol 6 (London: Amalgamated Press 1916) p.63

8 Mugridge, I. *The View from Xanadu: William Randolph Hearst and United States Foreign Policy* (McGill-Queen's University Press 1995) p.114

9 Wilson, H.W. & Hammerton, J.A. (eds) *The Great War* Vol 6 (London: Amalgamated Press 1916) p.65

10 Nicholson, C. *The Longman Companion to the First World War* (Edinburgh: Pearson Education, 2002)

11 Wilson, H.W. & Hammerton, J.A. (eds) *The Great War* Vol 10 (London: Amalgamated Press 1918) p.260

12 Corrigan, G. *Mud, Blood and Poppycock* (London: Cassell 2003) p.372

13 Henig, R. *Versailles and After: 1919–1933* (London: Routledge, 1995) p. 52

14 See Baker, R.S. & Dodds, W.E. (eds) *The Public Papers of Woodrow Wilson Authorized Edition* Vol. 1 (New York, 1924) pp.30–44

15 Barnett, C., *The Collapse of British Power* (London: Eyre Methuen, 1972) p.301

16 Kennedy, P. *The Realities behind Diplomacy* (Fontana, 1981) p 231

17 Defence Requirements Committee Report (DRC 14), 28 February 1934, CAB 4/23 in *Dilemmas of Appeasement: British Deterrence and Defense, 1934–1937* by Gaines Post Jr (Ithaca, NY: Cornell University Press, 1993) p.32

18 Overy, R. & Wheatcroft, A. *The Road to War* (London: Penguin 2000) p.311

19 Comments from the US Department of State Office of the Historian. Accessed at http://history.state.gov/milestones/1921-1936/Neutrality_acts

20 Overy & Wheatcroft p.343

21 Ibid p.315

22 Andresen, August H. Congressional Record. 19 February 1941, p.1185

23 Overy & Wheatcroft p.321

24 Ibid p.322

25 Quoted in the *New York Times* 16 September 1939, p.9

26 See Martin Gilbert, *Churchill and America* (New York: Simon & Schuster, 2005)

27 *New York Daily News*, cited by Robert Rice Reynolds, Congressional Record, 6 January 1941

28 Doenecke, J.D. 'American Isolationism, 1939–1941' *Journal of Libertarian Studies* Vol VI. No.3–4 (Summer/Fall 1982)

29 Short, Dewey, Congressional Record 29 May 1941, p.4567

30 www.generalpatton.com/biography.html

31 Brighton, *Masters of Battle* p.43

32 Ibid p.46

33 Corrigan, G. *Blood, Sweat and Arrogance and the Myths of Churchill's War* (London: Phoenix 2007) p.396

Chapter Two

From Breaking Out to Breaking Down

Two years later, the long demanded invasion of France began on 6 June under the direction of Eisenhower as Supreme Commander of the Allied Forces. Although the landing forces would be of roughly equal size, it was clear that US forces would eventually form the largest contingent of the Allied Expeditionary Force and Washington wanted an American to act as ground force commander in chief. Reluctantly, however, the Chiefs of Staff recognised that no US officer had the stature or experience of either Montgomery or Alexander and so the matter was quietly dropped for the time being. As a result, the actual air, sea and land assault phase was to be commanded by the British (Air Marshal Sir Trafford Leigh-Mallory, Admiral Bertram Ramsay and General Bernard Montgomery respectively) with the expectation that the land forces would remain under Montgomery until after a breakout had been achieved. All US ground forces in the assault phase would be under the command of Lieutenant General Omar Bradley, who in turn would be subordinate to Montgomery but with Eisenhower as the ultimate authority.

Prior to the invasion, Operation *Fortitude* had been underway to convince the Germans that the coming invasion would take place in the Pas-de-Calais, the area geographically closest to England. In response, the bulk of German forces in the west and especially the Panzer units, were concentrated into the area east of the Orne river and the zone earmarked for the British landing beaches. To keep them pinned down and allow the US forces to break out through the comparatively weaker German lines south of the beachhead, the British fought an attritional battle that saw casualty rates higher than during the bloodiest fighting at Passchendaele in the First World War. In 50th Division, part of XXX Corps, for example, fighting in Normandy cost the lives of two Brigadiers, twelve commanding officers and a large number of its more experienced company commanders.[1] In all, some 6630 all ranks of the Division became casualties in the 83 days between 6 June and 28 August. During the same period the eight British divisions making up the Second Army, each of around 7200 men in nine rifle battalions, lost an average of 341 officers and 5115 other ranks or some 75 per cent of their troops. The 3rd Infantry Division alone, Montgomery's old command, suffered 7267 casualties with even the lowest number of divisional losses (3639 in 53rd Division) accounting for half the formation's infantry strength.[2] In August, the situation had become so grave that the 59th (Staffordshire) Division had to be disbanded to try to provide reinforcements elsewhere. Despite this, US commanders began to complain that the British were failing to fully support American offensives and instead were leaving the fighting to their Allies.

Initial attempts to break out of the Normandy beachheads had been made on the 'broad front' principle favoured by the Americans. The application of a more concentrated thrust as advised by Montgomery had seen Bradley's Operation *Cobra* smash through the German lines around St Lô and the unleashing of General George Patton's armoured forces. Six US and one French armoured division had battered their way through two Panzer divisions and a heavily weakened infantry formation whilst the four British armoured divisions held back four SS and two Wehrmacht panzer formations along the eastern flank. Comparing Patton's seemingly spectacular advances through (it must be said) largely empty French countryside to the slower progress of the British and Canadians into the heavily defended Pas de Calais, acrimonious disputes developed between the British and Americans. Major General James Gavin, the newly appointed commander of the US 82nd Airborne Division, was one of those who was eager to disparage the British but seemingly unaware of the true situation.

> Aware of Patton's spectacular breakout and overrunning of Brittany, the Americans were at last beginning to see Montgomery as the 'do-nothing' general. They were beginning to tire of the publicity he was receiving for battles fought and won by the Americans. American wounded were returning in large numbers. They had won spectacular battles from Normandy on, but their casualties had been very high.[3]

The 'do-nothing' General Montgomery had just masterminded the greatest seaborne invasion in history and had set in motion a breakout that had far exceeded expectations, made possible because of enormous British losses around Caen in order to shield the beachheads and the American breakout. True, they had not captured one of their main D-Day objectives – Caen – but, as Eisenhower noted, in the heavily defended city 'ten feet in Caen is like a mile anywhere else.' Holding the eastern flank against the German counterattacks launched from their bases around the Pas-de-Calais, Montgomery knew that the enemy were using units thrown piecemeal into the assault and that he was wearing down the German forces north of the invasion area, which in turn would pave the way for a British-led breakout. Nevertheless, sources at SHAEF used the slower progress of the British to suggest that Montgomery was 'defence minded', especially when compared to Patton's apparently unstoppable drive across France – choosing not to notice that there were barely any Germans there to stop him.

As the Allies broke out of the Normandy beachheads, Patton's Third Army had bypassed areas of likely resistance in order to cover as much ground as possible but the practice meant, as Patton's men put it, 'we hold the road, they hold the shoulders.' Without Montgomery pinning down the main panzer force Patton's spearhead would have been cut off – as it so nearly was in early August when a German counterattack threatened the narrow corridor out of Brittany around Mortain. Despite desperate fighting, Bradley had received assurances that Mortain could be held and so, on 8 August, had presented Montgomery with a plan to create a giant pocket by having Patton's Third Army drive north to link with the British and Canadians around Falaise, thus trapping the Germans. Although Montgomery was already planning an even deeper envelopment to the Seine, he agreed to Bradley's plan and issued orders providing for a linkup between the Canadians and the Americans just south of the town of Argentan. On 10 August, General Haislip's XV Corps of the Third Army were at Le Mans and shifted their axis of advance to the north. With the Germans unable to exploit the 25-mile gap between Haislip's forces and VII Corps' flank at Mayenne, XV Corps reached Alençon on 12 August and continued their drive towards Argentan. The Canadians, meanwhile, were being slowed by fierce opposition north of Falaise.

Bradley halted Third Army short of Argentan, despite Patton's loud protests and suggestion that he could 'drive the British into the sea for another Dunkirk,'[4] a decision that remains the subject of considerable controversy, with many arguing that he should have crossed the army group boundary line and completed the encirclement but with Bradley himself blaming Montgomery for failing to act more vigorously to close the gap. Bradley could have recommended to Montgomery an adjustment of the army group boundary to permit the Americans to advance farther north but chose not to, later claiming that he had concerns about the potential for misunderstanding as Canadian and US units approached one another. More likely, Bradley was worried about overextending his forces and so, as he later put it, he settled for a 'solid shoulder' at Argentan rather than 'broken neck' at Falaise. Interestingly, General George Patton, commanding Bradley's Third Army, wrote in his journal on 13 August that 'this [XV] Corps could easily advance to Falaise and completely close the gap, but we have been ordered to halt because the British sowed the area between with a large number of time bombs [dropped from the air]. I am sure that this halt is a great mistake, as I am certain that the British will not close on Falaise.'[5] Given that it was apparently too dangerous for the Americans to advance because of the unexploded ordnance, the complaint about the British and Canadian failure to cover the same ground says much about the attitudes towards their Allies that the Americans were beginning to express by this stage.

The closing of the Falaise gap was not as complete as had been hoped but even so it led to a virtual dismantling of the German 7th and 15th Armies in France. Over 40,000 prisoners were taken and 730 of the estimated 880 available German tanks and tank destroyers were lost with only two Panzer divisions managing to extract more than 15 tanks each from the deadly trap. After weeks of stalemate, Allied armour began a pursuit of the shattered remnants of the German Army across France and into the Low Countries that saw advances of up to 70 miles a day by tank crews navigating by maps taken from garages and schoolrooms in newly liberated towns. From the lowliest private soldiers to high ranking generals, the mood was one of high optimism, the slogan 'win the war in '44' was on everyone's lips. In late August, Supreme Headquarters Allied Expeditionary Force (SHAEF) claimed that 'the enemy in the West has had it … the end of the war in Europe is within sight, almost within reach.' A few days later, Tuesday 5 September would go down in Dutch history as 'Dolle Dinsdag' – 'Mad Tuesday' – the day on which it seemed the Germans

British and US troops meet at the closing of the Falaise Gap. Behind the scenes, feelings were not as cordial as the press reports suggested.

bolted, stealing anything with wheels to help them escape their Allied pursuers; SHAEF confidently declared that the German Army in the west was 'no longer a cohesive force but a number of fugitive battle groups, disorganised and even demoralised'.[6] In Whitehall, the Joint Intelligence Committee considered that organised resistance under the control of the German High Command was 'unlikely to continue beyond 1 December 1944, and ... it may end even sooner.'

When the Allied armies landed in Normandy in June 1944, they had expected and planned for a costly 'bite and hold' style campaign reminiscent of the First World War in which progress would be slow but methodical. In the months before the landings, the French road and rail network had been systematically destroyed to isolate the area and delay reinforcements but planners knew that this would equally hamper their own logistical operations once they broke out of the beachheads. By working to a schedule, it was believed, the supply lines could be reopened in a rolling programme to meet the demands of the frontline troops. By D+90, for example, the Allies expected to reach the line of the Seine and halt for up to a month to allow time for their supply lines to be consolidated.

Instead, by D+90 British tanks had already crossed the river ten days ahead of schedule and were in Antwerp, 200 miles farther east of the Seine – exhausted and overstretched. Supply operations through the 'Mulberry' artificial harbours and across the invasion beaches performed far better than expected but, apart from Cherbourg, no port had yet fallen into Allied hands. The 'Red Ball Express', a continuous stream of trucks driving a circuitous one-way loop from the beaches to the front lines and back had been working around the clock to keep the lead elements supplied and already drivers of Red Ball convoys were making round trips of up to 1600 miles. Even this effort, however, wasn't enough to meet demand. By the beginning of September, 2137 ships had unloaded 2,825,769 tons of supplies at Cherbourg and there were 70,000 tons of stockpiled supplies sitting on the quays because there was no transport to move it forward. The French rail network had been brought to a standstill by pre-invasion air strikes that had proved more successful than expected and so it was not until 30 August that limited railway transport was resumed. The transport problem was becoming desperate. In the British sector, 1400 British 3-ton trucks – enough to move 800 tons and supply two divisions – were found to be useless because of faulty pistons in their engines. Three newly-arrived US infantry divisions found themselves stripped of their trucks in order to supply forces already at the front and even heavy artillery units of the 12th Army Group were left west of the Seine to allow their trucks to be used to move supplies for other units. An official report declared:

> Planning in early August 1944 visualised that until October a British force of nine divisions could be maintained as far as the Somme without the use of the Seine ports, and without rail facilities east of Caen. This force could be increased to 12 divisions after the opening of Dieppe and other minor ports ... It was anticipated that a maximum of 12 US Divisions could be supported as far east as the line Nantes-Orleans prior to October, and that by November, when railroads and ports should be sufficiently developed, approximately 18 divisions could be supported 100 miles further east ... [Until then] not more than six US Divisions could be maintained in an assault north or south of Paris.[7]

The capture of Paris alone would leave the Americans with a civil affairs commitment equivalent to the supply of eight divisions.

The supply situation for the US Army was complicated still further by an arrangement in which US supplies came through the Lines of Communication Zone or COMZ, a vast and sprawling organisation under the command of a lay preacher, Lieutenant General J.C.H. Lee (known behind his back and without affection as 'Jesus Christ Himself' Lee). Lee was not answerable to SHAEF but directly to Washington and it was he who decided what supplies each US Army commander could have. This in turn was determined by what the agreed equipment scales laid down stated they should have. 'If an item was not on the authorised scale of equipment it could not be issued. If a unit's demands exceeded its authorised scale, its operations should be modified since obviously the scale could not be changed.'[8] Stories circulated of Lee using an aircraft to ferry fresh oranges from Morocco every week and of a thriving black market once the COMZ headquarters settled itself in some 296 hotels – almost all the available accommodation – in Paris. By the time of Operation *Market Garden*, around 15,000 US deserters were believed to be in the Paris area, supporting themselves from the supply lines by hijacking trains and stealing truckloads of fuel.[9] Some corruption is inevitable in any army's supply lines but in the US COMZ it became endemic in an organisation that was effectively beyond the power of SHAEF to control. The fact that when Patton entertained Lee he laid on a band and Honour Guard is symptomatic of the degree to which the US supply tail had begun to wag the dog.

The British situation was somewhat easier with the logistics organisation under the command of Montgomery's staff and flexible enough to be able to respond to changes in requirements more easily. Despite this, by late August, with 19 British and Canadian and 22 US divisions in action far beyond the expected advance, supply lines were at breaking point, vehicles badly in need of maintenance and troops nearing exhaustion. Britain had no reserves and each casualty was irreplaceable. The Allied offensive in north-west Europe was losing momentum.

Other harbours should have been available by this stage but several were too badly damaged, Dunkirk would not fall until May 1945 and, although the massive port of Antwerp was in British hands, their advance had stopped short of sealing the causeways to the South Beveland peninsula where a force of around 80,000 Germans were holding out. The port was in Allied hands, but the Scheldt estuary leading inland to it was still under German

By late summer, the problem was not so much a shortage of fuel, but a shortage of transport to keep it moving.

The Allied air offensive designed to isolate Normandy and prevent the Germans bringing in reinforcements was more successful than anticipated. The French rail system was totally unusable and would not be restored for months. This hampered the delivery of stores to the front lines.

control. Tanks of the British 11th Armoured Division had raced ahead of the rest of the army and captured the city and port intact but short of fuel and ammunition, they concentrated on consolidating their prize instead of pushing a further 18 miles north. It was a colossal mistake and one General Brian Horrocks, commanding XXX Corps, freely admitted to.

> My excuse is that my eyes were fixed entirely on the Rhine and everything else seemed of subsidiary importance. It never entered my head that the Scheldt would be mined and that we would not be able to use Antwerp until the channel had been swept and the Germans cleared from the coastlines on either side … Napoleon would, no doubt, have realised these things but Horrocks didn't.[10]

He is frank in stating that had the advance been continued, the war would have been very different. Instead, in a spectacularly successful operation, an improvised evacuation of the Scheldt by the Germans brought around 65,000 men with their vehicles and guns out of danger. These men were in retreat, but the Germans had already proved themselves skilled at producing highly effective battle groups from the most unlikely forces.

Despite this, the German Army appeared to have been broken as a fighting force. As resistance crumbled, the Allied commanders began to chafe for an opportunity to lead the advance to victory. Eisenhower found himself holding together an increasingly fragile alliance and spending more and more time balancing the often insubordinate demands of his generals – so much so that in a private message to US Chief of Staff General Marshall, an exasperated Eisenhower confessed that he was tired of 'trying to arrange the sheets smoothly over several prima donnas in the same bed.'[11] In February, Eisenhower had been tasked with the invasion of Europe and the strategic goal of capturing Germany's main industrial sites in the Ruhr and thus crippling its means of production. A number of routes into Germany had been considered but

> … of the two axes considered feasible – north of the Ardennes on the general line Mauberge–
> Liege, and south of the Ardennes on the general line Verdun–Met –Saarbrucken – the northern
> route was preferred because there were more suitable airfield sites and because it led directly to

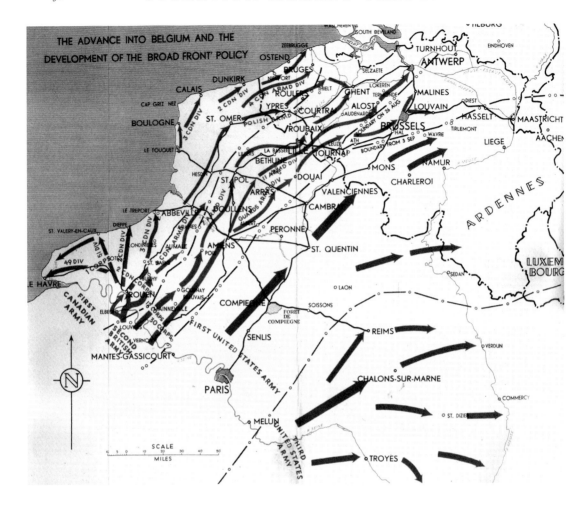

the Ruhr. The southern route led directly to the lesser Rhine cities and a turning movement through the Rhine valley would have been necessary to reach the Ruhr.[12]

Montgomery's 21st Army Group were assigned the northern route, Bradley's 12th US Army Group the southern. Having been told his route had in the pre-invasion planning been considered the preferred route, the emerging emphasis on the southern, apparently determined not by military strategy but by civilian news editors back in the US, exasperated Montgomery.

At the core of the problems facing Eisenhower, however, was a deep divergence of views on strategy. The British were of the opinion that a single thrust under Montgomery's leadership across a 20-mile section of the Rhine would break through onto the north German plain and provide relatively easy access to the industrial heartlands of the Ruhr. The Americans, on the other hand, argued for a broader front, attacking the border at various points and providing a choice of routes into Germany.

To the British, the broad-front plan smacked of a slap-dash, attack-everywhere-at-once approach summed up by one anonymous wag as 'have a go, Joe' – the usual salutation by London prostitutes to passing Yanks. The Americans, for their part, viewed the single-thrust plan as an attempt by Montgomery to hog the main show while the American role was downgraded. One of the British plan's provisions specified that those US troops not allotted to Montgomery's purposes were to remain in positions of static defence – in short, sidelined.[13]

'National political will and national interests play a tremendous role in the development of coalition strategy', as one later American analysis put it, going on to argue that

> Eisenhower, as the Supreme Allied Commander, understood the sensitivities and political ramifications of the Allied coalition. Montgomery, on the other hand, as the famed leader of *Overlord* and *El Alamein* saw only the British perspective and failed to understand that the United States, as the major provider in 1944 of manpower, materiel, and money, remained unwilling to allow the British to take the entire glory of an Allied push into Berlin.[14]

Montgomery himself, aware of the political pressure on the Americans, agreed that operations could only be successfully carried out under a single command and had declared that he was willing to serve under Bradley if that was what was required. Eisenhower's insistence on maintaining the 'broad front' strategy seemed to Montgomery to have been overtaken by events and by now appeared both unimaginative and dangerous. 'Administratively we haven't the resources to maintain both Army Groups at full pressure,' Montgomery argued.

> The only policy is to halt the right and strike with the left, or halt the left and strike with the right. We must decide on one thrust and put all the maintenance to support it. If we split the maintenance and advance on a broad front, we shall be so weak everywhere we'll have no chance of success.[15]

He was certain that the logistical problems now facing them would bring the broad front to a halt but that 'one powerful full-blooded thrust across the Rhine and into the heart of Germany, backed by the whole of the resources of the Allied armies, would be likely to achieve decisive results.'

With the war clearly nearing its end, Montgomery's thrust would also serve a more long term strategic purpose – to seize the vital ports of Bremen and Hamburg before the Russians. By then, the Soviet advance was rapidly closing on Germany and Churchill was concerned that they would overrun the entire country, reach those ports and thus gain a post-war foothold in the North Sea from which to threaten the security of Britain's long-time naval domain. British policy was to consider the long-term implications of their strategy. From their traditionally isolationist stance, the problems of post-war Europe were not an American priority. 'The motivation behind the Americans' plan was less subtle. It simply reflected their impatience. By attacking Germany on a broad front, they hoped to speed the end of the war in Europe, then turn to wrapping up the war in the Pacific, and go home at last.'[16] The US priority was to impose peace by superior firepower and to leave the consequences for Europeans to deal with later. Eisenhower, in a political position of having to balance these needs, chose to support the British but with a compromise – Montgomery would not have overall command of all Allied forces and the Americans would not go into static positions but would instead be put on 'aggressive defence' with an option for Bradley to undertake 'limited offence' operations. 'The more Germans we kill west of the Rhine,' he told Montgomery, 'the fewer there will be to meet us east of the river.'

Eisenhower's insistence on maintaining the 'broad front' served to divide his forces and to place his generals in direct competition for the available resources. In particular, it led to fierce rivalry between Montgomery and Patton, played out through Patton's superior, Bradley. Today, Montgomery, seeking to end the war through the unconditional surrender of the German military by the use of the combined forces available, stands accused in American histories of blinkered self aggrandisement on the basis that he did not realise that 'Allied' victory was only acceptable if it meant American-led victory. Even though both he and Bradley agreed that a single powerful thrust would be effective, the plan might involve sharing the credit – and that would not be acceptable to the American people.

The roots of the problem can be traced back to 1917 when, as we have seen, the United States entered the First World War and a sound military proposal that raw US troops be given battlefield experience under British and/or French command had been rejected on the grounds that America was no-one's 'ally' but an independent force. As a result, US forces did not take the field in large numbers until July 1918, leading some to criticise what they saw as the US providing too little, too late. If their military input was limited, the symbolic effect of their arrival undoubtedly influenced the German collapse by sending the message that a new, powerful and as yet untapped source of reinforcement was now available to the Allied powers. As a result of its sharing in the defeat of Germany, the US found a new sense of its own strength and could see no reason why, as such, it should be a team player on anyone else's side. By 1944, this had translated into a sense that America, with its huge resources not yet ground down by years of war, was the most powerful force involved. As such, many believed, it should take the lion's share of the glory. The real issue was less about how the war should be won and increasingly about who would be seen to have won it.

Nowhere was this attitude more clearly demonstrated than in Italy where, in May 1944, a multinational force under the overall command of British Field Marshal Sir Harold Alexander was involved in heavy fighting. After the breakout from Anzio, Alexander's plan was to send the American Fifth Army under Lieutenant General Mark 'Wayne' Clark north and east to cut off the escape route of Kesselring's 10th and 14th Armies as the British Eighth Army pushed northwards. Clark, however, had other ideas. Determined to be the first General to capture an enemy capital, Clark told Alexander that if men of the Eighth Army approached Rome before his men could, he would order his Fifth Army troops (of whom only around a third were American, the remainder British, Polish, French and Commonwealth units) to fire on them – a threat Alexander chose not to hear because of the need for US support. As a result,

> Clark's calculated act was to prove as militarily stupid as it was insubordinate. He deliberately committed what must rank as one of the most misguided blunders made by any Allied Commander during World War II. About to win a stunning victory that would not only have given him the flattering prize of Rome virtually without a fight, but would have earned him immortality as a great battlefield Commander, Mark Clark suddenly dismembered [Alexander's plan].

Watching his theatrically staged arrival in Rome CBS correspondent Eric Sevareid recalled that Clark's Corps commanders were red with embarrassment as they pretended to consult maps and a media colleague announced that 'on this historic occasion, I feel like vomiting.' Clark would only allow himself to be photographed from what he considered his best side and travelled with his own 50-strong publicity staff who, amongst other things, created a special Fifth Army song that began 'Stand up, stand up for General Clark, let's sing the praises of General Clark ...'[17]

Clark had graduated from West Point 109th of his class of 135 in 1917. His pre-war friendship with Eisenhower served him well and at 46 he had became the youngest Lieutenant General in US history. He was to receive the Distinguished Service Order for gallantry at Salerno, an action in which he retreated back aboard ship when the landings came under fire and ordered the Fifth Army to 'prepare to evacuate the beach.' A memorial at Salerno today records that message, along with the reply of his subordinate, Major General Middleton – 'leave the water and the ammo on the beach. The 45th Division is here to stay.' That a memorial should be so blatant in its disapproval of Clark's leadership is testament to the feelings of his troops but nevertheless, Clark was rewarded by promotion despite his failures. In his determination to take credit for the capture of Rome, Clark had openly disobeyed orders and allowed the German troops to escape and reorganise and in doing so had lengthened the war in Italy at a cost of thousands of Allied lives. When he died in 1984, however, he was reported in a UPI press release of 20 April as having been a 'four-star general, who led the Allied conquest of Italy'. In the introduction to his autobiography (modestly subtitled *Memoirs of a Great American General*), he is described as 'a major figure in World War II. He was prominent as one of the top American commanders. Together with Dwight D. Eisenhower, Omar N. Bradley, and George S. Patton, Jr., Clark was widely regarded as being responsible for victory on the European side of the conflict.'[18] What mattered, it seems, was not actual leadership ability but the skills of each general's PR team to spin the story.

Whilst Bradley recognised the sense in Montgomery's plan to focus on one strong thrust, when he met with Eisenhower to discuss it the New York newspapers were making much of the fact that Bradley's Army Group, comprising General Patton's 3rd US Army and General Hodges's 1st US Army, was still under Montgomery's operational control. While public opinion may have reluctantly accepted that the Normandy landings and initial operations were, as Eisenhower himself said, 'a single battle requiring the supervision of a single battleline commander', things had now changed.

General Marshall, the US Chief of Staff in Washington, wrote urgently to Eisenhower that the 'severe editorial reaction' to Montgomery's continuing influence over US troops must end and that Eisenhower should immediately 'assume and exercise direct command of the ground forces' himself. On 23 August he informed Montgomery that he intended to take over direct control of Allied operations from 1 September.

It is interesting to speculate on how this 'severe editorial reaction' came about given that the information supplied to editors came via the US military and correspondents were subject to censorship. Readers in the rural Midwest might not have objected if newspapers had also reported the simple fact that whilst US troops were fighting under a British general, that general himself was under the overall command of an American – as were all British, Canadian, Polish, French and other forces in Europe. Indeed, no such reaction was reported to Eisenhower's Deputy Supreme Allied Commander, RAF Air Marshal Arthur Tedder, nor to Alexander's control over US troops in Italy, nor to Britons Air Vice Marshal Sir Trafford Leigh-Mallory or Admiral Bertram Ramsay holding command of Allied air and naval forces. The editorial reaction, it seemed, was fuelled by stories fed to the press from SHAEF and aimed directly at Montgomery, making it difficult for him to see this as anything other than a deliberate personal attack. Having successfully led the invasion of France, he argued strongly that there remained a need for an overall ground commander and that he had the credentials for the job. When it became clear that he would not be considered, Montgomery had proposed that he serve under Bradley. Considering Bradley not up to the task, Eisenhower now intended to take command himself. This would leave Eisenhower as Supreme Commander of all Allied Forces with responsibilities to oversee the entire Allied

General George Patton carefully managed media reporting of his advance through France to make it appear that he was leading the fight against Germany. In fact, his rapid progress owed a great deal to the lack of organised resistance in eastern France. Most forces were deployed to prevent a breakout through the Pas-de-Calais.

strategy, direct air and naval operations, manage civilian affairs in the liberated areas and now, apparently in his spare time, directly control ground operations in what was a full time job in its own right. It was a daunting enough task for any man and particularly so for one with very little field command experience. Eisenhower's strength was as a staff officer and his career had been dominated by bureaucratic roles. He was many things, but he was not a battlefield commander.

Montgomery felt publicly humiliated by being removed as overall commander and was only slightly mollified by promotion to Field Marshal. What he saw as the American preoccupation with public relations led to an angry exchange between the two men when Montgomery proposed that his British advance should be given priority over that of the US Third Army: 'The American people', said the Supreme Commander, 'would never stand for it and public opinion wins wars.' Montgomery heatedly disagreed. 'Victories win wars,' he announced. 'Give people victory and they won't care who won it.'[19]

Montgomery's outburst was crass and petulant but on the matter of a need for a strong leader to control the Allied armies, he had a point. Eisenhower's directives had been vague, often contradictory and arguably too willing to compromise to smooth the ruffled feathers of Montgomery, Patton and Bradley. What was urgently needed was a commander willing to take – and enforce – difficult decisions and to get a grip of his subordinates. Someone who was prepared to ruffle nationalistic feathers in the interests of getting the job done. If that produced a rapid end to the war and the safe return of soldiers to their families, few would care who had been in command. From a military point of view, Montgomery was right. But this was an election year and the American public had to be given what it wanted.

In the Japanese, the Americans had an enemy who were racially and culturally distinct and who had attacked first. There was widespread anger; gaining public support for the Pacific war and the destruction of the Japanese people was not difficult. So commonplace was the hatred of the Japanese as an inferior race that on 22 May 1944 *Life* magazine felt able to publish a photo of an American girl at a desk gazing at a skull with the caption:

When he said goodbye two years ago to Natalie Nickerson, 20, a war worker of Phoenix, Arizona, a big, handsome Navy lieutenant promised her a Jap. Last week Natalie received a human skull, autographed by her lieutenant and 13 friends, and inscribed: 'This is a good Jap – a dead one picked up on the New Guinea beach.' Natalie, surprised at the gift, named it Tojo.

Although the armed forces were said to 'disapprove strongly of this sort of thing', public reaction was more mixed and such trophies appear to have been widely taken.

War against white Europeans, however, was a different matter. Reversing its isolationist stance and persuading Americans – many of them of German and Italian descent – to fight in Europe required an enormous propaganda effort to convince the American people that the war was even worth fighting. As custodians of the main source of news for most Americans, the influence of the press barons was enormous. When William Randolph Hearst sent an artist, Frederick Remington, to cover the war in the Philippines at the end of the nineteenth century, the story has it that Remington found the country at peace and telegrammed a message asking to return. Hearst responded that he should stay with the words 'you supply pictures and I will supply war.' The story – albeit probably apocryphal, gained currency, with journalists and editors aware just how much influence they as individuals had over policy.

Brought up to view isolationism as an ideal, a 1942 poll showed 59 per cent of Americans were unable to locate China – America's largest ally in the fight against Japan – on a world map.[20] The following year, *Collier* magazine sought the views of a variety of Americans on what fascism meant to them:

> A typist thinks 'Fascism means being ruled by a government and having part of your salary taken by the government. We just about have Fascism in America now.'
>
> A baffled Boston housewife commented: 'It doesn't mean much to me except a bunch of people rabid about something but I wouldn't know what.'
>
> A husky longshoreman confessed: 'I don't know what Fascism is and I wouldn't know a Fascist if I saw one.'

Speaking for many Americans, another interviewee simply responded, 'Why, we're way out here in Ohio, there are no Fascists here.'[21] That Americans had no awareness of, or even interest in, events in Europe was a fact not always fully appreciated by the British, whose homes had been directly attacked and who needed no convincing that they were engaged in a war of survival. In a bid to ensure favourable coverage at home, press relations had to assume a high priority.

'The official US Record,' wrote Colonel Barney Oldfield,

> ... carried by the Office of the Chief of Information, Department of the Army, names 1,828 people who were accredited by the War Department during the Second World War. There were actually more people than this who wrote, broadcast, and made photographs, but apparently many operated as 'specials'. An astounding thing about the British and the French, normally meticulous about recording everything, history or trivia, is that they did not consider this journalistic activity in the rear of their armies, navies and air forces sufficiently important to keep any accounts of it. In fact, when Brigadier A. Geoffrey Neville, who was Field Marshal Sir Bernard Law Montgomery's Chief of Publicity and Psychological Warfare at the 21st Army Group, found that I was asking each war correspondent headed for Normandy to write his own obituary, he was appalled. 'Whatever for?' he asked. An explanation of the way by-lines were followed in America, and of the fact that by-liners were interesting to readers, left him completely unconvinced. 'A lot of bloody nonsense,' he said.[22]

Already, with novelists like Hemingway and Steinbeck accredited as war correspondents, some journalists had achieved celebrity status themselves and the leading writers like Ernie Pyle would gain an enormous readership for their personal view of the war. The idea that an individual reporter could hold influence went against the British view that saw them at best tolerated as a regrettable nuisance by some officers. Others, however, saw things differently.

Eisenhower's decision to treat journalists as 'quasi-staff officers' was, militarily if not politically, a dangerous move. If, as von Clausewitz had claimed, war is a continuation of politics by another means, then it follows that generals are merely politicians with heavily armed campaign staff and they may be equally driven by the manipulation of power and status for their own ends. A symbiotic relationship grew as journalists cultivated their sources and rewarded access with favourable coverage. 'Generals Bradley and Patton', writes Philip Knightley, 'played unashamedly to a public that knew them from correspondents' reports.'[23] The more a general became a public figure, the more reflected glory those correspondents closest to him could gain and it was therefore in their interests that 'their' general gain celebrity status. During the invasion of Sicily, for example, Patton was front page news. The *New York Herald Tribune* told how 'Patton leaped ashore to head troops at Gela' whilst the *Los Angeles Herald Express* told how 'Patton led Yanks against Nazi tanks in Sicily.'[24] In the *Milwaukee Journal*, 'Patton waded ashore to lead attack that drove out tanks.'[25] It was exactly what Patton wanted the American public to read and it made the lead story across the country; in truth neither Patton nor the journalist left the ship on the first day of the invasion and it wasn't until day two that he went ashore to watch from a rooftop as US forces went into action in the distance. Even Patton struggled with the award of the Distinguished Service Cross for 'extraordinary heroism' on that visit and wrote to his wife 'I rather feel I did not deserve it but won't say so.'[26]

When Eisenhower had referred to the press as staff officers, he had also stated a belief that they were, to all intents and purposes, part of the war effort and certainly they themselves were aware that what they were selling was not fact, but was instead supplying a market back home for stories of Americans at war that would appeal to their audience. The relaxed attitude of the British to the presence of African-American troops was a source of conflict with white Americans used to open racial segregation. Fights broke out between white Americans and British soldiers and civilians triggered by GI anger that a white girl should be willing to dance with a black man. For a nation founded on stories of British oppression and ideals of standing for individual freedom, the story that African-American soldiers were being treated as equals by their British hosts was clearly one that would not play well in the colour-conscious US states. Although Eisenhower told the press they were free to report it, they themselves decided to censor the story.[27] Eisenhower claimed he wanted the press to be able to report freely but a 200-page censorship guide had been produced and those stories not regarded as showing the Americans in the best light swiftly disappeared.

Of course, the British were equally willing to manipulate the facts to suit themselves and much of the disdain shown to 'our Italians' in the early days of 1942 came from a perception of the Americans as reluctant to fight for democracy but quick to enter the war once it saw a profit. Americans, aware of their relative inexperience, were prepared to accept British direction at first but this soon became seen – with some justification – as a British attempt to treat the Americans as yet another colonial force to do their bidding rather than as independent allies. For their part, American officers could be equally rude and patronising. When Colonel Bill Stirling visited Patton's HQ in Casablanca in 1942, an aide listened to Stirling's strong accent before turning and asking loudly, 'Is there anyone here who understands French?'[28] The American press in particular struggled to accept the need to consider Allied sensibilities. After years of anti-British sentiment and the creation of the myth of the superiority of the American way over all others evident in the concept of manifest destiny, US newspapers were quick to find fault with their new allies. In August 1942, Eisenhower's aide, Harry Butcher, noted:

> Ike concerned about anti-British sentiment at home. A story which broke in the US that our airmen were not getting co-operation from the RAF is all wet. Probably will need a press conference to deny effectively. Ike's information all to the contrary. RAF is practically wet-nursing American fliers in sweeps over France. Our fliers learn quickly, but much more rapidly when flying in company with experienced British. They are very cocky when they first come over, thinking their methods and training are the best in the world. Apparently this isn't always true.[29]

Americans who took time to acquaint themselves with the British, Butcher wrote, 'had found that the lessons all Americans learn in their history books aren't true of the present day; believe it or not, the British are not really red-coated devils.'[30] Concerned about reports on the arrogant attitude of some Americans arriving in Britain in the belief that they had come to save the day, Eisenhower insisted on issuing a guide stressing to newly arriving GIs that 'This is no time to fight old wars'[31] and was furious when a radio programme about the Battle of Bunker Hill was broadcast on 4 July 1944. He demanded that if an American officer was responsible for having it broadcast in Britain he would take disciplinary action.[32]

The guide insisted; 'It is always impolite to criticize your hosts; it is militarily stupid to criticize your Allies' and warned US servicemen to avoid a variety of comments likely to cause offence such as boasting about having 'come over here and won the last one' or reminding Britons about war debts. 'The British will welcome you as friends and Allies', it told them. 'But remember that crossing the ocean doesn't automatically make you a hero. There are housewives in aprons and youngsters in knee pants in Britain who have lived through more high explosives in air raids than many soldiers saw in first class barrages in the last war.'

Where possible, US bases ensured that on arrival men were taken on a tour of bomb sites to see what the locals had had to endure during the previous two years. It was with embarrassment that it was discovered that British civilians had responded to a call to invite Americans into their homes but had frequently fed their guests the entire family's weekly ration. Aware that the Americans – 'overpaid, oversexed and over here' as the saying went – had never been subject to rationing, Eisenhower strove to impress on his men the need to show respect to a people who had already experienced war at first hand. As a result of the propaganda effort, relations improved but, far from home and unable to access US newspapers, a major complaint of US troops was that the British Broadcasting Corporation focused on British achievements and reported any American success as an 'Allied victory', leaving them feeling underappreciated. It was a sore point for the US Army, made worse by their experiences in 1918.

In June 1918, the American Expeditionary Force had been in action at Belleau Wood, north of Paris. Strict censorship was in place to prevent journalists revealing the identities of the units involved but on 6 June, correspondent Floyd Gibbons had filed a story that began, 'I am up front and entering Belleau Wood with the US Marines.' He was then badly wounded, losing his left eye and suffering serious injuries. Thinking that Gibbons was dying and had filed his last dispatch, censors allowed the story through unchecked. The American public, hungry for war news, seized upon the story that the Marines had saved Paris but worse, some newspapers also gave the Marines credit for the army's victory at Chateau-Thierry. According to Robert Leckie, the US 2nd Division later went into action to clear the edge of Belleau Wood:

They drove them out, and the first messenger of victory was a gigantic doughboy captain carried into a forward hospital with his legs in bloody splints. Sitting erect on his stretcher, groggy with ether, he cried out exhultantly: 'Oh, the goddam sonsabitches! The headline-hunting bastards! We showed the sonsabitches how to do it!' The captain was not referring to the defeated German enemy.[33]

Army anger at being denied credit for their actions was such that it is claimed that in 1942 MacArthur was asked to propose the award of a Presidential Unit Citation to units involved in the fighting in the Philippines. When questioned by President Roosevelt as to why he hadn't included the 4th Marines in his listing he is claimed to have answered: 'The Marines received enough credit during the last war.'[34] Like all soldiers, US troops wanted to believe that their efforts were being recognised. They needed to hear they were heroes. So did their generals.

The close relationship between the press and their 'own' generals, according to Reginald Thompson, a former captain in the British Intelligence Corps until being released to serve as a correspondent in 1944, was at times 'constrained, at others it instigated the very tactics of warfare', the notorious Montgomery clashes with the Bradley/Patton alliance being the prime example of what could happen when journalists used their influence. According to Thompson,

> The differences between Montgomery and Bradley were exacerbated by correspondents reports … As a result the feeling of unity in the Allied army which Eisenhower had done so much to protect was killed and a united effort made impossible.[35]

Whilst appearing to dismiss press attention, Montgomery had been elevated to national hero status by the efforts of a press corps ruthlessly utilised for that very purpose, although in marked contrast to the relationship of American correspondents to their generals, even Montgomery's closest admirers found him so aloof and condescending that few journalists actually liked him as a person. His greatest achievement to date had been the victory at El Alamein in 1942 that had finally put an end to the series of defeats inflicted on Britain in the first two years of war. He had arrived in North Africa to take over a demoralised Eighth Army and had turned them rapidly into an effective fighting force that swept the Germans and Italians out of North Africa in a campaign only he could have led. This was undoubtedly true – after all, he told the world so himself in what Gordon Corrigan has described as 'one of the most self-serving memoirs ever foisted on the reading public, and one that did immense harm to Anglo-American relations after the war.'[36] In fact, direct political interference by Churchill had caused many of the setbacks for the British Army in 1940–41 through a series of ill-considered operations in Norway, Greece, Iraq and Ethiopia that had weakened the already under-strength army elsewhere. It was only the arrival of General Alan Brooke as Chief of the Imperial General Staff and Churchill's closest military adviser that finally provided some measure of protection from Churchill's more Quixotic schemes. Montgomery was the first general in the Middle East to operate freed from political demands and able to follow military requirements and had been sent to replace Auchinleck, who had been forced into retirement by Churchill for his supposed inactivity. It was an unfair criticism. Auchinleck had just fought (and won) the First Battle of Alamein in July and had reported that he would go on the defensive until mid-September when his men would be ready to begin their offensive operation. Churchill had repeatedly shown an inability to understand that a tank offloaded at Port Said would not then be immediately available for use in the Western Desert. Similarly, he complained about a large RAF presence based on the relatively few aircraft without considering that pilots and aircrew needed to be fed or that planes needed to be repaired and maintained.[37] Convinced that any failure to implement his grand ideas must be because of bad leadership he sacked a string of competent men rather than face the simpler explanation that it might be because his own plans were impractical.

Remaining on the defensive was unacceptable to Churchill. Under pressure from both the Russians and Americans to launch a cross-Channel invasion that summer and having only just survived a vote of no confidence in Parliament, he was determined to turn the tide. At the Casablanca Conference, Roosevelt had said that regardless of any criticism of the secret meeting, he would still be in office for three more years. Hearing it, Sir Dudley Pound had earned a glare from Churchill when he muttered 'that's more than any other person sitting at this table can say.' But if Churchill needed a British victory to save his political career, Roosevelt also needed one to demonstrate to a reluctant American public that after so many defeats, Britain was still worth backing. So by the autumn of 1942, Churchill was very much aware that time was running short for the British to defeat Rommel before the first US troops arrived and both he and Montgomery were prepared to pay heavily for it. Montgomery knew that to do so he had to crush Rommel's panzers with overwhelming numbers of his own tanks. Even if it meant losing all his armour, Montgomery was certain they could be replaced by US vehicles supplied under the Lend-Lease agreement but it would come down to a simple matter of numbers – Rommel's overstretched lines of communication meant he would be getting no more panzers. A common misconception in accounts of the fighting in north-west Europe is that Montgomery was overly cautious of taking casualties as a result of his experiences on the Western Front in the First World War. As a humanitarian excuse for his approach it has its attractions but in fact it simply reflected his making the most of the limited resources available to him. If the potential outcome was deemed to be worth the price, Montgomery could be ruthless. With so much at stake in North Africa, he was willing to pay the butcher's bill. El Alamein would simply be a battle of attrition. Whoever could absorb the most casualties would win.

Under Montgomery's control, the Second Battle of El Alamein opened on the night of 23/24 October with a huge artillery barrage followed by a massed attack by eleven divisions and pitching 195,500 men and 952 tanks of his army against the 104,000 men and 550 tanks of the German and Italian armies.[38] Ironically, those critics not claiming he was trying to avoid fighting First World War-style battles of attrition have instead accused Montgomery of doing just that in the desert, but circumstances allowed no other way. Despite the reservations of some of his commanders, Montgomery kept pushing forward regardless of casualties and eventually, inevitably, after almost two weeks, the enemy began to retreat.

It had been Auchinleck's plan, but it was Montgomery's victory. In the wake, he traded the Australian slouch hat he had been wearing for the black beret of the Royal Tank Regiment at the suggestion of Captain Warwick Charlton, editor of *Eighth Army News*, and Geoffrey Keating of the Army Film and Photographic Unit. Photographed standing in the turret of an American-built Grant tank wearing the Tank Regiment beret, the picture made newspapers around the world. That image, of Montgomery apparently leading from the front, along with the dramatic scenes captured for the film *Desert Victory*, brought enthusiastic responses from audiences in Britain and America. The 'Monty' brand had been created.

El Alamein was the first British land victory of the war against Germany. It was also the last purely British and Commonwealth success. The Americans were coming and from then on, it would be an Allied war effort. In 1944, with the war clearly nearing its end, Montgomery's proposed thrust northwards would aim to outflank the prepared defences along the Franco-German frontier and deliver a powerful army to a position to directly threaten Germany's war production plants and to engage the enemy on the ideal tank territory of the north German plains. It was Monty's chance to consolidate his place in the history books.

Other factors were also at work. With the end of the war seemingly in sight, politicians of both nations began to look ahead. Churchill's son-in-law, Duncan Sandys, had been appointed to coordinate intelligence on the use of the German *Vergeltungswaffe* (retaliation weapon) – the V1 'doodlebugs' that had been striking London and the southeast. Perhaps in an effort to create a positive public image in anticipation of a return to party politics, on 7 September 1944, after five years and four days of constant air threat, Sandys declared London finally safe because, he said, Allied advances had put the static launchers of the V1s out of action. The next day his picture made triumphant headlines in all the papers but that night, explosions rocked Chiswick and Epping. Sandys immediately ordered a Secrecy Order to be imposed on the story. The first V2s had been launched from mobile trailers in an area around The Hague and Wassenaar, 100km west of Arnhem. Aware of the fact that these missiles could be launched from almost anywhere thanks to their mobile trailer launch rigs, Sandys wanted the threat eliminated fast and that meant a push into northern Holland.

By now Montgomery felt himself to be by far the most experienced Allied general and was certainly willing to remind people of the fact. He was a difficult man to manage, arrogant and rude, even to Eisenhower. His successes made him popular enough at home that he could even challenge Churchill – who described him as 'in defeat, unbeatable, in victory, unbearable'. His demeanour upset many who met him. Most significantly, he upset the US war correspondents by failing to show due deference to them. Impatient for an end to the fighting and keen to find a commander with more of an interest in the media, the press corps turned their attention to the man they decided was the rising star of the European war, the commander of the US Third Army, George Patton.

In his lectures on personality disorders at Wright State University, Dr Robert L. Gordon tells students:

> A person with a narcissistic personality disorder is characterised as one who frequently displays a pervasive pattern of grandiosity, shows a strong need for admiration, and lacks empathy. A 'Narcissist' is typically preoccupied by fantasies of unlimited success and power. They like to surround themselves with other successful people and show contempt for those they perceive as inferior. Clearly, General George Patton had strong narcissistic traits.[40]

The son of a wealthy family with strong connections to the Confederate Army, Patton grew up listening to the stories of John Mosby, a family friend and former leader of a guerrilla cavalry force during the American Civil War. By the age of ten, Patton had declared he wanted to be a famous general. Although he gained a place at West Point, Patton was not a popular cadet, frequently reporting others for any infringement of the rules and believing that other cadets were jealous of his superior knowledge of military matters. After graduating in 1909, he took up a cavalry commission and two anecdotes perhaps give a flavour of the man. In 1912, Patton took part in the Stockholm Olympics in the military pentathlon event and took fifth place. According to one biographer,

> He would have placed first … he had problems in the pistol shooting part of the event, having the same problem that he had had while training for football at West Point … he had trained too hard, having lost nearly 30 pounds in preparation for the Olympics.[41]

Having lost points for missing the target, Patton insisted that the fault lay with the judges. Unaware of just how skilled he was, they had failed to spot the obvious – it was impossible for him to miss. Unlike other competitors, he used the large calibre .38 pistol and so, he said, it should have been clear to them that one of his bullets had passed through the hole left by the previous shot.

After a self-funded period at the French cavalry school at Saumur, Patton saw service on the Mexican border before going to France as a Captain on the staff of General Pershing. It was in France that Patton saw the future of cavalry and he was instrumental in setting up the first tank school for the US Army, taking delivery of the first batch of tanks in March 1918, although as previously mentioned that has not prevented his admirers crediting him with having been responsible for the British success at Cambrai in 1917 – remarkable given that he was without tanks or tank crews to command at the time. On 26 September 1918, Patton watched as his tanks came to stop at a trench line under German artillery fire. Patton gathered a group of infantrymen to collapse the sides of the trench and later admitted he may have killed one of them by hitting him with a shovel to encourage the others to work faster. As the tanks pushed forward again, Patton was hit in the backside by small arms fire. Ever mindful of his priorities, he was heard to mutter 'at least I'll get my [Distinguished Service Cross]' as stretcher bearers carried him away.[41] He later enjoyed joking that his wound meant he could only be a 'half assed general'. Patton's life was saved that day by his orderly, Joe Angelo, who applied dressings and stayed with him under heavy fire for over an hour. Recommended for the Medal of Honor, Angelo was awarded the Distinguished Service Cross for his actions. In 1932, Angelo was among the thousands of veterans and their families taking part in a march on Washington to demand the 'bonus' promised to those who had served in the Great War. As a cavalry major, Patton along with his superiors, Army Chief of Staff General Douglas MacArthur and MacArthur's aide-de-camp, Major Dwight David Eisenhower, a friend of Patton's, were tasked with putting down the so-called 'Bonus March'. Patton was staunchly anti-communist at a time when communism was defined as 'any demand for higher pay than employers were willing to give.' At the head of a cavalry detachment, Patton drew his sword and twice charged the crowd. Later, when Angelo requested a meeting with him, Patton refused to recognise the man who saved his life.[42]

By 1944, Patton had established himself as an aggressive and successful commander but had been passed over for promotion when his one-time subordinate Omar Bradley was given command over his head; the relationship between the two men was complex. Bradley had originally served under Patton as deputy commander of II Corps in North Africa until Patton was tasked to return to command of I Armoured Corps for the Sicily invasion. Then, on 3 August 1943 at the 15th Evacuation Hospital near Nicosia, Patton became angry at finding Private Charles Kuhl, who was clearly uninjured. When asked what was wrong with him, Kuhl replied 'I guess I can't take it sir.' Patton, convinced that shell shock was, as he put it, 'an invention of the Jews', slapped Kuhl across the face with his gloves before dragging him to his feet and kicking him out of the tent.[43] Exactly one week later, on a visit to the 93rd Evacuation Hospital, he found Private Paul Bennett, who told him that he could no longer stand the shelling. A furious Patton drew his pistol and threatened to shoot him on the spot as a coward. It was only the intervention of the hospital commander, Colonel Currier, that calmed the situation. A written complaint from Colonel Currier reached Bradley the same day with a request that it be forwarded to Eisenhower. After checking whether anyone else had seen it and being told no, Bradley told his aide to seal the report in an envelope and lock it in the safe. 'Eisenhower was told of the slapping', Bradley wrote, 'though not through me.'[44]

The story was leaked to the press by a nurse at the hospital but, as 'quasi staff officers', the journalists took it to Eisenhower with the offer to 'bury' it[33] though only if Patton was fired. On 20 August, Eisenhower's aide Harry Butcher was presented with the details of the incident by journalist Demaree Bess. Soon afterward he heard Charlie Daly of CBS tell him that Patton had apparently gone 'temporarily crazy'. Finally, Quent Reynolds returned from Sicily and 'asserted that there are at least 50,000 Americans who would shoot Patton if they had the slightest chance.'[45] Eisenhower had no choice but to act by relieving Patton of command. A year later, in command of the US Third Army and now junior to his own former deputy, Patton regarded himself as the real power of the First Army Group but Bradley himself had not been consulted about Patton's assignment to his command: 'Had Eisenhower asked for my opinion', Bradley wrote,

> I would have counselled against the selection. For not only did I question George's conduct of the Sicilian campaign, but I seriously doubted the wisdom of forcing Patton to stomach this reversal of roles in command … Ike assured me that George would submit without rancour … Like Eisenhower, I did not dispute George's brilliant dexterity in gaining ground – and there was much of it to be gained between the Channel and Berlin. But even this striking talent of Patton's could not offset the misgivings I felt about having him in my command.[46]

Bradley, writing after the war, stated that during the Normandy campaign 'the choice of Montgomery as British commander for the *Overlord* assault came as a stimulant to us all'[47] and that throughout 'I had not asked to be freed from Montgomery's British Group command. He had neither limited our authority nor had he given us directives that might have caused us to chafe.'[48] In fact, Bradley claimed, he 'exercised his Allied authority with wisdom, forbearance and restraint … I could not have wanted a more tolerant or judicious commander.'[49] Realising that he could not remain in overall control, Montgomery had even proposed that Bradley take his place and announced himself willing to serve under him in a joint thrust. It is therefore a measure of the degree to which Bradley was in thrall to Patton that it was only after the latter's arrival in France that he allowed himself to be browbeaten into opposing the plan he had already agreed with Montgomery and began to openly undermine British command.

By careful use of his extensive press corps, Patton was steadily building a reputation for himself among readers at home as one of America's greatest ever combat leaders; but as his fame grew, his mental state grew more precarious with his grandson, Robert H. Patton later citing bipolar disorder or manic depression as being the underlying problem. His frequently stated belief that he was the reincarnation of a Roman legionnaire and of one of Napoleon's officers was at first seen as a mild eccentricity, but he began to display ever more disturbing signs of breakdown as the war progressed. This, coupled with a long running affair with his own niece (not the incestuous affair sometimes presented, Jean Gordon was the daughter of his wife's half sister and thus not a blood relative) did little to enhance his suitability for promotion to a role that often required tact and diplomacy as much as fighting ability. True to form, Patton again blamed the judges, claiming as one biographer puts it, that he was passed over because

> … at Patton's expense, other General Officers were building their careers and gaining undue praise. Patton himself, was being kept under wraps and he was being virtually ignored. Others of lesser ability were being promoted over him. In reality, he was pushing them up the ladder and they were taking the credit that was honestly due Patton … Initially Patton did not mind

Bradley stealing his ideas because as a soldier he realized that it would help the war effort. As time passed it became evident that the Allies would, indeed, win the war. Patton felt that he had been pushed far enough and that he had been taken advantage of too much. When Patton personally proffered his plans he was ignored. When Bradley put forth Patton's plans, as his own, they were readily accepted for consideration … On 14 August 1944, Patton wrote in his diary regarding the St. Lô breakthrough, 'It is really a great plan, wholly my own, and I made Bradley think that he thought of it.[50]

An alternative explanation for his failure to gain promotion comes from those who argue that other factors may have been involved. Throughout the 1920s, for example, Patton had demonstrated a lack of ability to perform staff duties and this was reflected in his annual efficiency reports. Although he uniformly received above average to superior ratings for his physical energy, endurance and initiative, he rarely rose above average in the categories of judgement, common sense and tact. In 1920, for example, during his tour of duty at Camp Meade, Patton was described by his commanding officer as 'an efficient officer' whilst Lieutenant Colonel E.G. Beurat of the Inspector General Department, in his assessment of the staff at Meade summarised him as 'efficient; keenly interested in the development of tanks. I consider him average.' That same year, Colonel W.C. Rivers, regimental commander of the 3rd Cavalry and Patton's immediate superior, rated him 'below average' in tact. So serious was this deficiency that his first tour of duty in Hawaii between 1925 and 1928 ended with him being sacked as the division G3 and he received an efficiency report in which the commanding general called Patton a 'disturbing element in peacetime'. Despite his self belief and the received wisdom today, Patton was not as highly regarded as is often supposed. When, in February 1945, Eisenhower ranked the abilities of his major generals in Europe, Omar Bradley and Carl Spaatz were rated as the best, followed by Bedell Smith. Patton was ranked third – although since he was closely followed by Mark Clark, the criteria for 'best' is unclear. In December of the same year, Eisenhower asked Bradley to carry out the same exercise. According to Bradley, Patton rated no higher than the sixth best US general in Europe.[51] Nevertheless, in the eyes of the US public at home, Patton was as untouchable as Montgomery was to the British.

   This, then, was the atmosphere in which the Allies began to prepare for the defeat of Germany. By the late summer of 1944, American reporters paid to report American successes began to support a view leaking from US officers at Supreme Headquarters Allied Expeditionary Force (SHAEF) that Montgomery was 'defence minded' – the 'do-nothing general' as Gavin later put it. For the American press, the breakout of the six US and one French armoured division through two weakened and heavily outnumbered Panzer divisions cut off from their own lines of communication showed dash and courage whilst the failure of four British armoured divisions to overcome four SS and two Wehrmacht Panzer divisions in an area prepared for the expected invasion was clear evidence of timidity. Surely this was proof that the British should no longer be allowed to take the credit for Americans winning the war.

   In Montgomery's proposal for an Allied strategy, 'an Allied push into Berlin' meant just that. Montgomery wanted the single thrust because it had been shown time and again to work. The breakout from Normandy initially failed when US troops attacked on a broad front. It was only when Montgomery argued forcefully for the application of what the military termed a *Schwerpunkt* that the spectacular success was finally achieved. In the early stages of the war, the German blitzkrieg had relied on the Schwerpunkt as the focal point of the maximum military effort. By the concentration of forces on one spot, a localised breakthrough would allow the highly mobile armoured forces to get behind the enemy lines, and it had proved devastatingly effective. Guderian, one of the chief proponents of the *Schwerpunktprinzip* (concentration principle) had summarised it as being governed by the adage '*Nicht kleckern, klotzen!*' ('don't tickle, punch!')[52] Montgomery had experienced the effects of this at first hand in 1940 and was quick to adopt similar methods. His approach required the build-up of massive forces able to overwhelm the enemy, but this delivered what he referred to as a series of 'colossal cracks' against the enemy – powerful, targeted punches designed to cause the maximum damage rather than the optimistic rain of blows that the broad front seemed to offer.

The fast, dramatic progress of Rommel had been headline grabbing in France and North Africa but in the desert he was operating at the end of a very long supply chain that saw him run out of fuel in the middle of operations in October 1942. Patton, too, would concentrate on pushing ahead at the expense of his logistics. Blitzkrieg took tanks far into enemy territory but, as one of Patton's men pointed out, they might hold the highway, but the enemy still held the country on either side of the advance. After generations of fighting colonial wars far from home, British generals were accustomed to paying close attention to their logistics and ensuring that they were able to provide heavy, sustained pressure until the enemy broke. It was slow and methodical in its preparation – but effective in practice.

To the American public, Patton's sweep across France fitted the plan for a quick end to the war perfectly. It was fast, dramatic and, if the figures supplied by Patton's admirers are to be believed, accounted for 55 per cent of the total German losses in north-west Europe (although Colonel Barney Oldfield later reported one incident in which the 20,000 prisoners already reported taken clearly hadn't been informed of their decision so correspondents had to be hastily recalled from an area where heavy fighting was quite obviously still going on). The claim played well at home. As journalist Chester Wilmot later put it,

> Eisenhower knew that his troops in the field and his people at home would see the issue in simple terms, almost in terms of American football. Patton was 'carrying the ball', and was making an 'end run' with every American cheering him on. As Eisenhower saw it, there was no justification – in football or in battle – for taking the ball away from him ... Neither the British nor the Canadians had yet shown a capacity for advancing with the dash and drive the Americans had demonstrated so brilliantly since the breakout.[53]

It might, however, be argued that an advance of 250 miles in four days by the British showed at least some 'dash and drive' and by the end of August, both armies were a similar distance from their starting lines.

In the late summer of 1944, however, as Montgomery's men approached the open tank terrain of the north German plains, Bradley was facing the first serious obstacles his men had encountered since the breakout as they approached the Maginot Line and the Siegfried Line defences in the rugged terrain of the Franco-German border. Although not manned by Germany's best troops, the fortifications would still prove a difficult barrier to penetrate and in October 1944, *Yank* magazine noted:

> It made an awfully good story, a wonderful story. 'GERMANY'S VOLKSTURM MADE UP OF OLD MEN, STOMACH CASES, CRIPPLES WITH GLASS EYES AND WOODEN LEGS.' Most people back home thought that was very funny. 'Those Germans are really scraping the bottom of the barrel, aren't they? Well it won't be long now.' But the GIs up front

didn't think it was very funny. 'I don't care if the guy behind that gun is a syphilitic prick who's a hundred years old – he's still sitting behind eight feet of concrete and he's still got enough fingers to press triggers and shoot bullets.'[54]

Gradually, blaming the British for diverting their resources, Bradley's Army Group's advance slowed. Eisenhower's problem was now to decide whether to pursue a broad logistical solution and clear the approaches to Antwerp or to concentrate on destroying German forces with a decisive tactical solution. With the battered German armies seemingly on the run, most Allied commanders were in favour of a pursuit and destroying them before they could regroup. The problem was where.

From hesitant beginnings in 1940, both the British and Americans had developed large-scale airborne formations and, on 2 June 1944, SHAEF had issued a proposal to draw together these units into a single First Allied Airborne Army. Eisenhower approved the plan 18 days later but both Patton and Bradley were among a group of senior American officers opposed to the new force. The plan, to coordinate Allied airborne operations under a single command, was rejected ostensibly on the grounds that they believed US airborne troops should only be used to support US forces. In reality, however, a major concern was that command of the prestigious formation might be given to General Browning of the British 1st Airborne rather than the promotion of an American. Again, Eisenhower chose a compromise solution to satisfy both camps. On Monday, 21 August 1944, under the headline 'Airborne Army', *Time* magazine reported;

> Announced by General Eisenhower was a new kind of command: an airborne army of close to 250,000 men. Presumably it would be used in the knockout blow against the Germans – who had first proved the devastating effects of air assault.
>
> To command the new army 'Ike' Eisenhower chose an airman; bright-eyed, 54-year-old, rakish Lieut. General Lewis Hyde Brereton, who had bossed the Ninth US (Tactical) Air Force in its scourging campaign in France in support of Allied ground troops. Annapolis-trained Lewis Brereton had seen more of World War II than most US generals. In the attack on the Philippines he had lost all but a fragment of his air force, had moved on to Java, then to India, where he organized the Tenth Air Force, then to the Middle East where he commanded the Ninth which made the first great raids on the Ploesti oilfields.
>
> As an airborne commander, 'Looey, dot dope,' as unorthodox, red-tape-hating General Brereton is called by old Army friends, was going to have more chance to try new tricks than an air force command had ever given him.
>
> For his deputy, Eisenhower gave him one of airborne's best: suave Lieut. General Frederick A. M. Browning, Britain's topmost airborne man, small-arms expert and husband of novelist Daphne (*Rebecca*) du Maurier. What the airborne army's assignment would be was still something the Germans would like to know.

Lewis Brereton had commanded the US 12th Aero Squadron on the Western Front in the First World War and had been involved with a plan to use American infantrymen dropped by parachute to seize Metz late in 1918. The plan had not progressed beyond the planning stage before the war ended and Brereton had instead become an advocate of strategic bombing, rising to command the US Far East Air Force. As news of the Japanese attack on Pearl Harbor reached Manila, many of Brereton's crews had just returned to their bases from a lavish party in town. Although he placed the air force on alert, Brereton neglected to order them to disperse so that the first air attack on the Philippines virtually wiped out all the available American air power. Escaping via Java to India, he briefly became Deputy Commander of American-British-Dutch-Australian Command (ABDACOM), which unified Allied forces in South East Asia and the South West Pacific.

> Brereton gets along well with his British colleagues in India. When the British in the Mid-East, India or the Pacific are criticised in his presence, he says: 'We have no right to pass judgment … We've shown nothing yet that stacks up to the Battle of Britain.' But he clings fiercely to his Americanism. He has commanded his secretary to fine him a rupee (50¢) every time he uses a non-American expression. Total fines up to last week: two rupees, for two 'Rightos' over the telephone. His unceasing fear is that he will catch himself describing an air battle as 'a jolly good show'.[55]

Brereton then went on to command the US 9th Air Force in the Middle East and remained with it when it transferred to operations in support of ground operations in Europe. During the Operation *Cobra* breakout from Normandy, the 9th flew in support of Bradley's forces but there had been problems. As one veteran recalled 'I always knew our Air Force was pretty good, because twice we were strafed by our own planes. We tried to put identification panels out where our pilots could see them, but in the apple orchard country of Normandy that was kind of hard to do.'[56] Dozens of other accounts support the claim of frequent 'friendly fire' incidents, the most serious of which killed General Leslie McNair and caused hundreds of American and French civilian casualties in a carpet bombing raid that went disastrously wrong. Days before *Cobra* began, General Bradley briefed the press at the 1st US Army press camp at Vouilly where reporters asked if the civilians had been warned. General Bradley later wrote:

> I shook my head as if to escape the necessity of saying no. If we were to tip our hands to the French, we would also show it to the Germans … The success of *Cobra* hung upon surprise; it was essential we have surprise even if it meant the slaughter of innocents as well.[57]

The operation called for the bombing of the Périers-St-Lô road and would require dangerously close air support. The vital issue was whether the aircraft were to attack parallel to the road or perpendicular to it. General Hoyt Vandenberg, in direct control of the operation, understood that General Bradley had insisted that the bomb run last no more than an hour, a requirement suggesting a perpendicular flight path. Triple-checking this with Air Marshal Trafford Leigh-Mallory, he was assured that Leigh-Mallory had 'spoken to Bradley and that the additional time to deliver the bombing attack [by means of a lateral approach] was too great for Bradley to accept and that, therefore, he [Bradley] had decided to accept the additional risk of perpendicular … bombing.'[58] The result was a disaster. Immediately Bradley blamed Vandenberg and, by extension, Vandenberg's chief, Brereton. There is evidence to show that Bradley was, to some extent, responsible for the error by insisting on a short bomb run, but he was determined to shift the blame elsewhere. The creation of the new post of commander of the Allied Airborne Army gave Bradley the opportunity to exert pressure on Eisenhower to sidetrack Brereton, at the same time undermining the new force and regaining for himself the use of the American airlift capability.

During preliminary discussions with Brereton in July, Eisenhower demanded that operations must be planned with 'imagination and daring' and Brereton promised results as soon as an opportunity arose.

The fact was that the paratroopers and glidermen resting and training in England had in effect become coins burning holes in SHAEF's pocket. That is not to say that SHAEF intended to spend the airborne troops in a wild or extravagant fashion. Rather, SHAEF had decided to buy an airborne product and was shopping around. The impetus to buy did not come from General Eisenhower alone. As late as August, [US Air Force Chief] General Arnold had again voiced his desire for an airborne operation that would have strategic implications. The War Department obviously wanted to see what airborne troops could do in actual combat; pursuit warfare, many believed, provided an excellent opportunity for their use.[59]

The German collapse meant that at last an opportunity to experiment with the use of airborne troops in pursuit warfare had arrived.

Whilst this was being played out at the top, the men of the First Allied Airborne Army stood by for operations. On 6 June, the British 1st Airborne prepared for Operation *Tuxedo* – a planned drop to reinforce the landings in Normandy. When this became unnecessary, they stood by to seize Carpiquet airfield outside Caen. It too was cancelled. Time after time, between June and late August, some 14 drops reached various levels of preparation, usually to be scrapped as ground forces reached the objective first. This constant state of preparation is blamed for having undermined 1st Airborne's morale and contributing to later problems at Arnhem but in fact only around half of these missions reached the stage of full readiness. Nevertheless, the round of briefings and cancellations was beginning to wear down the planners and corners began to be cut. On 3 September, Operation *Linnet II* was scheduled to block the German withdrawal from Normandy by seizing bridges on the river Escaut around Tournai and Lille. Brereton noted in his diary:

> ADVANCE HQ. SHAEF, 3 September 1944 (D-plus-89). General Eisenhower and [Air Chief Marshal] Tedder favored mounting Operation LINNET II, a drop in the Aachen-Maastricht Gap. However, the Supreme Commander left the decision to Bradley and Montgomery.[60]

Most sources report that the operation was scrapped when the British and Canadian ground advance overran the target area. In fact, as the official US history puts it:

> The most notable example of General Bradley's antipathy to an airborne operation occurred at Tournai. Though this city lay outside his 12th Army Group sector and inside the British zone, Bradley ensured its capture before an airdrop could be staged by ordering the First Army to rush ahead and take it. The ground troops arrived in good time to make an airborne operation there unnecessary. But Bradley had nevertheless lost a measure of air supply because the troop carrier planes had been withdrawn from supply missions to prepare for the drop. 'Although we had made good on our boast and Ike's air drop was washed out,' General Bradley later wrote, 'even our smugness could not compensate for the critical loss we had suffered in tonnage … During the six-day stoppage that had resulted from SHAEF's planned drop at Tournai, we lost an average of 823 tons per day. In gasoline, this loss would have equalled one and a half million gallons …'[61]

It was against this background of outright hostility towards airborne operations by Bradley that orders reached the 1st Airborne Division for a British-only attack in support of 21st Army Group's advance north. Operation *Comet* would consist of two lifts and three phases; the first phase consisting of coup de main operations before first light in the immediate vicinity of the Arnhem, Nijmegen and Grave bridges followed by a brigade-sized drop into each area; finally, the balance of the glider forces and the Polish airborne would be landed to reinforce the perimeters around each objective. Given the criticism that was to come later, the *Comet* plans were in many ways superior to those for *Market*. The coup de main assaults would land close to and on both sides of all the bridges and the drop zone at Arnhem would be five miles northwest of the town. Interestingly, no RAF objection was made to the landing of gliders south of the Arnhem bridge, nor to the selection of the drop zone there, nor yet to the decision to undertake two lifts in the same day by some of the aircraft involved. The operation was provisionally scheduled for 4 September.

As mentioned above, the following day, Tuesday 5 September, is known to the Dutch as Mad Tuesday, as it seemed that the German Army was in flight. Operation *Comet* may well have succeeded if it had been launched as planned but the supply problems caused by the dispute between the Americans and the British led to postponements – first from the night of 9/10 September and then to the night of 11/12 before the cancellation of *Comet* just as the decision was reached to place the entire First Allied Airborne Army at Montgomery's disposal. By then the opportunity of a quick and easy victory had passed.

Having decided to commit the Airborne Army to support of Montgomery's northern advance, on 4 September Eisenhower sowed the seeds for the Arnhem operation by directing Brereton to 'operate in support of the Northern Group of Armies (i.e., Montgomery) up to and including the crossing of the Rhine.' In a private memorandum written on the 5th, Eisenhower specified that, alongside the broad front strategy, 'we should use our airborne forces to seize crossings over the Rhine and be in a position to thrust deep into the Ruhr and threaten Berlin.'[62] With that in mind, on 10 September, aboard Eisenhower's personal aircraft at Brussels airport, Montgomery explained the concept of Operation *Comet* and then began to lay out plans for an even more ambitious scheme that seemed to fit perfectly with the growing demands for Eisenhower to make use of his airborne army. Very much aware of Bradley's influence over Eisenhower, Montgomery and his senior advisors had taken great care to exclude US liaison officers from their discussions about the plan to outflank the West Wall altogether and push the British Second Army into northern Germany. Initially, Eisenhower had insisted that the clearing of Antwerp and the establishment of a bridgehead across the lower Rhine was as far as he was willing to go at this point but listened patiently as Montgomery began to describe using the 1st Airborne Army to open a route to Germany's back door. It was a strong argument. As a US intelligence summary a few days later noted:

> 'The German High Command has given first priority to General PATTON's drive, second to General HODGE's, and third to the drive North by the British and Canadian Armies. The establishment of these priorities leaves the area North and West of MAASTRICHT free from Panzer units … This situation plus the fact that the German Seventh and Fifteenth Armies are hard pressed for manpower and equipment accounts for the odds and ends on the enemy's line from ANTWERP to MAASTRICHT.'[63]

Other senior US commanders had joined Patton's vociferous complaints that Eisenhower was favouring the British over his own side and it was clear to him that to go ahead with the plan meant he would need to draw supplies away from US troops. However, he could see that what Montgomery was proposing made sense. The broad front strategy had been intended to keep the Germans guessing about where the next attack would come from. If Eisenhower favoured the US forces, he would be attacking where the Germans were prioritising their defences and were most prepared. Instead, the new plan would attack where it was least expected and provide the ideal opportunity to make maximum use of the airborne forces available. 'I not only approved,' he later wrote, 'I insisted upon it. What we needed was a bridgehead over the Rhine. If that could be accomplished, I was quite willing to wait on all other operations.'[64] It was a brave decision, but a correct one. The Americans were about to assault the West Wall defences of the Reich and Eisenhower correctly believed Patton was being overly optimistic about his ability to break through. Montgomery's plan was exactly the kind of operation he had been waiting for to revitalise the advance and to give the airborne a chance to show what they could do. Ever mindful of the effect this would have on his old friend Bradley, however, Eisenhower sought a compromise. The attack, he said, must be a limited one that merely extended the British advance.

I'll tell you what I'll do, Monty, I'll give you whatever you ask to get you over the Rhine because I want a bridgehead … but let's get over the Rhine first before we discuss anything else.

Still arguing about what he saw as a half measure, Montgomery accepted. When Bradley heard about the proposal, he thought that

had the pious, teetotalling Montgomery wobbled into SHAEF with a hangover, I could not have been more astonished … Although I never reconciled myself to the venture, I nevertheless freely concede that it was one of the most imaginative of the war.[65]

Operation *Market Garden* was born.

Notes

1 Brigadier James Hargest quoted in *Firing Line* p.350
2 PRO WO 285/13 Casualties and Ammunition, Second Army 1944–45 quoted in French p.147
3 Gavin, General James, *On to Berlin* (New York: Bantam 1979) p.148
4 Account of the US Army in Europe prepared for the US Army Center of Military History by David W. Hogan. Accessed at: http://www.history.army.mil/brochures/norfran/norfran.htm
5 Province, Charles M. *The Unknown Patton* (Hippocrene Books, 1983) CMP Productions, 1998 (Electronic Version)
6 SHAEF intelligence estimates, quoted in Forrest C. Pogue, *The Supreme Command* (Washington, 1951) pp.244–45.
7 The General Board, European Theater. Study Number 1 'Strategy of the Campaign in Western Europe 1944–45' US Army. Not dated p.45
8 Graham, D. and Bidwell, S. *Coalitions, Politicians and Generals* (London 1993) p.203 quoted in Neillands p.73
9 Neillands p.75
10 Horrocks, General Sir Brian *A Full Life* (Collins 1960) quoted in Cornelius Ryan *A Bridge Too Far* (Book Club Associates 1975) p.54
11 Franklin M. Davis Jr. *Across The Rhine* (Time Life Books 1980) p.22
12 The General Board p.44
13 Davis p.23
14 Fox, Lieutenant Colonel Jennifer B. 'Lessons Learned From Operation *Market Garden*' USAF Air University Report April 1994 p.24
15 Hibbert, Christopher *The Battle of Arnhem* (New York: Macmillan 1962) p.14
16 Davis p.23
17 Whicker, Alan, *Whicker's War* (HarperCollins 2005) pp.180–184
18 Clark, General M.W. *Calculated Risk: The War Memoirs of a Great American General* (Enigma Books 2007)
19 Ryan p.61
20 *Time* magazine Monday 4 May 1942
21 *Colliers* 11 December 1943 p.14
22 Hibbert p.14

23 Knightley, P. *The First Casualty* (London: Pan Books 1975) p.323–4

24 Brighton, T. *Masters of Battle: Monty, Patton and Rommel at War* (London: Viking 2008) p.205

25 'Patton waded ashore to lead attack that drove out tanks' *Milwaukee Journal* 14 July 1943

26 Brighton op cit p.206

27 Eisenhower, *Crusade* p.58–9

28 Butcher, Captain H.C. *My Three Years with Eisenhower* (London: Heinemann 1946) p.206

29 Ibid p.41

30 Ibid p.206

31 War Department. Instructions for US Servicemen in Britain. Washington 1942 p.4

32 Butcher p.522

33 See Leckie, R. *The Wars Of America* (Harper & Row, 1968)

34 Clark, G.B. *Devil Dogs: Fighting Marines of World War I* (Presidio Press 1999)

35 Knightley p.324

36 Corrigan, G. *Blood, Sweat and Arrogance and the Myths of Churchill's War* (London: Phoenix 2007) p.417

37 Ibid p.365

38 Brighton p.146

39 See Dr Gordon's course notes at: http://www.psych.wright.edu/gordon/psy110/Psy110Module47-slides.pdf

40 Frank Stroupe 'General George S. Patton, III' accessed at http://www.freeinfosociety.com/site. php?postnum=517 see also Charles M. Province *The Unknown Patton* (Hippocrene Books, 1983)

41 Corrigan, G. *Mud, Blood and Poppycock* (Cassell Books 2003) p.72

42 See Patton, R.H. *The Pattons: A Personal History of an American Family* (Brassey's, 2004) p.184

43 Private Charles Kuhl was later found to be suffering dysentery and malaria. See Toplin, R.B. *History by Hollywood: The Use and Abuse of the American Past* (University of Illinois Press, 1996)

44 Bradley pp.160–161

45 Butcher p.336

46 Bradley p.229–30

47 Ibid p.209

48 Ibid p.351

49 Ibid p.319–20

50 Province, Charles M. *The Unknown Patton* (Hippocrene Books, 1983) CMP Productions, 1998 (Electronic Version)

51 Essame, H. *Patton: A Study in Command* (New York: Charles Scribners Sons, 1974) p.23

52 Freiser, K-H. *The Blitzkrieg Legend* (Anapolis, Maryland: Naval Institute Press 2005) pp.156–157

53 Wilmot p.520

54 Whiting, Charles, *A Traveller's Guide to The Battle for the German Frontier* (Windrush Press 2000) p.31

55 *Time* magazine Monday, 4 May 1942

56 Carafano, Lieutenant Colonel James Jay, *The Ethics of Operation Cobra and the Normandy Breakout*, http://www.usafa.edu/isme/JSCOPE00/Carafano00.html

57 Bradley, General Omar, *Soldier's Story* (Henry Holt 1951) pp.157–8

58 Shillingberg William B. 'A Gathering of Generals' Originally published in Johns' Western Gallery auction catalogue *14: The Vandenberg Military Collection* (San Francisco, 2005)

59 MacDonald, Charles B. *The US Army in World War II: The Siegfried Line Campaign* (Washington: Office of the Chief of Military History 1963) pp.435–6

60 DDE Office Memorandum, Sep. 5, 1944, *The Eisenhower Papers*, vol. IV, p. 2121.

61 Brereton, Lewis H. *The Brereton Diaries: The War in the Air in the Pacific, Middle East and Europe, 3 October 1941–8 May 1945* (New York: William Morrow 1946) p.337

62 McDonald p.437

63 Annex 6 to Field Order 4 US Troop Carrier Command 13 September 1944

64 Ryan p.78

65 Ryan p.80

Chapter Three

From *Comet* to *Market Garden*

The plan Montgomery brought to Eisenhower was essentially an extension of Operation *Comet* which itself was one of a number of options under consideration by 21st Army Group HQ and its cancellation meant that Montgomery was now actively considering other alternatives. Second Army commander Lieutenant General Miles Dempsey had been one of those opposing a strike towards Arnhem and was arguing instead for an offensive towards the east to aim for crossing the Rhine at Wesel in cooperation with the US First Army but, as he confided in his diary on 9 September, he did not consider the Second Army would be ready to fight a 'real battle for at least another ten days'.[1] As a result, when he heard about *Comet*, Dempsey wondered 'Are we right to direct Second Army to Arnhem or would it be better to hold a firm left flank along the canals and strike due east?'[2] On 10 September he phoned Montgomery to arrange a meeting which would finalise which objective they should set and remained 'convinced that we should go to Wesel'. For David Belchem, 21st Army Group's Operations Officer, at that point 'there was no question of going to Arnhem. Dempsey and Browning arrived [on 10 September] to finalise their master plan for Wesel.' On arrival, they found Montgomery 'standing at the door with a telegram from the War Office in his hand' and he greeted them with the news that 'we are going to Arnhem.' Belcham later recalled that Montgomery was fully aware that 'all of us from Dempsey downwards were against [it].'[3] Dempsey himself believed that this latest message from London to address the V2 threat had been the deciding factor. Montgomery, Dempsey believed, had not 'really made up his mind on Arnhem before he got this telegram'.[4]

In the later rush to disassociate themselves from the disaster, many senior Allied officers attempted to suggest that the plan was one forced on them by the rash decision of Montgomery acting out of character. In fact, although rather more bold than his other operations, it fit with his 'colossal cracks' approach. All indications were that the Dutch border was held by a thin crust of defenders but that there was no real in-depth defence. The Germans were in disarray and, if he could secure sufficient resources, this could prove a knockout blow. That said, it soon became clear in the preparations for *Comet* that overconfidence had virtually dismissed the possibility of the Germans regrouping effectively and that little credence was given to the growing body of evidence that the Germans were not out of the fight just yet. There is, however, a strong case to be made that the real degree of Montgomery's culpability for pushing forward what would turn out to be a flawed plan is open to question. The most likely candidate for blame in deliberately ignoring the true level of risk involved is Montgomery's trusted airborne protégé – Lieutenant-General Frederick Arthur Montague 'Boy' Browning.[5]

In *A Bridge Too Far*, Cornelius Ryan writes that 'like Eisenhower, Lieutenant-General Browning and the headquarters of the First Allied Airborne Army in England were, at this

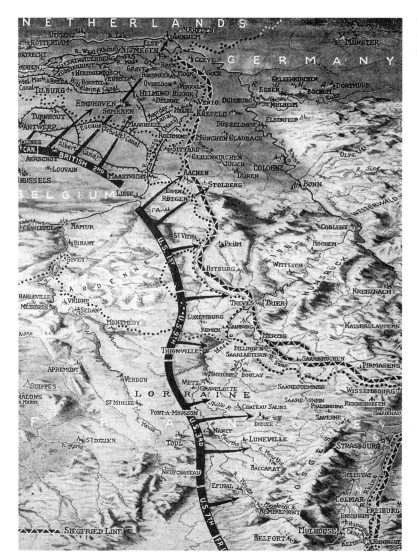

The situation in northwest Europe in September 1944.

moment, unaware of Montgomery's new airborne scheme.'[6] In fact, Browning knew full well that plans for Operation *Comet* were complete and indeed that the troops had only just been stood down at their bases in Britain. It is not even beyond the realms of possibility that his influence with Churchill had prompted the decision to push for the use of his airborne forces to remove the V2 threat. Whatever the truth, despite allegedly being caught by surprise by Montgomery's decision, Browning was able to report to First Allied Airborne Army HQ by 1430hrs on the 10th and by 1800hrs, newly appointed by Brereton to command the airborne operations, to give a detailed briefing to 34 senior Allied officers. Historian William Buckingham suggests that the usually calm and methodical Montgomery was presenting such a risky plan because his own lack of airborne experience meant he did not fully appreciate the degree of risk involved. Certainly it is clear that although the concept was Montgomery's, he and his staff at 21st Army Group had little or nothing to do with the actual detailed planning and there was a lack of liaison staff at First Allied Airborne Army, supporting the claim that he handed responsibility entirely to the judgement of Browning.

Major-General Browning, self styled father of the British airborne whose determination to be the first commander to land a Corps HQ by air diverted resources away from the primary objective.

Other sources suggest that Montgomery was very much aware of the risk, but that the potential benefits of the operation were so great that the gamble was considered worthwhile. Operation *Comet* had been considered practicable with just one airborne division albeit with severe doubts expressed by General Sosabowski of the Polish Brigade and Brigadier 'Shan' Hackett of 4th Parachute Brigade among others about the likely German reaction. The assignment of First Allied Airborne Army meant that each objective would now be attacked by divisional sized forces. If planners believed it possible before, surely now the risk of failure was negligible.

In an atmosphere of fierce inter-Allied and inter-service rivalry and competition for scarce resources, the airborne was a new arm, still regarded by many of the old school as a gimmick. It needed a man who could champion it and Browning appeared to be that man. Unfortunately, like so many of his contemporaries in all armies, the distinction between what was best for his command and what was best for him personally blurred considerably as the end of the war approached.

The 47-year-old 'Boy' Browning had served with distinction with the Guards in the First World War, earning a Distinguished Service Order and Croix de Guerre before his twentieth birthday and had first met Churchill in a dugout on the Western Front where, having resigned from the government over Gallipoli, Churchill was temporarily serving as a Lieutenant-Colonel in the 6th Royal Scots Fusiliers. Between the wars, Browning set about renewing his acquaintance with Churchill and using it to enter the world of the social elite and in the process became skilled in both the political and administrative roles necessary for success as the type of soldier usually dismissed as a 'Whitehall Warrior'. Personally given command of the airborne forces by his old friend Churchill, Browning was able to make use of his connections to ensure the delivery of supplies and material for his men and to bring with him a large number of senior NCOs from the Guards to ensure a high degree of discipline.

Taking control over almost every aspect of his division, Browning qualified as a parachutist and glider pilot and did much to create the popular image of the British airborne forces. It was he who decided in the summer of 1942 that they ought to have a distinctive beret instead of those of their former units (contrary to some claims, his novelist wife Daphne du Maurier did not choose the colour) and assigned the artist Major Edward Seago to design an emblem for the airborne forces, finally approving one inspired by Greek mythology showing the warrior Bellerophon riding Pegasus, the winged horse. Browning's own maroon beret was the only indication that he was an airborne officer having also found time to design his own personal uniform made of barathea with a false Uhlan-style front complete with medal ribbons, collar patches and rank badges, together with kid leather gloves and a highly polished 'Sam Browne' belt and swagger stick. He then commanded Britain's first airborne unit and had seen it through operations in North Africa before being appointed as Eisenhower's senior airborne advisor in 1943 just before the disastrous airborne assault on Sicily. When the First Allied Airborne Army was brought into being, Browning was, as he was quick to point out, the most senior and experienced airborne commander available – at least on paper.

Plans for the creation of First Allied Airborne Army had been proposed in May 1944 as an attempt to bring all Allied airborne troops under unified control. A consultation document was sent to 1st United States Army Group, 21st Army Group and the Allied Expeditionary Air Force, but the idea was immediately rejected by Major-General Leven C. Allen, Chief of Staff of 1st United States Army Group. Allen argued, amongst other things, that the larger number of US airborne troops, the differences in equipment and staff between British and US formations and the limited capacity of the available transport aircraft to carry only the total number of US airborne troops meant that there was no need for a unified command for both US and British airborne forces. On the other hand, 21st Army Group and the Allied Expeditionary Air Force both agreed to the recommendation with only a few minor changes. On 17 June Major-General H.R. Bull, the Assistant Chief-of-Staff, Operations and Plans of the Supreme Headquarters Allied Expeditionary Force, recommended that a combined airborne troops headquarter be created, although the original suggestion that it include control of the Air Force Troop Carrier Command was dropped.

Squabbles about who should command the force were founded on a fear among airborne commanders that air force control over soldiers might set a dangerous precedent and in turn the air forces complained about administrative problems involved in combining headquarters and resources. Despite this opposition, Eisenhower remained determined to create a single command that would control both airborne forces and troop carrier units, taking his proposal to General of the Army George Marshall and General of the Air Force Henry 'Hap' Arnold and asking for the assignment of a US Army Air Corps officer as commander of the unified headquarters. After a great deal of discussion they agreed that, as the British had already accepted, the air forces would control all airborne operations up to the point at which the airborne forces were consolidated on the ground, when control would revert to a ground commander.

Having agreed what the new commander would control, the problem became one of finding suitably qualified personnel. The Airborne Center at Camp Mackall was approached by the US Department of War to offer personnel and, in the UK, Headquarters Company of the Second Airborne Brigade would be disbanded and its personnel transferred to the new command. The US Strategic Air Forces in Europe would be asked to allocate ten officers and 50 enlisted men and, after discussion between Eisenhower, Arnold and Marshall, it was decided that the first commanding officer of the formation should be US Army Air Force Lieutenant General Lewis H. Brereton, who currently commanded the USAAF Ninth Air Force. Brereton was not a supporter of the idea of a combined HQ and thought that it should be brought under the control of his air force but eventually was won round by pressure from above.

Having finally and reluctantly agreeing to accept the post, it was Brereton who suggested the title of 'First Allied Airborne Army', and the name was accepted by Eisenhower on 16 August but opposed by Major-General Bull, who argued that such a name would be inaccurate, because, as he saw it, there was no intention to use the organisation as an army as such, only to use parts of it. This argument overruled, the new organisation was given operational control over the aircraft of US IX Troop Carrier Command and XVIII Corps (Airborne), which comprised the US 17th, 82nd and 101st Airborne Divisions along with the British I Airborne Corps comprising the 1st and 6th Airborne Divisions, 1st Special Air

Service Brigade and the Polish 1st Independent Parachute Brigade. It also gained control of the RAF troop carrier units on an operational basis, the RAF remaining independent on other operations as need demanded.

When General Eisenhower gave his approval to the establishment of the First Allied Airborne Army, Browning was the most senior British airborne officer and therefore a claim was made that this made him the senior Allied airborne commander as British airborne troops had been first into action as early as 1941. With resources for the Allied Airborne Army coming predominantly from the Americans it was clear this would not happen. Instead, responsibility was given to Brereton with Browning designated as his deputy and remaining as commander of 1st British Airborne Corps. By six months Brereton's senior and having been involved from the start in the development of Britain's airborne forces, Browning was not best pleased but unfortunately, his experience did not extend to actual combat command and his involvement to date had been entirely at staff level. Adept at playing the same political games as men like General Clark, Browning had managed to create an image of himself as the creator of the airborne concept that far outshone many with a greater right to the title – not least Colonel John Rock, the man appointed in 1940 to create the airborne corps and who had started from 'rock bottom' to bring together civilian sport gliders and RAF surplus parachutes and used them to develop the Parachute and Glider Pilot Regiments. Rock had died in a flying accident two years earlier and General Gale, the highly experienced commander of 6th Airborne, was only recently returned from Normandy as Browning pushed himself forward for the position as chief of all Allied airborne forces.

General James Gavin, newly promoted to command of the 82nd Airborne after its return from Normandy, would be one of those most directly affected by Browning's appointment but gives a confused impression of the man as seen through American eyes. In November 1943, Gavin met with General Matthew Ridgway before leaving Italy to prepare for Normandy.

> He cautioned me against the machinations and scheming of General F.M. Browning, who was the senior British airborne officer, and well he should have. For although the Americans had provided most of the troops and airlift, the British seemed determined to take command of the total Allied airborne effort. General Browning had not been in a command position so far but had been promoted to Lieutenant General; thus, because of his rank, he would automatically be given command of any combined British-American airborne force. I do not believe that he had any sinister design on our resources, but the British seemed to be convinced that they were better at planning and employing airborne troops than we were.[7]

General 'Jumping Jim' Gavin (right) newly promoted to command the 82nd Airborne with Browning's main rival for the command of the 1st Allied Airborne Army, General Ridgeway, seen here wearing the grenades that earned him the nickname 'Old Iron Tits'. (US Army)

Arriving in London, Gavin met with British General Frederick Morgan of COSSAC (Chiefs of Staff to the Supreme Allied Commander) on 17 November. In passing, he mentioned Browning and was told 'Ah yes, he is an empire builder.'[8] However, describing a visit to the fledgling 82nd in the US during 1942, Gavin recalls Browning as 'the senior British airborne officer, a dapper, handsome, charming man, who in combat turned out to be a first class soldier in every respect.'[9]

Gavin, as we shall see, had more cause to be critical of Browning than most and his memoirs are peppered with disparaging remarks about the British. Yet he describes Browning as 'a first class soldier in every respect' who did not have any 'sinister design' on American resources. Indeed many, even in the US military, saw Brereton – an Air Force officer with no experience at all of working with airborne troops and who regarded the position as beneath him – as being unsuited to command the Airborne Army in almost every respect bar his not being British (despite his pro-British leanings). A man fond of drink and a poor administrator, many held Brereton responsible for the loss of the US Far Eastern Air Force, believing it was his friendship with General 'Hap' Arnold in Washington that had kept him on the promotion ladder instead of being fired and that this was what earned him the command of First Allied Airborne Army.

When American intervention cost him the job of supreme commander of the Allied Airborne, Browning, relegated to his nominal deputy position as a Corps Commander, saw himself as being placed in direct competition with his rival, the newly promoted General Matthew Ridgway of the US XVIII Airborne Corps for the top job. Ridgway, himself cultivating his image as a fighting general by habitually wearing infantry webbing with hand grenades attached (and earning himself the nickname 'Old Iron Tits' amongst his men), had at least been dropped into Normandy and had some combat experience. Browning was very much aware that his position as airborne chief was becoming ever more precarious and that time was running out for him to take control.

Ironically, Bradley's intervention at Tournai had saved Browning and indirectly led to the operation that would bring his tanks to a halt. In the planning stages of Operation *Linnet* Browning had used the lack of available maps to delay preparations, eventually threatening his resignation over the matter when Brereton insisted on going ahead without them. The complaint was justified, but there is also some suggestion that Browning may have been inflating the problem as part of a deliberate ploy to undermine the operation in support of the US First Army in order to ensure the resources were available for Montgomery's Second Army to the north. Brereton immediately put Ridgway on standby to replace Browning but Bradley's intervention resolved the standoff by making the operation redundant. The incident left Browning with his position both in the airborne and, more importantly, in the post-war military hierarchy, under threat. It also made the employment of the airborne by the British vital. At the same time, the inclusion in the plan of two US divisions appears to have left Ridgway assuming that he should have command of the operation. That Browning was in command should not have been a surprise to Ridgway. The two divisions had been placed under command of 1st British Airborne Corps for Operations *Linnet I* and *II* and Browning had been given command of *Comet* from the outset so it seemed logical that he should remain in command, but when Ridgway arrived in Nijmegen on 20 September, his concern was not for the battle raging around him but for the (erroneous) belief that Browning was in command of 'his' divisions.

As Perret puts it in *Winged Victory*, the undermining of the airborne assault in Operation *Linnet* 'in turn put pressure on Montgomery: use them or lose them.'[10] General Gavin also noted the cancellation of *Linnet* and felt that by now 'the high command was hell bent on getting the First Allied Airborne Army into the fight, whether or not the commitment was decisive or even sound.'[11] As confidence in an early end to the war grew at SHAEF, Browning knew that the Arnhem strike, now known as Operation *Market Garden*, could be his last opportunity to take command of a large scale airborne attack.

The Plan

The concept behind Operation *Market Garden* was deceptively simple. There would be two mutually dependent elements. Operation *Market*: Two of the five divisions of First Allied Airborne Army, one British and one American, would drop to form an 'airborne carpet' across Holland to seize bridges and other features between the existing front lines and the town of Arnhem under the overall tactical command of General Browning.

Operation *Garden*: Another US airborne division would come under the command of the British XXX Corps under Lieutenant-General Brian Horrocks and would land immediately behind the German front line to secure a ground route across which XXX Corps would then spearhead a push by the British Second Army to move north and link with the airborne en route, reaching Arnhem and the Rhine within days.

With these bridges under Allied control over two million men of the British Second Army and US Ninth Army would cross the Rhine and smash into the Ruhr — Germany's industrial heartland. The dash would follow a narrow highway north and would be highly vulnerable to counterattack. To defend against this, Lieutenant General Neil Ritchie's XII Corps would advance on XXX Corps' western flank and Lieutenant General Sir Richard O'Connor's VIII Corps to its east.

The plan was largely a 'cut and paste' modification of *Comet* — so much so that many of the briefing papers and plans bore the name, hastily crossed out. The massive airborne operation would begin with the US 101st Airborne Division, under Major General Maxwell D. Taylor, dropping in two locations just north of the XXX Corps position on the line of the Meuse-Escaut Canal to take the bridges north-west of Eindhoven at Zon and Veghel. Then, north-east of them at Grave and Nijmegen, Major General Gavin's 82nd Airborne Division would take more bridges near those two towns, allowing XXX Corps to push on towards the British 1st Airborne Division under Major-General Robert Elliot 'Roy' Urquhart and the Polish 1st Independent Parachute Brigade under Major General Stanislaw Sosabowski who would drop to take the road bridge at Arnhem and rail bridge at Oosterbeek.

General Montgomery and General Brian Horrocks, commander of XXX Corps.

To achieve the breakthrough, the British forces at the extreme northern end of the route would need to hold their positions long enough for XXX Corps to make the 64-mile dash along the airborne carpet to link up with them. Experience in the previous weeks suggested it would take, at most, a matter of days. The premise was that German resistance along the start line would be confined to a 'thin crust' formed by men of Kampfgruppe 'Walther' with no more than an estimated ten weak battalions with ten assault guns. Once this crust was broken, the race would begin. Although the timescale did not allow for a great deal of planning, when Colonel Joe Vandeleur, whose Irish Guards Group would lead the charge, attended a briefing in Belgium he admitted wondering 'How much time do you really need to plan for a straight bash through German lines?'[12]

The Air Plan

Alongside inter-Allied politics, the British were hampered by inter-service rivalries between the Army and the Royal Air Force about who should control airborne operations. The RAF had been an independent service since 1918 and were determined to remain so. Whilst their American colleagues would not gain their independence until 1947 and were effectively a branch of the US Army, the British Army and the RAF had, during the cash- and resource-starved interwar years, been involved in frequently petty, tit-for-tat bickering about roles and responsibilities. The price of securing Air Ministry cooperation in the formation of parachute forces in 1940 had been an agreement that the RAF would remain in control of all airborne operations planning (including the selection of drop zones) until the troops were on the ground. It appeared to be a logical enough compromise for the small-scale operations originally envisaged – but now it would lead to disaster.

The conflicting priorities of the Royal Air Force and Army were highlighted in a post-war analysis by General Gavin who explained the need for airborne troops to be briefed, prepared and loaded onto their carriers as complete platoons, companies, battalions and regiments at the same airfields. They also needed to load as units so that they could maintain their unit integrity for the jump and to enable regrouping on the ground. This, he argued, meant they would be 'immediately ready for ground engagements as intact combat units. Their arrival at their objectives as tactical units ready to fight especially appears to be imperative and fundamental.' On the other hand, he acknowledged, troop-carrier units required exactly the same things. They would want to service their own aircraft and prefer to fly their own squadrons. They too would suffer command, control and administration problems if they had to break up squadrons or flights to accommodate an airborne organisation that couldn't fit into the usual number of aircraft in each flight.[13]

There has been a tendency to view the problems inherent within the air plan as being a solely British failing. David Bennett, for example, writes:

> The air plan was made by the air force in the light of what it perceived to be possible. The Americans did things differently, with the airborne laying down what it wanted and the air force delivering the goods. Whatever the theory, there was more harmonious co-operation among the Americans than there was among the British, where formalities of responsibility took precedence over the need to get the job done in the most effective way.[14]

On closer examination, however, this argument falls apart unless one accepts the possibility that Gavin and Taylor preferred their divisions delivered piecemeal over several days rather than to have second lifts on D-Day. Even though the US IX Troop Carrier Command was, in effect, an army unit, the Americans would face exactly the same difficulties as their British counterparts in arguing for a say in where, how and when their troops would land. Further, Bennett himself has pointed out that during the planning for Operation *Comet*, the Royal Air Force had already agreed to coup de main assaults, different landing zones, flying two lifts on D-Day and had shown a willingness to land gliders south of the Arnhem bridge.[15] These plans would only be overturned after the operation was expanded to include the IX Troop Carrier Command and on the insistence of its commander, General Paul Williams with the backing of Brereton.

The 1250 C-47 Dakota transports available to First Allied Airborne Army each had a capacity of 18–22 paratroopers depending on the equipment they carried, providing a lift capacity of 27,500 men at most. To take and hold the bridges, Operation *Market* intended to deliver over 34,600 men by air to the battlefield. The 36 battalions involved would need all 15 aircraft groups of the US IX Troop Carrier Command and 16 squadrons of the RAF's 38 Group – currently using converted bombers on special operations missions in support of resistance groups – and a transport formation, 46 Group. In addition, each division would need re-supply drops once on the ground. According to Gavin this meant each division would require 264 tons of supplies per day. Whereas *Comet* would have landed a single division, as Brereton wanted, 'with thunderclap surprise', it quickly became clear that the massive increase in troop numbers now assigned to the task meant that needs would far outweigh the capacity of the available aircraft. As a result, *Market Garden* would be a drawn-out affair over at least three days. The air force planners seem to have missed the irony of the fact that the new schedule would mean that if all went as well as hoped, the last groups of airborne troops would not be landing until long after XXX Corps had passed through their objectives.

Over the years the belief has grown that the airborne troops themselves were clear that they would prefer to take potentially heavy losses landing near an objective than to land and have to fight to it. For the Arnhem assault, Colonel George Chatterton, commander of the Glider Pilot Regiment, had proposed a coup de main by glider near the bridge, arguing that even if half the force were wiped out, the risk was worth it. After all, such an attack had already formed part of Operation *Comet*. 'I saw no reason why we could not do it but apparently nobody else saw the need for it and I distinctly remember being called a bloody murderer and assassin for suggesting it,' he later recalled.[16] Certainly some were of the opinion that the losses involved could be justified but, as we shall see, the belief was not as widespread as is often assumed.

The change in attitude towards what was regarded as possible can perhaps be traced to the increase in size of the operation. Operation *Market* would rely heavily on relatively inexperienced US troop carrier pilots, and US Air Force chiefs were still attempting to rectify the serious problems they had had on airborne operations and in particular the chaos of previous drops for which they had been heavily criticised. During the invasion of Sicily in July 1943, inexperienced or poorly trained aircrews had struggled to maintain formation and widespread panic caused by the fear of flak had meant the release of paratroopers at too high an altitude or at too great a speed. British gliders had been cut loose by their American tug planes at the first sign of anti-aircraft fire and as a result hundreds of men had drowned as they crashed into the sea. The Allied paratroopers were supposed to be dropped from C-47 Dakota aircraft slowing down to almost stalling speed of 100 miles per hour at a height of 600 feet. In reality, they were flung out at 1500 feet with the aircraft racing along at nearly their top speed of 200 miles per hour. Together with strong winds and navigation errors this meant that 3405 American paratroopers were dropped across 60 miles of south-east Sicily[17] and in the early stages of the landing, James Gavin, then a regimental commander in the 82nd Airborne Division, found himself on the ground with just 19 of his men having made the rendezvous.[18] He later estimated that no more than 425 of the 3405 men (about 12 per cent of the force), had actually landed somewhere near the planned drop zones.[19] In the same drop, Colonel Reuben Tucker of the 504th PIR could only account for about a quarter of his men 24 hours after landing. Similarly, just 27 men of the intended force of 200 British paratroopers landed close enough to take part in the fight for the vital bridge at Ponte Grande.[20] As the British survivors of the glider crashes were brought back to their North African bases, tempers were running high, especially when it was learned that the pilots who had panicked and caused so many Allied deaths were about to receive medals for bravery. General Sir John Hackett, then with the reserve brigade, wrote:

> Glider pilots who were recovered from the sea came back looking for tug pilots' throats to cut. I saw no option but to confine them to camp until after the American parade for the award of decorations for gallantry, by which time the admirable qualities always to be found in glider pilots had reasserted themselves and calm was restored.[21]

A year later the airborne assault in Normandy had seen 3500 of the 101st Airborne's 6600 paratroopers still missing by the end of the following day[22] and Lieutenant-Colonel Otway of the British 6th Airborne found himself attacking the Merville Battery with just a fraction of the force believed necessary for success. In August, the drop for Operation *Dragoon* in southern France had landed about 60 per cent of the US and 40 per cent of the British paratroopers too far from their drop zones to be considered to have made a successful drop.[23] Urquhart, newly appointed by Browning to command 1st Airborne, expressed doubts about his own lack of experience to command an airborne force but it has been suggested that his position was a political gambit by Browning to have an inexperienced (and therefore compliant) divisional commander who would not be able to challenge or question Browning's alleged abilities as an airborne leader. Indeed, the expert advice which Urquhart received was that heavy losses would be suffered if he attempted to make his initial landings south of the river close to the Arnhem bridge. The flak, it was said, would be intense, and the fenland here too soft for the landing of gliders. It was difficult for Urquhart to overrule this expert opinion, since he had no previous experience of airborne operations. Moreover, he had inherited a division which had suffered heavily in Sicily because its landings had been

A Douglas C-47 Skytrain or Dakota, the military transport aircraft used during Operation *Market Garden*.

scattered and strongly opposed. Since then, 'the doctrine had grown up within the Division that it was more important to land accurately and safely than to land close to the objective.'[24]

Aware of the problems involved in airborne drops and not willing to come in for still more criticism, air planners agreed with the prevailing thinking in 1st Division, deciding that the landings would be made in daylight over areas deemed to be relatively safe. This would avoid the aircraft stream becoming dispersed and would land the troops in a concentrated area. It is also true that the air forces were by now increasingly unwilling to risk their dwindling aircraft resources as the war neared its end. Reports suggested heavy flak concentrations in Arnhem and at the Deelen airfield to the north, ruling out those areas as far as air planners were concerned.

The period commencing 17 September would be moonless and the risk of another confused drop together with the awareness that Luftwaffe night fighter capability was still largely effective, ruled out night operations. The selection of drop and landing zones on these criteria meant that those chosen for the British were up to eight miles from the Arnhem bridge. This goes some way to explaining the seemingly contradictory refusal to land troops near the bridge on the basis that the drop zone was unsuitable, yet to use the same area to land the Poles later – once any opposition had been suppressed and thus when it would be safe for aircraft.

An important factor at this point, often ignored, is that it was the Wesel plan that was under active consideration by Montgomery as the preferred option for a strike across the Rhine but this was rejected out of hand by Brereton and his staff. They argued that the town lay in the belt of anti-aircraft defences around the Ruhr and was considered too dangerous for the slow moving glider tugs to fly over. (The town was taken by an airborne assault the following year.) Consequently, air planners pressed for the more lightly defended Arnhem, forcing Montgomery's hand. With an Air Force officer in command of the Airborne Army, it was not just the British paratroops who found themselves taking second place to air force priorities. 'The airmen had the final say,' wrote Major General Urquhart later, 'and we knew it.'[25]

When Gavin first heard that Urquhart's men would be landing so far from the bridge, he was incredulous.

> I couldn't believe my ears. It seemed contrary to all we had learned so far. I turned to Colonel John Norton, my G-3, and said, 'My God, he can't mean it,' and Norton replied, 'He does, and he is going to try to do it.' … but I felt very apprehensive about his prospects, since he would have to move on foot through the city of Arnhem and its suburbs where even a few German infantry could impose an almost indefinite delay upon him.[26]

After a later briefing, company commander Captain T. Moffatt Burriss of the 504th PIR wrote that the plan seemed puzzling and caused the 82nd to doubt the 'capacity of the British to wage conventional warfare'.[27] The British drop zones were between five and eight miles from the Arnhem road bridge and this has been rightly criticised. However, despite his criticism of the British plan, Gavin remains quiet on the subject of his own drop zones – also at least five miles from the Nijmegen bridge and requiring an advance through a buil-up area where, as he says, even a few German infantry could impose an 'almost indefinite delay'. In which case, presumably even a few American paratroopers on and around the Nijmegen bridge could do the same for any German response, yet as we shall see, no attempt was made to establish a presence there until it was too late, thus placing Gavin in exactly the same predicament as Urquhart at Arnhem. In the event, the Nijmegen bridge was eventually captured by the 504th PIR, who had landed up to ten miles away from it.

After accepting the drop zones Gavin then changed his priorities from the capture of the bridge to the consolidation of the Groesbeek Heights, later writing in his diary that 'I knew that I had to hold the high ground if for no other reason than to bring in the reinforcements so essential to continuing the battle, for that was where the drop and landing zones were.'[28] In other words, seizure of the bridge might be the crucial linchpin of the entire operation, but it would now take second place to the need to compensate for Brereton's refusal to undertake additional lifts on D-Day.

Another serious difficulty was caused by the decision to stagger the drops to accommodate the inexperience of aircrews and the maintenance of the aircraft at their home bases. The argument that more than one lift per day would risk losing precious aircraft to mechanical and human error by tired crews was reasonable up to a point but the distances involved should not have precluded additional flights. Indeed, staggering the drops made the risks even higher. As General Gavin later noted;

> Reacting quickly to the first landings, *the enemy is usually waiting for re-supply transports on their subsequent runs.* [Gavin's emphasis] None of us who saw the re-supply flights coming into the 82nd Airborne Division along the Merderet river in Normandy will ever forget the amount of flak and small-arms fire the troop-carrier formations had to take. It was 'murder on the Merderet' as some of the troopers described it at the time.[29]

Faced with a piecemeal insertion, in order to secure the landing zones valuable troops would have to be detailed to remain where they landed, thus significantly reducing the already depleted numbers available to achieve the objective. Far more experienced than Urquhart and dealing with a branch of the US Army rather than a fiercely independent organisation, General Gavin managed, albeit with great difficulty, to make some minor alterations to the drop zones for his 504th PIR for the capture of the Grave bridge, but otherwise was also pressured into working to a plan devised for the convenience of the air force that would deliver his men.

As soon as Eisenhower agreed to the plan the first operational conference on Operation *Market* was held at the headquarters of the First Allied Airborne Army at Sunnyhill Park at 1800hrs on 10 September. Amongst those present for Browning's briefing were Brereton,

as Commander of the First Allied Airborne Army, along with his troop carrier and airborne commanders and their staffs. After outlining the situation, Browning explained that the aim of the operation was 'to capture and hold the crossings over the canals and rivers on the main axis of advance of the British Second Army, ie EINDHOVEN-GRAVE-NIJMEGEN-ARNHEM.'[30]

To achieve this, the US 101st Airborne Division under General Maxwell Taylor would land north of Eindhoven to capture the bridges over the river

General Miles Dempsey, Commander of the British 2nd Army.

Aa, Willems Canal, river Dommel (St Oedenrode) and Wilhelmina Canal (Zon) and then go on to capture Eindhoven itself. Securing the road from Eindhoven to Grave would give the 101st a perimeter of some 40 miles to cover and Second Army commander General Dempsey later overruled Browning by allowing the 101st to halt at Veghel, leaving a gap of some 13 miles between the 101st and 82nd. The US 82nd Airborne Division under Gavin was to capture the bridges over the river Maas at Grave, the Maas-Waal Canal and the road bridge in the centre of Nijmegen as well as securing the Groesbeek Heights, an area of wooded hills about 8 miles long to the east of Nijmegen. The British 1st Airborne Division's landing zones were on the heath land west of Arnhem, and their targets would be the road bridge in the town centre, the railway bridge out to the west on the lower Rhine and a pontoon bridge which was later discovered to have been dismantled on the eve of the operation.

Priority would be given to the US paratroop divisions on D-Day with their being given the greater share of assets – 424 C-47s and 70 gliders – to be followed by 450 gliders on D+1 and a further 385 on D+2. The 82nd were given 480 C-47s and 50 gliders on D-Day to be reinforced by 454 gliders on D+1 and a further 258 gliders on D+2. In all, the US effort would use almost every available glider and use every glider pilot in the UK. On the first day the British would be allocated just 145 powered aircraft but 341 Horsa, 13 of the huge Hamilcars and 10 American-built Waco CG-4A gliders. The three British lifts to Arnhem alone would involve 697 tug aircraft of various types and almost the entire strength of the Glider Pilot Regiment to fly in nearly 700 gliders.

In keeping with the general American dislike of Montgomery, US glider pilot veteran John Lowden accuses him of having 'vacillated about a firm date to give the green light for *Market Garden* and during the two weeks that elapsed the Germans were able to resample and reorganize their chewed up combat units after the campaigns in Normandy and southern France.'[31] It is not clear, however, where this claimed delay of two weeks has come from. Having been given permission to go ahead and promised support on the morning of 10 September, the first briefing was held that evening, thus Montgomery stands accused of being both too rash in pushing forward too quickly and too indecisive in setting a date at the same time. In fact, on the 10th Brereton pushed for the operation to begin just four days later but the practical problems involved in simply moving the troops to their takeoff airfields were too complex. Finally persuaded, Brereton agreed a delay. The first drops would begin at 1300hrs on Sunday, 17 September.

82nd Airborne Plan

Some accounts suggest the conference did not take much more than an hour; Gavin remembers it as taking about three and at the end each commander returned to his own HQ to start his staff working on analysis and planning. 'Operation *Market* did not appear to pose any new type of problem that had not been encountered in the planning for Sicily, Italy, Normandy, or for the many operations we had planned but not carried into execution' wrote Gavin[32] and by the 13th, operational orders had been drawn up. These included the instruction that the 508th PIR under Colonel Lindquist were to prepare to seize the Nijmegen bridge 'on the orders of the Divisional commander'.[33]

The following day, as arranged, Browning gathered the commanders together and asked them to outline their plans. Gavin described how his division would

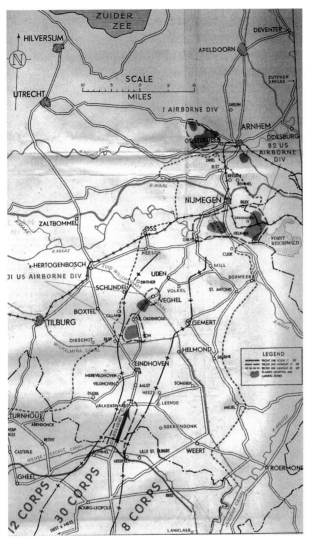

The intended route for Operation *Market Garden*.

... land by parachute and glider commencing D-Day south of Nijmegen; seize and hold the highway bridges across the Mass [sic] river at Grave and the Waal river at Nijmegen; seize, organize, and hold the high ground between Nijmegen and Groesbeek; deny the roads in the Division area to the enemy; and dominate the area bounded North by line running from Beek West through Hatert and thence Southwest to Eindschestraat, South by river Mass and the Mook-Riethorst highway, East by Cleve-Nijmegen highway and Forst Reichswald, and West by line running North and South through Eindschestraat.[34]

As the 82nd's historian Phil Nordyke explains, this would be 'the largest, most complex airborne operation ever attempted'[35] and would require the 82nd to seize four bridges over the Maas and Waal rivers and five over the Maas-Waal canal, 'be concerned' about an armoured attack from the Reichswald, wipe out any troops in the area and finally to 'be concerned' about a possible armoured attack from the Arnhem area.

The sole aim of the entire airborne operation was to seize control of bridges across Holland so that XXX Corps could reach the 1st Airborne at Arnhem as quickly as possible. It was later described in one report as

> ... resembling the difficult task of threading a piece of cotton through the eyes of seven needles in a row; lick your piece of cotton and try and thread it through all seven eyes but if a hole is missed and the cotton is splayed, some frantic licking will be required to get it through the next one.[36]

For a commander, the first and most important consideration is the 'selection and maintenance of the aim' or, put more simply, deciding what he is trying to do and how he will do it. At an early stage, the focus of the 82nd's efforts drifted away from the capture of perhaps the most vital of the seven needles.

During the planning phase, Browning ordered Gavin not to attempt to reach the bridge before securing the heights. 'I could not have agreed with him more,' Gavin recalled, 'but I was deeply troubled by the possibility of failing to accomplish some of my objectives.' He resolved that 'if I could possibly spare a battalion, I knew I had to commit it to the Nijmegen bridge as quickly as I could send it in that direction.'[37] The capture of the last, crucial element of the 'airborne carpet' was thus relegated to a chore to be completed once the Division was secure. The question now arises, why were the Groesbeek Heights – which were not going anywhere – suddenly more important than the crucial bridge that was key to the entire operation and already rigged for demolition?

The British, Gavin later claimed, were 'greatly preoccupied' with the roughly 25 square miles of heavily wooded area known as the Reichswald, just inside the German border. It provided excellent cover, and according to Gavin the British were convinced that there was a considerable German armour presence there. At about 300 feet, the Groesbeek ridge is the highest ground in the area and forms the boundary of the forest marking the German border and Gavin decided that the ridge had to be his first priority, arguing that 'in German hands, physical possession of the bridges would be absolutely worthless, since it completely dominated the bridges and all the terrain around it.' He went on to argue that

> it is a basic concept of airborne tactics that an airhead must first be established, from which further tactical operations can be conducted. This high ground provided ideally such an area. I personally considered it the key to the accomplishment of the entire mission; and thought that even if we were driven off the low ground around the bridges, if the high ground could be held, ultimately the Second Army could accomplish its mission.[38]

Conventional military thinking would agree that holding the high ground is almost always the safest action. However, this was not a conventional operation. Major-General John Frost – who, as a Lieutenant-Colonel commanded the paratroopers holding Arnhem bridge – has studied the campaign in detail. Speaking of the ridge, he argued:

> It is in fact a gentle slope and it's always nice to be a little bit higher than your enemy and as such it does perfectly control the exits from Germany through the rather wooded territory there but what happens on those Groesbeek Heights had absolutely no effect or no influence on what happened at the Nijmegen Bridge. The vital thing here was the bridge. It didn't matter how much you went and sat on the Groesbeek Heights, which were only about 300 or 400 feet high anyhow, if you haven't got the Nijmegen Bridge, and no German sitting on top of those heights can hurt anybody who's trying to take the Nijmegen Bridge. It's an irrelevant factor in my view.[39]

The justification given for prioritising the high ground was the threat of attack from the Reichswald forest east of the Groesbeek Heights although, as we have already seen, the main need was to protect the landing zones for the reinforcements planned for subsequent days. The briefing for the 82nd Airborne declared that the German forces from 'ROTTERDAM to the German frontier might comprise a Regt from 719 Div, a regt from 347 Div, remnants of 70 Div, a few mobile [battalions], some scraped up static troops and one Panzer Division, much the worse for wear'.[40] It also raised the possibility of some 4000 SS recruits in the Nijmegen area and suggested an 'estimate of a divisional strength in this area may not be far wide of the mark'. At some point, in addition, American planners began to talk of the presence of 1000 tanks in the area – a ridiculously high figure given the losses at Falaise – and the error is attributed to Gavin's Intelligence Officer, Colonel Winton's,

Aerial shots of the Nijmegen bridges in 1943 with the road crossing (left) and rail (right).

misinterpretation of the available information. There is no evidence to suggest that the British really were concerned about the presence of 'considerable armor' in the Reichswald. In fact, remaining intelligence reports for Operation *Market Garden* show that the British repeatedly downplayed the threat, questioning the effectiveness of what they saw as the battered remnants of Panzer divisions. The intelligence briefing provided to the 504th PIR claimed that no more than around 250 tanks were operational in the whole of Holland with a maximum reinforcement of 350 possible, albeit unlikely. The 21st Army Group estimate suggested that the Reichswald might contain the equivalent of 'two Home Guard divisions'.

The 82nd's plan, then, involved dropping in a triangle formed by the Grave bridge at bottom left, the town of Groesbeek as bottom right and the Nijmegen bridge as the apex. Between the 504th at Grave and the rest of the Division were thought to be some 4000 SS recruits in a heavily built-up area in which, Gavin said, 'a few well placed automatic weapons could hold up a battalion indefinitely in narrow city streets.'[41]

> The Grave bridge was considered the most important ... There was where the first link up would be made ... It was obvious that we had to get bridges across the Maas–Waal Canal ... Seizure and retention of the bridges in strength on the Canal would add to the defensive strength opposing ... an enemy effort. Due to the tremendous sector that the Division was to hold, it was first considered best not to attack the Nijmegen bridge until all other objectives had been captured and the Division well reorganized and well in hand.[42]

The possibility that this would also allow time for the SS to organise an effective defence of the bridge and thus defeat the mission is not mentioned.

Given that the initial plans had stated the 82nd should 'be concerned' with the possibility of attack from the Arnhem area and that, as Gavin states, a few well placed weapons could seriously impede progress through the city streets, it seems odd that it does not appear to have occurred to him that by ignoring the bridges he was in fact leaving the back door open to allow forces from Arnhem to enter Nijmegen, drive a wedge between Grave and the Groesbeek Heights and, with an attack from the Reichswald, encircle the 82nd with relative ease. Even a small blocking force around the bridges could have served to delay or even prevent this.

Another, more uncomfortable rationale behind the decision to focus first on the capture of the heights can be found in the influence of 'Boy' Browning, who, recognising his need to be seen as a battlefield commander if he were to keep his post, had further depleted the already weak British force at Arnhem by demanding the use of the Wacos and 38 Horsa gliders – enough to land a battalion of troops – to transport his Corps HQ into the Nijmegen area so that he could be the first commander to airland a Corps level staff. Why this was necessary remains a mystery since the US airborne divisions were slated to come under XXX Corps' control as soon as contact was made and, on the basis of Browning's own later criticisms of the ground elements, he fully expected this to be within about 24 hours of the start of the operation. So there was little his HQ could accomplish by landing in the first wave. Nevertheless, when Urquhart approached Browning with a request for 40 more planes for his division at Arnhem, 'Browning was pessimistic about my getting even a proportion of them.' Asked about the greater availability of aircraft to the American sectors, Browning told him that priority had 'got to be bottom to top, otherwise you'd stand a chance of being massacred'.[43] As the only high ground available from which to direct the battle, the Groesbeek ridge presented the obvious location from which to direct operations, and the attendant publicity Browning stood to gain would be a propaganda coup against Ridgway. So from the outset Browning insisted that the Groesbeek Heights be taken before any attempt was made on the bridges and Gavin was, for his own reasons, prepared to agree. In stating that the British were apprehensive about the potential for a large-scale counterattack, why, if they were truly concerned about a strong German tank force in the Reichswald, was their Corps HQ to be sited in the front line directly in the path of it?

By September, British forces had entered Holland and consolidated along the canal line, ready to jump off for the next phase.

From the outset, then, *Market Garden* was beginning to suffer from 'mission creep' – the tendency to drift away from the original intent that often plagues complex operations – and it may be that perhaps the oft quoted exchange between Browning and Montgomery following the meeting with Eisenhower demonstrates the lack of clarity. The exchange has an uneasy Browning asking how long it would take the tanks of XXX Corps to reach the northernmost bridge at Arnhem, 64 miles from the start line. Montgomery told him 'two days. They'll be up with you then.' To which Browning is said to have replied, 'We can hold it for four. But sir, I think we may be going a bridge too far.'[44] In light of what happened, the remark demonstrates a great deal of foresight on Browning's part and surely proves what an able commander he was to have been able to recognise the inherent problems. Since there are no other known witnesses to the conversation and the report comes from Urquhart (who was not present but heard it later, presumably from Browning himself), perhaps we need to treat it with caution. It has been alleged that Browning made the remark for posterity but this would have required remarkable foresight and a disturbing lack of understanding on his part of the significance of the Arnhem bridge if he made it before the operation he himself had masterminded. Alternatively it was perhaps astute political manoeuvring if he wanted to distance himself in the aftermath. John Baynes, in his biography of Major-General Urquhart, casts doubt on the phrase, suggesting it may actually have come from a meeting before Montgomery took the plan to his superior and that it was more likely Montgomery himself who used it. As it reaches the Dutch border, the Rhine is at its widest but then splits into branches: two thirds of the water volume flows into the Waal river with the rest following the Nederrijn (Lower Rhine) through Arnhem and into the IJssel. Knowing that Eisenhower would favour only a limited attempt to gain a bridgehead on the Rhine and that the Waal at Nijmegen is the major branch of it, together with the fact that the famous phrase has also been rendered as 'one bridge too far', the possibility exists that Montgomery may either have had his own doubts about the extent of the operation or alternatively was attempting to play Patton at his own game. On 17 September, as the operation got under way to the north, Patton remained determined not to allow resources to be diverted away from his own effort and decided to push ahead in defiance of his instructions from Eisenhower. Writing in his diary, he said 'To hell with Monty. I must get so involved that they can't stop me. I told Bradley not to call me until after dark on the 19th. He agreed.'[45] Just as siblings compete for parental affection, both men were now vying for Eisenhower's attention. Both knew that he would have to reward success but also that should any unit become endangered he would have to divert help to reach it.

If Browning genuinely believed that the operation was overly ambitious, it was his responsibility to say so. He had already shown a willingness to stand up to Brereton when he claimed that there were insufficient maps for the Tournai drop and, as the intelligence summaries developed a picture of greater forces in Arnhem than expected, Browning could have used this to change the plan. He did not. Brereton had called his bluff over Tournai and Browning knew that Ridgway was waiting eagerly to take over as Deputy Commander if he again threatened to step down. Instead, he pushed forward the existing plans with enthusiasm despite growing disquiet among his senior planners. Prior to the escape of the German forces on the Scheldt, advances of 50 or even 60 miles a day had been possible, even common. Reaching Arnhem in two days was well within the realms of possibility if, as was generally believed, the Germans could offer only a thin crust of defences behind which their forces were in chaos.

By September 1944, the pressure was on to produce an airborne operation before December and the expected end of the war. Eisenhower was facing increasing demands from Washington to use the Allied Airborne Army and, as Gavin claimed, was looking to go ahead whether or not the operation was sound. His own generals had made it clear that they wanted nothing to do with airborne operations so it fell to Montgomery to 'use them or lose them'. Political pressure from home, coupled with the refusal of Brereton to commit air forces to an operation towards Wesel, limited Montgomery's choices. With a plan already in place that would fit the bill, Browning saw a chance to consolidate his standing as the foremost airborne commander. The risk was growing by the day but so too were the potential rewards. Little wonder, then, that intelligence reports about the enemy situation were being quietly brushed to one side.

Notes

1 Bennett p.20
2 Liddell Hart Centre for Military Archives, Papers of Captain B.H. Liddell Hart LHP15/15, Papers of Chester Wilmot CWP/130 Notes on Dempsey's Diary – Meeting 27 June 46. Quoted in *Montgomery and Colossal Cracks: The 21st Army Group in Northwest Europe, 1944–45* by Stephen Ashley Hart (Praeger Publishers, 2000) p.136
3 Churchill College Archive, Cambridge. Papers of Ronald Lewin RLEW/2/13. Quoted in Hart op cit p.136
4 Liddell Hart Centre for Military Archives, papers of Captain B. H. Liddell Hart LHP15/15, Papers of Chester Wilmot CWP/130 Notes on Conversation with Dempsey 4 June 1946. Quoted in Hart p.136
5 Buckingham, William F. *Arnhem 1944* (Tempus Books 2002)
6 Ryan p.76
7 Ryan p.79
8 Gavin, *On To Berlin* p.90
9 Ibid p.91
10 Geoffrey Perret, *Winged Victory* (New York, 1993) p.322
11 Gavin: Personal Diary Box 8 Folder 'Diary Passages' James M. Gavin Papers US Army Historical Institute In Nordyke p.413
12 Ryan p.126
13 Gavin, *Airborne Warfare* pp.75–76
14 Bennett, *Magnificent Disaster* p.40–41
15 Ibid p.20
16 Ryan 104n
17 Breuer, W Drop Zone Sicily. Allied Airborne Strike, July 1943 Novato, CA: Presidio, 1983 pp.71, 89
18 Ibid p.57
19 Blair, C. *Ridgway's Paratroopers. The American Airborne in World War II* (New York: The Dial Press, 1985) p.88
20 Breuer, p.45
21 General Sir John Hackett in the Foreword to Shannon, K. & Wright, S. *One Night in June* (Airlife Publishing 1994) p.7
22 Crookenden, N. *Drop Zone Normandy* (London: Ian Allan Ltd. 1976) p.110
23 Blair, op cit p.314
24 Wilmott p.557
25 Urquhart p.18
26 Gavin, *On to Berlin* pp.165–166
27 Burris, T.M. *Strike and Hold* p.103
28 Gavin *On To Berlin* p.165
29 Gavin *Airborne Warfare* p.84
30 Task Force for Operation *Market*. Headquarters First Allied Airborne Army Document dated 11 September 1944 CGSC Library Ft Leavenworth, Kansas
31 Lowden, J.L. *Silent Wings at War* (Washington: Smithsonian Institute 1992) p.96
32 Gavin *Airborne Warfare* p.87
33 Briefing Order HQ 82nd Airborne Division dated 13 September 1944

34 Gavin *A Graphic History of the 82nd Airborne Division 1945*
36 Report on Operations at Nijmegen PRO WO 205/1125 p.2
37 Gavin, On to Berlin pp.162–163
38 Gavin, letter to Captain John C Westover, July 25 1945 quoted in Philip Nordyke *All American, All the Way* (Zenith Press 2005) p.418
39 John Frost, quoted in Major & Mrs Holt, *Battlefield Guide: Operation Market Garden* (Barnsley: Pen & Sword Books 2004) p.22
40 Briefing Order HQ 82nd Airborne Division dated 13 September 1944
41 Gavin, *On To Berlin* p.167
42 Nordyke p.418–9
43 Urquhart p.17
44 Urquhart p.16
45 Province, Charles M., *More Than a Tank General* www.pattonhq.com/textfiles/morethan.html

Chapter Four

Classless Killers and Yard Long Pedigrees

'Thus, in its early stages,' as Major General Urquhart understatedly put it, 'Operation *Market Garden* was not the best example of Anglo-American accord.'[1] Nor would things improve as the operation progressed, as the culture clash being acted out amongst the senior commanders was replicated at all levels below them. Above all, however, the events and accounts of *Market Garden* were affected by a deep-seated elitism amongst the participants, an attitude that has been replicated by historians over the years. The two formations that would play key roles in the coming battle – Gavin's 82nd Airborne and Major-General Allan Adair's Guards Armoured Division – were both considered, not least by themselves, to be elite units, and in order to understand the events at Nijmegen it is worth taking time to consider what that actually means and how it might have affected their behaviour in the battle.

Colonel Bernd Horne of the Canadian Airborne Regiment has written on the subject of elites[2] and argues that whilst the term is widely used in military history, there is no consensus on its definition. Broadly, sociologists refer to four traditional types of elite in civilian society, all linked to power and status and all devoted to limiting the membership of their group in order to preserve its prestige, the aristocracy, or any other group enjoying hereditary privileges being the obvious starting point. Next comes an elite of merit made up of intellectuals and others whose talents mark them out as special. Thirdly comes a functional elite composed of those who hold positions vital for society to function such as key civil servants and, in some instances, influential military figures. Finally, there is the power elite of business executives and others who exercise political and/or economic power. Each group holds and controls a particular sphere of influence in determining how a society functions and it is relatively easy for us to identify who these groups are and what power they wield.

In military terms, however, the situation is not so clear. The rule of the Prussian Junkers demonstrates how closely military and political power is exercised by the existence of cliques of senior officers forming a virtual – or actual – military dictatorship and it falls neatly into the definitions provided by sociologists, but as Horne points out, the term 'elite' when applied to military units is more confusing. What makes a unit 'elite' in terms of how it views itself and is viewed in turn by historians is often determined by that unit itself. At one level, former US soldier writer James Jones believed that 'an elite unit is only elite when the majority of its members consider themselves already dead.' This definition, shared by others, regards elites as a kind of doomed group of heroes willing to fight on to the end. In a similar vein, Eliot Cohen has written of very clear criteria for the existence of a military elite.

First, a unit becomes elite when it is perpetually assigned special or unusual missions – in particular, missions that are, or seem to be, extremely hazardous … [thus] airborne units have long been considered elite since parachuting is a particularly dangerous way of going into battle … [elites undertake missions that] require only a few men who must meet high standards of training and physical toughness, particularly the latter … an elite unit becomes elite only when it achieves a reputation – justified or not – for bravura and success.[3]

Alternatively, an elite may be defined by its role, a group of men specially selected and trained to respond to rapidly changing situations (such as Special Forces units), the individuals having greater skills and decision-making powers than their regular counterparts. Following on from this indirectly comes the concept of an elite as a military unit freed from the usual constraints of military organisation in which individuals undergo some rite of passage. French author Gilles Perrault insists that military elites are a kind of cult with their own jargon, uniforms and patterns of behaviour intended to clearly define those who are part of the group from those who are not.[4] Strategist Colin Gray argues that the term relates directly to the standard of selection of members and not the actual activity that the soldiers are selected to perform.[5] Elsewhere, military historian Douglas Porch uses measures of battlefield performance to determine elite status and this is supported by another historian, Eric Morris, who wrote of units becoming elite by the fact that 'they were required to demonstrate a prowess and military skill of a higher standard than more conventional battalions.'[6]

A broad definition therefore emerges from the literature of an elite being a unit which, by dint of its selection of members, training, role, performance in action, discipline or some other factor, is distinct from the rest of the military. At its broadest, Horne argued, 'the designation of elite was applied simply because individuals and units were not representative of their conventional brethren by virtue of the quality or type of personnel, training or mission. Quite simply, unique equalled elite.'[7] As a result, the term has been used to describe a wide range of specialisms – from military policemen, to submariners, to the RAF Regiment – and could equally be used to describe almost any unit at almost any

To some, 'elite' is defined by special uniforms and equipment. Intended from the outset to be an elite force, the US airborne adopted both, as seen here by this picture of a paratrooper wearing the specially designed 1942 jumpsuit and carrying an adapted M1 Carbine. (US Army)

time. Who but an elite group of specially trained men could produce a full English breakfast for a frontline battalion under fire? Generally, however, the term is mostly used in military history to sell books about 'classless, highly trained killers who have a wide popular appeal'.[8]

The Second World War was perhaps the high water mark of elite unit formation and demonstrated the best and worst of what such units could achieve. Winston Churchill had experienced service against Boer commandoes and was so captivated by the idea of special operations that he enthusiastically supported the development of units as diverse as the Special Operations Executive, SAS, the Commandos, Popski's Private Army and many other small, semi-independent groups within the British Army. His Chief of the Imperial General Staff, Field Marshal Sir Alan Brooke, never agreed with Churchill's sponsorship of special units, arguing that they were 'a dangerous drain on the quality of an infantry battalion.'[9] In Burma, where his 'Chindit' columns were developing an elite status, legendary Field Marshal Viscount Slim nevertheless fully agreed with Brooke, complaining that special units

> … were usually formed by attracting the best men from normal units by better conditions, promises of excitement and not a little propaganda … The result of these methods was undoubtedly to lower the quality of the rest of the Army, especially of the infantry, not only by skimming the cream off it, but by encouraging the idea that certain of the normal operations of war were so difficult that only specially equipped corps d'élite could be expected to undertake them.[10]

With this in mind, it is not difficult to speculate that during Operation *Market Garden*, the speed and response of ground troops was influenced in part by this attitude. The airborne element would gain the lion's share of the glory after spending the summer at home whilst the ground troops had been in action for months, so why not expect them to do the lion's share of the fighting now that these supermen had finally arrived? Certainly this is supported by anecdotal reports of survivors of the 1st Airborne being jeered by shouts of 'call that a battle?' from men for whom a week in action had become normal.

Both Brooke and Slim were aware of what had happened to the German Army in 1918 when it had scoured its regiments for the toughest, most experienced soldiers to form elite new 'Stormtrooper' units for the planned Kaiserschlacht offensive. These units proved highly successful at infiltrating gaps in the Allied defences and had contributed significantly to the initial success of the attack but had suffered heavy casualties in doing so. A second sift of the army was needed to reinforce Stormtrooper units for the next phase of the offensive – and a third for the next phase. The result was the removal from infantry regiments of their best men so that when the Allied counterattack came, it was against only the poorest quality troops who failed to resist as well as they might have if the supply of experienced men had not been so depleted. Fear of the weakening of regular army units and the diversion of much needed resources to units with a limited scope of operations became the main objections from high ranking officers of all armies who, whilst recognising the need for special operations, saw the creation of elites as potentially damaging to the military as a whole.

Whatever benefits elite units might bring in terms of specialist combat roles, for the military the main problem is that the process of selection and training of specialist units in itself instils a belief in those who complete it that everything else is second best. This in turn leads to the arrogant dismissal of members of other units. For many experts, there is agreement that the cult of the elite, if unchecked, produces a direct threat to the command and control structure of any force to which they are attached and they point to instances where a culture of poor discipline and antagonism towards regular army units is at times actively condoned by the elite's own hierarchy.

A prime example of the phenomenon is found in the case of the 'filthy thirteen', a sub unit of the 506th PIR of 101st Airborne Division. The group earned their nickname by refusing to wash or shave more than once a week and gained a reputation for violent disobedience, even towards their own officers. 'The reason the men got away with some of the questionable behavior was because of their combat skills' author Richard Killbane told *Stars and Stripes* newspaper in its 10 November 2008 edition. Their behaviour, however, preceded their first combat jump and seems to have been the result of an official tolerance of actions that would have been stamped on in other regiments. In writing about his exploits during *Market Garden*, the group's leader, Jake McNeice, follows the tone set by many US paratroop memoirs in assuming that no other soldier or force made the same impact on the war in Europe as the one to which he himself belonged. In this genre, no action by a foreign army is ever allowed to stand comparison to an American action. Thus, in dismissing the landing of the British 6th Airborne in Normandy in which highly successful actions were undertaken at Pegasus Bridge and at the Merville Battery and where, after days of hand to hand fighting around Breville, one company of 160 British paratroopers was reduced to just twelve men, McNeice claims with apparent certainty:

> The reason that Operation *Market Garden* had even come into consideration was that 'Sonny Boy' Browning, who was head of all English airborne forces, was a little ashamed because the British airborne forces had accomplished nothing and gained neither fame nor recognition from Normandy. In the first place, he used a very light contingent of his paratroopers and they jumped into areas that were not even defended by the Germans. Afterwards he wanted to gain the glory that had been achieved by the 101st and 82nd. So he came up with this wild scheme of dropping an airborne carpet all the way to the Rhine.

McNeice's co-author, who provides copious footnotes correcting McNeice's wilder claims, ignores the very full activities of the British 6th Airborne in Normandy and explains that *Market Garden* was needed because Patton kept overrunning planned airborne drop zones. He goes on to state that it failed because of 'a lack of British urgency'.[11]

McNeice's account is an extended discourse on the superiority of his group of misfits over even the rest of the 101st that insults the memories of thousands of Allied troops. His co-author frequently explains that there is no evidence to support his claims or that the available evidence flatly contradicts his version but despite its frankly ludicrous comments about the British airborne in Normandy, McNeice's memoir has sold well and has been positively received by American audiences.

However inaccurate its facts are, it merely provides a distilled version of the attitudes and beliefs that seem to have underpinned the self image of US paratroopers in 1944. With the corrosive effects of this type of elitism in mind, we need to consider the two units most closely involved in the crossing of the Waal.

504th Parachute Infantry Regiment, 82nd Airborne Division

The 82nd Infantry Division was formed on 25 August 1917 at Camp Gordon, Georgia and since the members of the Division were drawn from all 48 states, it quickly acquired the nickname 'All-Americans' from which came the design of the 'AA' shoulder patch. In the spring of 1918, the Division deployed to France and was involved in nearly five months of combat during which one of its men, Sergeant Alvin C. York, famously won the Medal of Honor for the capture of over 130 Germans during one patrol. After the Armistice, the Division was disbanded.

On 25 March 1942, it was resurrected at Camp Claiborne, Louisiana, under the command of the man who would, ironically, later undermine airborne operations, Major General Omar Bradley. On 15 August it was redesignated as the first airborne division in the US Army. From the outset, the intention was to create an elite and the problem of elitism surfaced almost immediately. At a Washington press conference in 1942 about the development of the US airborne forces, Major General Lesley McNair, then Commander of US Army Ground Forces, remarked that; 'They [paratroopers] are our problem children. They make lots of money, and they know they're good. This makes them a little temperamental, but they're great soldiers.'[12] 'Temperamental' is not a term often used by army officers, especially when describing a unit they are actively seeking to promote as an elite fighting force, and McNair's comment serves to underline the concerns already being expressed by other commanders about standards of discipline. The press, however, loved them. According to Larry Gough, writing in *Liberty* magazine,

> In the first place, they [parachutists] are perfect specimens. They have to be because their work is rough, tough and full of excellent opportunities to get hurt. Mentally they're quick on the trigger, again because their job demands it, because split seconds can make the difference between instant death or a successfully completed job.[13]

The sense of being an elite was reinforced by the treatment handed out to those who failed the rigorous physical demands of airborne training. At first, these men were spirited away from the camps as quickly as possible to prevent their failure 'contaminating' the others. Later, as the formations grew in size, the process slowed and they were forced to wait for reassignment. Anyone failing the course was routinely subject to abuse ranging from being forced to wait until last for meals and to sit in silence on separate tables to outright verbal and even physical abuse. Many were forced out of barrack huts into tents far from the main camp and forced to wear signs around their necks with the word 'Quitter' in bright letters. A culture developed that saw anyone not entitled to paratrooper wings as a failure and a lesser man. This created tension even within the airborne division between the volunteer paratroopers with their special insignia and extra flight and hazardous duty payments and the men of the Glider Infantry Regiment who received no recognition of their own extremely dangerous role. These men were not volunteers and were looked down on by the paratroops so much that it was not until July 1944, after the invasion of Normandy, that any recognition was made of the fact that they landed and fought alongside the paratroopers and shared every element of the danger. Even so, many resented the award of a glider badge based on the same design as their paratrooper wings.[14]

It was a source of annoyance amongst others that many of the officers occupying command of the airborne had not completed formal parachute training, often regarding the parachute as merely a means of delivery when other options were impractical. Ridgway, for example, intended to travel into Normandy by glider and he made a last-minute decision to make his first and only combat parachute jump. When the rules were then changed to allow one combat jump to count for the award of paratrooper wings there were many objections.

In April 1943, now under the command of Major General Matthew Ridgway, the 82nd Airborne Division set sail for North Africa in readiness for the upcoming invasion of Sicily, where Colonel James Gavin's 505th Parachute Infantry Regiment (PIR), along with 3rd Battalion of the 504th PIR landed on 9 July 1943 despite weather reports that conditions were unsuitable for a drop. Because the amphibious elements of the assault were already underway, it was decided to go ahead. High winds and inexperienced pilots scattered the paratroopers over a wide area and it was some days before units could reorganise fully. The drop was a success in that many of the scattered troopers used their own initiative to reach their objectives and attacked targets of opportunity en route, creating an impression of a far greater force having landed.

On the following night, the rest of Colonel Ruben Tucker's 504th PIR was due to land on Farella, an abandoned airfield three miles east of the town of Gela. As the aircraft passed over the invasion fleet in close formation, nervous gunners below, having experienced some 23 air raids already that day, opened fire; 23 planes were lost along with almost 400 paratroopers. When Eisenhower received the first reports on the 504th disaster, he was furious and immediately wrote to Patton, as commander of the US invasion force that

> if the cited report is true, the incident could have been occasioned only by inexcusable carelessness and negligence on the part of someone. You will institute within your command an immediate and exhaustive investigation into allegations with a view to fixing responsibility. Report of pertinent facts is desired and if the persons found responsible are serving in your command, I want a statement of disciplinary action taken by you.

Patton is reported to have confided to his diary: 'As far as I can see if anyone is blameable it must be myself but personally I feel immune to censure … Perhaps Ike is looking for an excuse to relieve me.'[15]

This incident in particular, and the heavy losses to the British airborne, was likened to the German invasion of Crete that had cost so many expensively trained lives that no more large-scale German parachute landings were carried out during the war. Now Sicily had a similar effect and almost caused the Allies to scrap the idea of airborne forces. After their initial landing, the US airborne were used as regular infantry but held back from the heaviest fighting to preserve what was left of the unit. On 16 August, Sicily fell.

On 7 September, the Italian-speaking Divisional Artillery commander Brigadier General Maxwell Taylor and Colonel Tuder Gardiner left Palermo and, disguised as prisoners of war, were escorted through enemy lines for a clandestine meeting with the Italian commander Marshal Badoglio. It was known that the Italians were keen to surrender but feared German reprisals against Rome unless the Allies could reach the city first, so a plan was made ready for the 82nd to drop onto airfields around Rome at the same time as a seaborne landing at Salerno. For the plan to succeed, the Americans would need to rely on Italian support. Taylor soon realised the Italians were in no position to provide it and immediately sent coded messages to cancel the drop. The message arrived as the first troopers boarded the planes for take-off.

Four days after the Salerno landings, General Mark Clark urgently requested assistance from the airborne to stem a possible German breakthrough on the beachhead. Having already prepared for the Rome mission, the Division's equipment was ready and advance elements of the 504th, briefed in flight, dropped just eight hours later, quickly followed by the 325th Glider Infantry. The following day the remainder of the 504th, together with Gavin's 505th and elements of the 509th, made drops. The 509th, widely scattered in mountainous terrain, lost 130 men before returning to Allied lines three weeks later, but in that time their actions tied down a huge number of German troops, estimated to be more than the size of the entire Allied landing force. Other elements of the 82nd arrived by sea on the 15th as Colonel Tucker's 504th consolidated positions around Altavilla, where German artillery positions had a commanding field of fire over the route of the Allied advance.

By the 17th, the 504th had taken its objectives but was now surrounded. Having received no information all day, the commander of the US VI Corps correctly guessed what had happened and sent a runner to find Tucker and relay the order to try to breakout and withdraw to nearby Albanella. Tucker ignored the order and when communications were restored, asked instead for his 3rd Battalion to be sent forward. It was and the position held. Tucker was awarded the Distinguished Service Cross.

When, on 1 October, Naples fell to the British XX Corps, attached units from the 82nd were amongst the first into the city. In November, as the bulk of the Division returned to the UK to prepare for the Normandy landings, the 504th PIR, the 376th Field Artillery and elements of the 307th Airborne Engineers remained in Italy at the specific request of General Clark.

On the night of 21/22 January 1944 Operation *Shingle*, a seaborne assault at Anzio that caught the Germans completely by surprise, began under the direction of the commander of the US VI Corps, Major General John P. Lucas. From the outset Lucas had been highly critical of the plans for the Anzio battle, arguing that his force was not strong enough to accomplish its mission – a point seemingly reinforced when it was scaled back by last-minute orders and he was allegedly advised by Clark not to 'stick your neck out'. Soon after landing, a Jeep patrol was able to drive unopposed to the outskirts of Rome and reported back that the road was clear, but rather than seize the opportunity, Lucas chose instead to wait until he had fully consolidated his landing. In the days that followed, the German response was swift and fierce. The open road to Rome was closed and, after four weeks of extremely tough fighting, Lucas was relieved by Clark and replaced with Major General Lucian K. Truscott.

Over the coming months, the 504th fought as infantry and were attached for some of this time to the British 1st Armoured Division around Carroceto as the Allies endured extremely accurate and effective German artillery fire that prevented any significant forward movement. Finally, on 25 March, they were ordered to sail for Britain to rejoin the Division.

Still refitting, the 504th did not take part in the Normandy landings but the rest of the Division dropped in the early hours of 6 June and spent the next 33 days in action, losing around half of its men by the time it returned to England in early July. Its sister division, the 101st, had suffered equally high casualties before they too were withdrawn in July whilst their British counterparts, also badly hit in the initial phase, would remain in action on the eastern flank for many weeks to come.

Following Normandy, the Division underwent changes. In early August, Eisenhower promoted Ridgway to command of the new US XVIII Airborne Corps comprising the 82nd, 101st and 17th Airborne Divisions and Ridgway recommended Gavin for promotion to replace him as divisional commander making Gavin, at 37, the youngest Major General in the US Army since Custer. This left a vacancy for the post of assistant division commander and, as the most experienced commander in the Division, both Ridgway and Gavin agreed that the obvious candidate was the 504th's commander, Reuben Tucker. After consideration, however, both agreed that whilst Tucker had proved himself an able battlefield commander he lacked the ability to grasp the wider picture. 'He didn't give a damn about administration and paperwork', Gavin said later. 'Ridgway and I talked about it and we decided we just couldn't promote Tucker.'[16]

As one of six children of a working class family, at 18 Tucker had passed the entrance exam for the Military Academy at West Point but could not get a place in 1929, instead spending a year working in Wyoming before joining the following year's intake. He failed to graduate as expected in the Class of 1934 after failing in mathematics and was required to undergo further examinations to gain re-admittance and finally was allowed to be 'turned back' to join the Class of 1935. After overcoming these obstacles to graduate from West Point and proven himself as an able commander, the response of 'the Little Colonel' (as his men called him) to the reasons for his being refused promotion is not recorded but this further rejection by the military establishment could not have been easy for him to accept. Instead he remained as the commander of the 504th until the end of the war.

By now, the 504th had won a Presidential Unit Citation for their actions in Italy and had adopted the nickname 'devils in baggy pants' after a comment found in a captured German diary. The veterans of the unit regarded themselves as the most battle-hardened of the Division and had certainly proved their value in combat. But alongside the justified pride in their achievements, a culture was developing that would have a direct impact on events in Holland.

In his memoirs, company commander T. Moffat Burriss describes his experiences with the 504th and clearly demonstrates the emerging elitism that was developing within the unit. Amongst the battle honours he claims for the 504th, for example, was credit for the rescue of a senior British officer from certain capture at Anzio. The man leading the patrol, Lieutenant James 'Maggie' Magellas, would win the Bronze Star for having taken a small group of men forward through German lines to extract the Brigadier and his staff from their surrounded position yet, as Magellas later recalled, 'I did not know the name of the British brigadier we were cited for rescuing, nor did I ever see him. I led the patrol that reportedly rescued him, but at the time I never knew that a British brigadier had been captured.'[17]

Burriss goes on to suggest that during its time at Anzio, the 504th 'sustained one of the heaviest bombardments in the history of warfare …'[18] a claim that might be disputed by veterans of the 'drumfire' bombardments of the First World War or by many Eastern Front veterans and which appears to imply that only the 504th were subjected to it. In fact, as another official US account of Anzio explains:

> Paradoxically in this strange place, the safest company was the one nearest the front lines because most of the German fire passed over it, to fall on the harbor and port; also, the Company at the front had room to disperse. In the crowded area around Anzio-Nettuno were the heaviest Ordnance casualties and the worst cases of 'Anzio Anxiety' or 'Nettuno Neurosis,' caused by the strain of constant shelling and bombing, added to overwork.[19]

After being relieved at Anzio, the 504th sailed back to England aboard the *Dunbar Castle*. Sergeant Ross S. Carter described the 'superbly disciplined' British guardsmen who shared the ship and recalled:

> By contrast the troopers [of the 504th] resembled a mob of pirates. Nearly all of us, dressed in anything from fatigues to tan jump suits, wore a handlebar mustache [sic] and shuffled around with a pistol or knife or both swinging on our shoulder or hip. I am certain that, in modern times, a more desperate-looking gang of ruffians had not sailed on a British ship. The British Guardsmen, knowing us to be one of the crack regiments of the US Army, surveyed us with undisguised amazement and curiosity. To them discipline was an important factor in war and if we had any they couldn't put their finger on it.[20]

The 504th (or 'the Legion' as he calls it) had discipline, he insisted, but not the 'lady-laced kind'. Playing up to their roguish self-image, Carter reports how the paratroopers refused to acknowledge the authority of anyone but their own officers during the voyage back to Britain. On arrival in the UK, he says, 'We all had big heads' and, after rejoining the Division near Leicester,

> the truth of the matter is that we conducted ourselves like uncouth barbarians … Not all of our boys were so rude or got drunk every night, but enough of them were to give many Britishers the impression that we were a mob of cloutish rubes. I can understand why we acted as we did but can neither condone nor justify it.[21]

Having been referred to in the press as the 'Anzio Roughnecks', the 504th became dismissive even of other US airborne units, and 'looked down on the 506th [their counterparts in the 101st Division made famous in the book and TV series *Band of Brothers*] as upstarts'.[22]

Units usually develop their character from the leadership of the commanding officer and Tucker appears to have been held in high regard as a no-nonsense fighting man. Gavin later quoted Carter's account of how Tucker exercised that command in a story that says much about the means by which he controlled the men of his regiment. During the fighting in Italy, the 'Little Colonel' ordered a Greek-American sergeant named Perici to lead a patrol into the town of Altavilla.

> Resolutely Perici replied 'No, sir, I can't go into that town.' The little colonel, gasping with rage, pulled out his .45. 'Perici, why can't you go into Altavilla?' 'Sir,' rejoined Perici calmly, 'I've been in this army for four years. I done learned that I can't go into town without a pass. The MPs would get me as shore as hell is red-hot.' With a tight smile on his lips, the colonel wrote out a pass for Sergeant Perici to enter the town with six men.[23]

Amusing – but if true, it seems odd that as a respected commander Tucker's first response was to assume he needed to enforce his orders at gunpoint. Perici was, after all, a sergeant and therefore presumably one of his more capable soldiers. A year later, having been asked by a senior non-commissioned officer for a written pass to allow his men into an enemy-held town, Tucker would criticise the British for their insistence on doing things 'by the book'.

In the wake of the Nijmegen battle, to ensure that his men did not soften, Tucker required them to remain on combat rations and to sleep in foxholes long after the need had passed. In October, he refused to allow them to light fires to cook the better quality rations available to them or to wear greatcoats against the cold. Although this latter had at least the rationale that it would avoid US paratroopers in greatcoats being mistaken for Germans in similar coats, to the British, who widely expressed the belief that any idiot can be uncomfortable, the behaviour smacked of masochistic posturing. Embarrassingly for Gavin, when General Dempsey visited the 82nd at Nijmegen, his men complained openly about the poor quality of food and Dempsey immediately ordered double supplies of British rations to be delivered, including repeated offers of the rum ration available to British troops. Gavin, however, declined the rum. 'I turned him down because our company commanders complained that most of the troopers were too young and did not drink rum, except for a few, and they invariably would collect the rations from the others and get drunk.'[24] Since the rum ration was a long established tradition in the British Army, the refusal on the grounds of concern for the moral welfare of young men trained and encouraged to think of themselves as cold-blooded killers seemed slightly hypocritical and the belief that a minority would 'invariably' get drunk helped foster the impression of poor standards of discipline. The British rum ration was, after all, issued under the supervision of officers and had not proved a significant problem.

Whilst the warrior ethos was useful in creating a strong and aggressive esprit de corps, it also meant that the 82nd were developing a highly egocentric viewpoint. Prior to the jump into Holland, Magellas recalled that the paratroops 'were all issued a small sum of invasion currency (in Dutch guilders), but I couldn't imagine for what purpose.'[25] A pause for thought may have helped Magellas to realise that whilst he may consider himself to be owed a debt by the people he had come to liberate, to the starving Dutch peasant watching his family's meagre food stock being taken from his house, a small payment would mark a huge difference between the behaviour of the Germans and that of the Allies – the difference between a liberator and a conqueror. It had long been a British military dictum that one does not loot from the civilian population of one's allies.

In the wake of its experiences in Sicily, Italy and Normandy, the 82nd had carefully fostered an image of the Division as 'a pack of jackals; the toughest, most resourceful and bloodthirsty infantry in the [European Theatre of Operations].'[26] Whilst as a formation it had gained a great deal of experience – the 504th had clocked up around 105 days of frontline duty since its arrival in North Africa the previous May with some men having volunteered for duty in Normandy as well – heavy losses meant that most were replacements and had far less experience than that. Up to half of them had only just arrived and were facing their first action. Nevertheless, by September 1944, the Division was showing all the negative traits associated with elitism, including poor discipline and a disregard for anyone outside their own unit. Even within the Division itself, the line between paratroopers and glider infantry remained rigorously observed and contempt for 'leg' (regular, non-airborne) units was widespread, as was a vehemently anti-British attitude following what was seen as a poor performance by British units in Italy.

There, was, however, another view. 'The 82nd was a good division,' wrote BBC correspondent Cyril Wray, who joined them for *Market Garden*,

> … extremely professional, but approached the battle like bloodthirsty boy scouts, armed to the teeth. Grenades hanging all over them. Our gliders landed in the centre of a circle held by paratroops who had dropped previously. The American soldiers stormed out of the gliders, armed to the teeth, and met two cows and a Dutch farmer.[27]

The habit of wearing an infantry webbing harness with grenades attached had already earned General Matthew Ridgway his nickname and Gavin himself wore a steel helmet even for ceremonial occasions, which again seemed oddly pretentious to the more casual British officers standing alongside them.

Colonel George Chatterton of the Glider Pilot Regiment was present at a meeting in Nijmegen and later recalled the contrast between the Allies.

> It was an extraordinary meeting and I have never seen men so contrasted in all my life. General Browning, standing, in his immaculate uniform; the brigade commander of the Guards Armoured Brigade, with clipped moustache, in his battle dress with the insignia of the DSO and MC on it, and wearing suede shoes, sitting on a shooting stick; and on either side of him three colonels whose black berets were adorned with the badges of the Irish Guards, the Grenadier Guards and the Scots Guards respectively. Their faces were covered in dust and mud thrown up at them as they stood up in their armoured cars or tanks as they dashed down the

road. Each of them had an old school scarf – I noticed Eton, Harrow and Winchester above the collars of their battledress tops, and each had a pair of faded corduroy trousers and suede Chukka boots. They wore a most amazing air of nonchalance and gave the impression that this was not a battle but an exercise near Caterham Barracks … In contrast to them, Colonel Tuck [sic], the American commander, had a tin hat on which covered his whole face, a jumping jacket on which there were several decorations (including our DSO), a pistol strapped under his arm, a knife on the right side, long trousers and lace-up boots. He chewed a fat cigar, and every now and then he spat. Each time he did this, faint looks of surprise flickered over the faces of the Guards officers.[28]

With a history dating back just two years and battle experience gained in 100 days of battle, the US airborne would now encounter a tradition built up over almost 300 years, where frontline service was measured in decades.

Guards Armoured Division, XXX Corps

Like the airborne, the brigade of Guards considered itself an elite but by an almost diametrically opposed standard. Whilst the Americans held their poor behaviour out of the line as a status symbol afforded to men who fought well, the Guards' reputation as fighters was regarded as the product of rigid discipline at all times. Formed to protect the royal household after the restoration of the monarchy in 1660, the Foot Guards and their mounted equivalent in the Horse Guards had always been regarded as a prestigious formation. In the wake of the Civil War, and fearing further threats of revolution, their officers had been drawn from the classes with the most to gain by maintaining the status quo and so were filled with members of the aristocracy and gentry. Purchase of commissions into any Guards regiment was beyond the price of all but the richest and even after the practice had ended, strict regulations regarding personal incomes ensured that only a select few could serve. At the turn of the twentieth century, for example, when a family home in London could be rented for £100 a year, a Guards officer needed a private income of £160 a year over and above his salary just to afford the extravagant lifestyle expected of him, and it is said that one newly arrived officer reacted with surprise when he learned that the War Office would actually be paying *him* for his service rather than, as he assumed, he paying them for the privilege.

Heavy losses in the First World War diluted the officer class of the British Army to a degree, but a peacetime commission in the Guards was still regarded as open only to a social elite and standards were only slightly relaxed in wartime. As Colonel Robert Sink of the 101st Airborne told his men at a briefing before *Market Garden*, 'Those Guards divisions – they're good outfits. Best in the British Army. You can't get in 'em unless you've got a 'Sir' in front of your name and a pedigree a yard long. But don't laugh at 'em. They're good fighters.'[29]

When war broke out in 1939, the Guards were once again called upon to spearhead the British response and served with distinction in the battle for France. In the wake of Dunkirk, however, a committee under Lieutenant-General Sir William Bartholomew sat in June 1940 to consider the lessons of the campaign. It concluded that vague verbal orders were responsible for the chaos and confusion that marked the retreat. Despite a strong argument in favour of allowing greater use of initiative among junior officers by Lieutenant-General Sir W.G. Lindsell, who had served as Quartermaster General to the BEF, the committee concluded that this would be 'too revolutionary' and that military operations should, in future, be carried out with an even greater level of prescription than they already were.

Prior to the war, a 'Gentleman Cadet' earned a place at either the Royal Military Academy at Sandhurst or RMA Woolwich by competitive examination and a short interview with the emphasis still being heavily on the candidate's qualifications as a 'gentleman' first and foremost. In 1939, with the introduction of conscription came a decision to require all potential officer cadets to serve first in the ranks – a politically motivated action intended to counter claims of class bias as the conscript army expanded. Responsibility for officer selection now fell to the commanders of training units, who would put forward any likely candidates.

In the 22 months between the outbreak of war and June 1941 the Royal Navy grew from 180,000 officers and ratings to 395,000, an increase of 119 per cent. In the same period, RAF numbers rose from 193,000 to 662,000, an increase of 243 per cent. The British Army mushroomed from a pre-war strength of around 207,000 to some 2,221,000 men, an increase of 1010 per cent.[30] The problem was that although an infantry private could be trained in a few weeks and a tank crewman in a matter of months, officers and NCOs took longer to cultivate. Former officers from the First World War could be recalled but, it was argued, they were not ready for a different type of war. They were also now middle-aged men with families and would be expected to return as second lieutenants on a pay of 18 shillings a day – which few could afford to do. There was a desperate shortage of leadership material.

A history in which soldiers had long been regarded as 'the scum of the earth' and a belief that the Royal Air Force and Royal Navy required more intellectual recruits meant that both those forces were hugely oversubscribed with volunteers and by those conscripts regarded as better educated than most. At the same time, those selected for the army were again sifted to redirect those with skills and qualifications into the more technical corps. Only three in ten were destined for the infantry, mostly men unsuitable for other roles. The creation of elite units such as the paratroops and commandos then skimmed off the most motivated and able of these infantrymen.

For a generation that had grown up in the political turmoil between the wars, there was a strong political awareness and with it a sense of class and trade solidarity. Trade unions had become powerful organisations and the concept of 'demarcation' of roles had been carried over into the military. A noted feature of operations by all armies throughout the war was the reluctance of one group of soldiers to help another if the other group was of a different trade. For example, infantry were often very reluctant to help engineers by acting as labourers. It was certainly not an attitude unique to the British. As John Nye has pointed out,

> Differences between the Allied and Nazi organization and tactics at the ground level were quite striking. Whereas the Germans stressed cohesion, coordination, and effective use of combined arms maneuvers, the Allies were plagued by inter and intra group bickering and backbiting. Though fiercely loyal to each other, American troops often complained about their officers and there continued to be great friction between the two major army branches of infantry and armor. On occasion the one refused to come to the support of the other. No doubt these differences were further exacerbated by the youth and inexperience of the American soldier as well as the fact that the majority of the American GIs had never trained with armor.[31]

Conscripts were prepared to do their bit but only their bit and only on their terms. For Joe Ekin, a tank crewman of the Northants Yeomanry,

Generally speaking, I had no time for the army. All the bullshit were an absolute waste of time. I knew what I were doing regards my job. First thing we did when we got over there was throw away the machine-gun ammunition and fill the boxes with fags … [We were] just making the best of it and skiving out of as much work as you could.[32]

It was an attitude summed up in the telling acronym 'FUJIAR' ('f*** you, Jack, I'm all right') that would mark Allied progress throughout the fighting in Europe.

By deselecting the best and brightest recruits from service in the infantry, the War Office demonstrated its emphasis on a war of materiel rather than combat, focusing on developing its logistic tail at the expense of its frontline teeth. In an analysis of British performance in Sicily, one observer wrote of the typical infantry platoon that it consisted of 'six gutful men who will go anywhere and do anything, twelve 'sheep' who will follow a short distance behind if they are well led, and from four to six ineffective men who have not got what it takes in them ever to be really effective soldiers.'[33] Training now focused on ensuring that the 'sheep' did what they were told.

On the Napoleonic battlefield, success had depended on the ability of a regiment to move and deploy in close formation and training centred around the importance of foot drill, at which the Guards excelled and which remains a core element of the training curriculum even today. The aim is to instil instant and total obedience to orders because the battlefield is no place for debate. But for an army still suffering the effects of pre-war cutbacks, drill also offered a cheap means of occupying time. It became, in many cases, a substitute for more effective combat training and, as a new generation of recruits arrived, they found themselves subjected to endless 'bull' and drill. Against this rigid background, men of all classes were made very much aware that they were, as countless sergeants have explained, 'not paid to think'. After a period of weeks spent in such an environment, designed to effectively stifle personal initiative and to instil the importance of obeying orders to the letter, potential officer candidates were sent for interview.

In 1941, as part of the expansion of the armoured corps, a number of infantry battalions found themselves suddenly converted into tank units. As Britain's oldest regiments, the Guards had always enjoyed a reputation as excellent infantry soldiers and an elite status in the military based on their steadfast performance on the battlefield. 'This standard', wrote Peter Carrington, who was commissioned into the Grenadiers in 1940,

> … was achieved by a tradition of discipline and order, perhaps a touch inflexible but in infantry combat assuredly effective. The tradition was less applicable to armoured warfare, or much of it. Where manoeuvre is required, so is speed and imagination and initiative. I never thought our system was perfect for breeding those qualities. Individuals possessed them – splendidly. But the army itself was differently designed …

When the decision was made to re-train infantry battalions as armoured units, responsibility for managing the change fell on officers and NCOs who frequently had themselves long service in the ceremonial duties of the peacetime Guards and generations of family contact with the regiments, but only as infantrymen. They were, Carrington thought, 'admirable men, but more in those days than today they were executants of pretty rigid orders, custodians of a fairly inflexible regime … Furthermore they themselves were in some cases less than rapid learners of new ways.'[34] In one case, Carrington recalled discovering why a certain sergeant-major always delayed before responding to radio calls to his tank. Every time he recognised an officer's voice, the man stood in his turret and saluted before reaching for the microphone.

The characters of individual units varied to reflect that of their commanding officer; some managed the change well, others less so. Some encouraged initiative and leadership amongst their junior officers; others sought to micro-manage every aspect of the battalion's daily activities. As late as January 1944, a British Army training manual advised that: 'The battalion commander must be able to control his battalion as a conductor controls his orchestra, bringing one part or another into play to give a harmonious effect to the whole.'[35]

There was no room in the doctrine for improvisation. On an operational level, his experience in North Africa had convinced Montgomery that

> it cannot be emphasised too strongly, that successful battle operations depend on the intimate co-operation of all arms, whether in armoured or unamoured formations. Tanks alone are never the answer; no one arm, alone and unaided can do any good in battle.[36]

The message that tanks could only be effective when supported by infantry and artillery, together with the expectation that senior commanders would have total control over operations, further reinforced the importance of simply following orders because someone, somewhere, was in charge and could take the larger view.

Knocked off balance by the sudden switch from the infantry warfare they understood so well to a role where they were still finding their feet, the criticisms that during Operation *Market Garden* the Guards Armoured were hide-bound is certainly justified. Routines such as using the hours of darkness to cease operations and carry out maintenance developed in Britain during training and were transferred without question to the combat zone. So when the operational orders issued to XXX Corps before *Market Garden* stated categorically that there would be

> NO movement on the main axis during the hours of darkness except:
>
> (i)   Where it is a tactical necessity.
>
> (ii) When a Group Commander is satisfied that his group can complete its move, without disrupting traffic arrangements, within two hours of last light[37]

for the Guardsmen, the orders (or any others) were not subject to negotiation.

Although Staff at Corps HQ had been together since Alamein, the three divisions were serving together in action for the first time. Elements of XXX Corps had been in the first waves of the assault in Normandy and had still been in action when the 82nd were withdrawn to England. The Guards Armoured Division had deployed to Normandy to join XXX Corps on 28 June, rejoining the 50th (Northumbrian) Division, who had been in action since the first wave of the landings. The 50th, a first line Territorial unit, had first seen action in France in 1940 and had served through the North African campaign and into Sicily before being withdrawn to make ready for the Normandy assault. It had been joined by the 43rd (Wessex) Division later in the month and with the arrival of the Guards Armoured was now ready to act as a corps in its own right. During the previous three months it had suffered heavily, with 50th Division alone losing over 7200 casualties – the equivalent of its entire infantry strength – whilst 43rd Division, who had suffered among the fewest casualties among the British forces in Normandy, had lost around half its strength.[38]

Morale had crumbled amongst the forces holding the Orne line. Fighting there had been vicious with even German veterans likening it to that on the Eastern Front and some claiming it to be worse. As the long Normandy summer bred swarms of insects to feast on the corpses littering the battlefield, 20 mosquito bites on one hand were common. Many became infected but few men could be spared from their units to have their boils and bites treated properly. Dysentery outbreaks affected up to 75 per cent of some units and lesser infections quickly spread. The combination of discomfort, disease and disquiet about their equipment all contributed to a slow down in their performance. Pinned down for much of the time, losses had reached levels that at times exceeded some of the bloodiest fighting of the First World War. For the young conscripts who made up the British Army, it often became too much. For that reason, in an attempt to bolster the frontline strength, paratroops who had dropped on 6 June remained in the line long after their American counterparts had returned to England. Still, the sheer effort of holding back the main German effort in the west was almost too much. The 6th Battalion of the Duke of Wellington's Regiment, for example, had suffered over 350 casualties when its commanding officer was replaced. After only four days in post, the replacement, Lieutenant-Colonel Turner, reported that with all the company commanders and most of battalion HQ staff lost, the battalion was no longer able to function. It was a brave move that cost him his career. A furious Montgomery ordered the battalion disbanded and the report suppressed. Later, during the battle for Hill 112, elements of 43rd Division had to be held in position by officers with drawn pistols. Battle fatigue cases across the Allied armies soared.

Morale was not helped by a serious problem that SHAEF had been aware of for some time. In 1944 the *New York Times* published a controversial article under the headline, 'American Tanks Inferior to German?' in which it argued that the thin armour and light weaponry of the standard issue M4 Sherman tanks made it almost impossible for US tanks to defeat the best German tanks, except on the basis of numerical superiority. A ratio of six to one was being widely spoken of amongst tank crews as being about right. In other words it was assumed that it would take six Shermans to destroy one German Tiger. In Normandy, for example, German tank ace Michael Wittman's Tiger tank had rampaged through a British armoured column and escaped unharmed. Indeed, he was only eventually killed later in the campaign when five British Shermans were able to surround him and attack simultaneously.

The article prompted an investigation which confirmed fears that the standard armour-piercing shells from the Shermans 'bounced off the front plate of the German tanks as if we were using pea shooters' while another report added that 'Our tanks are no damn good.' It emerged that at 1000 yards, the Sherman was incapable of penetrating the front armour of any German battle tank and a report by General Dempsey concluded that its 75mm gun could not penetrate German armour at a range of just 30 metres. The only hope for Sherman crews was to outflank German tanks and fire into the sides at close range. As a result, German tanks were considered 'practically immune' to the weapons of Allied vehicles. In turn the Sherman's high profile and thin armour made it an easy target for anti-tank weapons hidden in the bocage whilst the 88mm gun mounted on the Panzer IV, Tiger and Panther tanks or used in its ground role as an artillery piece could destroy a Sherman at 2000 yards; one report from the Russian front even claimed that a German group used the gun to destroy a Soviet tank at a range of nearly 5000 metres.[39] At anything under 1000 yards, they were virtually guaranteed to hit and knock out a Sherman. By contrast, a Sherman needed to be within 500 yards and on the flank of a German tank to even stand a chance of a lucky killing shot. Dempsey's report concluded that German tanks were 'infinitely superior' and that 'our armour is fighting under a considerable handicap.' As disquiet spread through the armoured divisions in Normandy, one tank commander tried to

The most widely used Allied tank of the war, the US-built M4 Sherman was not popular with its crews. In particular, its high profile and flat sides made it vulnerable to German anti-tank weapons and its own weapon was underpowered to the extent it was regarded as virtually useless against any German tank in use in 1944.

Sloping armour and a powerful gun made the Panther virtually invulnerable to Allied anti tank weapons.

The German Tiger tank – with its 88mm gun capable of destroying a Sherman at 2000 yards – instilled fear out of all proportion to the number actually encountered by the Allies.

comfort his crew by pointing out how much safer they were than the infantry. 'What would the infantry do,' asked his gunner, 'if they were sent into action with rifles which wouldn't penetrate the enemy's uniforms?'[40]

The Sherman's main, indeed only, advantage was in the ease with which it could be replaced – the 400 tanks of the British Second Army lost or damaged on Operation *Goodwood* in July were made good within 36 hours – but, according to one report on the US 3rd Armoured Division, US troops regarded Shermans as 'death traps' and overall combat losses were extremely high. Nominally, the table of organisation assigned a US division 232 Sherman medium tanks. During 1944/45, 648 Sherman tanks of the 3rd Armoured alone were totally destroyed in combat and a further 1100 needed repair, of which nearly 700 were as a result of combat. According to the report, the Division lost 1348 medium tanks in battle, a loss rate of over 580 per cent in the space of about ten months. Coupled with this was a casualty rate amongst trained tank crews so high that in some cases infantrymen were drafted in to replace crewmen and sent into action after only a few hours training, and crews were cut from five to three in an attempt to keep the tanks in action.[41]

A better tank than the Sherman was available, but the Army had chosen not to procure it. The M26 Pershing was rejected, in part of because of General Patton's insistence that armored divisions should avoid and bypass enemy armor. Tanks were not supposed to fight other tanks. The Sherman he felt, being lighter, would be more mobile, and could avoid head on

To US troops, all German guns were '88s'. Designed as a flak weapon, in its ground role it was deadly accurate at 2000 yards and reports even claimed it had knocked out Soviet tanks at up to 5000 metres.

engagements with the Panzers. Yet despite Armored Force doctrine, tank battles took place anyway, and the Sherman usually came off second best. In fact, as Cooper points out, the Pershing was not only better armed and armored, it was the more mobile of the two machines off road. Its wider tracks gave it a lower ground pressure, something that Patton failed to understand. Thus the Pershing was better able to maneuver when an armored unit was slowed by mud and mines.[42]

As the most widely used Allied tank, the Sherman was also supplied to the Soviet army but was routinely dismissed by the Russians and often relegated to supporting roles in the most serious fighting. Indeed, complaints about the quality of the Sherman tank brought suspicions that Americans were deliberately shipping Russia second-rate equipment.[43]

The high profile of the M4 made it an easy target for enemy gunners and in any situation where the Germans had time to locate their armour and guns in good defensive positions, even a heavily outnumbered German tank could usually take out two to four Allied tanks before being stopped. Only with the introduction of the high-velocity 76mm gun did the M4 begin to compete on more equal terms with the older Panzer IV late in 1944, but it always remained inferior to the Panthers and Tigers. Design flaws meant that ammunition aboard the Sherman was stored in unprotected stowage close to its fuel tanks and there were too few escape hatches for the crews. As a result, the tank was prone to 'brewing up' when hit and crews were lucky if they managed to escape. It soon gained a grim reputation. British crews called it the 'Ronson' after the cigarette lighter famous for its slogan 'Lights up the first time, every time!' The Poles simply called it 'the burning grave'. The German nickname was more telling – they called it the 'Tommy cooker'.

A common feature in memoirs of the war is that, to Americans almost every tank they ran into was a Tiger, especially after an unsuccessful encounter. A sometimes understandable mistake given the similarities in profile of the more common Panzer IV and the Tiger but, as Nye puts it,

The fact that the Tigers and Panthers were available in smaller quantities than many eyewitnesses claimed actually testifies to their value. But this speaks volumes about the psychological value of the weapon that even in small quantities, such great fear could be provoked in the minds of the opponents that fear of a Tiger often caused troops to hesitate even when their tanks outnumbered the Germans by ratios of as much as 10 or 20 to 1.[44]

In addition, the poor quality of US and British equipment and the resultant caution employed by the experienced soldier was interpreted by

Amongst British and US tankers, it was widely believed that it would take six Shermans to destroy one Tiger.

the Germans as reflecting on the quality of both the men and the machines. A German report on the experience of the post-Normandy battles dated August 1944 reads: 'The combat spirit of our tank crews and their training in tanks are far superior to those of the enemy tank forces. The enemy's superiority derives only from the number of his tanks.'[45] As a result, all Allied tank crews had grown to believe that any encounter with even a single German tank or gun would inevitably be fatal. In turn, the infantry alongside them also grew more and more wary of German firepower. By the late summer of 1944, tank crews, like everyone else, were aware that the war might soon be over. Faced with almost certain destruction if faced by German tanks or artillery, an increasing degree of caution began to set in.

Faced with this imbalance, Montgomery recognised the need to reinvigorate his forces and in particular, to take a grip of XXX Corps, whose performance under Lieutenant-General Gerard Bucknall had been widely criticised. Doubts had been expressed about his readiness to command at this level even before the landings, but Operation *Bluecoat* had shown XXX Corps to be slow and it struggled to keep up with other formations. In his place came Lieutenant-General Brian Horrocks, a North Africa veteran recently recovered from serious injuries sustained in an air attack on Bizerte whilst preparing for the Sicily invasion. Horrocks had already proved himself a very capable officer but also one who knew his limitations – prior to El Alamein he had been offered command of X Corps but had refused it because X Corps was an armoured corps and he believed that Major-General Herbert Lumsden, a cavalry officer, would be more suited to the role. In August 1944, he arrived to take over and immediately performance improved so that XXX Corps was able to take an active part in the advance through France and Belgium, but the habits of years of training and uninspired leadership would be hard to break. Horrocks was still putting his stamp of authority on the Corps as *Market Garden* began.

These then, were the forces that would spearhead the battle for Nijmegen. On the one hand a poorly disciplined but highly motivated division of US paratroops instilled with a belief that they were the best soldiers in the entire Allied army and a culture that looked down upon

A captured Panther driven by a British tank crew.

any man not qualified to wear paratrooper wings as a lesser form of life. The Anglophobic sentiments widely expressed among the US forces were even more pronounced among the 'All-American' 82nd Airborne to a degree that the men bitterly resented being seconded to the British. Writing later, Captain Carl Kappel of the 504th said that he was pessimistic about the airborne plan at Arnhem but

> When it came to the British armor, we felt better. They were a good outfit. Frankly, however, we would have traded them all for the 2nd Armored Division … I know we wished it were going to be them. Maybe because of the fights we were always having with them around Fayetteville; we knew they were a tough outfit.[46]

A good performance in drunken brawls in the United States was no basis for a judgement of combat performance but it is perhaps understandable that the 504th wanted to fight alongside their own countrymen rather than foreigners. To the young troopers, professionalism was expressed by looking, as modern British soldiers put it, as 'warry' as possible at all times – as in Carter's depiction of the men wearing weapons even aboard the troopship and Chatterton's description of Tucker's appearance at the briefing.

By contrast, the British forces sometimes appeared to be poorly motivated, battle weary conscripts very much aware of the inadequacies of the tools they had been given. On an individual basis, there were men and units within XXX Corps capable of outstanding performance in battle and these were very much to the fore, but equally there were others willing to do what they had to and no more. These men were led by an officer class that had adopted an elaborately affected insouciance that, if it looked down on the Americans as overenthusiastic amateurs, at the same time seemed to confirm every American prejudice against effete Britishers. Like many of his commanders, Montgomery had spent nine of the last 30 years fighting the Germans and this translated into a refusal to consider that their American counterparts, who after all had almost missed the first war and were late joining this one, could tell them anything about fighting in Europe. Having been denied the opportunity to inflict total defeat last time in favour of the politically expedient quick end to the fighting, this time the British wanted to do the job right. There was no need to rush.

Two types of force, both seeing themselves as elite but for very different reasons and by very different definitions. Now the two would need to agree on a common aim.

Notes

1   Urquhart p.15

2   Horne, Colonel B. 'The Dark Side to Elites: Elitism as a Catalyst for Disobedience' *Canadian Army Journal* Vol. 8.4 (Winter 2005), pp.65–79

3   Eliot A. Cohen, *Commandos and Politicians* (Cambridge: Center for International Affairs, Harvard University, 1978) p.17

4   Gilles Perrault, *Les Parachutistes* (Paris: Éditions du Seuil 1961) p.42

5   See Gray, Colin S. *Explorations in Strategy* (London: Greenwood Press, 1996) p.158. Gray defines three 'tiers' of elite forces with Tier 1 being the highly selective groups undertaking special operations ('Black Ops') with a pass rate for applicants of 10–15%. Tier 2 includes US Green Berets and the British SAS and involves 'high value tasks' who accept 20–30% of applicants. Tier 3 includes units such as the US Rangers or the British Royal Marines, for whom the pass rate is around 40–45% of volunteers. Thus the 82nd could be regarded as reaching the lowest rung of the elite ladder as defined by selection procedure.

6   Porch, Douglas, The French Foreign Legion: The Mystique of Elitism,' in *Elite Formations in War and Peace*, eds. A. Hamish Ion , and Keith Neilson (Wesport: Praeger, 1996) p.131

7   Horne p.70

8 Kitchen, Martin, 'Elites in Military History,' in *Elite Formations in War and Peace*, eds. A. Hamish Ion , and Keith Neilson (Wesport: Praeger, 1996) p.26

9 Morris, Eric, *Churchill's Private Armies* (London: Hutchinson, 1986) p.90

10 Slim, Field Marshall Sir William, *Defeat Into Victory* (London: Cassell and Company Ltd., 1956) p.547

11 Killblane, Richard and Jake McNiece, *The Filthy Thirteen: From the Dustbowl to Hitler's Eagle's Nest* (Casemate 2003) pp.120–1

12 Breuer, William, *Geronimo* (New York: St. Martin's Press, 1990) p.9

13 Gough, Larry, 'Parachutists Want it Tough,' *Liberty*, 4 December 1943

14 Devlin p.119

15 http://www.strikehold504th.com/

16 Gavin quoted in Clay Blair, *Ridgway's Paratroopers* (Dial Press) p.355

17 Burris p.94

18 Ibid p.94

19 Mayo, Lida, *United States Army in World War II: The Technical Services. The Ordnance Department: On Beachhead and Battlefront Center of Military History* (US Army Washington DC, 1991) p.196

20 Carter, Ross, *Those Devils in Baggy Pants* (New York: Bucaneer Books 1951) p.128

21 Ibid p.132

22 Bennett p.17

23 Carter p.23

24 Gavin, *On To Berlin* p.208

25 Magellas, James, All the way to Berlin (New York: Ballantine Books 203) p.108

26 Blair p.295

27 Saunders p81–82

28 Chatterton, G. *The Lion with Blue Wings* p.178

29 Ambrose, Stephen, *Band of Brothers* p.121

30 Corrigan p.352

31 Nye, John V.C., 'Killing Private Ryan: An Institutional Analysis of Military Decision Making in World War II' draft prepared for the ISNIE conference in Boston 2002 p.38

32 Longden p.21

33 PRO WO231/14 Lieutenant Colonel Wigram to Directorate of Military Training. Reports from Overseas No15 Section 1. 16 August 1943

34 Carrington p.27

35 General Staff. Infantry Training Part I (London: HMSO 1944) p.31

36 Imperial War Museum. Briggs MSS 66/76/1 Eighth Army Training Memorandum No1 30 August 1942

37 21st Army Group p.100

38 PRO WO 285/13 Casualties and Ammunition 2 Army 1944–5

39 Nye p.20

40 Longden p.32

41 Cooper, Belton Y. *Death Traps: The Survival of an American Armored Division in World War II* (Presidio Press, 1998)

42 Sheppard, Burke G. Review of above at http://www.strategypage.com/bookreviews/184.asp

43 Nye p.22

44 See Cooper, op cit

45 Sharp, Charles, *German Panzer Tactics in World War II* (George Nafziger 1998) p.80

46 Kappel cited at Cornelius Ryan archives held at the University of Ohio. Accessed at https://www. library.ohiou.edu/archives/mss/ryan-exhibit/Index.pdf

Chapter Five

The Operation: 'Best Possible Speed'

D-Day Sunday 17 September

At airfields across England, Sunday 17 September dawned bright and clear. Throughout the night, fighter and bomber aircraft had pounded known flak concentrations along the route of the airborne armada and the attacks continued as paratroopers and glider men assembled. For two days they had been sealed in their departure camps going over the mission and waiting. Then, at 1019hrs, the first aircraft carrying the pathfinders began to take off. As the force assembled in the skies over England, it created a 100-mile long sky train of troop carriers and gliders in three columns spread across ten miles of sky and constantly protected by swarms of Allied fighters. Below, as the huge fleet swept overhead, General Kurt Student, commander of the German Parachute Army now dug in along the canal line, watched in awe. 'This mighty spectacle deeply impressed me. I thought with reflection and longing of our own airborne operations and I said [to his chief of staff Colonel] Reinhard, "Oh if ever I'd had such a means at my disposal. Just once, to have this many planes".'[1]

Aboard his C-47, jumpmaster Lieutenant Meddaugh remembered 'the sun continued to shine brightly and as we passed over the Channel it reflected off the water into a blaze of fire. It was a Sunday afternoon that in other times we all would have been off to the local swimming hole for a picnic. But today would be no picnic.'[2] Despite the suppressing air attacks, some flak batteries along the route survived but as the massed US tow groups appeared even they fell briefly silent, awed by the sheer scale of the invasion. The respite was short lived. As they crossed the Dutch coast, the aircraft carrying men of H Company of the 504th Parachute Infantry Regiment were hit by a heavy concentration of fire and one C-47 fell out of formation. Aboard the other planes in the serial, men watched silently as it fell to earth. The pilot of the doomed plane managed to keep control long enough for the witnesses to see the

General Kurt Student, the father of airborne warfare, commanding the paratroop forces opposing XXX Corps.

camouflaged parachutes of the passengers opening and count the 'stick' out. The crew were not so lucky. The 82nd still had 45 minutes to their drop zone.

Elsewhere, a flak shell tore through the floor of a plane carrying paratroopers of the 101st. '*Now* they give us a latrine!' one shouted to his fellow passengers. Private Robert Bryce, braced in the door of a low flying C-47, saw Dutch civilians 300 feet below making the 'V-Victory' sign. 'They're giving us two to one we don't make it!' he told the men behind him.

Gavin, along with his communications and headquarters personnel, and Captain Brestebeurje of the Dutch underground were in the lead aircraft of the serial waiting to drop on DZ (drop zone) 'N'. Standing beside the door, he and his G-3 (Operations Officer), Colonel John 'Jack' Norton tried to follow their route from their unmarked maps and what they remembered of the aerial reconnaissance photos they had studied over the past week. Below them, mile after mile of monotonous landscape gave few clues. Suddenly they spotted a flight of aircraft below them and off to their right. As parachutes began to appear, Gavin wondered whether they had reached their DZ but couldn't recognise a single landmark. As the plane flew on, he realised they had strayed off course and were passing over the 101st zone. Soon, however, they spotted the first features of their objectives.

The 82nd were led in by two pathfinder aircraft who dropped their personnel ten minutes before the arrival of the main body. Only the two DZs around the Grave bridge, considered by Gavin to be the Division's primary objective, would be marked before the drop. No enemy were encountered on the DZs so they quickly set up their equipment and laid out the prearranged visual signals – a yellow panel '0' and violet smoke – but as the remainder of the Division arrived over the area, the Germans began to react. Donald Orcutt, flying a C-47 with 18 men of the 82nd into a DZ 500 yards from the edge of the Reichswald forest, dropped to 50 feet for a fast turnaround:

> It was only then I spotted a German 88mm anti-aircraft guncrew up ahead and only five hundred yards from the edge of the drop zone. The 88 was slightly off to my left and pointed directly at us. I distinctly remember the image of the gun crew. One man was naked from the waist up, the second guy had on only his long johns and boots, and the third guy, a sergeant who

US paratroopers drop on D-Day.

was completely dressed as though about to answer roll call, pulled the lanyard just a moment before we roared over. I didn't see the muzzle flash. The three Germans looked directly up at us as we barrelled by. They must have taken a hell of a blast from our prop wash and wing down wash. The shot missed, obviously, or I wouldn't be here to talk about it.[3]

Meeting limited resistance – in marked contrast to the chaos of Normandy – the daylight drop had been unusually successful. The 82nd Airborne Division had 89 per cent of troops on or within 1000 yards of their correct landing zones and it would be followed by an equally successful glider landing with 84 per cent reaching their landing zones. Initial ground resistance was negligible and Gavin's staff sections soon established radio communications with his regimental commanders. Immediately upon landing Captain Brestebeurje went to a Dutch farmhouse to ask about the local enemy situation and was advised that there were about 200 Germans guarding an ammunition storage area in a wooded area beside the DZ. A firefight was under way there when Captain Brestebeurje telephoned nearby communities to check on German reactions to the landings. For the next few days, commercial telephone calls were placed to Arnhem to check on the progress of the British landings as well as to Nijmegen and other nearby towns. 'In fact,' Gavin said, 'someone on the staff wanted to know why we didn't call Berlin and talk to Adolf Hitler. I suppose that we could have in the first 24 hours but there were other far more important things to do.'

On DZ 'T' the 508th PIR landed around a flak battery scattering the gunners in all directions, killing those that they didn't capture. One lieutenant of the Regiment landed near Wyler some distance away from the planned DZ and while moving toward the assembly area his platoon found another flak battery firing at the transports overhead. They quickly overran it since the Germans had not thought to place any trenches around the site to provide security against ground attack. Similar stories were reaching Gavin from across the area. The 82nd had landed and were in good order

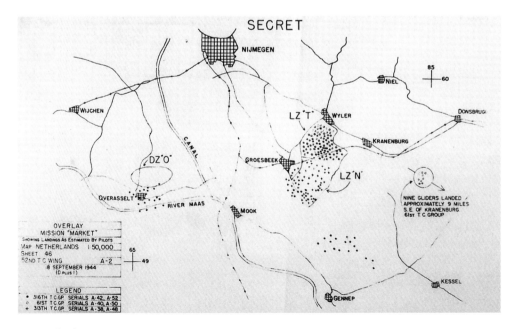

The US landing zones at Nijmegen.

Grave Bridge

There had been many nervous jokes at the briefing about the name of the 504th's first target until the troopers settled for calling it 'Gravy' (although more correctly it was pronounced 'Grarve'). The bridge, nearly 400m long, was one of the largest in Europe and its capture was considered essential if the 82nd were not to be cut off. The task would fall to the 2nd Battalion (2/504) and the presence of only light flak around it had allowed Gavin to persuade the air force to deliver their troops to two drop zones – E Company would land on DZ 'E' to the west of the objective and D, F and HQ Companies on DZ 'O' on the eastern side of the Maas river. To prevent confusion amongst other serials, E Company would be the last of the 504th to drop.

Having overshot DZ 'E', Lieutenant John S. Thompson and his men landed much closer to the bridge than expected.

The US War Department was keen to see what their elite airborne troops could do in combat.

Seeing that we were very close to the bridge and knowing that this was our primary mission, I sent a messenger back to where the Company was assembling and told the company commander that we were proceeding toward the bridge. We worked our way down various canals wading in water up to our necks. By this time, firing from the town and the buildings around us had increased considerably and there was now firing coming from a camouflaged flak tower on the southern approach to the bridge.

As we neared the bridge we could see German soldiers running to and from a power plant which was about fifty yards due west of the bridge. They made several trips carrying something in their arms. We waited until they made about three trips and then raked the area with machine-gun fire. Later when we overran the power plant we found four dead German soldiers and one wounded. They had apparently been carrying their personal equipment and blankets.[4]

The rest of the Company, under Captain Walter Van Poyck, assembled about a mile from the bridge and began to move up to support Thompson as the remainder of the battalion began to advance along the road from Asselt towards the eastern end of the bridge. As they began to lay down fire, Thompson's men were again moving forward.

As we got closer, we were surprised to see two trucks coming down the highway from Grave towards the bridge. My leading scout fired, killing the driver. The truck careened off the road with the German soldiers scrambling to get out. The second truck stopped and the soldiers in it jumped out and deployed. By this time my men had taken up firing at these Germans but they were evidently trying to get away. We continued to work our way along in defilade towards the flak tower and bridge. The flak tower continued to fire but by now the fire was going over our heads. My bazooka man worked his way forward and fired three rounds, two of them going into the top of the tower. The gun then ceased firing. In it we found two Germans dead and one wounded. We took over the gun and engaged the guns on the far side. All communication wires leading across the bridge were cut and a roadblock was set up at the southern end.

Shortly afterwards a patrol from the other side linked up with Thompson. The bridge was secure for the loss of just one paratrooper killed and 15 wounded.

That evening, VanPoyck heard the sound of approaching armour.

Our mission provided for our relief at the roadblock by British armor moving north on the Eindhoven road. Simultaneously, one of my men shouted 'Hold your fire, it's a Limey.' The tank was covered with camouflage netting and branches with the commander standing in the open hatch. I casually walked toward him, to our great relief. Simultaneously, as he realized I wasn't German, I realized he wasn't British. He fired a cannon round at me, which passed close to me and shattered a tree at my right rear.[5]

Behind VanPoyck, a group of paratroopers were caught by the fire and three were killed, eleven wounded by the shot. The tank escaped when the Americans opened fire with bazookas.

Maas/Waal Canal

On DZ 'O', three battalions were able to regroup and concentrate so easily that many compared it to an exercise back in England. As 2/504th moved off towards Grave, 3/504th headed north to secure the Grave-Nijmegen road whilst 1/504th moved east towards a series of bridges across the Maas/Waal Canal, numbered, from south to north, as 7–10.

Bridge 7, the Heumen Lock bridge, was attacked by B Company 1/504th under Captain Thomas Heldeson and they immediately hit heavy resistance. Crawling forward, paratroop engineers cut every wire they could 'with the urgency of men who knew that if they didn't succeed they were likely to go up with the bridge!' Unable to cross the waterway and close with the enemy on the far bank, all the men could do was use every weapon to pin down the Germans until help arrived from the 2/505th. They had been deliberately dropped over four miles away on DZ 'T' to avoid congestion over the much closer DZ 'N' and had had to cover twice the planned distance to reach the objective. Now surrounded, the Germans surrendered.

At Bridge 8, near Malden, German demolition parties had been alerted. Sergeant Ross Carter was among those who overshot DZ 'O' and landed in woods nearby.

The boys dribbled down the trail in two and threes until E Company was together. Nearly everyone had had a good jump. Within fifteen minutes after falling into Holland we were on the way to the bridge … Soon we emerged from the comfortable cover of the evergreens and hurried over the mostly open countryside towards our objective. We were within five hundred yards of it when a tremendous explosion lifted the bridge high into the air and scattered it over a wide area … Inasmuch as our objective had been blown up, it was pointless to risk our lives in daylight on the level terrain which could be machine-gunned from several directions. So we lay in the ditch and waited for darkness.[6]

Damaged during the attempt to capture it, Honinghutie Bridge (Bridge 10) was reduced to one lane, slowing traffic heading for Nijmegen. (Courtesy Jan Bos)

A longer view of Bridge 10, the road and rail bridges at Honinghutje. (Courtesy Jan Bos)

It was a similar story at Bridge 9, blown up as A Company 1/504th approached. There too the expected help from 3/508th had been delayed by their being dropped at Groesbeek.

Bridge 10 – the Neerbosch/Honinghuite road and rail bridge – had been identified as the strongest and thus most able to carry the weight of XXX Corps' tanks. Although Gavin regarded the bridge as 'of the uttermost importance', and knew it was heavily defended, only a platoon each from the 504th and 508th were deployed. Oddly for such an important bridge, it was only a secondary objective for C Company 1/504th after the failed attacks on bridges 8 and 9. Attacking from the west, the plan was that they would be joined by a platoon from E Company 2/508th attacking from the east but would not begin to move towards their objective until 0330hrs on the 18th – over 14 hours after the landings started.

Lieutenant Lloyd Polette Jr, a platoon commander with E Company, received orders that he and his 25 men were 'to remove my roadblock south of Nijmegen and move to Bridge Number 10, take the bridge, and organize a defense.'[7] Eight men were killed and several wounded as the platoon approached the bridge and Polette requested help from mortars. At around 1100hrs a section of 81mm mortars arrived and began to lay down fire on the German defenders. Joined by Lieutenant Tomlinson's platoon from D Company of the 508th, Polette's twelve remaining men stormed the bridge and held it until 1730hrs when they were recalled to their battalion. The expected support from the 504th did not materialise. The attack had cost half of the platoon and all of the machine-gun crews borrowed from HQ Company were killed or wounded but Polette would later receive a well earned Distinguished Service Cross for his leadership. During the battle, however, German engineers destroyed the rail link and damaged the road bridge so that when the crossing was finally secured, it was found to be unsafe for use by XXX Corps.

Mook Railway Bridge

The rail bridge across the Maas at Mook had been identified as a potential alternative route for XXX Corps and men of 1/505th PIR dropped on DZ 'N', two miles northeast of the bridge to capture it. Unfortunately, the delay caused by the distance gave the Germans plenty of time to prepare and as the first Americans overran the defences at the northern end, the bridge was blown.

Groesbeek Heights

The bulk of the 82nd's effort on D-Day would be to secure DZ/LZs 'N' and 'T' on either side of the village of Groesbeek. The landing was not quite as expected. The glider LZs had been expected to be opposed by up to 4000 SS cadets rumoured to be in the area but resistance was light. Instead of the fanatical cadets many had feared, the Americans found a group of bewildered Dutch civilians in their Sunday best approaching with white, frightened faces. The welcome for others was rather warmer. US glider pilot Arthur Kaplan landed in a field nearby under sporadic mortar fire. He helped unload his cargo and set off with his passengers towards their rendezvous (RV). Passing a barn, they heard suspicious noises from inside and burst in.

> There – in one of the stalls – a paratrooper was making love to a very willing Dutch girl. He was quite profane at being interrupted, so we apologized and left ... The guy couldn't have been on the ground more than an hour.[8]

The sheer scale of the planned landings would require every available glider pilot and the decision had been made to allocate just one pilot to each aircraft instead of the usual two. Passengers found themselves undergoing on-the-job training during the flight with a brief explanation of how to land if the pilot was hit. Flight Officer John Lowden, approaching the Nijmegen LZ in a later lift with an infantry sergeant as co-pilot, recalls being told quietly 'I wouldn't presume to fly for you, but I think you're about to land in a minefield.' A very rapid pull on the controls lifted the glider into the next field and into a gentle landing.

Despite the relative lack of reaction, German forces were in the area. Immediately, patrols were sent out from 1/505th PIR.

> The big threat for the Regiment was the tanks and troops which, according to the report we had received in England should be concentrated in the forest Reichswald. As First Battalion had the area closest to the Reichswald, it was very much concerned as to the correctness of the report. Therefore, at once they questioned civilians about the enemy in the forest. And they were glad to be informed that the report about the 1000 tanks in the Reichswald was false – a statement that was later confirmed over and over again.[9]

By the end of D-Day, the 82nd were digging in and the Division, Gavin thought, had 'the situation well in hand'. At around 1800hrs, however, he became aware that one objective had been overlooked. No attempt had been made to move against the bridges in Nijmegen itself.

Waal Bridges

As the 82nd dug in around Nijmegen, almost all its allocated objectives had been taken but, as the Official History records,

> In the hands of the remaining battalion of the 508th Parachute Infantry rested a special destiny. This battalion, the 1st, commanded by Lieutenant Colonel Shields Warren Jr., represented the 82d Airborne Division's best chance for a cheap and rapid capture of the highway bridge over the sprawling Waal river at Nijmegen.[10]

After prioritising the capture of the Groesbeek Heights, Gavin had had second thoughts about the overall aim of his mission and 48 hours prior to take off had given orders that a battalion-sized attack should be made on the Nijmegen bridge. Gavin later claimed

> I personally directed Colonel Roy E. Lindquist, commanding the 508th Parachute Infantry, to commit his first battalion against the Nijmegen bridge without delay after landing but to keep a very close watch on it in the event he needed it to protect himself against the Reichswald.[11]

In his own memoirs, Gavin states that he also told Lindquist on 15 September

> … that if, in his opinion, the situation along the Groesbeek high ground was quiet in the late afternoon of the day of our landing, he was to send a battalion against the Nijmegen bridge that night. I further cautioned him to send it off over the flat ground under cover of darkness and not through the city.[12]

Yet another history has Gavin advising Lindquist to 'move into Nijmegen to capture the highway bridge if practicable after capturing the initial objectives.'[13] Conspiracy theorists may be interested to note that the Official History of the campaign states that 'Although extensive combat interviews were conducted with personnel of the 508th Parachute Infantry, they are inexplicably missing from Department of the Army files.'[14] Lindquist had effectively been given four very different orders: attack at once after landing; attack when ordered to do so by Gavin; wait until after dark; wait until all other objectives had been

The Waal River bridge.
(Courtesy Jan Bos)

taken. He interpreted the second two versions to mean that no battalion was to go for the bridge until the Regiment had secured its other objectives and established a defensive line protecting his assigned sector of the high ground and the divisional glider LZ. Instead of moving immediately toward the Nijmegen bridge, Colonel Warren's battalion was ordered to take an 'assigned initial objective' in the vicinity of De Ploeg, a suburb of Nijmegen a mile and a quarter southeast of the city, organize this objective for defence, and to 'be prepared to go into Nijmegen later'.[15]

At around 1830hrs, five hours after landing, 1/508th began to dig in around De Ploeg. As the Battalion prepared its position, Lieutenant Robert Weaver's rifle platoon of C Company and the Battalion intelligence section were provided with a SCR300 radio and received orders to 'make an aggressive reconnaissance, investigate reports from Dutch civilians that only 18 Germans guarded the big bridge, and, if possible, capture the south end of the bridge.'[16] On hearing that only a single platoon had been sent into Nijmegen, Gavin is said to have angrily demanded that Lindquist 'delay not a second longer and get to the bridge as quickly as possible with Warren's battalion.'[17] At around 2000hrs, A and B Companies were ordered to abandon their positions and move towards Nijmegen. The order caught Warren by surprise. 'This was the first time the battalion was told it was to secure this bridge. By the time the battalion minus [its reserve C Company] was assembled from its rather wide defensive positions, it was well after dark.'[18]

Following a young Dutch resistance fighter, A Company reached their initial point and waited for B Company to catch up. When they had failed to do so by around 2200hrs, Captain Jonathan Adams, commanding A Company, was told to go ahead anyway. With their Dutch guide cycling ahead as a scout, they made good time until they reached the Keizer Karel Plein roundabout. Suddenly, an unmistakably German voice shouted 'Halt!' and a machine gun opened fire. Many accounts claim that the Dutch guide disappeared at this point and seem to imply that he ran away but in fact he had warned Adams about the guard post and according to Adams, 'this was where the Dutchman was moved aside.' His job complete, the guide went off, no doubt to other tasks. As the firefight developed, the Americans heard the sound of approaching armour.

> No one could have said so with any finality at the time, but the chance for an easy, speedy capture of the Nijmegen bridge had passed. This was all the more lamentable because in Nijmegen during the afternoon the Germans had had nothing more than the same kind of 'mostly low quality' troops encountered at most other places on D-Day.[19]

That afternoon, Nijmegen had been held by a weak company sized NCO training unit, three infantry companies of 6th Ersatz (Reserve) Battalion of 406th Infantry Division and a company of the Herman Goering Paratroop Training Regiment under Colonel Henke, together with assorted flak crews, railway guards and military policemen. By that evening, the entire garrison numbered fewer than 1000 men. The 406th Division itself was an administrative collection of scattered training units whose headquarters were mobilised in a matter of hours to put together Kampfgruppe Henke. Many of the men now forming a defensive ring around the Nijmegen bridges were veterans of 1914–18 hastily conscripted back into service, but even as Weaver's platoon prepared to begin their patrol, vehicles of the 9th Hoenstaufen SS Panzer Division's Reconnaissance Battalion under Captain Gräbner had raced across the bridge at Arnhem heading south to Nijmegen. They arrived just as the Americans came within reach of the bridge. From his HQ at Oosterbeek, Field Marshal Model had watched the British paratroopers dropping from the sky and quickly recognised the importance of the Nijmegen bridge if he were to prevent reinforcements reaching them by land. He agreed with SS-Gruppenführer Willi Bittrich that Nijmegen had to be the focus of II SS Panzer Corps' counterattack. The Reconnaissance Battalion was dispatched immediately, to be followed as soon as possible by the 10th SS Panzer Division of Kampfgruppe Frundsberg under SS-Brigadeführer Heinz Harmel whose mission was 'to block the threat in the south long enough to enable the 9th SS to settle with the British Division in Oosterbeek–Arnhem. This was the main task.'[20] The 9th was in the process of a move back to Germany to refit and its vehicles had already been loaded onto transport trains. Many had been disabled to prevent them being commandeered by their 10th Division comrades but even so the Battalion was ready to move after just five hours.

As the first units of the 10th SS Panzer Division (an infantry battalion and an engineer company) made ready, the plan was that they would relieve the 9th SS Panzer Division's Reconnaissance Battalion, which would then be freed to return to Arnhem, but by this time British troops of 2nd Battalion Parachute Regiment under Colonel Frost had reached the Arnhem bridge and prevented movement across it. Troops of Kampfgruppe Frundsberg were too late and were forced to take a detour to a ferry near Huissen, southeast of Arnhem and a long march into the Nijmegen area.

In the city, the SS counterattack had so disorganised the men of A Company that it was only the sudden arrival of B Company that helped stabilise the situation. Colonel Warren then reported the encounter to Lindquist and asked for reinforcement by C Company. Meanwhile Captain Adams had received a report from Dutch civilians that the detonator mechanism for destroying the highway bridge was hidden in the city's main post office, only a few blocks north of the Keizer Karel Plein, so he led a platoon-sized patrol to find and destroy the mechanism. After a brief fight, the paratroopers stormed the building and destroyed what appeared to be the demolition circuits but by then returning to the roundabout was no longer an option. The Germans had closed in behind them and for the next three days Adams' men and their civilian helpers were trapped inside the post office until relief came.

As the fighting continued, Gavin realised his men could make no headway in the street battle and gave the order to 'withdraw from close proximity to the bridge and reorganize'. The bridge was lost.

Meanwhile, XXX Corps had begun their advance. The plan put in place by Second Army stated clearly that the airborne attack would begin at 'H-Hour' and was provisionally set for 1300hrs on 17 September. The ground forces were to move at 'Z-Hour' which was 'likely to be one hour after 'H-Hour' and would, in any case, *not be earlier* [author's emphasis]'.[21] Browning's orders, signed on 16 September, are specific: Z-Hour was to be '70 minutes' after the 101st began to drop. It has been claimed that Horrocks was not informed that the airborne armada was on its way and so waited until the aircraft appeared overhead before giving the order to move. This may be possible given the generally poor communication between First Allied Airborne Army and the ground formations but seems unlikely. Rather, Horrocks watched the air armada passing overhead as he waited for the start time he had been given by Second Army.

In the historiography of *Market Garden*, the delayed start of XXX Corps is an accepted fact to the extent that in his book *Arnhem 1944*, the strongly pro-airborne William Buckingham claims that there was a pointless delay of 'two hours after the first airborne troops were on the ground' before the first move by the Guards, caused, he suggests, because the Irish Guards were simply not ready to move.[22] Like many delays blamed on XXX Corps, it's worth doing the maths. The ground forces were not supposed to begin the operation at H-Hour as critics have imagined. H-Hour was at 1300hrs but some units, such as the 508th

Tanks of XXX Corps in Valkenswaard.

at Nijmegen, did not drop until almost 1330hrs. Z-Hour was scheduled for not less than one hour later and Buckingham himself states that XXX Corps preliminary barrage began at 1400hrs (i.e. exactly on time) and that the tanks began to move at 1435hrs.

Nor was it, as many have suggested, mishandling by Horrocks. As his orders explained: 'Zero Hour: I will give Zero Hour as soon as I know for certain that the Airborne Divisions are on their way. Timings must depend, therefore, on weather.'[23] If Horrocks had to wait until he saw the aircraft overhead before ordering his advance, XXX Corps must have been in a state of high readiness to be able to react as they did.

Even assuming that the Guards should have advanced without a barrage to suppress the enemy artillery positions (Buckingham also explains that this wiped out the 'entire contingent' of towed anti-tank guns covering the main axis north and clearly this was therefore a wise precaution), the most that can be claimed is a delay of 25 minutes after the time set by Browning. He goes on to claim that there was 'little utility' in timing the attack to coincide with the drops. Whilst it is true that an earlier attack could draw reserves away from the landing zones, it would also alert and increase the garrisons of the bridges before the 101st's attempts to take them intact. If, despite every effort on their part, the Zon bridge was blown in the face of the surprise attack by the paratroopers, is there any chance that the bridge's defenders might not have noticed the clanking approach of an armoured division rather sooner?

As XXX Corps prepared to advance, the German paratroops deployed opposite were strengthened by an SS unit that had arrived undetected into the battle zone.

The Irish Guards moved forward behind an artillery barrage and with air support from rocket firing Typhoons. 'To start with,' Horrocks later recalled, 'everything seemed to be going our way. But suddenly nine of the Irish Guards tanks were knocked out almost all at once and a furious battle began in the woods in front of me.'[24] Resistance proved heavier than expected and it emerged that two battalions of the 9th SS had arrived to bolster the paratroopers holding the canal line defences. The after action report of 21st Army Group says that these troops came as a 'complete surprise' and slowed the advance. Adding to XXX Corps' problems was the fact that the attacks by VIII and XII Corps had not gone ahead as planned, leaving the Germans able to move reserves into XXX Corps' path. Although the loss of the Irish Guards' tanks has also been attributed by some sources to friendly fire, in the fighting that afternoon at least two German tanks were known to have been destroyed. Whatever the cause, the Guards pressed on and reached the outskirts of Valkenswaard by 1700hrs. They had covered seven miles. This is frequently cited as a failure on their part but the official US history explains,

> In view of the fact that woods and marshy ground confined the attack to a front not much wider than the highway leading to Eindhoven, progress was remarkable, though not sufficient to take the tanks to Eindhoven. As night came the British stopped in Valkenswaard, their 'formal' objective. The objective of Eindhoven, which General Horrocks had indicated he hoped to reach on D-day, lay six miles to the north.[25]

At a meeting on 13 September, General Taylor of the 101st had told General Dempsey that his division would reach Eindhoven at 1800hrs and would rendezvous with XXX Corps on the southern outskirts at 2000hrs. The lead tanks of the Irish Guards entered Valkenswaard some time after 1930hrs and stopped for the night, still some six miles south of their expected link up with the 101st. The reason for the decision remains the subject of much debate even now but reference to the War Diary of the 2nd Armoured Battalion Grenadier Guards gives us a clue. In it, the objective given for D-Day is for the Guards to seize Eindhoven and to link up with the 101st the 'next day'. In other words, the Guards had not been told about the planned rendezvous south of the city.[26]

The 101st had dropped as planned 'in an area to include Eindhoven' and had got within 50 yards of the bridge over the Zon canal when it was blown up in their faces. Two smaller bridges nearby were also found to have been demolished. Responding quickly, engineers rigged up a crossing using ropes and timber supplied by local civilians and even managed a raft to ferry men of the 506th to the southern bank. A post-war American analysis of airborne operations noted that 'although a makeshift bridge over the canal was completed by 1730, the troops *for no apparent good reason* [author's emphasis] did not attempt to advance any further on D-Day.'[27] Aware of the risks, Taylor is claimed to have warned the British that it might not be possible for the 101st to take Eindhoven on the first day and clearly there was confusion about whose responsibility the city was.[28] Intriguingly, writing about four weeks later, Brereton wrote:

> The original plan as demanded by 21 Army Group proposed a much further extension to the south of the drop of the 101st Airborne Division than I eventually agreed to. The 21 Army Group demanded originally that at least two drops should be made to the south of Eindhoven. The drop furtherest [sic] south would have been within artillery range of our own forces along the general line of the Meuse-Escaut Canal. I refused this and submitted a modification which would concentrate the 101st Airborne Division in the area generally from Veghel northeast to Grave with the 82nd Airborne Division dropping in its approved areas. I felt that the advance of the armor to Eindhoven was a simple task. As a matter of fact, I was assured by General Dempsey that they would be in Eindhoven about six hours after H-hour. The airborne drop could not be expected to do it any sooner.[29]

Put another way, Brereton assumed the British were to take Eindhoven and link up with the 101st further north.

The 101st were, indeed, initially assigned an impossibly large area of operations and this was modified after the early briefings. However, most historians have attributed this modification to a discussion between General Taylor and General Dempsey, not to Brereton's intervention. In fact, as commander of the Allied Airborne Army, it was Brereton's job to protect the interests of his subordinate, Taylor. If Brereton was of the belief that the British would be in Eindhoven faster than the airborne troopers could manage, surely it was his responsibility to ensure that Taylor was relieved of that responsibility and Eindhoven left to XXX Corps. Clearly, as both the 101st and the Guards Armoured believed Eindhoven was an airborne responsibility, Brereton had not pointed out the changes he felt necessary in the plan.

> Concentration of the two divisions [82nd and 101st] in the general area indicated would result in establishing contact with each other in a minimum of time and would furnish a strong combat force to assure the crossings of the Maas and Waal at Grave and Nijmegen and would establish in that general area a force of two divisions closely coordinated and capable of strong offensive action against any objective. I was not so optimistic as 21 Army Group concerning the enemy combat efficiency in the northern part of the salient, although I agreed that the advance to the general line Eindhoven-Helmond should be able to over-run any resistance encountered without delay.

Unfortunately, he does not explain how this 'strong combat force' of two closely co-ordinated divisions would be able to abandon their widely dispersed positions in order to 'assure the crossings'.

Thus, with Eindhoven still firmly in enemy hands and the bridge at Zon destroyed, the Irish Guards had valid reasons for not pushing on that night, but the debate centres on how much of that information was available to them at the time of the decision to halt. What is clear is that there was confusion about what was happening. The Guards were tasked with the capture of Valkenswaard on the afternoon of D-Day and had accomplished the task. There is a strong possibility that General Taylor's warning that his men might not capture Eindhoven on D-Day had translated into a situation where, as David Bennett has argued, the Guards were not even aware of the planned link up at 2000hrs and that in fact the 231st Infantry Brigade of 50th Division was expected to leapfrog the Irish Guards and to halt at the 'Judas Line' between Valkenswaard and Eindhoven, to await orders to move forward, presumably to make contact with the 101st.[30] Later explanations about allowing bridging equipment to pass appear to have been a convenient explanation but there are several different accounts, casting doubt on what information was known at the time.

D+1 Monday 18 September

After the bitter criticism Gavin had heaped on Urquhart's plan to land his closest troops five miles from the Arnhem bridge, as dawn broke on the morning of D+1, the 508th PIR were embroiled in a stalemate in the streets of Nijmegen, over five miles from their drop zone.

The situation around the 82nd's perimeter was confused. Just before dawn, Lieutenant William Hays of F Company 2/505th heard the sound of a freight train approaching. 'First the machine guns opened up; then it hit the Gammon grenades, which derailed the train. The engine came to a stop with steam hissing from the holes made by the machine guns.'[31] The troopers had been ready and the Gammon bombs put in place after an incident at dusk the previous evening. The 505th had occupied Hill 81.8 overlooking the railway tracks running east from Nijmegen into Germany and had heard the sound of a train approaching. 'Everyone was so taken by surprise that they just stood dumbfounded as the train passed.'[32] Orders were immediately issued to mine the tracks using the Gammon grenades to prevent further incidents.

At about the same time, Gavin and Lindquist met to discuss the situation. With no real information available about the enemy and the arrival of the second lift due that morning, Gavin felt it was essential to secure the landing zones but also that the attack on the bridges should continue. The two men agreed that one company could perhaps succeed if the advance was made along the more open streets of the southeastern and eastern fringes of the city and G Company 3/508th, under Lieutenant Colonel Louis G. Mendez Jr, was tasked with the mission. Currently defending the stretch of high ground centred on the village of Berg en Dal, four miles away, G Company had previously occupied Hill 64, little more than a mile from the south end of the highway bridge.

At 0745hrs G Company moved out under Captain Frank J. Novak

Gliders on D-Day.

toward the bridge. As they did so, Colonel Warren ordered B Company to hold its positions in and around the city hall as A Company fell back through them to try to consolidate their line. Along G Company's route, civilians crowded the roads and showered them with fruit and flowers but as they drew closer to the bridge the crowds markedly thinned. The reason soon became clear as, from dug-in positions on a roundabout south of Hunner Park, on the southern approaches to the bridge, the Germans lay in wait around the historic observation tower known as the Belvedere and the medieval walls surrounding it. They allowed the Americans to draw close before opening fire.

Captain Novak quickly deployed his men and attacked, forcing their way to within a few hundred feet of the defences, but they were beaten back by artillery from across the river. At that point, however, despite the incredible progress they had made against heavy odds, the reinforcement of G Company could not be considered. Colonel Mendez could not commit further troops without jeopardising his defensive line near the Hotel Berg en Dal and Colonel Lindquist had only a company in reserve, already earmarked to clear one of the Division's glider landing zones for the glider lift due at any time.

Then, at about 1000hrs, he received new orders from regimental headquarters to break off the action in town and countermarch both companies back to the drop zone to meet a growing threat to the glider landing zones where 454 gliders carrying 1899 men of the 319th, 320th and 456th Glider Field Artillery (GFA) along with 60 guns, 206 jeeps and 123 trailers were due to land. His already exhausted men began the long march back. At 1400hrs Colonel Mendez finally ordered G Company to break off and rejoin the Battalion on Hill 64.

Back in England, the bad weather that would plague the entire operation was making itself felt. As the second lift made ready, takeoff was put back from 1000 to 1500hrs, a delay that undoubtedly saved many lives. Copies of the operational plan had been found by a German patrol in a wrecked Waco CG-4A glider. (Although usually attributed to an American breach of security, three of the Wacos allocated to Browning's Corps HQ failed to reach their LZ and this may have been one of them.) The plans were now in the hands of Generals Model at Arnhem and Student near Nijmegen. Both suspected them to be fake because they were too detailed, too precise. The Luftwaffe, however, accepted them and at 1000hrs, as the gliders were expected to arrive, scrambled every available fighter to intercept. They found nothing.

German doctrine at that time was to counterattack airborne assaults as quickly as possible with any force available to try to disrupt any attempt to regroup; therefore General Feld, responsible for the German 406th Division, was under instructions from Model to push forward with the forces at his disposal. 'It was an almost impossible task,' he later wrote, 'for 406th Division to attack picked troops with its motley crowd. But it was necessary to risk the attack in order to forestall an enemy advance to the east, and to deceive him in regard to our strength.'[33] An attack by Kampfgruppe Gobel against Riethorst in the southeast of the 82nd's perimeter was beaten back when its armour attempted to manoeuvre off the roads into the low lying land. As XXX Corps would later find, the ground would not support the weight of the vehicles and they soon became easy prey for paratroopers with bazookas. At the northeast end, Feld had just 24 medium mortars to back up his infantry attack and was himself surprised when his 'motley crowd' of pressed amateurs made some progress. They were, however, no match for the highly trained paratroopers. When one battalion commander reported that he was pinned down, Major Rasch of Feld's staff went forward to investigate. He found

… old boys lying there, veterans of the First World War, who had just been called up to relieve the younger soldiers manning POW camp battalions. Now they too had been put into the front line. Somebody in the line called out to me, 'Major, we've already stormed the Craoneer Heights in 1914!' 'Ja', I was able to answer, 'can't you see that it's up to us old boys to run the whole show again; and we will do it exactly as we did then. First of all we have to get Tommy on the run, then we've cracked it.'[34]

The old boys moved forward.

With 30 minutes to go before the first gliders landed, Warren's men of the 1/508th launched another attack to clear the landing zones. In the face of heavy fire, the assault almost stalled as they made a dramatic bayonet charge using the downhill slope to increase their momentum; only the sudden appearance of the gliders overhead carried the day as the Germans broke and ran but the stronger groups could not be dislodged completely. A warning was sent to land on the western edge, away from the tree line, but contact could not be made with the incoming gliders. The second lift arrived under heavy fire. Some tug pilots failed to spot the previous day's LZs and General Gavin watched helplessly as tow combinations flew overhead carrying badly needed guns into Germany itself. Nine gliders carrying B Battery of the 320th GFA were released twelve miles east of LZ 'T', deep in Germany and were never seen again. Nine more were released over the German village of Wyler and their passengers of the 320th GFA were forced to defend the landing position until nightfall and then try to make their way 10 miles back to US lines, bringing with them 160 airborne troopers, 22 glider pilots, 10 jeeps and 2 field guns. Despite these failures, 85 per cent of the expected reinforcements had arrived.

Later, even the official US history would cast doubt on Gavin's priorities.

Whether the prospect of difficulty in holding the high ground in the 82nd Airborne Division's sector justified delay in renewing the attack on the Nijmegen bridge … must be a matter of conjecture. Few concrete indications that the Reichswald was rife with German armor, or even infantry, had developed. Civilians had told men of the 505th Parachute Infantry on D-Day that the Germans had no armor in the Reichswald. Patrols from the 505th had found no armor. One patrol reported that the 'high ground' in the Reichswald was unoccupied. 'Towers are empty, woods are tank obstacles – too thick.' The 82d Airborne Division's G-2 estimated that the enemy had 'probably two battalions of mixed L[ine] of C[ommunications] Troops' in the Reichswald, though he modified this low evaluation by listing first among enemy capabilities the likelihood of continuing piecemeal attacks, 'but in increasing strength,' from the forest. No tangible incidents of armor in action had developed; most vehicles reported as tanks turned out to be flak wagons.[35]

On the other hand, Gavin says he was still receiving reports from the Dutch resistance that the enemy had strong armoured and infantry units in the forest and civilians were said to have told his men about Germans massing for a new attack. In the late afternoon, nearly 100 Allied fighter bombers carried out strafing attacks and the 82nd's artillery began harassing fire into the forest.

Browning's Corps HQ, meanwhile, had managed to establish radio contact with the adjacent 82nd Division and with the Airborne HQ at Moor Park in England but not with the 101st at Eindhoven or the 1st at Arnhem. Given that the 82nd's HQ, codenamed 'Champion', was located nearby and that a lack of trained cipher operators meant that sensitive material could not be passed directly between Moor Park and Corps HQ, their role was now almost completely redundant. By then, a message had been received via a telephone call from Arnhem that the 1st Airborne had encountered stiffer resistance than expected and that support was needed as soon as possible. Conscious of the expected arrival of XXX Corps, Browning began to pressurise Gavin to move against the bridges.

> Browning had warned me, the Nijmegen bridge must be taken today. At the latest, tomorrow. The capture of the Nijmegen bridge was squarely on my shoulders. This I knew. But most important to me were the lives of General Urquhart and the British First Airborne.[36]

It was a spectacularly bad example of man management by Browning. Gavin had injured his back in the landings and was in great pain as he had attempted to fight a widely dispersed battle for the last 24 hours and was fully conscious that each passing hour allowed the enemy to reinforce the bridge defences and reduced his chances of success. In response, during the afternoon he presented Browning with a plan to use a battalion each of the 504th and 508th PIR to envelop the bridge from the east and west under cover of darkness that night. Browning initially approved but then changed his mind.

> On giving it more thought, [and] in view of the situation in the 30th Corps, he felt that the retention of the high ground S[outh] of Nijmegen was of greater importance, and directed that the primary mission should be to hold the high gr[ound] and retain its position W[est] of the Maas–Waal Canal.[37]

Gavin issued orders to concentrate on defending the existing positions.

As the Americans dug in deeper around their landing zones, SS Sturmbannführer (Major) Leo Reinhold had set up the headquarters of Kampfgruppe Reinhold on the northern banks of the Waal river and assigned responsibility for the defence of the railway bridge to Colonel Henke and the road crossing to SS Hauptsturmführer (Captain) Euling. An outpost line was established along the dual carriageway and two roundabouts south of the river with strongpoints at key junctions. These would be steadily strengthened over the next 48 hours as SS infantry, armour and artillery reached them via the Pannerden ferry operation. Despite opposition from Bittrich, who argued that blowing the bridges would not only stop and advance but would also cut off the British at Arnhem from any hope of rescue, Model stubbornly insisted that the bridges should not be blown unless they were about to be lost to the enemy so that, if possible, German forces could use them for counterattacks.

The situation by the end of D+1 was that the Nijmegen highway bridge – so vital that Model and Student had immediately grasped its significance – had not been reached. Three attempts had been made but the first, patrol-sized attack had been far too weak and its communications failed; the next, involving a two company-sized force had been beaten back because the Germans had been given time to reinforce their weak garrison; finally, a single company had been sent against a defence that had already seen off double that number. With civilians reporting that the bridge had been held by just 18 men when the Americans landed, at least the first two attempts could have succeeded if they had been launched whilst the 9th SS Battalion were still aboard their transport train at Arnhem. Even now, no attempt at all had been made against the nearby railway bridge.

To the south, XXX Corps had resumed its advance along separate routes. The Household Cavalry and Grenadier Guards had set out at 0530hrs on the central 'Club' route whilst the 32nd Guards Brigade had moved east along the 'Heart' route but had been stopped by strong defensive positions around Geldorp and Helmond and had had to rejoin the main axis of advance. By noon a link up with the 101st had been achieved and at 1900hrs the first Royal Engineers recce party had arrived to assess the damage to the bridge. An hour later, the first bridging vehicle arrived and work to build a Class 40 bridge capable of carrying the weight of the tanks could begin. A group of German POWs were pressed into service and one story tells of a Royal Engineer officer asking about progress and being told to go away by a distracted German prisoner because he was holding up the work.[38] The first vehicle crossed the bridge at 0615hours the next morning and at 0645hrs, the Guards began rolling again towards the Grave bridge, now visible in the distance.

D+2 Tuesday 19 September

According to the official US history,

> Spearheading the 30 Corps ground column, reconnaissance troops of the Guards Armoured Division linked with Colonel Tucker's 504th Parachute Infantry at Grave at 0820 the morning of D plus 2, 19 September. Major formations of the British armor were not far behind. From that point priority of objectives within the sector of the 82d Airborne Division shifted unquestionably in the direction of the bridge at Nijmegen. Already at least 33 hours behind schedule because of earlier delays south of Eindhoven and at Zon, the ground column had to have a way to get across the Waal.[39]

The timing given is curious and again it is worth doing the maths. In the wake of the failure of the operation, XXX Corps came in for a great deal of criticism for their apparent lack of urgency in attempting to reach Arnhem and the claim that they were a day and a half late reaching Nijmegen reinforces that sense of their being dangerously slow to move. According to various accounts, XXX Corps set out from Zon 'at least twenty four hours behind schedule', 'about thirty hours behind schedule' or, as above, 'thirty-three hours behind schedule'. Cornelius Ryan's seminal *A Bridge Too Far* even claims a delay of 36 hours. The link up with the 101st on the evening of D-Day did not take place and it was indeed 24 hours before the two units were able to meet in Eindhoven. If we add the 11-hour delay caused by the loss of the bridge, we get a figure of up to 35 hours. But were XXX Corps really so far behind schedule?

The claims made about expectations for XXX Corps' advance make confusing reading. Urquhart, for example, claims Frost's 2 Para were hopeful that 'the Bridge would only have to be held for twenty-four hours before XXX Corps came through.'[40] Montgomery had told Browning that the link would be made in two days. Browning allegedly said the bridges could be held for four and, during the battle itself, Urquhart optimistically predicted that 1st Airborne could manage up to eight days. The only timetable put forward that could achieve the goal of two days comes from Albert A. Nofi[41] who states that the expected rate of advance would mean that XXX Corps would reach

Eindhoven	by 1715hrs on 17 September
Veghel	by 2359hrs on 17 September
Grave	by 1200hrs on 18 September
Nijmegen	by 1800hrs on 18 September
Arnhem	by 1500hrs on 19 September

No contemporary evidence has been produced to support the idea that this timetable was ever put forward during *Market Garden* but it has been widely used by others and would seem to fit the schedule needed to reach Arnhem in the required timescale. Horrocks' own orders state simply; 'Speed absolutely vital, as we must reach the lightly equipped 1st British Airborne Division *if possible in forty-eight hours*.'[42] Of immediate note is that Nofi's timings required XXX Corps to reach Eindhoven by 1715hrs, three hours before it was scheduled to meet with the 101st south of the city. Neither group made the rendezvous that night as the Guards paused to the south whilst the 101st was forced to halt overnight to the north of the city. But although the link up was delayed by 24 hours, this does not mean that XXX Corps had been idle on D+1. The schedule above allows them almost seven hours to pass through Eindhoven after the link up and reach Veghel (on the north bank of the Zon). In fact, the meeting of the 101st and the Guards in Eindhoven took place after the first bridging vehicles began work on the Zon bridge several miles to the north. Horrocks' original idea was that XXX Corps would set out from Veghel on the morning of D+1 and, according to Nofi, reach Nijmegen by evening, around 28 hours after Z-Hour. It would not be until D+2 that this could be done but we can see that if they were 24 hours late leaving Veghel, by Grave they had clawed back around 4 hours and by Nijmegen had reduced the delay by around 6 hours, reaching Nijmegen 18 hours later than planned.

XXX Corps had crossed their start line at 1435hrs on Sunday 17 September. The lead elements reached the 82nd at Grave at about 0820hrs on 19 September and by 1200hrs 'major formations of the British armor' had reached Nijmegen whilst the official history of the 82nd reports that a joint British and US force began to move into the attack at 1100hrs, indicating that, allowing even a very short time for a briefing, the tanks must have reached the start line well before 1100hrs. The lead elements therefore made the link up 42 hours after crossing the start line and by noon were within 11 miles of Arnhem. The 'major formations' were in Nijmegen no more than 45 hours after starting out. In order for the column to be 'at least' 33 hours behind schedule when they reached Nijmegen, the time allowed for them to break through the German defence line along the Meuse-Escaut Canal and fight their way along 50 miles of a single highway would have been just nine hours and would have meant XXX Corps reaching bridge 10 – the Neerbosch/Honinghuite road and rail bridge several hours before the first men of the 82nd began their attempt to seize it and over twelve hours before it was actually taken. This would also have meant that XXX Corps would have to reach Nijmegen at least ten hours before the second lift was due to bring in the men needed to open the way for them. According to Ryan's claim of a 36-hour delay, XXX Corps were seemingly expected to be in Nijmegen about six hours after Z-Hour, placing them at the bridge at about the same time as the first patrol from the 508th began heading for it.

Using Nofi's schedule, the Guards Armoured reached Nijmegen no more than 18 hours later than expected – 11 hours of which resulted from the loss of the Zon bridge for which even the most ardent critic could not blame XXX Corps. Construction of a 190-foot Class 40 bridge could involve almost 350 vehicles, all needing to use the same narrow highway as the tanks, and movement forward was no easy feat. In the many accounts of the operation, no-one appears to consider the time taken to build the bridge to be unduly slow. As the schedule shows, it was assumed that the Guards would overnight in Nijmegen before setting out at first light for what was expected to be a nine-hour journey to Arnhem. On that basis, it is arguably possible that had the Nijmegen bridge been open, after reaching Nijmegen by noon the Guards could have pushed on to reach Arnhem by around 2100hrs on D+2. Late certainly, but only by some six hours rather than the 24 or 36 that so many writers have unquestioningly assumed. Ridgway's complaint – frequently echoed – that XXX Corps were 'inexcusably slow' thus becomes difficult to sustain once those factors outside their control (the loss of the Zon bridge by the 101st and the failure of the 82nd to secure the Nijmegen bridges) are removed from the equation.

It is undoubtedly true that some elements within XXX Corps underperformed but nowhere in the available plans for the operation are they asked to make anything other than 'best possible speed'. The pace of ground operations was different to that of the airborne forces and consequently the progress of the tanks appeared reasonable enough. After three months of battle, a couple of days seemed a very short time and anecdotal evidence suggests that many of the ground troops regarded the airborne as prima donnas expecting to be relieved after such a short time in action. Major Edward Thier of the Irish Guards later recalled a newly evacuated paratrooper who had escaped Arnhem and reached Nijmegen sarcastically asking a tank crewman 'Having a good rest, chum?' The response was immediate: 'Glory be to God, and haven't we been fighting since D-Day NOT Friday!'[43] Elsewhere Major Charles Farrell of 6th Guards Tank Brigade, found his men had little sympathy for the paratroopers escaping Arnhem: 'Call that a f---ing battle? Seven f---ing days up the sharp end and then back to Blighty?'[44]

The ground forces had been asked to reach Arnhem in two days if possible but had also been told by Browning that the 1st Airborne could hold for four. With 6 hours left to cover 11 miles they were late, but it seemed they could still make it in time. They were, after all, still over 48 hours ahead of the final deadline.

Notes

1 Student quoted in Ryan p.217
2 Nordyke, P. *All American, All the Way* (Zenith Press 2005) p.342
3 Lowden, J.L. *Silent Wings at War* (Washington: Smithsonian Institute Press 1992) p.38
4 Thompson, Captain John S. 'The Holland Jump.' 82nd Airborne Division War Memorial Museum
5 Nordyke p.448
6 Carter, R. *Those Devils in Baggy Pants* (New York: Bucaneer Books 1951) 141
7 Nordyke p.466
8 Dank, M. *The Glider Gang* (London: Cassell 1977) p.176
9 Saunders, T. *Nijmegen Barnsley* (Leo Cooper 2001) 63
10 MacDonald, C op cit p.162
11 Letter from Gavin quoted in MacDonald, op cit p.158
12 Gavin op cit p.167
13 Nordyke p.458
14 MacDonald Op cit Notes for Chapter 7
15 MacDonald p.163
16 MacDonald p.158
17 Saunders p.96
18 Nordyke p.459
19 MacDonald p.164
20 Saunders p.128
21 21st Army Group 'Operation *Market Garden*' 1945 p.7
22 Buckingham p.97
23 Horrocks p.88
24 Horrocks p.91
25 McDonald p.148–9 Based on a combat interview with Col Curtis D. Renfro, Liaison Officer, 101st Abn Div. McDonald also suggests that Wilmot, C. *The Struggle for Europe*, 'provides a lucid account.' Wilmot also claims Valkenswaard was the actual objective of the Irish Guards on D-Day.
26 PRO WO 171/1254 War Diary 2 Grenadier Guards (Armoured Battalion)
27 US Army Weapons Systems Evaluation Group (WSEG) Staff Study No3 'A Historical Study of Some WWII Airborne Operations' 1951 p.87

28 Koskimake p.122

29 Brereton's letter of 24 October 1944 to General 'Hap' Arnold, Commanding Genral US Air Forces regarding the attached 'Narrative of Operations in Holland' by HQ First Allied Airborne Army dated 9 October 1944

30 Bennett p.69

31 Nordyke p.468

32 Nordyke p.456

33 Saunders p.99

34 Kershaw, Robert *It Never Snows in September* (Crowood Press 2009) p.142

35 MacDonald p.168

36 Gavin, *On To Berlin* p.170

37 82d Airborne Division Chief of Staff Journal, 0700hrs, 19 September 1944, reporting a conference held at 1530hrs on 18 September 1944

38 Holt p.88

39 MacDonald p.174

40 Urquhart p.129

41 Albert A Nofi (ed) *The War Against Hitler: Military Strategy in the West. New York* (Hippocrene Books 1982) quoted in Powell p.87

42 Horrocks p.88

43 Interview with Major Edward G. Thier, 2nd Armoured Battalion, Irish Guards quoted at the Cornelius Ryan archive site at http://www.library.ohiou.edu/archives/mss/ryan-exhibit/panel_19.pdf

44 Neillands p.152

Chapter Six

A Change of Plan

By noon on D+2, the tanks of XXX Corps had linked with the 82nd Airborne and stepped on to the second element of the 'airborne carpet'. At this point, we need to consider two very telling but largely overlooked statements that speak volumes about the situation. The first came on the morning of D+1, when according to Charles McDonald in the official US account,

> No matter what the true situation in the Reichswald – which no one could have known with any certainty at this point – General Gavin endorsed the corps commander's view that the best practice for the moment was to focus upon holding what he had. General Gavin's confidence in the ability of his paratroopers made the decision easier. 'To those on the ground,' he recalled later, 'there was no doubt … that the bridge would be captured and it would be captured in time to relieve the Arnhem forces.' General Gavin's earlier experience in airborne combat reinforced this view. He recalled later: 'Experience indicated that we could expect a linkup in about two days and we felt quite sure of one in three. If, therefore, by the end of the third day the bridge were in my hands, and I had fought a good battle with whatever might develop in the remainder of the area, I felt that I would have been fortunate enough to have done a good job as planned.' On the basis of this theory, General Gavin had another full day in which to tackle the Germans at Nijmegen.[1]

Although the casual reader might be confused at this point about how Gavin's theory fits with the requirement stressed throughout the briefings that the bridges be taken 'with thunderclap surprise', it is perhaps a testimony to Gavin's confidence in his men that he felt he could allow the enemy to build up its forces for another 24 hours without being unduly inconvenienced in his mission. Thus McDonald, who made the claim of a delay of 33 hours, also demonstrates that Gavin himself considered that if the bridge were in Allied hands 'by the end of the third day' (i.e. the end of the 19th), then he would have done 'a good job as planned'. If his aim was to have the bridge in Allied hands by the end of the third day, Gavin also fails to explain how this would achieve the aim of relieving 1st Airborne in two. The Guards were expected to be in Arnhem before Gavin believed he could deliver his objective and they arrived certainly well within the timescale Gavin appears to consider not only acceptable, but good going.

The second statement comes from Browning, who apparently informed the Grenadier Guards battalion (with whom he had once served) that

XXX Corps tanks passing through Eindhoven. Wild celebrations blocked the streets for a time but the city was to suffer during retaliatory air strikes shortly after.

The American Division had secured the high ground south of the Waal but that he had insufficient troops to attempt to capture Nijmegen itself. He could do one or the other but not both – and he appreciated that the high ground was the more important of the two. From information supplied by the Dutch Underground Movement and civilians it seemed that the town was not strongly held, that the Bosche had very little artillery and that their morale was low. Under the circumstances he therefore decided that the best and quickest method would be to rush the bridge with tanks. By this time Brig Gen Gavin, Commander of the US Airborne Forces, had arrived and he readily agreed to provide a Battalion to form a bridgehead on the far side of the river. From information available it seemed that the Southern side should be easily dealt with.[2]

It is an extraordinary admission of failure on Browning's part and worth examining.

On D-Day, the 82nd reported a good and accurate landing against minimal opposition. By the end of the day the situation was considered to be well in hand. On D+1, the second lift – albeit delayed – had brought in the expected reinforcements. The third lift was scheduled to take place on D+2, by which time it was anticipated that XXX Corps would already be in the area. As a result, Browning had the number of troops he was expected to have according to the plan he himself had made. If he had insufficient troops, it could be for no other reason than because he had planned poorly. It also demonstrates his complete failure to prioritise.

Both Browning and Gavin failed to observe the fundamental principle of command that 'the selection and maintenance of the aim' was their primary responsibility. Simply translated as the question 'what are we supposed to be doing?' the aim selected for the airborne divisions was to open a pathway to allow the armoured divisions to pass as quickly as possible up an 'airborne carpet' to Arnhem, where they would join the 1st British Airborne Division in forming a bridgehead across the Rhine in readiness for future operations. The job of the 82nd was to take a series of bridges along that route, very specifically including the Nijmegen bridges themselves, and hold them until XXX Corps arrived. This they had not only failed to do, but they had chosen to completely disregard the whole point of the operation. Gavin writes repeatedly of allowing XXX Corps to take the bridges themselves and Browning's comments reinforce this. If the town was not strongly held and the southern side 'should be easily dealt with', why hadn't it been done? As we have already seen, Gavin criticised the British plan to advance through a built-up area into Arnhem on the basis that even a relatively weak force could delay them for long periods. By that token, the highly trained paratroopers could equally have held Nijmegen against German counterattacks long enough for the tanks to arrive. Knowing that bridges were a priority, Gavin had emphasised to his men that they should attack both ends at once but had made no provision to allow them to do so except at Grave, where the capture of the bridge would ensure XXX Corps would relieve the 82nd. Having condemned the 'defence minded' Montgomery, Gavin had seemingly prepared for a purely defensive battle, which placed force protection over achieving the aim.

Yet force protection alone should have made Gavin aware of the risk of German reinforcements building up in Nijmegen as quickly as possible after the landings and using the bridges to bring in those reinforcements. Self interest alone should have made the need to block that approach obvious. From the outset, without the bridges, *Market Garden* was pointless and, of all the bridges, the Germans had immediately recognised the pivotal role of those at Nijmegen. Both Gavin and Browning chose to ignore this simple fact. Now Browning, whose experience of commanding armour was even more limited than his experience of commanding paratroops in action, decreed that the 'best and quickest' method was to rush the bridges from one side before the demolition charges could be triggered. How exactly the tanks would be able to clear the buildings of infantry armed with anti-tank weapons in order to rush the bridge is not stated.

The shortage of manpower he complained of was worse than it needed to be. Fifty gliders had landed on D-Day and on the afternoon of D+1, delayed by poor weather over England, the 82nd had been reinforced by the second lift of 454 gliders bringing in artillery and anti-tank guns. This was scheduled to be followed on D+2 by the arrival of further infantry

On 'Hell's Highway', British and American medics tend to the wounded whilst behind them a stalled convoy comes under attack. The vulnerability of 30 Corps' route is very clear. (US Army)

in the form of the 325th Glider Infantry Regiment but poor weather prevented the fly in. Nevertheless, by the end of D+1 Gavin should have been able to call on extra men in the form of over 500 glider pilots. He could not.

Unlike their British counterparts, US glider pilots were regarded merely as 'aerial truck drivers' and expected to take no part in ground actions but instead to return to base as quickly as possible. When America entered the war, the need for an expansion of the US Air Force was obvious but quickly hit a stumbling block on the issue of what rank pilots should hold. The British Royal Air Force had large numbers of non-commissioned pilots but American airmen were horrified at the thought that the pilot commanded the aircraft and this meant that in some crews, a Sergeant pilot was in a position of authority over, for example, an officer acting as navigator. Such a scenario was intolerable to men who had served in the peacetime air force with its rigid hierarchy. Yet at the same time, commissioning large numbers of new officers could interrupt the careers of established men.

The solution was the creation of a new rank of 'Flight Officer'. Falling somewhere between a senior NCO and a junior officer, the rank has been equated to that of a third lieutenant. Falling between the established rank categories, they enjoyed the privileges of not being eligible for the extra duties of senior NCOs on the basis they were officers, but as a new rank were not required by regulations to undertake the additional duties expected of officers either. Equally their pay reflected senior enlisted rates which, with flight and combat bonuses, meant they were frequently better paid than their seniors.

A further benefit was the expectation that they would not have to face ground combat. Glider pilot John Lowden flew into the Nijmegen area on 23 September with the final lift. He describes landing near Groesbeek and making his way to the planned rendezvous but becoming lost when night fell. He sheltered for a time with a mixed group of pilots, glider infantrymen and paratroops who had also become separated from their units and were now looking to re-establish contact with the Division. During the night he describes how he became involved in an argument with 'an eager nineteen-year-old glider rider' who insisted that, as an officer, Lowden should lead a scouting patrol. Lowden recalls that he made it very clear that, as an officer, he had decided that the risks involved in a night patrol were too high. He was going nowhere.[3]

The next morning, before reaching the rendezvous, he describes meeting a British convoy returning to Brussels for supplies. He then claims he and eight other pilots were asked by a British Sergeant-Major to provide an armed escort for the convoy.

> A signal was given and off we went. Considering how close the fighting was all around us, I didn't think we had a prayer of getting through. But we did. We had been roaring down the road for about thirty minutes when the convoy suddenly came to an abrupt stop. Those of us behind the tailgates thought it was an ambush so we bailed out to take cover. However the British had simply stopped for late-morning tea …[4]

After a delay as they waited for British infantry to clear the road ahead, the glider pilots reached Brussels without firing a shot and went their separate ways.

After several days enjoying the hospitality of civilians welcoming their liberators, Lowden complains that

> The British considered Brussels their exclusive turf, and it wasn't long before they ordered all American glider pilots out of town. American MPs flown over from England helped with the round up.[5]

In the wake of the roundup, Lowden reports that it was only the ambiguous reply to a question during the briefing about what the pilots should do after landing (allegedly the reply being, 'don't worry, you'll find plenty to do') that saved many from courts-martial for desertion. In all, around 2000 Waco CG-4 gliders were made ready to support the American effort in Holland by the equivalent of an additional Parachute Infantry Regiment's worth of pilots. The standard rifle company in an airborne unit was around 126 officers and men, three companies forming a battalion. Thus, at Nijmegen by the end of D+1 the equivalent of over four companies were, to use Gavin's later assessment, causing confusion and getting in the way.

In a report after the operation, Gavin wrote:

> I do not believe there is anyone in the combat area more eager and anxious to do the correct thing and yet so completely, individually and collectively, incapable of doing it, than glider pilots.

They were, he said, 'definitely a liability to me', complaining that they had arrived untrained and ill-prepared and

> ... frequently became involved in small unit actions to an extent that satisfied their passing curiosity, or simply left to visit nearby towns ... Glider pilots without unit assignment ... aimlessly wandering about cause confusion and generally get in the way and have to be taken care of.[6]

Taylor, too, complained of glider pilots having simply 'disappeared' after landing to head for nearby liberated towns. In reply Ridgway refused Gavin's suggestion that glider pilots should be assigned to airborne units so they could be given infantry training. He remained content to allow the problem to continue but even Lowden himself was of the opinion that 'some studiously casual American glider pilots would have benefited greatly from the discipline and intense infantry training required of their British opposites, who fought with the glider-troop units.'[7] Lowden's experience may not have been typical in that he landed after the corridor had been opened and thus had the opportunity to escape the battle zone. Gavin did form an ad-hoc battalion from the pilots available in order to release men from

Artillery pieces being loaded into a Waco Glider.

duties such as guarding prisoners and to bolster quieter sectors of the defence perimeter, but the story stands poor comparison with the efforts of their British counterparts to the north. Whatever their contribution, however, each and every US glider pilot who took part in Operation *Market Garden* was awarded the Air Medal, announced in the recipient's home town newspaper by a highly effective PR organisation. In earlier operations, US Air Force decorations for glider pilots had been awarded by squadron lotteries but awards for ground actions had been refused. Since glider pilots were not combat troops, it was reasoned, they could not earn medals for ground combat. Unsurprisingly perhaps, Lowden explains that this had an impact on their motivation; 'What the hell. If I'm treated like a second class clown, I'll act like one.'[8]

With four companies of men he could not use, Gavin claims he was short-handed for a task that had proved less challenging than expected. The 82nd had jumped into Nijmegen expecting to be met by up to 4000 SS cadets and 'considerable armour' and were prepared for heavy combat. They met neither. A post-war US analysis reported that on D-Day, 7477 men of the 82nd had landed and had been in contact with a German force put at 1244. On D+1, a further 1300 US troops had landed but the entire force encountered just 675 Germans during that day.[9] Another report by Brereton stated that 1000 German POWs had been taken by the end of D+1. Reports from the Dutch stated that many of the defenders were First World War veterans recalled to service or were fifteen and sixteen-year-old boys hastily trained.

Despite the lighter than anticipated resistance, the first attempt on the Nijmegen bridges had been made by just two companies and on D+1 the entire effort to take the Nijmegen road bridge consisted solely of G Company of 3rd Battalion 508th, who withdrew at about 1400hrs. No attempt at all was made against the nearby rail bridge because it was felt no unit could be spared from the perimeter.

Having stated that the bridges could not be defended without control of the Groesbeek Heights, the elite paratroopers had failed to dislodge apparently poor quality troops even though they were attacking from the Heights without the control of which they claimed Nijmegen could not be held. By D+2 they seem to have remained convinced that Nijmegen was held by a relatively weak force that could easily be dislodged. Yet the bridges had not been taken.

Notes

1 McDonald 1963 p.169 quoting a letter from Gavin dated 17 January 1954
2 PRO WO205/1125 p.3
3 Lowden p.109
4 Ibid p.110
5 Ibid p.112
6 Devlin *Silent Wings* (1985) p.279
7 Lowden p.114
8 Ibid p.113
9 Weapons Systems Evaluation Group Study No 3 1951 p.109

Chapter Seven

'A Very Iffy Situation'

With the Guards now in Nijmegen, Browning needed to be seen to be doing something to get them across the Waal and once again began putting pressure on Gavin to act. Gavin, of course was in no need of reminding. Having previously presented Browning with a plan to send his men across the river by boat under cover of darkness only to have it rebuffed, Gavin now met with Lieutenant-Generals Browning and Horrocks and Major-General Allan Adair of the Guards Armoured Division on the evening of the 19th and suggested a revised version. If the British could supply boats, then he would send his 504th PIR across the river to attack the northern end of the bridges. According to Buckingham, 'this was an impressive piece of lateral thinking, although it says little for Browning, Horrocks and Adair or their combined staffs that it was left to a hard-pressed airborne commander fully occupied with fighting his own Division to come up with it.'[1] It was nothing of the sort. The failure to secure the bridges on D-Day meant that such an assault was the only option left. There was already a contingency plan in place for such a crossing, but to be made by 43rd Division rather than the 82nd. Unfortunately, the timescale was now such that a crossing was needed before the 43rd could be brought up. Gavin was, indeed, fighting a hard pressed battle but the British generals were not in Nijmegen as tourists. Horrocks was fighting a battle to keep his main axis of advance – now christened Hell's Highway by the men of the 101st – open against increasing attempts to sever his lines of communication. That was a difficult enough task for his thinly spread force. Having expected to roll straight across the Waal bridges he was also now fighting a second battle to secure a crossing and having to prepare for a third simultaneous battle at Arnhem. Gavin was not the only one with problems that night.

In the final analysis, it was Gavin's responsibility to secure the bridge and it says little for the 82nd Airborne's planners that they had not considered it necessary to provide their men with any means of crossing the numerous waterways in the Division's sector. At planning sessions in England Gavin had repeatedly told his men that the best way to capture a bridge was to attack from both ends at once, but the preoccupation with securing the Groesbeek Heights had diverted attention away from the problems concerning the Division's most important objective. Although there would be no drop north of the river to allow an attack from both ends, no-one had considered the possibility that the paratroops might have to make a crossing of any of the many waterways in their sector.

In Normandy, a similar scenario had existed when a force was assigned to capture the Orne river and canal bridges by a glider assault to allow tanks of the seaborne force to reach the men of the 6th Airborne east of the two waterways. Then it had been decided to reduce the size of the attacking force to allow the gliders to carry additional equipment. As part of an emergency plan in case the bridges were blown, a folding canvas assault boat and

General Gavin briefs General Horrocks on the river crossing plan.

an inflatable dinghy were added to ensure that the troops had alternative means of crossing if necessary.

If the bridges could not be captured, a contingency plan was for 7 Parachute Battalion, dropping north of Ranville, to secure a bridgehead to the west of Benouville and the canal which would involve ferrying the troops across the water gaps. A small detachment of four sappers under the command of a Royal Engineers sergeant would drop with 7 Parachute Battalion; 30 inflatable RAF issue dinghies and 500 fathoms of rope would be carried during the drop by 7 Para troops in their kitbags. Two hours after the first drop, the remainder of 2 Platoon's engineers would land in four gliders carrying lightweight rafts capable of taking the 6-pounder anti-tank gun. More RAF dinghies and rope made up the rest of the load together with two 30-foot rolls of 'chespaling' (a temporary road surface laid on hessian sacking sprayed with oil paint) which would be rolled over the muddy banks. In the event that the coup de main was a success, this equipment would be stockpiled on the east bank of the river Orne in case a counterattack was launched to destroy the bridges after capture. The 82nd made no similar preparations.

Nor was Gavin's plan unprecedented. On the first day of the war in the west, German assault pioneers had crossed the Albert Canal in daylight and under fire on rafts made from doors, tables and other materials salvaged from nearby buildings. At Sedan, Sergeant Walther Rubarth and a small team of six infantrymen and five assault pioneers had crossed the Meuse under heavy fire and for three hours had created such chaos amongst the defenders on the far bank that the French eventually broke and ran. The gathered generals all knew it could be done, but also that it was risky. The day before Gavin suggested the crossing, men of 9 Brigade, VIII Corps had undertaken a night crossing of the Meuse-Escaut Canal in support of XXX Corps. C Company of the 2nd Lincolns had suffered over 70 men killed and wounded in the attempt.

Interestingly, in a post-war analysis, Captain Carl Kappel of the 504th conjectured that the crossing might have been better made using the amphibious DUKW trucks of XXX Corps' engineers. Faster and armed with .50 calibre machine guns, he suggested that the crossing would have been even more successful if they had been brought forward. Equally, the concentration of the troops into fewer, larger targets may have actually increased the casualty rate but the fact was that Gavin had not asked for DUKWs, he had asked for boats.

Later that evening, Gavin discussed the operation with Browning, Horrocks and members of the Guards regiments and his divisional staff in the meeting Chatterton recalled for the difference between the appearance of the two forces. It would be, Gavin later wrote, 'a very iffy situation.'[2] If, he explained, the boats could be brought up and if the south bank could be cleared and if everything could be organised in the hours of darkness, then he would want to attack early the next morning. Gavin told them that speed was essential; there would be no time even for reconnaissance and 'Tucker seemed to be the only man in the room who seemed unfazed. He had made the landing at Anzio and knew what to expect. To him the crossing was like the kind of exercise the 504th had practised at Fort Bragg.'[3] Browning was, Gavin wrote, 'by now filled with admiration at the daring of the idea' and immediately gave permission to go ahead. Returning to his 'Champion' command post, Gavin says he gave orders for the operation to the 504th's executive officer to pass on to Tucker at about 2300hrs.

Captain T. Moffatt Burriss, commander of I Company, claims to have been at the meeting. He says that the level of risk involved was obvious and that both Horrocks and Browning kept asking whether they could do it, writing later that they realised they were 'asking us to lay down our lives for British soldiers'. Burriss goes on to claim that Colonel Tucker asked what assurances they could give that XXX Corps would continue on to Arnhem immediately and that General Horrocks replied that his tanks would be lined up ready to go the moment the bridge was taken. 'All of us took that as a solemn pledge, one that made the whole operation meaningful.'[4] For Burriss, the plan put forward by his own commander had by now been translated into a British demand that the Americans undertake what he thought looked like a suicide mission but no other record of the meeting makes any mention of the exchange or the 'solemn pledge' – indeed Burriss's counterpart in H Company, Captain Kappel, who would follow I Company across the river, was not at this point aware of the briefing or the task and certainly not present to hear the 'solemn pledge'. He would not even hear of the mission until 0900hrs the following morning – at least an hour after the 0800hrs start claimed elsewhere. Nor do any other accounts seem to feel that it needed such a pledge to make the operation meaningful. The 82nd were, after all, simply being asked to deliver the objective they had been set.

Following this meeting, accounts by veterans of the crossing become at best confused and at worst deliberately misleading as they become increasingly damning of their British colleagues. Gavin, for example, claims he had agreed the plan at 2300hrs and expected the boats to be brought up immediately so that the attack could be made soon after daylight believing the situation required an attack at the earliest opportunity, although also that he would have preferred to wait until dark the following night. When the boats were not available at first light, he says the attack was postponed until 1100hrs, then to 1330hrs, 1400hrs and finally 1500hrs.

British troops at rest waiting to make the crossing.

Burriss, meanwhile, writing in 2000, claims that a 'promise' was made to deliver the boats by 1100 but that he and his men 'watched 1100 come and go, then 1200, then 1300. We cursed the British high command. Finally, at 1400, they arrived.'[5] Lieutenant Magellas, writing in 2003, states that 'H-Hour was planned for 0800, then advanced to 1100, then to 1400.'[6] The implication is that the delays were solely caused by the British failure to deliver the boats. Gavin is described as becoming increasingly angry at Horrocks and Bennett writes that 'the boats did not arrive, to Gavin's disgust.'[7]

'Disgust' is a powerful term and accounts like these suggest that the 504th were ready to go at first light but were let down by British incompetence. In fact, had the boats arrived before 0800hrs they would have been kept waiting. The 504th did not clear the area around the launch site on the south bank of the Waal until midday and were in no position to mount the attack before then. Having said that the attack was planned for 0800hrs, Magellas goes on to say that his company did not even arrive at the assault site until noon, an unusual approach if the boats really were expected to reach them at any time during the morning. Captain Carl Kappel states that the battalion had moved from Jonkers Bosche to Hill 81 the previous evening and had received a warning order at 2130hrs to be ready to move back to Jonkers Bosche at 0730hrs the following morning, which they did aboard British trucks. Then, 'at 0900hrs, the Third Battalion received a warning order that they would make an assault crossing of the river Waal *that afternoon* [author's emphasis] to secure the Nijmegen Highway Bridge.' Kappel then goes on to say that the plan was for air support to 'bomb and strafe' between 1445 and 1455hrs and that the north bank was to be 'smoked at 1455 by artillery and mortars.'[8] He states that he and his men arrived at the launch site at about 1400 but the boats did not arrive until 1430hrs. This fits with the account given in 1946 by XXX Corps that 'it was not until two o'clock in the afternoon that the Americans could get down to the river bank at the place chosen for the crossing.'[9]

A 'Report of Action, 307 A/B Engr. Bn, to Commanding General, 82nd Airborne Division, 25 September 1944,' written in the field by Captain Robert K. Williams of the 307th Airborne Engineer Battalion, whose men would control the boats during the assault noted:

> On Sept. 20 at 0600 Capt. Harris received orders from the CO, 504th PIR, to prepare to make a river crossing at 1400 today. Col. Tucker told Capt. Harris he could pick up 26 assault boats

An 88mm gun knocked out on the southern approach to the Waal River bridge. (Courtesy Jan Bos)

near bridge No. 7 near the railroad at Nijmegen. The British were furnishing these boats, plus an officer and men for instructors in the use of the boats. Col. Tucker indicated the approximate crossing site about 600 yds. west of Nijmegen railroad bridge over the Waal river … Lt. Sabia arrived with the boats at 1315 and the Co. arrived at the factory at 1330. The recon party stayed and located a forward assembly area, plus dispersion areas for boats, noting the current of the river, and the loading area for the second lift. By 1330, Capt. Harris reported to Col. Tucker at his forward CP and found that he had set back the crossing one hour to 1500. He then conferred with Maj. Julian A. Cook, assault battalion commander, and made final arrangements for the assault.[10]

Note the times of both H-Hour and the delivery of the boats to the 307th. In terms of considering the evidence, it is worth bearing in mind that Williams' report was written within days of the event. Kappel wrote his account in 1949. Gavin provided his version over 30 years later and, for Burriss and Magellas, over half a century of regimental reunions would pass before they gave their accounts.

Whatever the truth of the matter, the men of the 504th were gathered at the site as H-Hour approached, anxiously awaiting the arrival of their boats and speculating about what lay ahead. Captain Kappel 'doubled the initial estimate of enemy strength' recalled Magellas, 'from 500 to 1000 when he briefed us platoon leaders.' 'Anything less', said Kappel, 'would be pure gravy.'

As the men waited, Gavin was suddenly called away by news that the Germans had overrun the villages of Mook and Beck and hurried back to his command post. It was here that he describes a surprise meeting with General Ridgway. Ridgway had no function in Operation *Market Garden* but he and Brereton had flown to Antwerp and then driven to join the 101st at Eindhoven to see what was happening for themselves. During a raid on the town, he and Brereton had separated and Ridgway had set out by jeep to reach the 82nd. At some point in the journey (accounts differ about the location but seemingly on the morning of the 20th he had been driving from Eindhoven to Zon en route for Nijmegen), he reported encountering a British tank officer who warned him that the road ahead was under fire. After waiting for some 40 minutes and not seeing any sign of action, he proceeded on foot for a while before calling his driver forward and continuing his journey. Donald R. Burgett of the 101st Division, later recalled 'General Ridgway and his group made it to the 101st command post without seeing a single German or being shot at on the way.'[11] The story is frequently repeated as an example of the seeming timidity of the British and is worth examining. General Ridgway did not see a single German but it would have been a poor ambush if he had. The experience of Allied air superiority in Normandy had taught the Germans to stay under cover in daylight and they would have been unlikely to make their positions obvious. A lone infantryman or even a jeep presents very little threat to a concealed gun position and would not be worth disclosing the gun site for or wasting limited ammunition on when the far more attractive targets offered by the Sherman tanks would be the Germans' main priority. Ridgway did not see Germans but the range of the 88mm was over a mile. From the passenger seat of a jeep, could he really be expected to be able to see a camouflaged gun position over a mile away? As any researcher will know, absence of evidence is not evidence of absence. Just because the general did not see them does not mean they were not there.

Nevertheless, Ridgway arrived in Nijmegen 'brimming over with resentment at perceived British failings'[12] and his mood was not improved when Gavin explained that he had something of a crisis on his hands and could not spare the time to chat with him. Gavin excused himself and left but 'sensed that he was quite unhappy with the fact that both his divisions were now under British Airborne Corps.'[13] They were not. The 101st, as planned, had come under the command of XXX Corps as soon as the linkup had been made and would remain so throughout the fighting. The 82nd were, again as planned, now also under XXX Corps. Browning may have had some influence but he was not now, or indeed ever had been, in a position of authority to control the ground battle. The 82nd were still very much engaged in the ongoing fight and it is difficult to see who (besides himself) Ridgway thought should have been in command of the paratroopers at that point. Ridgway's concerns appear only to reveal his preoccupation with the coveted role of Airborne Deputy Commander rather than the success of the highly risky operation US paratroopers were about to undertake. After all, he had agreed, in accordance with the plans set out by First Allied Airborne Army, that the 82nd were acting in support of the British and it was logical that as such they would be under British command.

Back at the launch site, 33 boats had been despatched but one lorry had been hit during an air attack – a further reminder of the difficulty in moving equipment up 'Hell's Highway' – and only 26 arrived. When they finally appeared, the men were shocked to find small, collapsible canvas and wood boats. 'American boats were plywood' noted Gavin, although he fails to explain how that might make them better suited to an assault crossing. 'It was arranged that the Guards Armoured Division would call up their assault boats,' a contemporary report noted,

> … but since they were of a type to which the Americans were not accustomed, it was thought that it might be as well to supply British crews as the handling of them requires some experience. However, Brig Gen Gavin said that his own Engineers would be quite happy to undertake the operation, although perhaps it would be of assistance if an Officer Instructor from the Royal Engineers were present to give advice on how to use them.

Major Neil, the Squadron Leader of 615 Field Squadron Royal Engineers arrived to give a crash course in boat handling.[14] Having refused the offer of experienced crews, seemingly for no other reason than unit pride, much is then made of the lack of experience the

The view from the road bridge. In the foreground is the railway crossing and behind it the power plant and site of the crossing by the 504th. (Courtesy Jan Bos)

The Waal railway bridge and launch site as it is today.

paratroopers had in making a river crossing but, according to Gavin himself, the 504th had practised just such a task at Fort Bragg, albeit under very different circumstances.

At H-Hour minus 30 minutes, British rocket-firing Typhoon planes began strafing runs. 'Rivers and I watched in awe from our concealed front-row seats as the planes attempted to neutralise enemy resistance,' remembers Magellas, 'More awesome, however, was the amount of fire the enemy threw up. The sky was black from puffs of exploding shells.'[15] At H-15, British tanks lined up along the river bank opened up with a barrage of shells and were quickly joined by artillery from the outskirts of town. With just ten minutes to go, the rounds were switched to include smoke and white phosphorous to create a smokescreen but the wind picked up and the smoke began to clear.

At 1500hrs, Major Julian Cook checked his watch, stood up and blew his whistle. All hell broke loose.

Notes

1. Buckingham p.135–136
2. Gavin, *On To Berlin* p.190
3. Ryan p.323
4. Burris, Strike and Hold p.110–111
5. Ibid p.111
6. Magellas p.134
7. Bennett p.115
8. Kappel, C.W. *The Operations of H Company, 504th Parachute Infantry (82nd Airborne Division) in the Invasion of Holland 17–21 September 1944 (Rhineland Campaign)* (US Army Infantry School Fort Benning, Georgia 1949) p.24
9. Captain Robert K. Williams. 'Report of Action, 307 A/B Engr. Bn, to Commanding General, 82nd Airborne Division, 25 September 1944' Accessed at http://www.usaaftroopcarrier.com/Holland/H-Waal%20River%20Crossing.htm
10. Gill, R & Groves, J. *Club Route in Europe: The Story of XXX Corps in the European Campaign* (Hannover 1946) p.74
11. Burgett p.84
12. Buckingham p.134
13. Gavin, *On To Berlin* p.193
14. PRO WO205/1125 p.7
15. Magellas p.137

Chapter Eight

'Hail Mary, Full of Grace …'

When Major Cook gave the signal, the men of H and I Companies of 3/504th and the engineers of C Company 307th Airborne Engineer Battalion grabbed the cumbersome assault boats and began to drag them across the embankment and across the flat, open ground towards the river. Captain Kappel, leading H Company, almost immediately ran into a large chain link fence blocking their way. Placing a Gammon bomb on one of the metal supports as Lieutenant Magellas did the same further along, the fence was forced down by the weight of the men pushing against it. Instead of running across the open space in a line, the paratroops were now channelled into the gap made by Kappel. After the first Americans neared the water's edge, the Germans reacted. A small, three-foot escarpment slowed the men down but gave them a chance to lift the boats onto their shoulders. Once past this, they ran full speed for the water as every weapon on the far shore turned toward them.

Sergeant Albert Tarbell, following closely behind Kappel, saw his officer strip off his harness and throw it into the boat. Tarbell followed suit, not knowing why. It was then he realised that a man was down and Captain Kappel was attempting to save him. It was probably this incident that inspired war correspondents to report later that men had stripped off their equipment to swim the river. As they reached the water, the men tried to clamber on board. The 19-foot boats already had a crew of two engineers as groups of 13 fully equipped paratroops tried to get in. Dangerously overloaded, several of the boats became lodged on a mud bank, forcing men to climb back out and push the boats back into the swift current.

The boats had been delivered with only a few paddles and the paratroops used the butts of their weapons to try to give them extra speed. Watching Oxbridge graduates amongst the Guards commented on 'some remarkably bad rowing' but the sight deeply impressed all who saw it. Captain Keep remembered

The water all around the boats was churned up by the hail of bullets, and we were soaked to the skin … By now, the broad surface of the Waal was covered with our small canvas craft, all crammed with frantically paddling men. It was a horrible picture, this river crossing. Set to the sound of a deafening roar of omnipresent firing, this scene of defenceless, frail canvas boats jammed to overflowing with humanity, all striving desperately to cross the Waal as quickly as possible, was fiendish and dreadful. We were soaked, gasping for breath, dead tired, and constantly expecting to feel that searing sensation as the bullet tore through you. I wanted to vomit; many did.[1]

US troops crossing the
Waal. (Courtesy Jan Bos)

Kappel had rowed at Princeton University and tried to establish some sort of rhythm in his crew but found himself nervously counting '7-6-7-7-7-8-9'. Nearby, Major Cook, a devout Catholic, was trying to pray, using the words to match his rowing; 'Hail Mary – full of Grace – Hail Mary – Full of Grace.' '"The Lord is with thee" was too long,' Cook recalled, 'so I kept repeating "Hail Mary" (one stroke), "Full of Grace" (second stroke).'[2] Chaplain Delbert Kuehl had asked to come along, knowing that the chances were high that the men would suffer badly and believing that his place was with them. As he rowed, Kuehl heard a sickening thud as the man next to him was hit by a 20mm round and 'had the middle part of his head blown away, so that his skull dropped on what was left of his lower face.'[3] The chaplain developed his own cadence, repeating over and over, 'Lord, Thy will be done.'[4]

Everywhere the heavy fire was taking its toll. By the time it neared the far shore, Kappel's boat was filled with casualties. As they reached the shallows, he jumped out to push it into the bank and found that of the 13 men in the boat, 6 were dead and 4 badly wounded. Only Kappel, Staff Sergeant James Allen and medic Seymour Fox were able to move. Behind them, boats filled with dead and wounded drifted in the current. Private Leonard Trimble would later be rescued downriver by Dutch civilians and brought back to safety, the only survivor of his packed boat.

As Cook neared the shore, he noticed a commotion in the water. Lieutenant Ernest Murphy and eleven men of H Company had struggled ashore after their boat was sunk. One man was missing. Murphy looked back across the river as Cook's boat approached. Then both men saw movement in the water. 'I thought I was seeing things when the top of a helmet broke the surface and kept on moving.' Cook recalled, 'Then a face appeared under the helmet, Private Joseph Jedlicka. He had bandoliers of .30 calibre machinegun bullets draped around his shoulders and a box in either hand.'[5] Sinking in eight feet of water, Jedlicka could not swim but, with incredible presence of mind simply sank to the bottom and walked out of the river, soaked but alive.

Nearby, Chaplain Kuehl and battalion surgeon Lieutenant Hyman Shapiro immediately began tending to the wounded at the water's edge and, as he was trying to help a man with a serious stomach wound, the chaplain was hit in the back. Kuehl recalled the concern the badly wounded man showed when he asked 'Oh chaplain, did they get you too?' Together the surgeon and the priest worked to gather the wounded and get them back onto the boats to be taken back across the river.

From the ninth floor of the power plant, Lieutenant-Colonel Giles Vandeleur, commander of the 2nd Armoured Battalion of the Irish Guards, watched the crossing.

> It was a horrible, horrible sight. Boats were literally blown out of the water. Huge geysers shot
> up as shells hit and small arms fire from the northern bank made the river look like a seething
> cauldron … I saw one or two boats hit the beaches, followed by three or four others. The men
> got out and began moving across an open field. My God! What a courageous sight it was! They
> just moved across that field steadily, I never saw a single man lie down until he was hit. I didn't
> think more than half the fleet made it across. The boats started back and it was obvious half of
> them had been lost.[6]

Along the shoreline, paratroopers struggled onto dry land, many vomiting with a
combination of exertion and fear but their attitude had hardened somewhere out on the
river; those who survived were now overwhelmed by anger and a thirst for revenge. With
all unit cohesion lost, men began to move forward on their own initiative, heading for
an embankment and hedge line around 800 yards inland. Captain Keep reports that the
2nd Battalion and the tanks across the river provided 'marvellous support' by maintaining
a constant fire into the German line. Kappel found the first line of defences along the
riverbank 'generally deserted' and the few remaining defenders were killed at bayonet point
before the paratroops moved steadily forward, firing from the hip across the wide open
space towards the distant embankment.

Reaching it, the men took shelter and paused for breath. By now, they were 'at a
fever pitch' according to Keep and all accounts describe 'a murderous rage' amongst the
Americans. Burriss ordered the men on either side of him to use grenades to clear the
far side of the bank. The bombardment was followed by a moment of silence before the
screams of wounded Germans could be heard. Along the line, the enemy troops stood up,
hands raised, 'but it was too late.' Burriss wrote, 'Our men in a frenzy over the wholesale
slaughter of their buddies, continued to fire until every German on the dike lay dead or
dying.'[7] Arriving a few minutes later, signaller Corporal Jack Bommer, laying a telephone
cable to maintain contact across the river found

> … dead bodies everywhere, and Germans – some no more than fifteen years old, others in their
> sixties – who a few minutes before had been slaughtering us in the boats were now begging for
> mercy, trying to surrender … [some] were shot out of hand at point blank range.[8]

The wounded
are collected on
the southern
approach to the
bridge.

A Sherman prepares to cross the Waal bridge during the battle.

Taking over the German positions, the men of the first wave lay down protective fire to cover the eleven boats able to make the second crossing. Two were lost but the remainder brought much needed reinforcements. Gradually regrouping into cohesive formations but still intermixed, H and I Companies then began to push eastwards towards the Fort Hof Van Holland defences beside the railway bridge. As one force of four men under 'Maggie' Magellas attacked the squat fortress, Burriss and Kappel led their respective companies in a dash for the bridges.

Fort Hof Van Holland was a major obstacle with two sets of dual 20mm guns mounted towards the rear and thus protected from the covering tank shelling and now able to fire into the rear of the Americans. Kappel ordered the single remaining 60mm mortar to engage but with only eight rounds of ammunition there was little it could do. Instead, whilst the mortar was used as cover, Sergeant Leroy Richmond stripped off his equipment and swam across the moat to reconnoitre a way into the fort itself. Peering over the parapet, he found a causeway spanned the moat on the other side of the building. Lobbing hand grenades over the walls to keep the Germans under cover, Magellas led them around to the far side. There they found Privates Dunlop, Davis and Legacie (the man Kappel had saved from drowning at the start of the crossing). The men, all part of a machine-gun section, had made their own way to the fort and had not been aware of Magellas' approach. As Richmond asked where they had been, Dunlop told him, 'Buddy, we were here before you.'[9] Lobbing more grenades and firing their machine gun into the fort without provoking any response, Magellas decided that the defenders posed no further threat and could be left to 1st Battalion to mop up. For the rest of the afternoon the defenders continued to harass the attacking troops until the fort was finally cleared later in the day and taken over as the Regimental Command Post.

'It was somewhere near the fort that Col Tucker came across about fifteen Bosche of the Hitler Jugend cowering in their foxholes,' a British report states.

> The Colonel ordered them to come out which they refused to do. After a brief explanation in German that they would be taken prisoner and treated as such, they still refused to move. So the Colonel, by now rather exasperated by these 'krauts', pulled one of them out by the scruff of his neck. He was shaking all over and crying profusely, but as soon as the Colonel released his grip he disappeared back into his fox hole like a miserable rabbit. The Herrenvolk were clearly not at their best and there was insufficient time to bother with the chosen race so, as they did not wish to be taken prisoner, there was only one alternative, and no doubt the fuehrer would be flattered that they were true to the last.[10]

The attack plan had called for the first wave to fight their way onto the railway embankment and along it to a point where it intersected with the highway heading north from the road

British Sherman
tanks crossing the
bridge after the
battle.

bridge, then to turn south back towards the river with H Company taking the right flank, I Company the left. G Company, in the second wave, was to follow behind and block the road. Lieutenant John Holabird and his engineers were to fight their way to the bridges and disarm any demolition charges they found there. Still intermixed, the paratroopers moved towards the first bridges in their scattered groups.

Kappel, with Lieutenants Richard 'Rivers' La Riviere and Ed Sims led his force towards the northern end of the railway bridge, about a mile from their present position. Sergeant Theodore Finkbeiner and his group reaching the intersection and took shelter behind the embankment. Lifting his head to peer over the obstacle, he found himself staring at the muzzle of a German MG34 machine gun. 'I think he was as surprised as I was.' Finkbeiner wrote, 'I ducked, but the muzzle blast blew the little wool line cap off my head.'[11] The Americans threw grenades, the Germans did likewise and followed it by charging the American position but the attack was beaten off. Then a vehicle-mounted 20mm flak gun arrived at the junction and opened fire on the group from behind. Private First Class Walter Muszynski edged within 15 yards of the vehicle and attacked it with grenades, wiping out the crew before himself being killed by rifle fire moments later. The action would win him a richly deserved Distinguished Service Cross.

A vicious battle for control of the embankment was underway but although the defences were well prepared for a frontal assault, there were few, if any, measures against a flanking attack. Turning his men south, Kappel sent them to search for culverts or tunnels through the embankment and it was during this phase that a group of Dutch civilians sheltering in a concrete bomb shelter in the embankment were severely wounded when the Americans threw Gammon bombs inside. Moving along the embankment, they reached the railway bridge, passed beneath it and were able to advance along the German flanks towards the highway bridge using the shelter of a dyke to protect their flank. It was now about 1600hrs. Across the river, the second wave had been delayed when the boats drifted downstream and had to be manhandled back to the start line. As fast as possible they were operating a ferry service to bring across the 1st Battalion.

Joining them was nineteen-year-old Sapper Roy Tuck who had travelled up in a canvas topped 3-ton truck, its roof covered with a bright orange cloth to identify it as an Allied vehicle. With him were a corporal, lance corporal, ten sappers and their driver, all members of 3 Troop, 615 Field Squadron, Royal Engineers. The truck had passed through Eindhoven

Captain Kappel's
sketch map of the
Waal crossing.

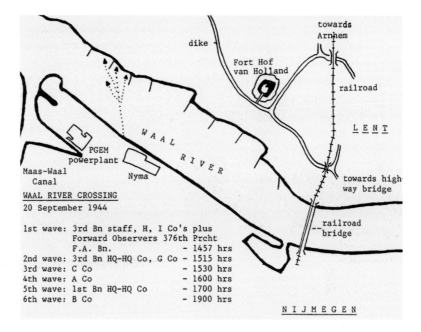

towards
Arnhem

dike

Fort Hof
van Holland

railroad

L E N T

W A A L

R I V E R

PGEM
powerplant

Maas-Waal
Canal

Nyma

towards high-
way bridge

WAAL RIVER CROSSING
20 September 1944

1st wave: 3rd Bn staff, H, I Co's plus
        Forward Observers 376th Prcht
        F.A. Bn.   - 1457 hrs
2nd wave: 3rd Bn HQ-HQ Co, G Co - 1515 hrs
3rd wave: C Co   - 1530 hrs
4th wave: A Co   - 1600 hrs
5th wave: 1st Bn HQ-HQ Co   - 1700 hrs
6th wave: B Co   - 1900 hrs

railroad
bridge

N I J M E G E N

the night before where a young Dutch girl had given Tuck a ring. Word was reaching them that the town had been heavily attacked a short time later and Tuck wondered whether she had survived. His thoughts turned to the task ahead. The group were about to take part, he remembered, 'in what, we were forewarned, could turn out to be a traumatic assault crossing of the river Waal.'

It was early afternoon when, clinging precariously to the top of a pontoon carried by a 'transporter' provided by our specialised 14 Field Park Engineers Squadron we entered the outskirts of Nijmegen. We had arrived in the middle of a battle. Several houses in the close vicinity were already burning furiously. Hurriedly dismounting, I experienced the familiar sudden inner clutch of fear as we learnt that the approaches to the river were under direct enemy fire. There was a frightening crackle from small arms as we left the shelter of buildings and raced for the nearest cover … By the time I had finished crawling the length of a long, dry, shallow ditch – negotiating, as I did so, my way past not only numerous tree roots but also the lifeless body of an American paratrooper – my confidence was virtually non-existent.

Tuck was not the only one. As the group made a dash for the river, the man in front froze. Even threats to shoot him failed to get him moving and the men edged around him, even more shaken.

As we reached the huge road embankment running parallel to the river, we came across two American paratroopers standing at the doorway of a small brick hut, in an obvious state of high tension and excitement they blurted out that their battalion had just been cut to pieces while carrying out a suicidal crossing of the river. Such startling news, coupled with the ever-increasing sounds of conflict about us, did nothing for my morale.

Pausing, the men watched in surprise as a bomb-like object crashed to earth a few yards away. With relief they realised it was an empty long-range fuel tank, released by one of the

British tanks on the north side of the Waal bridge moving forward after the battle. (Courtesy Jan Bos)

supporting aircraft overhead. Apart from that, they seemed cut off from the battle around them. Then they set to work to build their Class 9 Folding Boat Equipment Raft, designed to carry up to nine tons.

A paratrooper Lieutenant, all too aware of the horrific ordeal his battalion had just suffered, prepared to take command. It was obvious from his comments that he was undergoing an understandable crisis of confidence; anxious not only about tackling an extremely dangerous crossing of the river, but, also, as to where, if at all, it might be possible to attempt a landing on the other side. Very much sharing his doubts and concerns, it came as a great relief to me, when, instead of ordering us to load the [infantry support] artillery piece on to the raft, he decided to wait upon further developments. Respite, however, was short-lived. A tall, helmeted, American Colonel, wearing dark glasses, strode belligerently down the bank to commence an exchange of words, which are forever etched on my memory.

'Why is this gun still here and not over the river?', he demanded angrily. The young officer started to explain his dilemma, 'Lieutenant', the Colonel interrupted furiously, 'Our boys are hurting over there and need that gun; under threat of court martial I am ordering you take it across!'

'OK boys, let it roll', was the laconic response from the Lieutenant. I was totally dismayed – the whole idea seemed completely insane! Every instinct was urging me to seek cover and stay there. Yet, instead, loaded with a considerable amount of explosive material, we were about to attempt the crossing of a huge expanse of open water under enemy fire – and all this on the slowest of unwieldy craft. Hastily loading the gun and cases of shells on board, we flattened ourselves on the deck. In a high state of nervous tension, I checked to make sure that there was a round in the breech of my rifle. Alas, because of high stress I inadvertently put pressure on the trigger before applying the safety catch. Even allowing for all the extraneous noise about us, the single shot, which buried itself into a wall, echoed loudly under the close lee of the power station, startling everyone. All eyes turned in my direction, and I felt distinctly embarrassed.

Shortly afterwards, the two diagonal outboard engines burst into life and we inched our way out of the creek on to the vastness of the river Waal. Immediately, our cumbersome raft, caught in the grip of the fast flowing current, turned full circle. On board was the American Lieutenant, our Lieutenant and some fourteen men from our section. Tense moments passed before the straining engines finally overcame the racing tide. The response from the enemy was both immediate and aggressive; a salvo of mortars sending up fountains of water as they exploded uncomfortably close by. There could be little doubt; we had embarked on a perilous enterprise.

Between our under-powered craft and the distant bank stretched a daunting four- to five-hundred-yard mass of powerfully surging water. Upstream, towards Nijmegen, the mighty river curved towards the huge rail and road bridges, its surface gleaming in the late afternoon sunshine. Much of the town seemed to be on fire. Flames reflected in the river and glowed on the underside of a vast billowing column of smoke as it towered an enormous height into the sky, before drifting away over the flat countryside. Against a background chatter of automatic weapons and the crump of shells, we headed, alarmingly exposed and all too slowly towards the opposite bank In mid-stream, a rowing boat, constantly turning in the swiftly flowing water, approached us rapidly from the town. Our Lieutenant, suspecting it might contain fleeing Germans, opened fire with a borrowed rifle as it swept by, but there was no discernible reaction.

It did not escape me entirely that, with the bridges still held by the enemy, we would be the *very first land troops of the British Second Army* to be crossing the river. Consequently, with this in mind, as the raft finally reached the shallows, inspired by a youthful enthusiasm to be one of the first ashore, I grabbed a rope and, with a totally unexpected and momentary sense of personal drama, plunged into the water to help pull the ungainly craft into the bank. We beached to the left of the landing area. Once across the river, we dug in and waited. It was an area of rough uncultivated marshy grassland and was almost directly opposite to the power plant.

Our arrival immediately attracted mortar fire. After hurriedly helping to disembark the gun, I frantically sought cover by diving into one of the shallow foxholes recently vacated by American paratroopers who, by this time, had moved away towards the bridges. The shelling eventually ceased. Twilight gave way to darkness, and an uneasy calm settled over the scene of recent conflict. High overhead a full moon sailed serenely in the clearest of skies, while nearby the silent river was dark and impassive, with thin mists beginning to form upon its surface, and threading the long grass upon its banks. For a time, guns crackled and tracers weaved their intricate patterns as our tanks finally stormed the distant Road Bridge – then all was still. The surrounding flat marshy ground, bathed in a cool light, appeared strangely peaceful, yet we knew only too well that, not far away, an unseen enemy would be watching and waiting, and that careless noise or reckless movement could spell disaster.

As we waited alone and vulnerable, we received orders to recover an American officer, a Captain [possibly Captain W. Stanley Burkholder of HQ Company] reported to be lying badly wounded against a distant fence. Four of us, accompanied by our corporal, set out to find him. Moving as silently as possible, dragging a stretcher and keeping very low, we crawled, with no little apprehension on my part, towards the reported position of the stricken man. Eventually, we discovered him face down in the wet grass. This fence was on the far right extending inland from the Waal river, dividing up the large area of rough grassland. The officer was lying at the fence, which was some hundred yards from the river. The Captain was clearly in dreadful pain from a serious back injury.

Before we carefully eased him on to the stretcher, face down, Ron gave him a shot of morphine to help ease his agony. 'Be as gently as possible and keep him off the ground', he whispered. Such urging was not needed, the man's low pitiful moans providing all the necessary motivation for providing as smooth a progress as possible. However, I soon found lifting and moving at the same time – while struggling to keep a heavily laden stretcher just inches above the grass – required a technique entirely outside my experience. The totally unaccustomed repetitive movement – one, where my right arm was used to lift and move the surprisingly

Seen from Lent, looking back across the river to the launching side at Nijmegen. The boats were launched in the shadow of the factory. (Courtesy Jan Bos)

heavy stretcher forward before the left was required to lever my body in the same direction – resulted in a most unnatural contortionist twisting crawl.

It did not take long before I suffered a severe reaction. Complaining muscles rebelled to such an extent that the close presence of the enemy, which – up until then – had been an overriding concern, was totally ignored as an intensely painful cramp gripped my right shoulder and biceps. Not only was the pain acute, but I felt increasingly unable to lift the stretcher properly. In the end, it was only the life and death situation of our casualty, which gave me the will to struggle on. How much longer, I agonised? At last, after what seemed an eternity, we arrived back at the raft, it was at the same location where we had beached. The ordeal was over. Now came the tricky bit – a return to the other side. Thankfully, within minutes, a thick fog, quite miraculously, blanketed the whole area, muffling the sound of the engines and cutting visibility to a few feet.

Once we had re-crossed the river without incident, we hurried the wounded man up the embankment to where a temporary casualty station had been set up in the power plant. By the time we lowered him on to the bare concrete floor, dimly lit by its one hanging naked electric light bulb, he had lapsed into unconsciousness. I turned away, feeling far from confident about his chances of survival.[12]

Meanwhile, at the northern end of the railway bridge, Lieutenant Sims had found the resistance light and quickly took control, sending men to search for any leads connected to the demolition charges. As he did, La Riviere arrived to reinforce his small group just as the two men saw a large group of Germans attempting to escape the battle at the southern end by running north across the bridge. 'We let them come – two thirds of the way' La Riviere recalled. Lieutenant McClain of HQ Company estimated as many as 500 Germans in headlong flight towards them. With two machine guns, two Browning automatic rifles and the firepower of the riflemen, the men opened up.

> Before it was over they were leaping into the swift current of the river below. Some wounded fell through between the ties. Hardened by over two years of combat and the loss of many of my men, I still felt sick at this inhumanity to man.[13]

In a blood lust, paratroopers were shooting at Germans as they jumped from the bridge until Kappel ordered them to stop wasting ammunition. During a lull, one of the German prisoners already in American hands was sent to tell the trapped men to return to the southern side and surrender but was shot by someone on the bridge before he could deliver his message. 'They were again swept by machine-gun fire, and many leaped from the bridge even though they were not over the river. None surrendered at this time.'[14] McClain noted that 267 bodies remained on the bridge the next morning. Lieutenant Sims recalled that his men had 'little concern' about destroying the hopelessly trapped Germans but admitted it was 'not something to be proud of or brag about. It continues to bother me that I had to make the hasty decision that led to the deaths of so many young men, our own and those opposing us.'[15] At 1700hrs, Kappel tried to contact Colonel Tucker to tell him that the bridge was secure and ask for tanks to be sent across. Leaving Sims at the railway bridge, La Riviere joined Burriss in a move against the highway bridge. At 1830hrs, 1st Battalion arrived in sufficient numbers to relieve the small garrison and Sims and his men set out to follow.

Burriss reached the northern end of the highway bridge at dusk.

> An eerie silence had fallen at the north end, and we didn't see any enemy troops. Could it be that the Germans posted no defense at this end of the bridge? Across the river, the city of Nijmegen was ablaze, and there was a great deal of firing around the bridge's southern end.[16]

Peering across the length of the bridge, the silhouettes of tanks could be seen approaching.

As Burriss approached the northern end, Sergeant Peter Robinson led his troop of Shermans onto the bridge's southern ramp. Earlier, the 29-year-old Dunkirk veteran had been told by his troop commander, Major Trotter, that 'the bridge has to be taken. Don't stop for anything.' Both men knew that the bridge would be prepared for demolition and that it was extremely likely that it would be blown as the first tank crossed so Trotter added encouragingly that he would let Robinson's wife know if anything happened to him.[17] According to Robinson's watch it was 1813hrs. Ahead lay 600 yards of steel and concrete bridge running straight ahead above the river, defended by at least three anti-tank guns and a number of Panzerfausts on this side alone and already primed for demolition.

As the troop moved out of Hunner Park, Robinson saw the huge bridge looming ahead. Around them, the whole town appeared to be burning. Edging forward towards the bridge, an 88mm round ricocheted off the road in front of Robinson's tank and hit one of the idler wheels, the blast damaging the radio set. Pulling back, the 88 switched its attention to Lance Sergeant Billingham's tank but the remaining vehicles were stationary and ready to give covering fire. A single shot from Sergeant Pacey destroyed the gun before it could do any more damage. Reorganising, Robinson needed a working radio and ordered Billingham out of his tank and to follow behind in Robinson's damaged tank. Billingham tried to argue but accepted the order and the troop set out again. Under increasing pressure from his commanding officer to get across the bridge, Robinson again pushed forward to the ramp of the bridge. 'We had barely travelled 50 yards' he later said

> … when a Panzerfaust struck a nearby girder. It seemed projectiles were coming from every angle, yet strangely we remained intact. Not only was the bridge defended from both flank and front, but we suffered repeated attacks from the air in the form of men hanging from girders dropping grenades, while snipers endeavoured to keep us running 'blind' [ie closed down inside the vehicle][18]

Sergeant Pacey was following behind Robinson:

> Our happiest moment was when we saw the Germans actually on the bridge, firing at us from behind the girders and supports. 'Well anyway,' he said, 'if they are going to blow the bridge, they will blow up some of their own people with it.' Half-way over, there was a piece of piping across the road. That worried us. We thought it might be some sort of an igniter which would touch off the moment a tank passed over it.[19]

Advancing anyway, they found it was a harmless piece of tubing.

North of the bridge, SS Brigadeführer Harmel watched the tanks start across. General Model had issued specific orders that the bridge should not be blown so that it could be used for a counter attack but it had been prepared for demolition in case of emergency.

> As the crisis came I watched from the bunker on the riverbank. When I lost radio to Euling, I knew that the bridge was going to be taken. Everything seemed to pass through my mind all at once. What must be done first? What was the most important action to take? It all came down to the bridges. They must be destroyed. If Bittrich had been in my shoes, he would have blown the main bridge. In my view, Model's order was now cancelled because the situation had changed. I had no intention of being arrested and shot by Berlin for letting the bridges fall into enemy hands – no matter how Model felt about it. I waited, watching and then saw one tank on the centre of the bridge, then another following behind and to a side. I ordered the pioneer with the firing mechanism to 'Get ready' and when two more tanks reached the

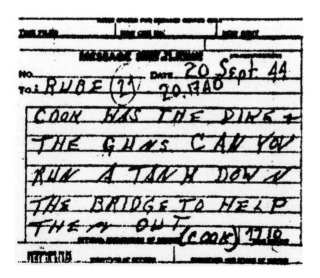

The message from Major Cook to Colonel Tucker. (Courtesy Jan Bos)

Major Julian Cook, commander 3rd
Battalion 504th PIR.

centre, I gave the order, on my own responsibility 'Let it blow!'
Nothing happened. 'Again' I shouted to the pioneer. I waited
to see the bridge collapse with the tanks into the river. It failed
to go up – probably because the initiation cable had been cut
by artillery fire. Instead, the tanks kept moving forward getting
bigger and closer.[20]

Crossing closely behind the tanks was Lieutenant A.G.C.
'Tony' Jones, reconnaissance officer of 14 Field Squadron
Royal Engineers, whose job it was to neutralise the
demolition charges. Later described by Horrocks as 'the
bravest of the brave', Jones worked under heavy fire and
was amazed at the standard of the preparations. It seemed
impossible that they had not been detonated.[21]

Watching from the city, Colonel Vandervoort saw an 88mm open fire at the lead tank
from the northern bank.

> It was pretty spectacular. The 88 was sandbagged into the side of the highway about 100 yards
> from the north end of the bridge. One tank and the 88 exchanged about four rounds apiece
> with the tank spitting 30 calibre tracers all the while. In the gathering dusk it was quite a view.[22]

Pumping out rounds as fast as the gun could be loaded, Guardsman Leslie Johnson,
Robinson's gunner, put the 88 out of action. Racing across the bridge, the tanks were then
engaged by a second 88. Believing that they had knocked it out, Robinson's driver drove
towards a 10-foot gap between the huge concrete blocks set on the bridge as a roadblock.
Robinson remembers that

> visibility was terrible. I was shouting like hell, trying to direct the gunner, the driver and inform
> headquarters all at the same time. The noise was unbelievable, with all sorts of fire clanging off
> the girders.[23]

Engineers remove the
demolition charges from
the Nijmegen bridge. The
bridge was later found to
have been fully prepared
for demolition. The
reason for the failure to
detonate has never been
conclusively found.

Once through the gap, Robinson spotted another 88 about 300 yards ahead. Johnson fired and hit the gun with his first shot and sent the infantry around it running. As the Germans fled, Johnson mowed them down with the tank's machine gun. 'It was a massacre', he recalled, 'I didn't even have to bother looking through the periscope. There were so many of them that I just pulled the trigger.' The tanks carried on, 'bumping over the bodies in the road'. Standing in his turret, Robinson urged his troop on. As they neared the northern end, a self-propelled gun fired. 'There were two big bangs in front of us. My tin hat was blown off but I wasn't hit.'[24] Johnson fired back, hitting the gun and a nearby house. Suddenly, the tanks were across. 'Just as I got round the corner and turned right I saw these helmets duck in a ditch and run,' Robinson said later. There was an explosion and he realised he had been hit by a gammon grenade but he ordered his crew to cease fire and saw figures in the ditch stand up. From the shape of their helmets he knew they were American. From all around, jubilant paratroopers swarmed onto the tanks. Burriss stepped forward and told him 'You guys are the most beautiful sight I've seen in years.' It was 1915hrs; Arnhem was just eleven miles away.

R obinson recalled:

Well my orders were to collect the [American] Colonel who was in a house a little way back and the first thing he said to me, 'I have to surrender. I can't carry on. I've lost nearly all my men. I haven't got many left.' Well I said, 'I'm sorry. My orders are to hold this bridge to the last man and the last round. I've only got two tanks but if you'd like to give me the ground support for a little while until we get some more orders then we can do it.' He said that he couldn't do

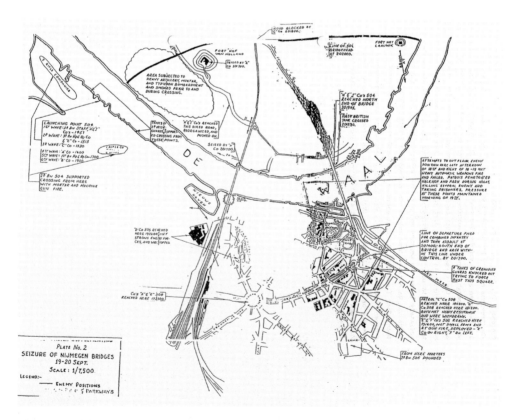

The seizure of the Nijmegen bridges on 19/20 September 1944.

it, so I said that he better come back to my wireless and talk to General Horrocks … so he came over and had a pow-wow with General Horrocks. The Colonel said, 'Oh very well then' and I told him where I wanted the men but of course you can't consolidate a Yank [i.e. establish a defensive perimeter] and they hadn't been there for ten minutes before they were on their way again.[25]

South of the bridge, British reinforcements began to cross. Captain P. Shervington's troop of self-propelled anti-tank guns of Q Battery 21st Anti-Tank Regiment went first, followed around 45 minutes later by infantry of Number 2 Company of 3rd Battalion Irish Guards and shortly behind them came the battalion's Number 1 Company. The infantry moved across the bridge on foot, still under fire from die-hard defenders tied to the highest girders. Others held out in positions under the roadway and sporadic fighting continued throughout the night.[26]

Robinson's troop now pushed forward towards the village of Lent and as they did so, they were hit by a hail of Panzerfaust fire and pulled back. As the firing started, Sergeant 'Rocky' Knight's tank collided with the vehicle ahead and was hit and set alight. He and his crew bailed out and took shelter at the side of the road. A German patrol checked the vehicles and a soldier kicked Knight, apparently thinking him dead. The rest of the crew were captured and marched away. Knight then checked the tank and found that the fire had been confined to the camouflage nets stowed across the rear deck; he was able to restart the vehicle and follow after the rest of the troop. As word spread that Knight now needed a crew, paratroopers with previous experience of the Sherman came forward and formed a joint US/British crew.

Having run a gauntlet of fire into Lent, Robinson's leading tanks approached the intersection where the road and railway met and where the paratroopers had earlier intended to turn south towards the bridges. The area was filled with SS troops and the Shermans' machine guns were in constant use. Then, the luck that had brought them this far ran out. In the growing darkness, they passed beneath the railway bridge and rounded a corner. 'We went round at 15mph', Johnson said,

… machine-gunning as we went. Suddenly there were two terrific explosions right in front of the tank. The blast from them came down the periscope and into my eyes and I thought for a minute that I had been blinded.[27]

The landing beach on the north bank of the Waal at Lent, the bridge in the background. (Courtesy Jan Bos)

The Nijmegen launch site today.

The tanks had hit a roadblock formed by two mutually supporting anti-tank guns. Unable to deploy off the road at that point and by now operating in complete darkness, the tanks had no choice but to pull back. Retreating back under the railway bridge, Robinson linked up with an isolated group of paratroopers and prepared to hold the position. There was no question of continuing the attack. Both the British and the Americans were short of ammunition and the exhausted paratroopers were in no state to provide the infantry support needed to tackle the roadblock. Even if Robinson made it through the trap ahead, it was clear that his tiny force would be picked off by Panzerfausts along the exposed roadway that formed the only route the tanks could take through the low lying and boggy terrain north of Lent.

Robinson had been ordered to secure the northern end of the bridge and the roadway. Now the tanks stopped at the limit of the American bridgehead. At 2200hrs, the Guards reported that consolidation was complete.

Notes
 1 Nordyke p.535
 2 Ryan p.326
 3 Nordyke p.535
 4 Ryan p.346
 5 Ryan p.348
 6 Nordyke p.539
 7 Burris p.115
 8 Ryan p.349
 9 Magellas p.154
10 PRO WO205/1125 p.14–15
11 Nordyke p.548
12 Personal account by Roy Tuck, 3. Troop, 615 Field Squadron, Royal Engineers, Guards Armoured Division. Courtesy of Jan Bos
13 Nordyke p.550
14 Kappel p.34
15 Nordyke p.550
16 Burris p.122
17 Ryan p.354

18 Saunders p.173–4

19 Hilary St George Saunders *The Left Handshake* (London: Collins 1949) p.8

20 Saunders p.174–5

21 The real reason the bridge demolition charges failed has never been fully established but credit has been given to a young former Boy Scout, 22-year-old Jan Jozef Lambert van Hoof, a member of the local intelligence gathering network who was killed during the battle on the Nezelstraat as he was directing a British armoured car, number No. F. 195193 crewed by Lance-Sergeant William Berry and Guardsman Albert Shaw through Nijmegen. The vehicle was hit and all were killed or wounded as they escaped. Jan van Hoof was captured alive but executed on the spot. According to Hilary St George Saunders, *The Left Handshake* (London: Collins 1949) p.8–9: 'Jan van Hoof was dead but the bridge still stood. Secretive to the end, he had, it would appear, made no report on his exploit or, if he had, none reached the headquarters of the American 82nd or the Guards Armoured Division.' A year later, van Hoof was officially credited with saving the bridge and a plaque erected to his memory. Although doubt has been cast on the story, in 1945 he was awarded The Medal for Freedom with Bronze Palm by the American government; in 1946 the Dutch government awarded him the Order of William Knight 4th Class; and in 1947 the British announced the award of The King's Commendation for Brave Conduct with silver laurel. He is remembered today by three Scout groups in Nijmegen, Nieuwegein and Gouda.

22 See Ryan p.355

23 Ryan p.357

24 Ibid p.357

25 Robinson in Holt p.180

26 Captain The Earl of Rosse and Colonel E. Hill, *The Story of the Guards Armoured Division*. (London: Geoffrey Bles 1956) pp.140–141

27 Saunders p.184

Chapter Nine

A Legend is Born

What happened next remains the subject of bitter recriminations almost 70 years later and we need to look closely at the prosecution case.

After their encounter with the German roadblock, the British tanks pulled back to rejoin the US paratroopers. According to Burriss, the British tank crews then, inevitably, brought out their teapots. In his book there follows a bitter exchange in which Burriss says that the tank troop commander, Captain the Lord Peter Carrington, refused to accept Burriss's authority to order the tanks to move on Arnhem immediately, claiming that infantry would need to clear the 88mm gun position before the tanks could go on. Infuriated that Carrington refused to move because of what appeared to be a single gun, Burriss writes that he called him a 'yellow bellied son of a bitch', cocked his weapon and threatened to kill him if he did not get the tank moving.[1] According to Lieutenant Magellas, in a story he claims comes from Sergeant Jimmy Shields, it was Lieutenant La Riviere who allegedly threatened the tank commander, ordering him to get going or 'I'll blow your head off and take the tanks myself.'[2] The story is dramatic and certainly paints Burriss (or La Riviere) as a man willing to do anything to save his fellow paratroopers, but when asked about it, Peter Carrington, whom one suspects would remember the incident, has stated that 'the story is simply lunacy and the alleged exchange did not take place.'[3]

Although Burriss rather grudgingly admits in retrospect that Carrington was perhaps not the real culprit, he claims that the 82nd were determined to get to their brother paratroopers at Arnhem and that nothing else mattered. He goes on to say that he saw no such determination among the British, stating that 'Twenty four hours later, the tanks were still sitting there and the surviving British paratroopers at the Arnhem Bridge were forced to surrender.'[4] Magellas agrees:

Lieutenant James 'Maggie' Magellas.

The British tanks eventually did move towards Arnhem, but it was more than twenty-four hours later. They had gone about two miles over the narrow road when a German 88mm gun hit the lead tank. It started burning and spun around, blocking the road. Instead of pushing the disabled tank off the road and continuing the attack, the rest of the British tank column turned around and headed back to the safety of Nijmegen. I personally witnessed this action.[5]

The Americans, reasonably enough, had assumed that the British tanks would immediately push through their bridgehead and on to Arnhem and were furious that this did not happen. Colonel Tucker later wrote:

> We just stood there, seething, as the British settled in for the night, failing to take advantage of the situation. We couldn't understand it. It simply wasn't the way things were done in the US Army – especially if it had been our guys hanging by their fingernails eleven miles away. We'd have been going, rolling without stop. That's what Georgie Patton would have done, whether it was dark or not.[6]

It is a theme echoed throughout American accounts of the operation – 'Georgie' Patton would have pushed his tanks down the road immediately. So why didn't the British?

'Georgie' Patton may have ordered his tanks forward. That other famous cavalry commander 'Georgie' Custer may even have ordered his men not to take prisoners as the Sioux closed in on him at Little Big Horn. Ordering something and it being possible are not the same thing. The evidence used by veterans of the 504th to condemn the Guards Armoured instead demonstrates how poorly prepared the paratroopers were for all arms warfare and evidences their refusal to look beyond their own concept of what was possible. The Nottinghamshire Yeomanry, for example, were operating near the Groesbeek Heights and as its history recounted,

> The Americans had not as yet had any experience with tanks and General Gavin asked Colonel Christopherson to 'clear the Reichswald' – just like that; as if all we needed to do was to buzz around for a few minutes playing hide and seek among the trees for the German paratroops to come out screaming for mercy.[7]

This is the same area, it should be remembered, that patrols from the 505th had reported to Gavin as being thick woods forming a tank obstacle impenetrable for German armour.

US troops of the 504th move through Nijmegen, returning from the north bank. (Courtesy Jan Bos)

A British 17-pounder anti-tank gun set up with an Anglo-American crew on the approaches to the Waal River bridge. The gun was one of the few Allied weapons capable of penetrating German armour.

After the battle, British tanks head north to 'the Island', passing US troopers on the bridge. (Courtesy Jan Bos)

As so often with statements of fact in the story of *Market Garden*, one again needs to do the maths. The delay of 24 hours claimed by the Americans would, of course, mean that the British did not move until late in the evening of the 21st when it was already after dark although, according to the accepted myth, the British refused to operate at night. The tanks did indeed stay put longer than expected but the claim that it was more than 24 hours before they resumed the advance is wrong and, as before, the delay is exaggerated to twice the actual time lapse. Indeed, in his history of the US airborne Devlin exaggerates this still further: 'On Friday, D-plus-5, after an incredibly long delay – nearly two days after the capture of the Nijmegen bridge – the British began rolling toward Arnhem.' In doing so, he increases the actual delay five fold but also appears to believe that Frost's men had held the bridge until D+4.[8] The problem was in moving 43rd Division up the corridor in order for them to provide the infantry support needed for any progress across the Island. Aware of the traffic jams and constant attacks on 'Hell's Highway', Browning had already signalled Urquhart on the night of the 20th that the advance of Guards Armoured would be delayed and that 'First Airborne will be first priority but do not expect another advance possibly before 1200hrs.'[9] Many historians have since drawn on German accounts to argue that there was only a thin screen available to block the route north that night and that this could have been forced by the single available troop of tanks. The fiercely airborne-oriented Buckingham reports that there were

Troopers of the 82nd
cross the bridge.
(Courtesy Jan Bos)

… virtually no German troops between Nijmegen and Arnhem. Nor were there for around sixteen hours, until the Germans were able to push armour over the Arnhem Bridge after finally overwhelming the British force clinging to the north end at midday on 21 September. The delay at Nijmegen handed the initiative to the Germans and allowed them once again to erect an effective defence where none had existed in time to counter Guards Armoured's leisurely advance.[10]

Given that preventing the breakout from Nijmegen had become the focus of the German effort, we need to ask where the suggestion that there were 'virtually no German troops' to oppose the advance comes from. Where, for example, had all the Germans gone who had laid down such fierce fire to the re-supply drop and strafing runs witnessed by Kappel? Many had certainly been killed on and around the bridges, but it is impossible to believe that they represented the whole of the German forces between Nijmegen and Arnhem.

Captain Kappel recalls witnessing a re-supply flight to Arnhem shortly before the Waal crossing as being met by a 'veritable wall of small arms and flak', indicating, he says, large numbers of the enemy across the river.[11] The official US history expands on this, stating that:

> At the village of Ressen, less than three miles north of Nijmegen, the Germans had erected an effective screen composed of an SS battalion reinforced with eleven tanks, another infantry battalion, two batteries of 88-mm guns, twenty 20-mm antiaircraft guns, and survivors of earlier fighting at Nijmegen, all operating under General Bittrich's II SS Panzer Corps. Arnhem lay seven miles north of this screen. The British could not pass.[12]

Whether the screen was as strong as the US history claims or as weak as others have suggested, the British could not, at that point, have known. What was clear was that in the terrain they now faced, a single 88mm gun had the capacity to halt an armoured column if it did not have infantry support – and that there were no infantrymen available.

Some versions have the Americans stating that they would mount the tanks and provide the support. It is not at all difficult to believe that the highly motivated troopers would do so. However, short of ammunition and exhausted after the events of the day, they could have been of limited use in a sustained operation. There are accounts claiming that when the tanks failed to move, the paratroopers talked about pushing forward on foot but it appears they did not request permission to do so as they assumed Gavin would refuse. If true, this raises the uncomfortable fact that the Americans did not push forward because they did not have orders to do so from their Divisional HQ but that they condemned the British for behaving in the same way.

Andrew Gibson-Watt was with the Welsh Guards Group waiting to head north:

> My own complaint is the thesis (which has been propounded by other historians) that Guards Armoured Division should have gone on to Arnhem on the night they captured the Nijmegen bridge. The Division, 'off-balance' and still heavily embroiled in Nijmegen town, could not have done so. There was nothing to go on with: the main preoccupation was now to defend the bridge against the expected counter-attack. Any element which had gone on would have found it very hard to get over the Arnhem bridge, which was not (and never had been) held by John Frost's gallant force; and if it had got over it would have been met by the greatly superior German forces in that part of Arnhem. An advance that night was 'not on' and general military historians have erred greatly in assuming that it would have been possible and should have been done. We have always been fed the story about fired up American paratroopers railing at the British tankers for not going straight on ... It is time for this accusation, which does not stand up to detailed examination, to be finally refuted.[13]

After a hurried briefing on a captured map during the morning of the 21st, Captain Ronald Langton of the Irish Guards led his tanks forward at 1100hrs, pushing north. From here to Arnhem, there was no possibility of operating off the embanked roads and the tanks would have to advance on a single vehicle front. Under orders not to stop for anything, the Guards moved steadily forward but on the narrow raised highway, the tanks presented an easy target for the Germans' highly effective anti-tanks weapons. Ryan writes that on the outskirts of Elst, about half way between Nijmegen and Arnhem, massive explosions rocked the lead tanks. Four Shermans were hit in succession by a self-propelled gun in the woods to the left of the road and blocked any further progress. The attached infantry were unable to reach the gun across the open ground between the road and the wood against heavy machine-gun fire and repeated Typhoon strikes failed to dislodge the enemy. The entire advance halted. Back in Nijmegen, tanks of the Welsh Guards spent an uncomfortable afternoon sat on the exposed bridge waiting to move forward. Contrary to what the Americans believed, the British tank crews were eager to reach their airborne comrades. Lieutenant John Gorman, trapped outside Elst, summed up his feelings:

British tanks on the north side of the Waal River bridge at Nijmegen. (Courtesy Jan Bos)

Letter to *Stars and Stripes* newspaper complaining of the lack of coverage of US involvement in Holland, October 1944. (Courtesy Jan Bos)

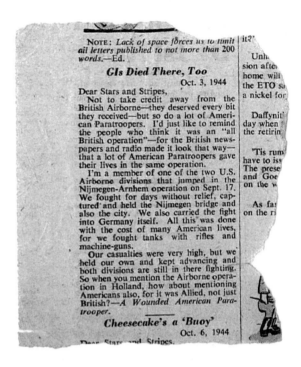

NOTE: *Lack of space forces us to limit all letters published to not more than 200 words.—Ed.*

GIs Died There, Too

Oct. 3, 1944

Dear Stars and Stripes,

Not to take credit away from the British Airborne—they deserved every bit they received—but so do a lot of American Paratroopers. I'd just like to remind the people who think it was an "all British operation"—for the British newspapers and radio made it look that way—that a lot of American Paratroopers gave their lives in the same operation.

I'm a member of one of the two U.S. Airborne divisions that jumped in the Nijmegen-Arnhem operation on Sept. 17. We fought for days without relief, captured and held the Nijmegen bridge and also the city. We also carried the fight into Germany itself. All this was done with the cost of many American lives, for we fought tanks with rifles and machine-guns.

Our casualties were very high, but we held our own and kept advancing and both divisions are still in there fighting. So when you mention the Airborne operation in Holland, how about mentioning Americans also, for it was Allied, not just British?—*A Wounded American Paratrooper.*

Cheesecake's a 'Buoy'

Oct. 6, 1944

we had come all the way from Normandy, taken Brussels, fought halfway across Holland and crossed the Nijmegen bridge. Arnhem and those paratroopers were just up ahead and, almost within sight of that last bloody bridge, we were stopped. I never felt such morbid despair.[14]

Magellas complains that the armoured column should have pressed on and that any knocked out tank could be simply pushed aside by the following vehicle. A short consideration of the problem should have made it clear that a knocked out Sherman tank is not something to be brushed aside lightly. It is a 32-ton steel roadblock filled with fuel and explosives. The task of pushing it is relatively simple, but as General Sosabowski famously asked at the *Market Garden* briefing, 'but what about the Germans?' Magellas seems to assume that the Germans would not take advantage of the easy target presented by the second vehicle being slowed by the effort of pushing the first aside. The third tank is now faced with two knocked out Shermans, 64 tons of steel in its path. And so on. At what point, one wonders, would Magellas accept the road was blocked?

What emerges is the by now familiar claim that XXX Corps were simply not making the effort, either because of lackadaisical attitudes or over-caution. Apparently determined to portray the British as cowards, Tucker later described how he joined the group at the bridgehead. As the tanks remained in position,

I remained at a farmhouse at the intersection of the railroad and main road that night, and although the British tank commander kept screaming most of the night for close in security, we had two battalions well out in front of him and our small group (at the C[ommand] P[ost]) could take care of any group attempting to get to his tanks ... I asked him what it was he feared since there was a whole American battalion 1,000 yards to his front. He said he wanted people dug in around his tanks – that we didn't have. I knew we had to get well out, then clean up the area in back of us.[15]

(Left to right) Colonel Reuben Tucker, CO of the 504th PIR, Major Julian Cook and Captain Wesley Harris receive the Distinguished Service Cross for their part in the capture of the Nijmegen Bridge, 20 January 1945. (US Army)

Using the word 'screaming' to describe the requests for support appears to be intended to illustrate this alleged timidity on the part of the tank crews but instead further serves to illustrate Tucker's inexperience in working with armour. Sergeant Spenser Wurst of the 505th could have explained. Asked to take up position across the street from some tanks during the battle in Nijmegen, he had been reluctant. 'At night, a buttoned up tank is practically blind. To advance around and move in front of those tanks would expose us to friendly fire as well as heavy fire from the enemy.'[16] Tucker's men, 1000 yards out in front, would have had no way of identifying themselves or their positions without close-in support around the tanks to direct fire. At the same time, small groups of the enemy, armed with Panzerfausts, had escaped the fighting and could do a great deal of damage from much less than 1000 yards. The experiences of the tank crews the previous night when American sentries simply slept behind doors to trip intruders did little to raise their confidence and even by this standard, Captain Kappel later admitted that 'Keep, Cook and I were together that night and we discussed it. We felt our job was done and I'm afraid we were a bit careless about setting up protection around the British; but we expected them to move out, not stay there.'[17]

This, too, was a matter of concern. It was clear to the British that the American perimeter was not secure. It was also at the end of a long and very insecure salient. Horrocks had to consider the fact that if his tanks did advance to Arnhem, there was a very real possibility of being cut off by a counterattack somewhere along the road behind them – and Nijmegen was clearly the point of maximum effort for the Germans. Indeed it would remain so for some time (Magellas describes his unit's withdrawal on 22 September and their handing over to the British as being made under fire and being 'touch and go') and fierce fighting would continue around the bridgehead for several weeks. The risk of the Guards Armoured simply joining the 1st Airborne in their predicament and being destroyed in detail was very great. But to the lightly armed paratroops, all tanks were invulnerable and they could see no reason for caution, telling each other that there was no reason to hold back.

Burriss complains that the British would not move because of one gun whilst his men had faced dozens. Again, a point worth considering. The road north of the Waal is raised because of the low water table in that area. In an analysis of the terrain prepared by the Assistant Chief of Staff of the US Airborne Corps on 11 September, the military evaluation of the area of 82nd Airborne's responsibility noted, 'Only feasible approaches are along the roads and railroads. Cross-country movement in the area varies from impractical to impossible.'[18] In other words, the tanks could advance only along the raised embankments of roads and railways and had little, if any, room to manoeuvre if they encountered enemy forces. No sane infantry commander would march his men in single file along an exposed track towards a single rifleman yet, in effect, this is what Burriss now expected of the Guardsmen. The area between Nijmegen and Arnhem – the 'island' as it became known – was known to be ideal defensive country and this had been made clear in the operational briefings given to the 504th. Indeed shortly after dawn on the 21st, Private John Towle of the 504th won the Congressional Medal of Honor for an action near Oosterhout when a company of German infantry supported by two Tiger tanks and a half-track attempted a counterattack. Towle engaged the infantry with bazooka rounds. In his account of the action, Sergeant Ross Carter claims to have personally witnessed the attack as being made by as many as five Tiger tanks, writing that '300 tons of mobile metal forts were being opposed by one man and one bazooka! Finally the stout hearted trooper forced the tanks to withdraw to the town. His bravery had saved our company and the left bank of the Rhine.'[19] Though Towle's achievement was rightly acknowledged for the superb action it was, no-one in the 504th seems willing to consider that if a lone paratrooper armed with a weapon Gavin considered largely ineffective against armour could stop an attack by a company of enemy infantry and two (or five) Tiger tanks, then what could the Germans accomplish with a prepared position armed with highly effective anti-tank artillery?

Horrocks later commented;

> Gavin told me afterwards that he and the men of his Division felt bitterly disappointed that we had not sent a task force straight for the Arnhem bridge after the capture, intact, of the two Nijmegen bridges. In fact, at the time, he felt that the British had let them down badly. This sort of criticism is a constant phenomenon of battle. The forward troops always think that those in the rear are leading a life of ease and should be doing more, but even Jim Gavin, the Divisional Commander, could have had no idea of the utter confusion which reigned in Nijmegen at that time, with sporadic battles going on all over the place, and particularly on our one road to the rear, where chaos reigned … I now began to feel as though I was in a boxing ring, fighting a tough opponent with one hand tied behind my back. I was, in fact, trying to fight three battles at the same time.[20]

On the morning of the 21st, according to Gavin,

> Tucker was livid. I had never seen him so angry. He had expected that when he seized his end of the bridge, the British armor would race on to Arnhem and link up with Urquhart. His first question to me was 'What in the hell are they doing? We have been in this position for over twelve hours and all they seem to be doing is brewing tea. Why in hell don't they get to Arnhem?' I did not have an answer for him.[21]

The exchange is interesting for two reasons. Firstly, Burriss talks of a 'solemn pledge' by the British to move on Arnhem immediately but when Gavin writes about his meeting

General Horrocks (left) and General Gavin (in helmet) introduce King George to veterans of the Waal crossing.

with Tucker, he says 'He [Tucker] had expected ...' Given that Gavin had been part of the meeting at which the alleged pledge was made, why does he say that Tucker had expected it and not '*we* had expected ...'?

Secondly, Horrocks has generously explained that Gavin could not have been aware of the chaos on 'Hell's Highway' but surely he could not fail to have been aware that the force available to press on to Arnhem was busy fighting in support of his Division in and around Nijmegen in what he himself describes as a widespread perimeter of some 25 miles. That he had no answer for Tucker is not true. However, we can speculate that he made the comment for entirely human reasons. Gavin had only recently refused to promote Tucker and this cannot but have affected their relationship to some degree. Gavin now had enough on his plate without taking time to debate the details of British armoured warfare with his subordinate and his response could have been enough to allow the two men to reunite against a common enemy – the British. A reasonable comment at the time, it is less so repeated over 30 years later in Gavin's memoirs when the reason for the delay should have been known to him.

Amongst the men of the 82nd, the story of the Waal crossing began to develop into a story of American heroism and British indifference. Years later, that story had taken on a life of its own. Lieutenant Thomas Pitt, administrative officer of 3/504th, for example would later recall the events of 20 September:

> So the first thing that was to occur prior to the actual crossing was that we were to get some air cover. British Spitfires that had long range capability were operating (I believe) out of somewhere in France. Finally after some delay, two Spitfires came over and started to strafe the opposite banks and on the opposite dike where the Krauts were dug in and all. About the second pass, they got one of the Spitfires and the other one went home. So that was the end of the air cover. The British had these large tanks; I forget the name of it. They were going to give us some artillery fire and first laid down some fire. There were about some eight or ten of them that dug in up closer to the bridge from us. They opened fire and they put a lot of iron down in a short period, but in a couple of minutes the counter battery came. I think about four or five of the tanks got hit and the others pulled out.[22]

The men waiting to make the crossing had already begun to form an image of what lay ahead. Major Cook, for example, referred to the assault as 'an Omaha Beach landing all by ourselves'.[23] Later, CBS war correspondent Bill Downs reported on the crossing as: 'A single isolated battle that ranks with Guam, Tarawa, Omaha Beach. A story that should be told to the blowing of bugles and the beating of drums for the men whose bravery made the capture of this crossing over the Waal possible.' Many reports told of troops tearing off their equipment and swimming the river to get at the enemy and of horrendous casualties among the attackers. No correspondents were eyewitnesses to the attack and neither those who wrote about it later nor the men they heard the story from had been at Omaha Beach or Tarawa.

Lieutenant Pitt did not take part in the crossing but caught up with the battalion later:

> We got down it must have been another third of a mile or so and came up where the Highway Bridge was across the river. By the time we got there Cook, who was the Battalion Commander was there. And then the first British tanks came roaring across the bridge. They cleaned it out there. Most of H Company (my old company) and G Company and what not came a little shortly afterwards. I don't know how many of them. Then came a couple of jeeps and what not and there was Gavin, the Division Commander and his radio man. They came over in the jeep and came in this house and we had taken over like the command post that was right by the edge of the bridge. They had come in there to get the information and how we were and how the situation was and things like that. We had begun to take some probes out to see what was out in front of us there as from Arnhem. By then, it was dark practically and there came a British staff car along and out got the British commander. He was, I guess, the corps commander. I'm not sure who he was. But one of the wheels and he came on in with his folks with him and what not. Tucker was there and Gavin was there and Cook was there, myself and one of the communications officers. We were sort of in the background when you get wheels like that around. Gavin said 'We will put some men up on the tanks and in front of the tanks and let's head for Arnhem.' I think it was 20 some miles or so, it wasn't far, you know. This British commander said 'We don't move our tanks at night.' Gavin said, 'You don't move them at night? Well if we wait till day light then they [the Germans] will move some stuff in.' The Brit said 'Well we can't move tanks at night.' Gavin said something to him, he said, 'If they were my men in Arnhem we would move tanks at night. We would move anything at night to get there.' This guy said 'We are not. We will move them in the morning.' So we had a front out there oh, 500 yards to 1000 yards or more perimeter. Then morning came and that road to Arnhem was nothing but German armor and what not and everything. We got no more got started half way up the road. We didn't get a couple of miles outside the place and that was it.

Interviewed 50 years later, Stanley Kaslikowski recalled his service with the 82nd and claims

> I made the jump in Holland. We were supposed to be reinforcements for some British and Polish paratroopers who were dropped miles from their zone. They were slaughtered. We were supposed to take a bridge. The Germans controlled one side of the bridge so we had to cross the river and fight them on the other side. Rubber boats were dropped in and we crossed. We were loaded with equipment and if anything happened to our boat we wouldn't be able to swim. We were under fire but our boat made it across without too much trouble. By the time we got across it was getting dark and we fought most of the night.[24]

Kaslikowski appears unaware of the 82nd's task for *Market Garden* and remembers inflatable rubber boats being dropped by air rather than canvas boats being delivered by lorry. Yet Kaslikowski, like the others whose accounts the legend relies on, can claim authority because he was there. We need to look at the legend objectively.

British armour heading north across the Waal River bridge.

Pitt's somewhat confused account demonstrates many of the problems involved in relying solely on eyewitness statements gathered years after the event. His account sets the scene for a desultory British contribution to supporting the American attack. Just two fighters are sent as air cover and the tanks withdraw as soon as the enemy fire back. The two 'Spitfires' he refers to were actually flights of rocket firing Typhoons. The 'eight or ten tanks' he could not remember the name of were in fact 30 US-built M4 Shermans, the most widely used Allied tank of the war. (Elsewhere, Staff Sergeant Ross Carter calls them 'Churchill tanks') and he neglects to mention the artillery support from the British and US gun batteries. His inability to recognise Allied equipment is symptomatic of a common problem amongst the paratroops and a factor in the incident at the Grave bridge when a German tank was mistakenly greeted by the 504th. What may seem like a fairly pedantic point is actually highly relevant. Few of the paratroopers seem to have had any ability to distinguish between different types of vehicle or gun and in almost all memoirs of the time, any German armoured vehicle is a Tiger tank, any artillery piece an '88'. This disregard for the importance of briefing the men accurately to distinguish between vehicles and aircraft meant an inability to appreciate the capabilities of each. As a result, paratroopers expected even the lightly armed reconnaissance vehicles of XXX Corps to be able to engage and destroy emplaced artillery across the river or to take on far heavier targets than their weapons were capable of. Equally, they assumed that the Shermans could simply barge through any road blocks and shrug off enemy fire.

British infantry crossing the Waal River bridge. (Courtesy Jan Bos)

The consequences of the failure of XXX Corps to reach Arnhem in time are well known and have been described in detail many times by other writers. Suffice it here to say that when it became clear that further resistance was useless, the men of 1st British Airborne were ordered to evacuate their perimeter and make their way back across the Rhine to Allied lines. Aided by the Polish Airborne Brigade south of the river and XXX Corps' artillery, the bulk of the Division escaped on the night of 25 September with many more following over the coming weeks. Members of the US Airborne were also involved in rescue patrols to collect bands of stragglers as they made their way by whatever means they could find back across the river to Allied lines.

Operation *Market Garden* was over. Magellas notes that despite the apparent bitterness between them, coming under the command of XXX Corps 'hardly caused a ripple' for the 82nd, other than frequently reported complaints about the quality of British rations especially the 'sawdust sausages', 'meat and kidney pudding' and of course the tea. They appear to have worked well with the British during the weeks to follow when, in the absence of any demand from First Allied Airborne or SHAEF for their return, the US Airborne Divisions remained in the line, just as the British 6th Airborne had in Normandy. It would not be until 13 November that the last elements of the 82nd boarded a fleet of British trucks and left Nijmegen.

Notes

1 Burriss, T.M. *Strike and Hold* p.123–4
2 Magellas, J. *All the Way to Berlin* p.163
3 Carrington, quoted in Neillands p.121
4 Burriss p.124
5 Magellas p.163
6 Ryan p.359
7 Saunders, T. *Nijmegen* (Barnsley: Leo Cooper 2001) p.120
8 Devlin p.508
9 Ryan p.361
10 Buckingham p.141
11 Kappel 1947
12 MacDonald, C. *The Siegfried Line Campaign* (Washington: Department of the Army 1961) p185. (Figures compiled from Evening Sitrep, *Army Group B*, 1845hrs, 21 September 1944, *Army Group B, Letzte Meldung;* Daily Sitrep, *Army Group B,* 0135hrs, 23 September 1944, *A Gp B KTB, Tagesmeldungen;* Bittrich Questionnaire, held by Office of the Chief of Military History (OCMH).
13 Neillands p.120
14 Ryan p.371
15 Nordyke, P *All American, All the Way* p.554
16 Ibid p.504
17 Cornelius Ryan archives held at the University of Ohio. Accessed at https://www.library.ohiou.edu/archives/mss/ryan-exhibit/Index.pdf
18 Operation 'Market': Preliminary Tactical Study of the Terrain. HQ US XVIII Corps Airborne 11 September 1944
19 Carter, Ross *Those Devils in Baggy Pants* p.151
20 Horrocks p.103–4
21 Gavin, J. *On to Berlin* p.200
22 'The Waal River Crossing.' An interview with Thomas Pitt, S-1, Third Battalion, 504th Parachute Regiment Interview by Thomas Pitt Jr. with his father in 1992. Accessed via http://www.101st-airborne.net/holland/interviewcrossing.htm
23 Ryan p.342
24 Pavia, T. *An American Town Goes to War* (Nashville: Turner Pub Co 1995). Accessed via Stamford Historical Society website at http://www.stamfordhistory.org/ww2_kaslikowski.htm

Chapter Ten

Aftermath

On 26 September, as the battered survivors of 1st Airborne straggled back to Allied lines, the higher echelons of First Allied Airborne Army began to fight for their careers by establishing their own public relations spin on events. It was the beginning of what Robin Neillands has called

> … the relentless and skilful propagation of … myths which place the blame for the failure of *Market Garden* squarely on XXX Corps, General Urquhart and the Guards Armoured Division. For some reason, although a number of accounts do mention the failure to take the Nijmegen bridge, no-one has analysed the reasons advanced for that failure, reasons which fail to provide even the shadow of an adequate excuse.[1]

For decades, countless smoke-and-mirrors accounts have taken the failure of the ground forces for granted. As we have seen, the evidence does not support the view. So why has the legend become so potent?

Writing to Urquhart on 26 September, Browning described how Horrocks would express his appreciation of the efforts of the airborne troops:

> He will explain to you, and in his expression of opinion I absolutely concur, that without the action of 1st Airborne Division in tying up, pinning down, and destroying in large numbers the German forces in the ARNHEM area, the crossing of the Waal, the capture of the bridges at Nijmegen and, above all, the advance from the bridgehead would have been quite impossible.[2]

The theme was taken up in the official history of the British airborne which argued that the British presence in Arnhem

> … forced the enemy to devote large resources, among them the remains of two SS Panzer Divisions, to the task of ejecting the audacious Urquhart and his men. Had the Germans not been under this necessity, their counterattacks farther south against the American 82nd and 101st Divisions would have been pressed with much greater vigour and might possibly have succeeded, at least for a time.[3]

Why 1st Airborne would need to draw large numbers of the enemy away from the 82nd is unclear given the supposed aim of the operation, but the sub text can be interpreted to mean Urquhart will be credited with a heroic defence against large numbers of the enemy

The city of Nijmegen after the battle. (US Army)

who otherwise would have been available to oppose XXX Corps. That means, of course, that opposition to XXX Corps was therefore lighter than it could have been.

Brereton, meanwhile, in an almost embarrassingly self serving report submitted on 9 October 1944 claimed that:

> Operation *Market* was a brilliant success … It was the breakdown of Second Army's timetable on the first day – their failure to reach Eindhoven in six to eight hours as planned – that caused the delay in taking the Nijmegen bridge and the failure at Arnhem … The decision to carry out a bold daylight operation was one which the Army Commander alone could make. His experience as Commanding General of the Ninth Air Force convinced him that it could be done. The success of the airborne operation testifies to the soundness of his judgment … [The airborne operation] held the bridge for seventy-two hours, twenty-four hours after the time that 30th Corps of the Second Army had promised to establish contact.[4]

True enough up to a point, although in an echo of Burris's 'solemn pledge', nowhere does the evidence suggest XXX Corps had 'promised' to be there; Horrocks' orders state simply they would head for Arnhem 'if possible within forty-eight hours'.

The failure to reach Eindhoven did cause delay, but as we have seen, neither of the expected formations reached it on the evening of D-Day. The Guards' halt at Valkenswaard is frequently criticised and, although it appears to have been part of the plan set for them, the implication is of a failure to seize the initiative. Those criticisms have some validity but need to be placed alongside an understanding that Eindhoven itself was not the problem. The Zon bridge was. Had XXX Corps reached Eindhoven earlier, it is likely that the bridge could have been reached and repaired more quickly and at some point recovered. But that would have meant yet another instance of tanks overrunning areas assigned to airborne troops and begs the question of why the 101st were assigned Eindhoven if it could have been taken by the tanks themselves as easily as is generally assumed. Any tank commander will agree that tanks do not operate well in built-up areas. They lose manoeuvrability and

General Lewis Brereton, commander of the
1st Allied Airborne Army.

the close quarters of street fighting removes the option of air
and artillery support. It is an infantry assault task.

In a covering letter to a narrative of the operation produced
two weeks after it ended and when he had had time to meet
with Browning, Brereton set the agenda for the claim that *Market
Garden*'s failure was due to the slow advance of the Guards. 'On
D plus 2, I arrived at Eindhoven after dark and about six hours
before elements of the Coldstream Battalion of the Guards
Armored established contact with 101st Airborne Division.' In
doing so, he appears to have personally made the link up with
101st 'after dark' – i.e. in the evening and six hours before the
Guards – thereby moving the meeting of the two forces to
the early hours of D+3. Later, his report states clearly that the
Guards met the 101st at the village of Nieuw Acht, northwest of Eindhoven itself at 1100hrs
on D+1, somewhere in the region of 36 hours before Brereton claims he arrived and
witnessed it. The 'breakdown of Second Army's timetable' theme has already been discussed
but Brereton's report adds a new dimension. It states that although General Horrocks was
established in Nijmegen by 1415hrs, 'advance elements' of the Guards Armoured did not
even cross the Maas-Waal Canal until 1800hrs on D+2. According to the same American
evaluation of airborne operations, the 'rate of movement of the armor to Eindhoven was
slow and the whole operation immediately fell 24 hours behind schedule because of the
slowness of these two forces [Guards Armoured and the 101st] in the Eindhoven part of the
operation.' This, it claims, fatally undermined the planned movement of the tanks across the
Nijmegen bridge, stating that 'had the *Garden* forces crossed the Nijmegen bridge at around
noon of D+1 as planned, they would have reached the Arnhem highway bridge in time to
take advantage of its north end being held by airborne forces.'[5] In other words, rather than
the 48 hours given elsewhere, XXX Corps were actually apparently expected to cover the
journey in little more than 24.

The situation then arises that according to Urquhart, John Frost's 2nd Battalion of the
Parachute Regiment had been given to understand that relief would arrive in 24 hours.
Somewhere along the line, seemingly within First Allied Airborne HQ, it had been decreed
that the Nijmegen bridge would be taken by noon on D+1 'at the latest' and Browning and
Gavin had decided that the task would be undertaken by the Guards Armoured themselves
to such a degree that even Gavin himself describes the efforts of the 82nd to take the
bridges prior to XXX Corps arrival as an 'extremely marginal performance'.[6] The American
evaluation report of 1951 noted that the 'possibility of exploiting the initial surprise and
taking the bridge with a small force had already disappeared on the night of D-Day.'[7] Thus
the measure by which the Guards are accused of failing is that they were required to meet
with the 101st (who weren't coming) south of Eindhoven at 2000hrs. Their detractors then
suggest they should have continued on to take Eindhoven and cross the Zon Canal (whose
bridge had been destroyed). This, it appears, should have been followed by a link-up with
the 82nd at Grave and later Nijmegen and for the tanks to be in a position to launch their
own attack to capture the bridges by the morning of D+1. Montgomery had been given
to understand relief should be possible in 48 hours and had briefed Dempsey and Horrocks

on that basis. As the Guards advanced with their eyes on Arnhem, they stand accused first of failing to secure the 101st's objective of Eindhoven for them and next of failing to secure the 82nd's objective of the vital Nijmegen bridges for Gavin's men. Unsurprisingly, they failed. On the basis that ultimately XXX Corps did not effect the relief of 1st Airborne, the Guards are guilty as charged. They were late. Horrocks could not deny that they were late and did not attempt to pass the buck for his own responsibility. As often happens in the Criminal Justice System, once there is an admission by one party, no-one looks too closely at the details. For generations of historians, XXX Corps were late, but by whose timetable or for what reason is rarely discussed.

Adept at political games, Browning had spun a web of patronage around himself and now began to use it to fend off criticism. He began to paint a picture of a highly successful airborne operation let down solely by the failures of the ground forces. Urquhart, through his connections with Browning, had been given command of 1st Airborne over the more suitable and experienced Brigadier Eric Down who had temporarily commanded the Division in the Mediterranean. Down, on the basis of his being a highly competent officer, whom Urquhart describes as 'saturated in airborne experience', was too much of a threat to Browning's self proclaimed status as Britain's leading authority on airborne warfare to be allowed a chance to realise his full potential. Instead he was seemingly sidelined in favour of Urquhart and posted off to India – allegedly at the behest of the War Office and despite Browning's claims to have made every effort to have him assigned to command of 1st Airborne. Urquhart, who it must be said, made no secret of his lack of experience in airborne operations, his propensity to airsickness or the fact that he had never made a parachute jump or flown in a glider, openly expressed his own doubts about his suitability and experience. Now Browning, having given Urquhart the promotion, was making sure that he understood what he was expected to say about events at Arnhem. Fourteen years after the event, Urquhart reported Browning's famous 'bridge too far' comment and wrote of how XXX Corps had reached Nijmegen and fought their way across the river to link up with the 504th:

> In this bridgehead – they paused.
> Later in the evening Boy Browning drove across the bridge and found the Guards held up. He met two Guards officers there and asked how things were going.
> 'The leading Irish Guards tanks have been knocked out and they're blocking the road', one of the officers replied.
> 'Can't you get off the road?' Browning asked.
> 'We can't. There is an eight foot drop on either side.'
> Browning had been given cause to remind the spearheads of XXX Corps that they still had some way to go, and he certainly had the feeling that they lacked the right sense of urgency. If the Guards Armoured Division had been on time, he felt sure he could have secured the bridge with their leading group and a US combat team forty-eight hours earlier.[8]

Since Urquhart was in Arnhem at the time, the only source for this story can be Browning himself. Yet again, it is an account worth examining. The tankers say that the road is blocked by the wrecks of the leading tanks. Browning asks if they can go round. It seems unlikely that the officers hadn't thought of this for themselves but they explain that there is an 8-foot drop on either side of the road. Browning should have known this; it is, after all, quite hard to not notice an 8-foot drop. His own intelligence briefings before the operation had warned that tanks could not operate off the road in that area. Yet that does not stop Browning

Some idea of the risks facing the tank crossing can be gained from this modern shot of the Waal bridge today. From here, any vehicle would be highly vulnerable to attack.

presenting this as still more evidence of a lack of urgency among XXX Corps. He then goes on to say 'he' could have secured the bridge 'forty eight hours earlier' if the tanks had been available. Why then did he design an airborne operation that needed armoured support to achieve its primary objective?

The true nature of Browning's relationship with Horrocks is unclear but Horrocks' letter to Urquhart dated 28 September perhaps falls somewhat short of Browning's hopes. Expressing regret at the high cost, he tells Urquhart:

> We realise that, had it not been for you, we would have had no chance whatever of securing the NIJMEGEN bridges intact … you prevented any reinforcements from moving down towards NIJMEGEN. This just gave us time to secure these vital bridges.[9]

Also on 28 September, Montgomery wrote to Urquhart: 'There is no shadow of a doubt that had you failed, operations elsewhere would have been gravely compromised. You did not fail, and all is well elsewhere.'[10] The following day, Second Army commander Dempsey joined the congratulations: 'Thanks to the way in which you contained the enemy at Arnhem, we were able to secure the bridge at Nijmegen intact.'[11] Arnhem, it seems, was not a defeat, it was an extravagant diversion from the real objective. Few people were fooled.

Eisenhower had told Montgomery to establish a bridgehead on the Rhine. Montgomery had allowed Browning to command the operation to secure such a bridgehead. Courtesy of the US Army, Eisenhower now had a bridgehead over the Rhine. American correspondent Bernard J. McQuaid wrote in the *Indianapolis Times* of Tuesday 10 October 1944 of how he had been

> … one of a party of war correspondents who came from France to study this northern extremity of the western front, I had the honor of crossing the river Rhine and looking back on the historic Nijmegen bridge … Every GI in the outfit takes time to inform you that it was the first bridge across the Rhine that any allied troops secured. They are indignant at news accounts which fail to explain that the river at this point – which the Dutch call the Waal – is actually the lower and major confluence of the Rhine itself. To men of the 82nd it is never the Waal, it is the Rhine, and they are the ones who got across it, let no historian forget that.[12]

Although in retrospect it seems an unlikely prospect that the British airborne was sacrificed to enable the capture of the Nijmegen bridges, the question raised by Browning's letter is to what extent the Nijmegen bridgehead really could be seen as being the true objective of Operation *Market Garden*. Some historians have suggested that the 1st Airborne were given the objective of Arnhem in the expectation that their loss would have fewer political ramifications than the potential sacrifice of a US division under Montgomery's command would have done. The claim that the 1st Airborne were sent to prevent German moves against Nijmegen could be seen to support this, especially when added to the famous 'bridge too far' remark claimed by Browning, which adds weight to the argument by implying that Nijmegen was far enough. Given that without the Arnhem bridge the 'airborne carpet' would cover a road to nowhere, it seems far more likely that the remark was never made and that the letter was the product of a need to hide the massive failing to which Browning's glory hunting had directly contributed. In the end, Browning's powerful friends were able to obtain suitable alternative employment for him away from the airborne army and his place was taken by the far more capable General Richard 'Windy' Gale. Under Gale's direction, a joint US/British airborne force would drop around Wesel in 1945 in a highly successful operation to support the Rhine crossing in the area originally proposed by 21st Army Group.

Browning, however, was not the only one to redefine the outcome of Operation *Market Garden*. Gavin, as noted above, reported how the US Military Academy at West Point set about 'perpetuating the myth that Arnhem was a great victory, but this time an American victory'.[13] Much scorn has been poured on Montgomery's claim that the operation had been '90 per cent successful' though not, oddly enough, on Brereton's claim of a 'brilliant success' masterminded by himself, which testified to the soundness of his own judgement. In the coming months, the Nijmegen area would be under heavy attack and reduced, like Arnhem, to ruin. Prince Bernhard of the Netherlands, one of the many who had been offended by Montgomery's lack of social skills, had never been an admirer. Afterwards, he told Ryan that 'My country can never again afford the luxury of another Montgomery success.' Had the high risk gamble succeeded, the possibility that the Allies could have ended the war by December 1944 would have been very real. Indeed, as we have seen, had Operation *Comet* been able to go ahead in early September, there was every chance of success. Instead, Operation *Market Garden* was a costly failure. For many observers the loss of over 7500 men of the 1st Airborne Division at Arnhem alone provides proof of the incompetence of Montgomery and the British high command and justification for the American view that their strategy was the correct one.

The emphasis on Montgomery's failure, however, provided a useful smokescreen to hide errors elsewhere. The insistence on maintaining the 'broad front' approach had become so entrenched that nowhere were the Allies strong enough to punch through the West Wall. To the south, Patton had become fixated on the capture of Metz for no other reason than because he thought he could. According to his grandson,

> The sixty-five reporters attached to Third Army pestered him for positive news and action, and his ego, accustomed to headlines, was rankled. Patton wrote his wife: 'I fear I am off the first page for the moment as we are not going so fast. Metz is hard to take.' He continued to strike the city with inadequate company- and battalion-sized units with the excuse that he was trying to maintain his army's attitude of aggressive initiative. Gen. Omar Bradley, his superior, urged him to quit 'this pecking campaign' and accept the so-called October Pause imposed in the aftermath of *Market Garden*'s 12,000 Allied casualties. But Patton claimed a need to 'blood' his

newer recruits to the realities of combat. As if hoping to generate a self-fulfilling prophecy, he declared Metz conquered on several occasions, only to have to retract the claim in the face of continued German resistance.[14]

The successes of the previous weeks had created a mood of overconfidence:

> From September to December, Eisenhower, Bradley, and Patton had their sights set firmly beyond the Rhine. Consequently, they underestimated the obstacles and opposition that their soldiers would have to overcome along the way. Thus, a difference in outlook arose between the higher commanders who drew large arrows on maps and the tactical units fighting for yards of muddy ground … General Patton can also be faulted for neglecting to practice economy of force. We have noted several instances in which Third Army's forces were spread out on a broad front in an attempt to be strong everywhere with the result that they were decisively strong nowhere. In retrospect, the important battle in September was XII Corps' fight around Nancy, and in November, the main effort was XX Corps' assault against Metz. And yet Patton failed to concentrate Third Army's resources in reinforcement of the corps engaged in decisive operations. Furthermore, Patton never made an attempt to punch through the German defenses with divisions in column, even though he received approval for such an operation from his superior, Lieutenant General Bradley. One rule of thumb for mechanised forces that emerged from World War II was to march dispersed but concentrate to fight. In Lorraine, Third Army fought dispersed … to capture the province of Lorraine, a problem which involved an advance of only 40 to 60 air miles, Third Army required over three months and suffered 50,000 casualties, approximately one-third of the total number of casualties it sustained in the entire European war …
>
> Ironically, Third Army never used Lorraine as a springboard for an advance into Germany after all. Patton turned most of the sector over to Seventh Army during the Ardennes crisis, and when the eastward advance resumed after the Battle of the Bulge, Third Army based its operations on Luxembourg, not Lorraine.[15]

Further north, during the period of the British-led operations in Holland, General Hodges' First Army were to take 30,505 casualties in the battle for the Hurtgen Forest. The cost was high,

> Yet to General Hodges, his staff, and his corps commanders, there was no alternative. They admittedly might have bypassed the forest; but under the kind of conditions existing at the time, should an army with absolutely no reserve expose its flank to counterattack in this manner? Furthermore, when the First Army first entered the forest, nobody expected any real trouble. After the hard fighting developed, the Germans had to endure the same kind of hardships as the Americans did and were infinitely less capable of replacing battle-weary formations with rested units. The expectation was always present that one more fresh American division would turn the trick. As the First Army G-3, General Thorson, put it succinctly: 'We had the bear by the tail, and we just couldn't turn loose.' More than 8,000 men from the First Army fell prey in the forest to combat exhaustion and the elements. Another 23,000 were either wounded, missing, captured, or killed. That was an average of more than 5,000 casualties per division … What had been gained at this cost? The Americans had battered at least six German divisions. They also had eliminated hundreds of individual replacements. They had conquered a formidable forest barrier by frontal assault. They also had forced the Germans to commit some of the forces intended to be held intact for the Ardennes counteroffensive. Beyond these, the fight in the

forest had achieved little in the way of positive advantages – no German industry, limited roads. The basic truth was that the fight for the Hurtgen Forest was predicated on the purely negative reason of denying the Germans use of the forest as a base for thwarting an American drive to the Rhine. In the process the fight thus far had failed to carry the only really critical objective the forest shielded – the Roer River Dams.[16]

Operation *Market Garden* had advanced 50 miles at a cost of 18,000 casualties and is remembered as a costly blunder. Hodges lost over 30,000 in a battle to control a forest that could arguably have been bypassed. Patton lost 50,000 men to cover a similar distance to no advantage. The politically expedient broad front strategy was failing, just as Montgomery had predicted, yet it was his narrow front strategy that would come to be presented as the wrong approach.

Notes

1 Neillands p.107
2 Museum of Army Flying archives. Report of 1st Airlanding Brigade, Annexure 'P' Number 3 Letter, Browning to Urquhart dated 26 September 1944
3. *By Air To Battle* HMSO 1945 p.133–4
4. Brereton, Narrative of Operations in Holland
5. Ibid p.24–5
6 Gavin. 'Lessons Learned' Report to Commander of XVIII Corps 3 December 1944 in 'Report of Airborne Phase (17–27 September 1944) Operation '*Market*' XVIII Airborne Corps' December 1944
7 WSEG Report p88
8 Urquhart p.127–8
9 Museum of Army Flying. Number 4 Letter Horrocks to Urquhart 28 September 44
10 Ibid Number 1 Letter Montgomery to Urquhart, 28 September 1944
11 Ibid Number 2 Letter Dempsey to Urquhart, 29 September 1944
12 'Nazis Died like Flies in Battle of Nijmegen Bridge: Tougher and Bloodier than Salerno' Report dated Tuesday 10 October 1944 By B.J. McQuaid. *Indianapolis Times* and the *Chicago Daily News* Inc. Found on http://www.nijmegenweb.myweb.nl/)
13 Gavin, *On to Berlin* p.207
14 'When a Dash Becomes a Siege' By Robert Patton *New York Times* 5 April 2003
15 Gabel, Dr Christopher, *The Lorraine Campaign: An Overview, September–December 1944* US Army Command and General Staff College 1985
16 MacDonald p.493

Chapter Eleven

Stories and Histories

Today Operation *Market Garden* remains the subject of heated debate and controversy. In the aftermath of the disaster, accusations and counter accusations flew, and now, 70 years on, some of these claims have taken on the mantle of unassailable truth. But viewed more objectively, the evidence shows that many of the arguments put forward for the failure of the operation are, as we have seen, the product of almost breathtaking double standards. Timings are vastly altered, tactical considerations are ignored and airborne failings quietly pushed to one side.

Montgomery, (almost) everyone's favourite hate figure, is blamed for ignoring intelligence reports and pushing through the operation too quickly. He is also, at the same time, accused of 'prevaricating for two weeks' about the decision to go ahead. The fact is that the plan he offered made sound military sense and even his harshest critics have admitted that the audacity of it impressed them. SHAEF was under pressure from Washington to use the expensively trained airborne divisions and Montgomery in turn was given the option to 'use them or lose them'. Later, Montgomery accepted some blame for the disaster himself, but primarily saw it as the result of Eisenhower's half-hearted backing and his failure to provide the resources needed, complaining about the lack of flank protection provided by O'Connor's VIII Corps in particular. Already having lost his heavy artillery because their transports were needed just to maintain the tanks of VIII Corps, O'Connor had pushed forward with limited resources but had been unable to maintain his momentum when his supply situation became critical, leaving XXX Corps isolated and open to attack from the east. 'In my prejudiced view,' Montgomery wrote later,

> if the operation had been properly backed from its inception, and given the aircraft, ground forces, and administrative resources necessary for the job, it would have succeeded in spite of my mistakes, or the adverse weather, or the presence of the 2nd SS Panzer Corps in the Arnhem area. I remain *Market Garden*'s unrepentant advocate.[1]

In the immediate post-war period, even some American participants agreed. Writing in 1949, Captain Kappel remained of the opinion that had VIII Corps been able to take the pressure off XXX Corps and the airborne been delivered faster, the plan would have worked. Yet the enthusiastic supporters of the idea were quick to distance themselves from its failure. It is to Eisenhower's great credit that he later took responsibility for his own part in the decision to undertake a very risky operation, but others sought desperately for some explanation for the failure that could not be linked to them personally.

In the memoirs of those who took part, the issue of the drop zones comes up time and again. Veterans of the 82nd are very vocal in their condemnation of the British decision to drop so far from their targets. British veterans complain of RAF intransigence. Yet, as we have seen, the RAF were willing to take risks for Operation *Comet* and to undertake most, if not all, the coup de main operations, closer drop zones and two lifts on D-Day asked of them. The situation only changed with the inclusion into the expanded plan of the US Troop Carrier Command, who would provide the bulk of the extra aircraft. Those objections were raised via Brereton as head of the First Allied Airborne Army but acting, it seems, only as champion of the US Army Air Force. At the same time, following a series of confused landings, the belief was gaining credence – in 1st British Airborne at least – that a concentrated drop was more important than proximity to the objective. Given that the US Airborne had suffered similar problems in their previous drops, just how much did the airborne staffs of the three divisions actually openly object to the proposals the air forces put forward? Were they, too, focused on concentrated drops at a distance rather than scattered drops near the objective? Smaller units could land in smaller drop zones near their objectives. Divisional drop zones needed space for a division to land in and that meant looking further afield. What did divisional commanders want most?

Urquhart, commanding an airborne division for the first time, is regarded as having shown his inexperience in allowing his men to be dropped between five and eight miles from the Arnhem bridge and being delayed reaching the main objective; but his men seized and held positions around the Arnhem bridge. Gavin, commanding the 82nd for the first time, also dropped several miles from the Nijmegen bridge and failed even to send the first patrol against it for over six hours. Urquhart is presented as a somewhat ineffectual general, Gavin as a superb one.

General Brereton, as commander of the First Allied Airborne Army, in his report of 9 October complained bitterly that he should not have come under the command of 21st Army Group for the operation but instead that they should have taken direction from him. 'Many of the ground force commanders', he wrote,

A US-built M4 Sherman of the Guards Armoured Division at the Waal River in Nijmegen. (US Army)

… have indicated a desire for purely local and tactical employment of the airborne forces. In this respect their vision and education can be compared to that of the average senior ground commander concerning his conception of air support four years ago. Once placed at the level of lower echelons for planning, I am dominated by the scheme of the ground force commander concerned. So far as 21 Army Group is concerned I have been compelled to arbitrarily refuse to consider many of the projects submitted.

… I would like to present a few of the conditions which must be fulfilled to increase the chances of success of a large-scale airborne operation. The first: 'Don't send a boy to do a man's job', 'concentrate the maximum force on the principle objective.' This sounds trite but the ground force planners persist in presenting a multitude of objectives. An all-out effort with everything that can fly must take advantage of the initial surprise by dropping the maximum of supplies and reinforcements before the enemy can muster his air, ground and flak defences. All troop drops and landings from the outset must be in combat teams, no matter how small the combat team is.[2]

Note the use of the word 'arbitrarily' in respect of his refusal of 21st Army Group proposals. The word is usually defined as being a random decision, made on a whim without regard to the evidence or facts. Thus Brereton proudly boasts of refusing to consider objectives without any reference to their actual military value, merely to make a point that he is in charge of the air forces and will not be treated as an underling by 21st Army Group. He then goes on to talk of an 'all-out effort'. This, it should be remembered, comes from the man who, one month earlier, had hamstrung the commanders on the ground by prioritising the needs of his aircrews over those of the paratroops, forcing them to break up combat units to fit with lift capacity and to leave large portions of their forces on the landing zones as protection for the later lifts, necessary because of concerns that US aircrews were not up to an 'all-out effort' on D-Day. Nevertheless, he reported to Washington that whilst *Market* had been a brilliant success, it had been let down by the *Garden* element. Bradley agreed, blaming Montgomery's planning and the slow advance by the British between Nijmegen and Arnhem.

During the planning phase, it had become clear that enemy strength in Arnhem was greater than expected but intelligence-gathering was patchy. The expectation was that resistance would be heaviest at the start of the ground operation and would become progressively lighter the further XXX Corps advanced along the airborne corridor. As a result, although the presence of additional SS troops along the canal line was missed, reconnaissance of the area between the start line and Eindhoven was relatively good. Beyond that, though:

The major primary Air Force enemy intelligence interest at this time appears to have been in strategic bombing targets. Nothing here is intended to suggest that considerable efforts were not made to gather and disseminate the information required, only that it was not generally a primary mission for the agencies involved. In accordance with the foregoing, it is suggested that more effective efforts were made to collect and disseminate knowledge of the enemy's strength and disposition in the depth required for planning an airborne assault whenever such information was also of vital and primary interest to the collecting agencies. In general, intelligence of the enemy appears to have been … less than adequate in *Market*. In *Market* inaccuracies in such intelligence were responsible to a high degree for the defeat at Arnhem. The suggestion is made that it is possible that detailed information of enemy strengths and dispositions was available to airborne forces in direct proportion to the importance of such information to ground and air force agencies responsible for its collection.[3]

Put another way, the intelligence given to airborne planners was largely second-hand material gathered for an entirely different purpose in support of bombing operations. That said, such intelligence as was made available showed a greater enemy presence than previously thought. Staff at Browning's HQ decided to suppress the information to push the plan through. Cynically, Browning's after action report blamed XXX Corps for what he saw as their underestimation of the strength of the German forces in the area as well as the slow progress they had made up the highway; the bad weather; his own signals staff; and the Second Tactical Air Force for failing to provide adequate air support. For good measure, he also campaigned to have General Sosabowski dismissed from his command of the Polish Airborne Brigade on the basis that the Pole had not been fully supportive, setting in motion what must rank as one of the most distasteful examples of passing the buck of the entire war.

Major General Urquhart is often blamed for the fact that the drop zones for British 1st Airborne were too far from the bridge but, to his credit, he accepted responsibility for his own actions on the first day as contributing to the failure to secure Arnhem. The Germans agreed. Reports by the German High Command and the Luftwaffe both blamed the decision to spread the drop over several days as being the main reason for the failure and, whilst General Student thought the drops were successful, their reinforcement by ground troops was too slow. Student and Model – both highly experienced officers – had immediately recognised the significance of the Nijmegen bridges and had marshalled their limited resources with great effect. Whilst searching for reasons why the Allies failed, it is easy to adopt the same air of overconfidence that had affected SHAEF and to assume that the outcome was a foregone conclusion. This frequently leads to an assumption that the lack of success must therefore be due to massive failings on the part of the Allies rather than, as was actually the case, a superb example of improvisation in the field by two very competent commanders.

Operation *Market Garden* was a bus with a great many hands on the steering wheel but, in the poisonous atmosphere of SHAEF, no-one was allowed to emerge as the designated driver, though several contenders assumed they should be in control. With no consensus on how it should be driven or at what speed, a crash was arguably inevitable. Of the Allied commanders directly involved, only General Taylor of the 101st had previous command experience at the level asked of him. Browning had no airborne combat experience at all. Brereton had come from an air force command and had assumed control of the Airborne Army just a few weeks before. Although Gavin had seen combat with the 82nd he had only taken over the Division in August (in the process becoming, at 37 years old, the youngest Major General since Custer) and was leading his first operation. Horrocks, too, had only recently assumed command of XXX Corps after 14 months recuperation from wounds received in North Africa and had been seriously ill during August. Urquhart, as we have seen, was also new and inexperienced. All had yet to make their mark on their commands, as Horrocks' furious attempts to instil a sense of urgency on the Guards Armoured Division demonstrated.

The 'fact' of a poor performance by XXX Corps is taken for granted even in the few histories where the extremely difficult circumstances of attempting to hold 'Hell's Highway' are taken into account. Buckingham, for example, writes:

> Poor to non-existent forward planning was also a feature of XXX Corps' performance, as shown by the fact that it does not appear to have occurred to anyone to have the corps and divisional allotment of assault boats on hand until US and Polish airborne commanders asked for them. This was an amazing oversight for formations advancing across multiple water-courses, and supports the suggestion that for some unfathomable reason Guards Armoured and the 43rd Division did not really consider what was happening north of the Waal and Lower Rhine to be their affair.[4]

The monument to the men of the 504th PIR at Nijmegen. (Courtesy Jan Bos)

The 'unfathomable reason' might be that the plan for *Market Garden* required XXX Corps to roll across an 'airborne carpet' laid over a series of bridges captured by air assault. It did not call for XXX Corps to lay that carpet. By the time XXX Corps arrived at a watercourse, the crossing should be available. Perhaps more unfathomable is why airborne planners failed to provide some means of crossing these barriers to the forces that actually needed them.

In retrospect, *Market Garden* is a catalogue of errors but most, even in combination, would not have proved fatal. If any one error, however, can be said to have sealed the fate of the 1st Airborne Division at Arnhem, it was Browning's decision to prioritise the Groesbeek Heights over the capture of the bridge and Gavin's willingness to agree. Model and Student immediately saw that without the bridge Arnhem was isolated and so poured all available resources to its defence. Gavin, almost certainly under pressure from Browning, instead chose force protection as his main priority over the rapid relief of 1st Airborne. The bridge at Grave, linking his men with the approaching XXX Corps, was the focus of a major effort. The Waal bridges were not even approached until late in the day, and then by a single patrol. By the time any serious effort was made, the Germans had had time to alert their forces in the area, unload their vehicles from a train in Arnhem, rearm and reequip them and drive to Nijmegen and establish defences. The bridge, lightly guarded that afternoon, had by evening become virtually impregnable. Knowing the bridges to be prepared for demolition at any time, the 82nd did not rush to attack and instead focused their attention on securing the Groesbeek Heights so they could dominate the approaches to Nijmegen and, in Gavin's words, 'ultimately the Second Army could accomplish its mission.' The threat of counterattack from the Reichswald was far less than the 82nd's Intelligence Officer had claimed and Gavin should have questioned why, if the risk were really so high, Browning was prepared to site his Corps HQ directly in the front line.

Despite being held up by the loss of the Zon bridge, XXX Corps reached Nijmegen at 0820hrs on 19 September (D+2), about 42 hours after crossing their start line. Their schedule – based on Browning's statement that the bridges could be held for that long – allowed for a delay of up to four days in reaching Arnhem and an optimistic signal from Urquhart had suggested that it might even be possible to hold until the 25th (D+8).[5] At that point, they were only some eleven miles from the Arnhem bridge and the full German defensive screen was not yet in position. Reaching 1st Airborne within 48 hours was still (just) possible. The failure to secure the bridge on D-Day or later meant that XXX Corps became embroiled in a long battle to secure its own crossing. In the course of that battle, the tenuous grip on the Arnhem bridge was lost and German armour raced across it to deploy north of Nijmegen.

Much is made in accounts of the US airborne of General Dempsey's visit to Gavin at Nijmegen. 'He greeted me warmly,' Gavin recalled, 'with the statement, "I'm proud to meet the Commanding General of the finest division in the world today."' A staff officer nearby overheard the remark and it quickly became part of the 82nd's mythology. Gavin, however, was not so sure. 'I accepted it with reservations,' he later admitted, 'believing that he was being too kind.'[6] Perhaps he was.

Notes

1 Montgomery, Field Marshal Sir B.L. *Memoirs* p.267
2 Brereton, *Narrative of Operations* October 1944 p.3
3 WSEG Report p.127–8
4 Buckingham, p.202
5 Signal from Urquhart. Museum of Army Flying. Report of 1st Airlanding Brigade. Annexure 'P' Number 8
6 Gavin op cit p.204

Chapter Twelve

The Myth of False Gods

The historian's first duties are sacrilege and the mocking of false gods. They are his indispensable instruments for establishing the truth.

Jules Michelet. *Histoire du France* 1833

This book began with du Picq's statement that man is the first weapon of war and that by studying the smallest incident in a war we can learn far more than by reading the great histories of campaigns and generals. It took as its focus the alleged exchange between a Captain of the 504th Parachute Infantry Regiment of the US 82nd Airborne Division and a Captain in the Grenadier Guards Battalion of the British Guards Armoured Division on the evening of 20 September 1944. By analysing the way in which this exchange has been reported and by placing it in its widest social, cultural, political and military context, we have seen how that one incident encapsulates the factors that underpinned – and undermined – Allied strategy in the European theatre of war. We have also seen how elitism, a problem common to any army in any age, so crucially affected how events were perceived both at the time and, more importantly, even today, that any lessons to be learned have already been lost beneath layers of carefully managed mythology. That mythology, handed down by members of 'the greatest generation', has become to some an unquestionable truth so powerful that it is accepted even when, as we have seen, it is patently at odds with the facts.

There is no objective truth in the study of history, and military history in particular. In the field of social studies, 'myth' and 'history' are closely intertwined to produce 'the story a people tell about themselves.' Myths are not lies; they are merely the interpretations we give to events. In Britain, the 'blitz spirit' is a myth. It is the version of events passed down from generation to generation based on what we believe about the time, not what the reality might have been. Key to understanding events is to recognise that 'story' is the biggest part of 'history'. As Jacques Thibault put it, 'When a history book contains no lies it is always tedious.' So what does the meeting of the two captains tell us?

The author is painfully aware of the irony bordering on hypocrisy of an Englishman accusing another nation of xenophobia but in this case, the claim is valid. Although it was, of course, never universal, many American writers freely admit that Anglophobia was rife at all levels of the US military from the ordinary GI to the offices of Washington. Condemnation and even outright hatred is commonly expressed almost as a matter of course in so many memoirs that it is impossible to ignore as a major problem that had a direct impact on the American will to support her British allies. That opinion is not based on the author's nationalistic bias. What is obvious from a reading of the memoirs of British and American veterans is a vast difference in the ways the two viewed each other. Certainly

Lieutenant John Holabird, 307th Airborne Engineers.

anti-American sentiments appear in some British texts, but as a minority voice and nowhere with the same frequency or the same casual venom that run through virtually every American account and especially in the memoirs of the men of the airborne divisions.

It should be remembered that America entered the European war reluctantly and only after Hitler had declared war on the United States. Prior to that large numbers of Americans had fiercely resisted any attempt to assist Britain and were quite content to carry on business with the Nazi regime. The senior US generals responsible for preparing for war had begun their service at a time when Congress seriously debated whether to enter the First World War on the German side to crush its natural enemy, Britain. The decision to enter the war on the side of Britain and France was motivated by profit, not ideology. For almost 200 years, Americans had viewed the British as their greatest threat and the myth of the mistreatment of colonists by the hated redcoats ran deep. In the 1930s, these same generals had based their annual exercises on a hypothetical invasion of the US by Britain. Suddenly, they were allies – if only on the basis that 'my enemy's enemy is my friend.'

The young Americans coming to Britain came from a society where racial discrimination was not only widespread but in many states legally mandated. Their army was racially segregated and strict rules controlled any interaction between black and white troops. Arriving in the UK, many white Americans were shocked to find black soldiers treated equally and often defended by British soldiers and civilians appalled at the overt racism of the Americans. Black GIs were welcomed into the homes of white British families, further proof that these were two very different societies. Tensions ran high and gun battles between black and white Americans broke out in several British towns. For anyone socialised to believe that human beings should be segregated, it was possible to transfer the belief that non-whites were lesser beings to a belief that non-Americans were also of no importance. That could, and did, translate into resentment of the British, on whose behalf the GIs had been conscripted and dragged far from home. After 150 years of isolationism, few saw the problems of Europe as being any of their responsibility and they were vocal enough in their complaints that their commander was forced to order the publication of a guide to explain why the British might seem somewhat underwhelmed by their arrival. As previously mentioned, GIs were taken on tours of bomb sites to press home the message that mere arrival in Britain did not make them knights in shining armour come to the rescue of a defeated people. Throughout the accounts of these young men, a sense that they were not shown enough gratitude or attention by the British is evident. In particular, after the Normandy invasion we can see complaints that the British media concentrated on the British effort. US troops felt their sacrifices were going unnoticed.

The media of any country is parochial; it looks first and foremost at the local angle. The problem, of course, was that US troops in Europe had easier access to the British media than

The cost of war: an unidentified US casualty. (Courtesy Jan Bos)

to their own press. In Britain, US troops felt they were being ignored but by the same token, in the US any British story took second place. In the years since, Hollywood and popular culture in the United States has pretty much erased Britain's contribution and instead promoted 'the greatest generation' as having stood up to Nazism. In 2006, for example, screenwriter David Ayer told BBC radio that his script for the film *U571* (which depicted the capture of a German Enigma code device by a crew of American naval specialists) was 'a distortion … A mercenary decision … to create this parallel history in order to drive the movie for an American audience.'[1] Similarly, producer David Puttnam admitted that his film *Memphis Belle*, although filmed in the UK, would not have been funded had it featured an RAF bomber crew because American audiences would not identify with it. This ignorance of military history in a general audience in the United States is perhaps understandable, but on the sixtieth anniversary of the Normandy invasion, historian Robin Neillands acted as a battlefield tour guide for several groups of visiting Americans who, presumably, had some prior interest in the Second World War. Of some 200 visitors in total, he reports that he 'did not find one who was remotely aware of the full extent of the British/Canadian participation on D-Day. One visitor, making his third visit to the D-Day beaches, had never been east of Omaha beach.'[2] The museum at the Normandy town of St Mere Eglise is dedicated to the US airborne forces. It shows films throughout the day in two languages: French and 'American'.

Amongst the servicemen arriving in the UK were those of the US airborne divisions. Trained to consider themselves an elite and encouraged to look down on anyone not wearing paratrooper wings, these men found a natural target for the carefully fostered arrogance that marks any designated elite. In order for the airborne to be elite, they needed someone to be better than. The less capable the men they contrasted themselves with, the greater their sense of professionalism could become. It is a feature of airborne units that they routinely equate non-membership of the 'airborne brotherhood' as a sign of failure on the part of the outsider. At different times in the history of a unit, the culture can change according to the style of command it operates under and Phil Nordyke, historian of the 82nd Division, records how,

> after seven months of gruelling training under Colonel Gavin, the 505th was probably the best parachute regiment in the US Army. It had received the benefit of Gavin's intimate knowledge of airborne operations … There was a fierce unit pride that rose above even the other parachute regiments. The 505th were a tight-knit family, and Gavin was the patriarch. In fact, the 505 troopers had such a fierce loyalty to the 505 and to Gavin that the Regiment had trouble fully integrating into the 82nd Airborne Division.[3]

This, it should be noted, records events in late 1942. Gavin's 'intimate knowledge' of airborne operations was entirely theoretical at that point but what he had managed was to create such a strong unit culture that the 505th found it difficult to cooperate even with members of their own division. Given that, we can see that the potential for such a unit to work effectively with non-airborne troops was compromised even before they deployed to an active theatre of war. If they had difficulty in working alongside other US paratroopers, what chance they would accept the directions of a foreign tank commander?

Military journals have been filled with discussions about the problems of elitism and the effects of the phenomenon on all arms operations. In terms of general military history, however, elitism sells. History is, as has already been said, a commodity. The image of the elite soldier as a heroic renegade is attractive and is popularised in comics, films, computer games and, not least, in the massive SAS brand, which, attached to books or even toys ,will guarantee sales. For a certain audience, this is not a problem. Unfortunately, however, elitism is not confined to the mass market. The 'greatest generation' paradigm generated by Tom Brokaw's 1998 book creates the impression that the Americans who went to war in 1941–45 were, in themselves, an elite group simply by having served in some capacity. The book was closely followed by a flood of memoirs written ostensibly for the benefit (most claim) of grandchildren as a kind of inheritance of grandfather's war experience and a sense of ownership of the war itself. They were, however, published commercially. As already pointed out, in order to be an elite, one has to have someone to be better than. If every American who served was of the greatest generation, how then were the paratroopers going to stand out as 'extra-elite' in what was becoming a crowded marketplace? Viewed in this light, we can see a vested interest in a certain mythology being maintained.

Within the field of general popular history it is unavoidable that certain preconceptions will be repeated and accepted as concrete fact. In more specialised military history, it is a problem rarely acknowledged. History is a commodity. Elite histories sell. Therefore, there is profit to be had in writing about elites. There is also an element of reflected glory in writing about Special Forces and heroic actions. Given a choice between a book about paratroopers and one about army cooks, publishers will always go for the former.[4] The result is the emergence of specialist military histories with their own vested interest in promoting a particular view of their subject.

At the beginning of his detailed history of the 82nd Airborne, Nordyke spells out his view of his subjects as being 'held in awe' not only by their airborne colleagues but by everyone who ever encountered them. His work can be seen as an extended hagiography rather than an analysis and it can be read accordingly. Others, however, approach the subject

A German casualty at the side of the road bridge.

more subtly but with a bias towards the airborne every bit the equal of Nordyke's hero worship. Some are histories written by veterans themselves based on interviews with men they served with. Others are memoirs written with varying degrees of accuracy from a limited viewpoint. Yet others are presented as the product of academic research. William Buckingham, for example, completed a PhD on the development of the airborne forces and went on to write about airborne operations, including Operation *Market Garden*. No fan of Browning, Buckingham rightly criticises the empire building antics of the man who, more than any other, undermined the entire plan in an attempt to establish himself as the leading airborne commander of the war.

However, he also, in the author's opinion, ignores much of the evidence in respect of XXX Corps and inflates the professionalism of the airborne element at the expense of the ground troops. Like many others, Buckingham makes inferences based on only one side of the story, thus XXX Corps' advance becomes 'leisurely' and its fighting abilities poor. Whilst one can argue about its speed, not even the veterans of the 82nd who fought alongside the Guards in Nijmegen itself had anything negative to say about their willingness to take risks and casualties.

During the battle in Nijmegen, Private First Class Earl Bolling of the 505th had given a pack of gum to the driver of the second of three Shermans moving up with them towards a traffic roundabout in the city centre. Seconds later, the first tank was hit and caught fire. As the second tried to move past it, it too was hit. The crew attempted to reverse but the vehicle burst into flame and Bolling stood unable to help as the man he had spoken to died in the inferno. A third tank tried to locate the hidden gun but was hit within seconds, its crew pulling back. Bolling's officer, Lieutenant James Coyle, saw the third tank as it

> … went into reverse and backed up about fifty feet to the houses we had just left. I went storming back to the third tank shouting at the commander to get back with us. He said he was hit. I told him he was not hit. I could not see a mark on his tank. A British Sergeant jumped out of the tank and said, 'What's that then mate?' pointing to a large hole on the other side of the turret which I had not seen. I felt about two feet tall. I don't know how that tank took that hit without suffering any wounded or catching fire.

Bolling then witnessed a British Sergeant-Major order another tank to continue up the street. The driver argued that the Germans would destroy it. 'And the Sergeant Major said, "So what. The Yanks will send us another on lend-lease."'[5] These were not the actions of the type of unit the Guards Armoured is so often implied to be in histories of *Market Garden*.

In the final analysis, despite its name, Operation *Market Garden* was not a joint operation to deliver the tanks of XXX Corps to the north of the Rhine. It was an airborne operation to which the tanks of XXX Corps were expected to conform. The concept was of an airborne carpet across which the tanks could speed to Arnhem but that concept fell apart when, instead of finding a series of bridges held open for them and the roads ahead defended, XXX Corps found themselves forging their own path and fighting a running battle to keep their lines of communication open. In order to protect the Airborne Army from the detractors who were increasingly arguing that the days of parachute operations had already passed, Operation *Market* had to be seen as a success. Any failure could not be on the part of the airborne and blame quickly shifted onto the ground forces, a myth grew and continues to grow. XXX Corps were late but by how much no-one seems able to say. No two witnesses seem to agree on just when XXX Corps were meant to be where, or why.

The student of history will search long and hard to find an account of Operation *Market Garden* that gives equal prominence to an analysis of the problems facing the ground forces. At the risk of becoming repetitive it is worth, just once more, doing the maths. The first tanks of XXX Corps crossed the start line on schedule at 1435hrs on D-Day. They crossed the Nijmegen bridge – the final major obstacle to Arnhem – by 2000hrs on D+3. It had taken just under 78 hours. That time is the evidence that condemns them. However, eleven hours had been spent building a bridge after the 101st were unable to capture the Zon crossing. The lead tanks then reached Nijmegen by noon on D+2 but could not secure the bridge until 2000hrs on D+3, 32 hours later. Thus 43 of those 78 hours were delays resulting from the failures of Operation *Market*. If those failures not of XXX Corps' making are discounted, we can see that the lead tanks could have reached the north bank of the Waal within 35 hours of crossing the start line – leaving 13 hours to cover the last ten miles to Arnhem. After deciding to sit by and wait for the tanks to take the bridges themselves, Browning and Gavin made at best a token effort to secure the crossings in advance of the arrival of XXX Corps and yet managed to foster the belief in the rest of the Airborne Army that it was Horrocks' men who lacked a sense of urgency. Because as an elite the airborne were, and are, regarded as the more professional soldiers, the myth quickly spread. Someone had to be seen to be at fault. Therein lies the problem. Politically and commercially, elites are valuable commodities. If anyone was to be held to have failed, too much was invested in the airborne for them to take the fall.

In-fighting and intrigue at all levels blocked communication at every stage of the planning process. Montgomery had even felt the need to exclude American officers from the early stages of planning because he felt sure they would undermine him – as it appears they ultimately did. Meanwhile Washington wanted the paratroops sitting idle in England used for any reason that could be found. SHAEF was looking for an opportunity to experiment. Montgomery had a sound strategic goal and a need to get back at Patton's clique for the loss of face when he was removed as ground commander. Brereton had a new air force and a reputation for breaking his old ones that he needed to dispel if he were to get away from the second-rate position he now saw himself in. Browning was in direct competition with Ridgway and knew his position as Deputy was tenuous. Landing a corps HQ would be a first and put him a step ahead. With all these pressures, Operation *Market Garden* had to go ahead, even if the intelligence reports were beginning to reveal serious German opposition. Into

A body lies amongst stores and silent guns after the battle at Nijmegen.

this mix were placed paratroopers trained to think of themselves as the best of the best; men who owed loyalty first to their unit and to the 'airborne brotherhood' and who regarded all other soldiers as lesser beings. A powerful mix of Anglophobia, anti-Americanism, ambition and the arrogance that marks airborne elitism combined to ensure that to this day, histories of *Market Garden* are almost entirely histories of the airborne operation in which the failure of the ground forces is assumed but never explored.

The story of Operation *Market Garden* is a story of the heroic defence of Arnhem by 1st Airborne, of the opening of 'Hell's Highway' by the 101st and, of course, of the Crossing of the Waal by the 82nd. It is a story of doomed courage and of the skill and determination of the men of the airborne forces. All that is true and nothing here is intended to detract from that. But at the same time, because that story is true, it also serves to preclude any suggestion that Operation *Market*, the phase for which these same men were responsible, was a failure. In the popular imagination, Operation *Market Garden* is all about the quality of the story, not the history.

From the evidence, it would not be difficult to infer that the history of *Market Garden* has been manipulated into something it never was. Firstly, the story of a brilliant airborne success let down by the poor performance of the British was largely one created by the American Commander of the First Allied Airborne Army – with the aid of the American contender for the post of deputy commander – to cover the decision of the American commander of the 82nd Airborne to change the object of the exercise. Further, this cover-up was, of necessity, supported by the British Deputy Commander of the Allied Airborne Army to avoid embarrassing questions about his own competency in interfering with the plans. The British, it could be argued, were in no position to upset their affluent allies.

Eighteen months earlier, in April 1943, the British Eighth Army were about to capture Tunis. Eisenhower's aide, Harry Butcher, noted in his diary for 17 April:

> Mindful of American public opinion – an opinion undoubtedly built up from wishful thinking, that the Americans under Patton should have pushed through to the sea and cut Rommel off as he was retreating in front of the Eighth Army – Ike insisted that General Alexander give the Americans their own sector in the forthcoming and, we hope, final phase of the Tunisian battle … Ike explained to Alexander the home front in America. Ike emphasised the danger to Britain and America if Americans were given to feel that they had not taken an effective part in the conclusion of the Tunisian campaign. Much of our choice equipment, Sherman tanks, as well as ammunition and food, had gone to the British for their use. If the Americans feel we have not played a substantial part they will be even more intent upon prosecution of the war against the Japs and commensurately less interested in the grand strategy of beating Hitler first and Japan second. Alexander was quick to realize this possibility – actually approaching a probability – and readily acceded to the suggestion. So Americans will have their own front and a chance to take a more conspicuous part in the final push … There will be monumental problems of supplying four instead of two divisions.[6]

The message Alexander was given was clear – if the Americans were not seen to be winning the war they would, effectively, pack up and go home. As a result the capture of Tunis was delayed to accommodate US public opinion. Although by late 1944 US troops were too deeply embroiled in Europe for a complete withdrawal to be possible, the threat of a split between the Allies and the impact this might have on British logistics could not be ignored. The failure of *Market Garden* was due to problems in the US sectors but any open criticism would inevitably bring a repeat of the threat to Alexander and so the story of the failure of the ground forces was allowed to grow to avoid a fatal rift in the relationship with Britan's major supplier. Whether this was actually the case should be the subject of further investigation but for now, perhaps it is sufficient to question whether, for Brereton, Ridgway, Gavin et al, the will ever really existed to make the plan work.

It was not in American interests that *Market Garden* should succeed. If it had, Eisenhower might have been forced to throw his weight behind the despised Montgomery. In an election year, what was militarily sound was not politically sound. The American public, it was claimed, would not tolerate the thought that the war might be ended under British leadership. Far better to prolong it and have an American victory. If this seems absurd, it should be remembered that only ten years before, American business interests had been shown to have been the dominant reason for US entry into the First World War, with claims that they too had prolonged hostilities for their own ends. No soldier fights as well for a cause he does not believe in. It was in American interests for Montgomery's plan to fail. It was in Ridgway's interest for Browning to fail. It was in Gavin's interests that Ridgway took the senior post in the Allied Airborne. It was certainly in the Allied Airborne Army's interests that they were not seen to have failed. Gavin described how, after the war, the US Military Academy at West Point claimed Arnhem as an American victory. It is easy to see why some might see it as such.

The crossing of the Waal by the 504th PIR has rightly earned a place in military history as an example of what can be achieved by well led, aggressive infantry. But, like so many examples of spectacular courage by the men on the ground, it was brought about by the failure of their leaders. For Brereton, Operation *Market Garden* was a chore taking him away from the bombing offensive where he felt he really belonged. For Browning it was a chance to find personal glory in the deeds of others. For Bradley and Patton, drawing resources away from the British and undermining the airborne meant they could watch Montgomery fall on his face. Montgomery himself, so determined to be proved right, chose not to see the warning signs. Eisenhower, pouring oil on troubled waters, tried to please everyone and ended up pleasing no-one.

And, as their commanders bickered, brave soldiers died. John Holabird, who had led the 307th Engineers during the crossing later recalled how impressed he had been when, during a period he and his 'were doing nothing constructive', he watched a column of British tanks halt for a break. The crews produced a football and began an impromptu match. The sight impressed Holabird who saw them as motivated, professional soldiers. It was much later on, though, that he would he would look back on that moment and reflect that he and his men were sitting around watching the British play soccer. Neither group seemed in any particular hurry to get to Arnhem and if the British could be accused of taking a relaxed approach, he said, there had been no sense of urgency amongst the Americans either.[7]

The men who fought in Operation *Market Garden* were not, despite how they are now sometimes remembered, supermen. They were ordinary young men from ordinary families who were asked to do extraordinary things and, somehow, did them. They deserve to be remembered with pride but they also deserve to be remembered honestly for what they truly were – frail, fallible and all too human – not for what others have tried to make them. That is the debt history owes them and one that stories cannot pay.

Notes

1   'U571 Writer regrets "distortion".' BBC News 18 August 2006.
2   Neillands p.36
3   Nordyke p.23
4   As an example of an 'heroic' attempt by a publisher to swim against the tide, see Spellmount's *No Labour, No Battle: Military Labour in the First World War* by John Starling and Ivor Lee (2009). A fine history but perhaps commercially perilous.
5   Nordyke pp.498–9
6   Butcher pp.243–4
7   Sliz, J. *Assault Boats on the Waal*. Published by Lulu.com 2009

Bibliography

Books

Adams, M.C.C., 'Postwar Mythmaking About World War II,' in Stoler and Gustafson, ed., *Major Problems in the History of World War II* (Cengage Learning 2002)

Astor, G., *The Greatest War: Americans in Combat, 1941–1945* (Presidio Press 1999)

Barnett, C., *The Collapse of British Power* (Eyre Methuen 1972)

Bennett, D., A Magnificent Disaster (Casemate 2008)

Blair, C., *Ridgway's Paratroopers: The American Airborne in World War II* (The Dial Press 1985)

Bradley, General O., *Soldier's Story* (Henry Holt 1951)

Brereton, General L.H., *Narrative of Operations in Holland 1944*
The Brereton Diaries: The War in the Air in the Pacific, Middle East and Europe, 3 October 1941–8 May 1945 (William Morrow 1946)

Breuer, W., *Drop Zone Sicily: Allied Airborne Strike, July 1943* (Presidio Press 1983)
Geronimo (St Martin's Press 1990)

Brighton, T., *Masters of Battle: Monty, Patton and Rommel at War* (Viking 2008)

Brokaw, T., *The Greatest Generation* (Random House 1998)

Burriss, T.M., *Strike and Hold* (Dulles: Brassey's 2000)

Butcher, Captain H.C., *My Three Years with Eisenhower* (Heinemann 1946)

Carter, R., *Those Devils in Baggy Pants* (Bucaneer Books 1951)

Chatterton, G., *The Wings of Pegasus* (London 1962)

Clark, G.B., *Devil Dogs-Fighting Marines of World War I* (Presidio Press 1999)

Clark, General M.W., *Calculated Risk: The War Memoirs of a Great American General* (Enigma Books 2007)

Cohen, E.A., *Commandos and Politicians* (Harvard University Press 1978)

Cooper, B.Y., *Death Traps: The Survival of an American Armored Division in World War II* (Presidio Press 1998)

Corrigan, G., *Mud, Blood and Poppycock* (Cassell 2003)
Blood, Sweat and Arrogance and the Myths of Churchill's War (Phoenix 2007)

Dank, M., *The Glider Gang* (Cassell 1977)

Davis, F.M. Jr., *Across The Rhine* (Time Life Books 1980)

Devlin, G.M., *Paratrooper!* (Robson Books 1979)
Silent Wings (New York 1985)

du Picq, Colonel A., *Battle Studies: Ancient and Modern Battle* (translated from the eighth edition by Colonel J.N. Greeley and Major R.C. Cotton, US Army 1921)

Dupuy, T.N., *Numbers, Predictions and War: The Use of History to Evaluate and Predict the Outcome of Armed Conflict* (Fairfax 1985)

Eisenhower, D., *Crusade in Europe* (New York 1947)

Eltinge, Captain L., *Psychology of War* (Department of Military Art, the Army Service Schools Fort Leavenworth, Kansas 1911)

Essame, H., *Patton: A Study in Command* (Charles Scribners Sons 1974)

Fleming, P., *Invasion 1940* (Rupert Hart Davies 1957)

French, D., *Raising Churchill's Army* (Oxford University Press 2000)

Gavin, J., *Airborne Warfare* (Washington DC 1947)

 On to Berlin (Bantam 1979)

General Staff, *Infantry Training Part I* (HMSO 1944)

Gilbert, M., *Churchill and America* (Simon & Schuster 2005)

Gill, R. & Groves, J., *Club Route in Europe: the Story of 30 Corps in the European Campaign* (Hannover 1946)

Graham, D. and Bidwell, S., *Coalitions, Politicians and Generals* (London 1993)

Hart, S.A., *Montgomery and Colossal Cracks: The 21st Army Group in Northwest Europe, 1944–45* (Praeger Publishers 2000)

HMSO, *By Air to Battle: The Official Account of the British Airborne Divisions* (London 1945)

Hibbert C., *The Battle of Arnhem* (Macmillan 1962)

Hogan, DW., *Account of the US Army in Europe prepared for the US Army Center of Military History*, accessed at: http://www.history.army.mil/brochures/norfran/norfran.htm)

Holt, Major and Mrs, *Battlefield Guide: Operation Market Garden* (Pen & Sword 2004)

Holmes, R., *Firing Line* (Jonathan Cape 1985)

Horrocks, General Sir B., *A Full Life* (Collins 1960

 Corps Commander (Magnum Books 1977)

Howlett, P., *Fighting with Figures: A Statistical Digest of the Second World War* (HMSO 1995)

Jones, J.P., and Hollister, P.M., *The German Secret Service in America 1914–1918* (Small, Maynard & Co. 1918)

Kershaw, R., *It Never Snows in September* (Crowood Press 2009)

Killblane, R. and McNeice, J., *The Filthy Thirteen: From the Dustbowl to Hitler's Eagle's Nest* (Casemate 2003)

Kitchen, M., 'Elites in Military History' in *Elite Formations in War and Peace*, eds. A. Hamish Ion and Keith Neilson (Praeger 1996)

Knightley, P., *The First Casualty* (Pan Books 1975)

Leckie, R., *The Wars Of America* (Harper & Row 1968)

Longden, S., *To the Victor the Spoils* (Arris Books 2004)

Lowden, J.L., *Silent Wings at War* (Smithsonian Institute 1992)

MacDonald. C.B., *The US Army in World War II: The Siegfried Line Campaign* (Office of the Chief of Military History 1963)

Magellas, J., *All the Way to Berlin* (Ballantyne Books 2003)

Mayo, L., *United States Army in World War II: The Technical Services* (Center of Military History. US Army Washington DC 1991)

 United States Army in World War II: The Ordnance Department (Center of Military History. US Army Washington DC 1991)

 United States Army in World War II: On Beachhead and Battlefront (Center of Military History. US Army Washington DC 1991)

Montgomery, B.L., *Normandy to the Baltic* (Hutchinson & Co 1947)

 Memoirs (Cleveland 1958)

Moorehead, A., *Eclipse* (Hamish Hamilton 1945)

Morris, E., *Churchill's Private Armies* (Hutchinson, 1986)

Mugridge, I., *The View from Xanadu: William Randolph Hearst and United States Foreign Policy* (McGill-Queen's University Press 1995)

Nofi, A.A., (ed) *The War Against Hitler: Military Strategy in the West* (Hippocrene Books 1982)

Nordyke, P., *All American, All the Way* (Zenith Press 2005)

Overy, R. and Wheatcroft, A., *The Road to War* (Penguin 2000)

Patton, R.H., *The Pattons: A Personal History of an American Family* (Brassey's, 2004)

Perrault, G., *Les Parachutistes* (Éditions du Seuil 1961)

Pogue, F.C., *The Supreme Command* (Washington 1951)

Powell, G., *The Devil's Birthday* (Leo Cooper 1984)

Province, C.M., *The Unknown Patton* (Hippocrene Books 1983)

Rosse, Captain the Earl of, and Hill, Colonel E. *The Story of the Guards Armoured Division* (Geoffrey Bles 1956

Ryan, C.A., *Bridge Too Far* (Book Club Associates 1975)

Saunders, T., *Nijmegen* (Leo Cooper 2001)

Seth, R., *The Lion with Blue Wings* (Panther Books 1959)

Shannon, K. and Wright, S., *One Night in June* (Airlife Publishing 1994)

Shillingberg, W.B., 'A Gathering of Generals' originally published in Johns' Western Gallery auction catalogue 14: *The Vandenberg Military Collection* (San Francisco 2005)

Toplin, R.B., *History by Hollywood: The Use and Abuse of the American Past* (University of Illinois Press 1996)

US War Department, *Instructions for US Servicemen in Britain* (Washington 1942)

Whicker, A., *Whicker's War* (HarperCollins 2005)

Whiting, C., *A Traveller's Guide to the Battle for the German Frontier* (Windrush Press 2000)

Wimott, C., *The Struggle for Europe* (London 1952)

Wilson, H.W., and Hammerton, J.A. (eds) *The Great War* Volume 6 (Amalgamated Press 1916)

Articles/Reports

DDE Office Memorandum, 5 September 1944, *The Eisenhower Papers*, Volume IV

Doenecke, J.D., 'American Isolationism, 1939–1941' *Journal of Libertarian Studies* Vol VI No.3–4 (Summer/Fall 1982)

Foster, J.B., 'After the Attack ... The War on Terrorism' *Monthly Review* 53 (6): 7 (November 2001)

Gough, L., 'Parachutists Want it Tough' *Liberty* 4 December 1943

Horne, Colonel B., 'The Devil's Playground: The Airborne Battlefield in World War II' *Canadian Army Journal* 7.4 (Winter 2004)
'The Dark Side to Elites: Elitism as a Catalyst for Disobedience' *Canadian Army Journal* 8.4 (Winter 2005)

Leland, A. and Oboroceanu, M.J., 'American War and Military Operations Casualties: Lists and Statistics' (Congressional Research Service 26 February 2010)

Steele, J.L., 'Time Essay: How real is Neo-Isolationism?' *Time* 31 May 1971

Nye, J.V.C., 'Killing Private Ryan: An Institutional Analysis of Military Decision Making in World War II' draft prepared for the ISNIE conference in Boston 2002

Newspapers/Magazines

Colliers 11 December 1943
Milwaukee Journal 'Patton waded ashore to lead attack that drove out tanks' 14 July 1943
New York Times 16 September 1939
New York Daily News, cited by Robert Rice Reynolds, Congressional Record, 6 January 1941
Time 4 May 1942

US Army Command and General Staff College Combined Arms

Research Library, Fort Leavenworth

Operational Orders
Operation *Market*: Preliminary Tactical Study of the Terrain. HQ US XVIII Corps Airborne 11 September 1944
US Troop Carrier Command, Annex 6 to Field Order 4 13 September 1944
82nd Airborne Division, Orders 13 September 1944
    Chief of Staff Journal, 1944
504th PIR, Administrative Order 13 September 1944
    Intelligence Briefing
508th PIR, Administrative Order No1)

Reports
21 Army Group, 'Operation Market Garden 17–26 September 1944'
US War Department, 'Headquarters 1st Allied Airborne Army: Task Force for Operation Market 11 September 1944'
    'Operational Study No.17 Bakery and Coffee Roasting Operations 1 November 1945'
    'A Graphic History of the 82nd Airborne Division *c*. 1945'
US Air Force, 'Airborne Operations in World War II European Theatre Historical Study No 97'
US Army, 'A Historical Study of Some WWII Airborne Operations' Weapons Systems Evaluation Group (WSEG) Staff Study No3 1951
    'Strategy of the Campaign in Western Europe 1944–45' European Theater Study Number 1
    'Report on Airborne Phase' 17–27 September 1944 Headquarters XVIII Corps 1944
    'Combat Lessons of 82nd Airborne Division AGF Report 440' HQ ETO War Observers Board
Carpenter, D.C., 'A Failure of Coalition Leadership: The Falaise–Aregentan Gap' (US Army War College 2002)
Fox, Lieutenant Colonel J.B., 'Lessons Learned From Operation Market Garden' USAF Air University Report April 1994
Green, Major W.V., 'Operation Market Garden' USAF Air University Air Command and Staff College March 1984
Jefferson, J.J., 'Operation Market Garden: Ultra Intelligence Ignored' School of Advanced Military Studies, US Army Command and General Staff College, May 2002

Infantry School, Fort Benning, Georgia

Johnson, K.L., 'Supply Operations of the 508th Parachute Infantry Regiment in the Invasion of Holland Arnhem Operation 15–19 September 1944' (Rhineland Operations) (1950)

Kappel, C.W., 'The Operations of H Company 504th Parachute Infantry (82nd Airborne Division) in the Invasion of Holland 17–21 September, 1944' (Rhineland Campaign) (1949)

Phillips, J.D., 'Operations of the 3rd Platoon, Company 'E' 505th Parachute Infantry Regiment (82nd Airborne Division) in the Seizure of the Nijmegen Bridge 19–20 September 1944 (Operation of the 1st Allied Airborne Army in the Invasion of Holland)' (Holland Campaign) (1948)

Sickler, R., 'Operations of Company 'D', 2nd Battalion 508th Parachute Infantry Regiment (82nd Airborne Division) at Nijmegen, Holland, 17–18 September 1944' (Rhineland Campaign, European Theatre of Operations) (1948)

Imperial War Museum

Briggs MSS 66/76/1 8th Army Training Memorandum No.1, 30 August 1942

Museum of Army Flying, Middle Wallop, Hampshire

064/83 Operation Market Garden

National Archives. London

PRO WO 171/1254 War Diary 2 Grenadier Guards (Armoured Battalion)
PRO WO 205/1125 Report on Operations at Nijmegen)
PRO WO 231/14 Lieutenant-Colonel Wigram to Directorate of Military Training. Reports from Overseas No.15 Section 1, 16 August 1943
PRO WO 285/13 Casualties and Ammunition, 2nd Army 1944–45

Internet Sources

Pavia, T., 'An American Town Goes to War' (Turner Pub Co 1995) accessed via Stamford Historical Society website at http://www.stamfordhistory.org/ww2_kaslikowski.htm
Pitt, T., 'The Waal River Crossing', an interview with Thomas Pitt, S-1, Third Battalion, 504th Parachute Regiment Interview by Thomas Pitt Jr with his father in 1992 Accessed via http://www.101st-airborne.net/holland/interviewcrossing.htm

Index

Adair, General Allan 77 125
Adams, Michael C.C. 5
Alexander, Field Marshal Sir H. 30, 38, 39
Allied Airborne Army 51–68 passim, 75,
    107, 110, 130, 160, 162, 169, 180–1
Antwerp 33–35, 51, 54, 129
Anzio 38, 83–85, 127
Argentan 31–2
Arnhem 9–10, 13–14, 53–4, 57, 63, 65
    68–70, 72–4, 113–121, 127, 148–57,
    164–5, 169–70, 172–3, 179–8

Bradley, General Omar 12, 16, 27, 30–38,
    47–56, 62, 74, 81, 165, 170, 181
Brereton, General Lewis 51–3, 58, 60–75
    passim, 110, 124, 129, 161–2, 165,
    169–71, 179, 181
Bridges
  Grave 53, 63, 67–70, 72–3, 99, 102,
    110, 121, 115–6, 158, 162, 172
  Heumen Lock (Bridge 7) 102
  Honinghutie (Bridge 10) 103, 116
  Malden (Bridge 8) 102
  Mook Railway 70, 104
  Nijmegen 9, 67, 69, 70–2, 113–4, 116,
    143, 150–4, 160–169, 179, 186
  Zon (Son) 63, 108–110, 115–7, 161–2,
    172, 179
British Units
  21st Army Group 36, 41, 53, 57–8, 60,
    72, 75, 97, 109, 145, 150, 152, 155, 165,
    169–70, 183
  Second Army 13, 30, 54, 57, 62–3,
    68–71, 93, 107, 161–2, 164, 172
Corps
  1st British Airborne 60–2, 130

VIII Corps 13, 63, 109, 126, 168
XII Corps 13, 63, 109, 166
XXX Corps 13, 30, 35, 63–5, 70, 73–4,
    87, 90, 95–6, 98, 103–4, 107–10, 112,
    114–7, 119–21, 126–8, 130–1, 153,
    158–64, 170–3, 178–9
Divisions, Airborne
  1st Airborne 9, 51, 53–4, 63, 66, 69–70,
    79, 113, 115, 117, 119, 154, 160, 163,
    165, 171–3, 180
  6th Airborne 60–1, 66, 80, 125, 159
Divisions, Armoured
  Guards Armoured 9, 77, 86–7, 90, 110,
    115–6, 125, 130, 147, 149–52, 154,
    160, 162–3, 171, 174, 179, 185, 187
  11th Armoured 35
Divisions, Infantry
  3rd Infantry 30
  7th Infantry 6
  43rd Infantry 90–1, 125, 150, 171
  50th Infantry 6, 30, 90, 111
  59th Infantry 30
Brigades
  32 Guards 114
  Polish Airborne 53, 59, 61, 63, 157, 159,
    171
Regiments
  Grenadier Guards 86, 89, 109, 114, 119,
    174, 187
  2nd (Armoured) Battalion 109
  Household Cavalry 114
  Irish Guards 64, 86, 107, 109–11, 133,
    145, 152, 163
  Nottinghamshire Yeomanry 149
Other units
  Glider Pilot Regiment 65, 69, 86

Royal Engineers 81, 114, 126, 130, 136, 143

'Broad Front' Strategy 31, 37–8, 49, 50, 54, 165–7

Brockaw, Tom 4

Browning, General F.A.M. 'Boy' 51, 57–64, 68–9, 71, 73–5, 107–8, 112–21, 125–7, 130, 141, 150, 160, 162–5, 167, 171–3, 178–9, 181

Burriss, Captain M.T. 9, 14, 67, 84, 127–9, 134–5, 141, 144, 155, 159, 183

Butcher, Captain Harry 43, 45, 48, 56, 181–3

Carrington, Captain Lord P. 89, 97, 148

Carter, Sergeant Ross 6, 84–5, 96, 102, 155, 158

Chatterton, Colonel G. 65, 86, 96, 127

Churchill, Prime Minister W. 12, 24–5, 27, 37, 44–6, 58–9, 79

Clark, General Mark 38–39, 49, 61, 82–3

Coffee roasting operations 8

Cook, Major J. 129, 131–3, 142–3, 154, 156–7

Dempsey, General Sir M. 13, 57, 68–9, 85, 91, 109–10, 162, 164, 173

Down, Brigadier Eric 163

Du Picq, Colonel Ardant 11, 13, 174

Dupuy, Colonel Trevor 6

Eindhoven 63, 68–9, 102, 109–11, 113, 115–6, 120, 129, 136, 161–3, 170

Eisenhower, General D.D. 12, 27, 30–1, 39–55, 57, 60–1, 68, 74, 82–3, 164, 166, 168, 181–2

El Alamein 37, 44–5, 90, 95

Elitism 77, 80–1, 84, 86, 96, 174, 177, 180

Falaise 31–2, 71

Gavin, General J. 8, 11–4, 31, 49, 61–77 passim, 82–3, 85–6, 99–107, 111, 113–4, 119–31, 149, 152, 155–7, 162–3, 165, 169, 171–3, 177, 179, 181

German Forces

Armies

  7th Army 32

10th Army 38

14th Army 38

15th Army 32

Corps

  II SS Corps 107, 114, 151, 168

Divisions, Infantry

  406th Ersatz 106, 112–7

Divisions, Panzer

  9th Hoenstaufen SS 106, 109, 114

  10th SS 106

Kampfgruppe

  Frundsberg 106

  Gobel 112

  Henke 106

  Reinhold 114

  Walther 64

'Greatest Generation' 4–7, 174, 176–7

Groesbeek 68–73, 122, 124–5, 103–5, 172

Hodges, General 39, 166–7

Holabird, Lieutenant J. 136, 175, 182

Horrocks, General B. 35, 63, 95, 107–9, 116, 125–8, 143, 145, 154–5, 171, 179

Isolationism in the United States 15–26, 41, 175

Italy 4, 6, 21–2, 27, 38–9, 61, 69, 83–6

Jones, Lieutenant A.G.C. 'Tony' RE 143

Jonkers Bosche 128

Kappell, Captain C. 11, 96, 126–9, 131–7, 141, 151, 154, 168

Keep, Captain 132, 134, 154

Kuehl, Chaplain Delbert 133

Lee, General J.C.H. 33–34

Leigh-Mallory, Air Marshal Sir T. 30, 39, 52

Lend-Lease 24–25

Lindquist, Colonel Roy E. 69, 105–7, 111–2

Magellas, Lieutenant J. 9, 14, 84, 86, 128–9, 131–2, 135, 148, 153–4, 159

Market Garden see Operation *Market Garden*

Metz 11–2, 14, 51, 165–6

Model, Field Marshal 16, 106, 112, 114, 142, 171–2

Montgomery, Field Marshal B.L. 9, 10, 12–3, 28, 34–75 passim, 90–1, 95–6, 115, 121, 162, 164–5, 167–8, 170, 179, 181–2
Mook 70, 104, 129

Nijmegen 9, 12–3, 53, 62–3, 67–74, 85–6, 95, 100–28 passim, 137–56, 160–80 passim
Nordyke, Phil 6, 70, 77, 178
Normandy 7, 27, 30–1, 33, 35, 39, 41, 48–9, 52–3, 61–2, 66, 68–9, 80–1, 83, 86, 90–1, 95, 100, 125, 129, 153, 159, 175–6
Norton, Captain John 67, 98

Operation *Cobra* 31, 52
Operation *Comet* 57–77, 165, 169
Operation *Fortitude* 30
Operation *Husky* 41
Operation *Linnet* 53, 62
Operation *Overlord* 37, 48
Operation *Market Garden* 7, 9–13, 16, 18, 20, 22, 24, 26, 28, 32, 34, 36, 40–129 passim, 130, 134, 136, 138, 140–181 passim

Patton 10, 12–4, 27–8, 31–2, 24, 38–55 passim, 74, 80, 82, 93–4, 149, 165–6, 179, 181
Profiteering in WW1 19, 20, 22, 175
Press 12, 36, 39, 41, 42, 49

Ramsay, Admiral B. 19, 21, 30, 39
'Red Ball Express' 33
Ridgway, General M. 27, 61–2, 73–4, 81, 83, 86, 116, 123, 129–30, 179, 181
Robinson, Sergeant Peter 141–146
Royal Air Force 39, 43, 45, 54, 61, 64–5, 78, 88, 122, 126, 169, 176

Sherman Tank M4 91–94, 129, 135–6, 141, 145, 152–3, 158, 169, 178, 181
Siegfried Line 51–2
Sosabowski, General 59, 63, 153, 171
Supreme Headquarters Allied Expeditionary Force (SHAEF) 13, 31–4, 39, 49, 51, 53, 55, 63, 91, 108, 159, 171, 179

Taylor, General M. 63–4, 68, 82, 109–10, 123, 171
Towle, Private John 155
Tuck, Sapper Roy 136–140
Tucker, Colonel R 66, 82–85, 96, 115, 127–9, 135, 141–2, 149, 153–7

Urquhart, General R. 63, 66–8, 73–4, 77, 96, 111, 114–5, 150, 155, 160, 162–4, 169, 171, 173

US Army
Army Groups
 First Army Group 48
 12th Army Group 33, 53
Armies
 First Army 48, 53, 57, 62, 166
 Third Army 31, 40, 46, 48, 165–6
 Fifth Army 38–9
Corps
 XV Corps 31–2
 XVIII Airborne Corps 62, 83, 155
Divisions, Airborne
 17th Airborne 83
 82nd Airborne 5–6, 8–9, 12, 31, 61, 63, 66, 68–9, 71, 77, 80–1, 96, 100, 110, 113, 119, 125, 128, 155, 174, 177, 180
 101st Airborne 5, 60, 63, 66, 68, 80, 87, 110, 162
Regiments
 307th Airborne Engineer 83, 128, 132, 175
 504th Parachute Infantry Regiment (PIR) 9, 11, 66–8, 72, 80–6, 96, 98, 101–3, 114–5, 125–32, 143, 149, 154–8, 172, 174, 181
 'H' Company 98, 127, 132–3, 136, 157
 'I' Company 127, 136
 505th PIR 82, 102, 104, 111, 113, 149, 154, 177–8
 506th PIR 80, 85, 109
 508th PIR..8, 13, 69, 100, 103, 105–7, 111, 113–4, 116, 124
 509th 82
US Army Air Force 60, 169
 IX Troop Carrier Command 60, 65
Valkenswaard 108–11, 161
Vandervoort, Colonel 143
Warren, Colonel S. 105–7, 112–3
Wurst, Sergeant Spencer 154

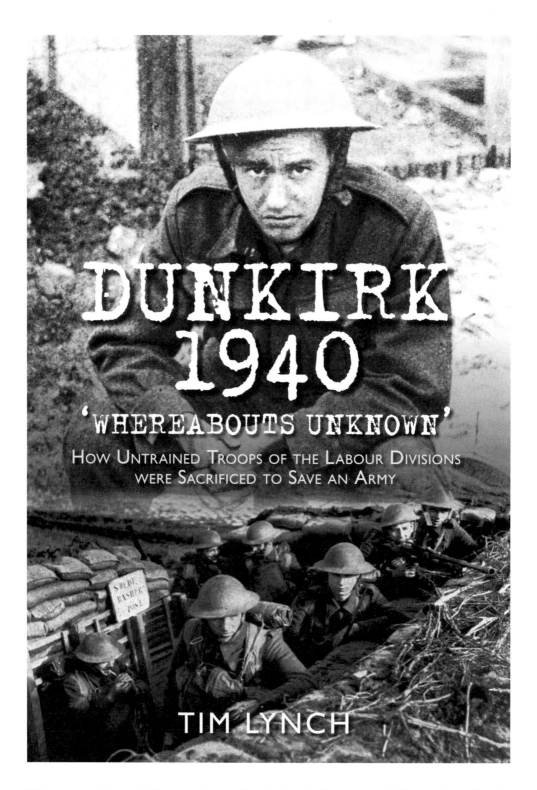

DUNKIRK 1940

'WHEREABOUTS UNKNOWN'

How Untrained Troops of the Labour Divisions
were Sacrificed to Save an Army

TIM LYNCH

Visit our website and discover thousands of other Spellmount and History Press books.

www.thehistorypress.co.uk

THE CHURCH OF ST MARY THE VIRGIN

ELLAND

A HISTORY

Anthony Murphy

Anthony Murphy

for Joan with best wishes.

Published by Elland St Mary's Parish Church Council

www.acny.org.uk/elland-st-mary-the-virgin

ISBN 978-1-3999-3869-3

Printed by

The Amadeus Press

Printed by Amadeus Press, Ezra House, West 26 Business Park, Cleckheaton, West Yorkshire BD19 4TQ

www.amadeuspress.co.uk

CONTENTS

All photographs were taken by the author except where stated otherwise.

Preface iv

Foreword. v

Introduction and Acknowledgments. vi

Glossary of architectural terms. viii

Plan of St Mary's Church. x

Chapter 1. *Beginnings: The Eland Family and the Foundation of St Mary's.* 1

Chapter 2. *The Church Building, exterior and interior: Chancel, Chapels, Nave* 3

Chapter 3. *Elland Charter and the fall of the Eland family* 9

Chapter 4. *The Savile family and the extended east end and west tower.* 11

Chapter 5. *Medieval stained glass: the Great East Window and other fragments.* 14

Chapter 6. *Victorian painted glass.* 32

Chapter 7. *Interior burials and memorial tablets.* 42

Chapter 8. *Interior furnishings: font, pulpit, seating.* 51

Chapter 9. *Former galleries, organs, choir, bells and clocks.* 55

Chapter 10. *Vestries, sculpture, masons' marks, 19th and 20th century restorations.* 63

Chapter 11. *Parish chests, Parish records, silver plate, graveyard burials.* 72

Chapter 12. *Canon Winter and the foundation of All Saints.* 81

Chapter 13. *List of St Mary's incumbents.* 84

List of Books and Sources consulted 91

About the author 93

PREFACE

by REV'D CANON DAVID BURROWS, RECTOR OF ELLAND

It is perhaps surprising that the story of the Church of St Mary the Virgin, Elland, in all its 850 years, has never really been told. It is an unpretentious building from the outside, giving little hint of the glories within. There exists a learned article or two here and there, and a brief volume from the 1950s, which, together with a colour brochure produced to mark 800 years in 1980, do surface from time to time. I am delighted that Tony Murphy has been able to bring this current work to publication, and ensure that the story of St Mary's is now made available to a wider audience. He has an historian's understanding of the bigger picture and the wider context, together with an artistic fascination for the beauty of the detail, especially of the coloured glass, and brings out the human fascination of the characters who have found a spiritual home in this place.

Elland in the 21st Century remains, paradoxically, both a popular place to live, and a community within the top 10% nationally of deprivation. Seemingly overlooked by more powerful and noisy neighbours, it is still what keeps Halifax and Huddersfield apart. Its ancient Parish Church tells the story of this community in a way that no other building can, and is above all else a place of encounter with the divine; it was built to the glory of God, and God is still worshipped here in all the changes and chances of life.

I hope that you will enjoy reading this book.

FOREWORD

We were thrilled and honoured when asked to write a Foreword to Tony's latest work. As members of the Greater Elland Historical Society, we are delighted to support this project.

Tony Murphy has produced a masterpiece of historical evidence. His diligence and determined research has allowed him to give the reader a deeper understanding of the growth of St Mary's Church over the centuries. Even if you have visited the church regularly this book will enhance your knowledge and help you to focus on the skilled craftsmanship and beauty of this most valuable of Elland's buildings. If St Mary's Church and the local area are new to you this book will give you a greater understanding of its development and importance.

We were able to pass a little information on to Tony regarding his text. As a genuine historian he gratefully accepted these additions and passed on his thanks. His work is informative and easy to read, beautifully illustrated and acts as a guide and reference book. Tony is an historian who by researching the past is helping to preserve our heritage – Elland's Heritage.

Read, reflect, and rejoice that a local author has such respect for - and desire to promote - our history.

**Andrew Gilmour (Chair) and David Glanfield (Life Member)
of the Greater Elland Historical Society.
GEHS Founded 1974**

INTRODUCTION AND ACKNOWLEDGMENTS

My interest in and love for St Mary's Church goes back to my teenage years when I first joined its large, mixed choir and was prepared for confirmation. In those early 1960s there was plenty to engage young people. In addition to the choir and Servers' Guild, most of us were in the AYPA - the Anglican Young People's Association - and attended regular dances in the Parochial Hall where there was also an annual pantomime. The Church Lads' Brigade was thriving, meeting weekly in the hall at All Saints and organising summer camps and supporting its own brass band. There were opportunities, too, for service and several of us visited the housebound and unwell, with Bible readings and prayers and assisted with Sunday School teaching. I early on made many friends in the church and even wrote a (very) short history of the St Mary's in my school's magazine, The Ealandian: my first venture into writing about history.

Today, sadly, most of these organisations are gone, along with a lively presence of young people, many of whom nowadays do not tend to join societies and communal ventures. Indeed, the congregation itself consists largely of more mature people, many of whom have grown up in Elland and worshipped in St Mary's all their lives.

What struck me in researching the history of the church was the recurrence of several family surnames through the ages. Some names have died out but more remain to this day. It is highly likely that there are hundreds of people in Elland and in the surrounding villages - for Elland's parish stretched for miles around - have ancestors who were baptised, married and buried at St Mary's. It is a fact that, until the early 19th century, St Mary's Church was the *only* legal place for these rites of passage for those who lived in the extensive Parish of Elland.

My own family on my mother's side (the Haberghams) is a case in point. On the second page of the 1559 Church Registers I noticed that John Clay of Clay House married Marjery Savile of Bradley Hall, the sister of Sir John and Sir Henry Savile, who both figure in this book. John Clay and Marjery's granddaughter, Elizabeth, co-heiress of the Clays, married John Habergham of Habergham Hall near Burnley, in St Mary's Church in 1649. Their son Clay Habergham married local girl Jane Bairstow also in St Mary's and from then on their descendants continued to figure regularly in the parish records. This kind of connection is, I'm sure, replicated in scores of other local people's backgrounds and is not at all unusual. St Mary's Church played a vital role in everyone's lives down the centuries from its foundation in late Norman times.

St Mary's Church is by far the oldest building in Elland. When it was founded in the 1170s it would probably have been the only stone edifice for miles around as most dwellings, including Elland Hall - the seat of the Lord of the Manor - would have then been built of timber. Its position at The Cross would have given St Mary's prominence amongst the humble dwellings of its parishioners. This prominence would be further enhanced once the west tower was added in around 1490. Today, it may seem less conspicuous against the 1970s blocks of flats ranged along its south face. That decade changed fundamentally the appearance of 'Olde Elland'. Nevertheless, St Mary's still stands as a witness to the long history of Elland and remains a constant presence of Christian worship in the town. Long may this continue.

This book is aimed primarily at the general reader with an interest in history, though I hope that the specialist historian and art historian will also find it of interest. My own academic background is partly in medieval art and architectural history and I do adopt the terminology of these disciplines. I hope that the glossary of terms and plan of the church at the front of the book will help those who are less familiar with this somewhat esoteric language. I considered including an index but as the contents page and chapter headings are fairly descriptive I decided against it. I also rejected footnotes as I felt these would be a distraction though a list of the sources I consulted can be found at the end of the book. I have followed a roughly chronological plan in this history, weaving architectural detail with the leading families - the Elands moving on to the Saviles and Thornhills - as their influence on the development of the church up to the 17th century was crucial. This means that I return to discuss areas of the church already visited as changes took place through time, particularly in the restoration of the church in the mid 19th century.

I am extremely grateful to a number of people who have given invaluable help in the research and writing of this history. First and foremost I thank Fr David Burrows, our Rector, for his encouragement and his assistance in providing crucial information about various aspects of the church's history and of many of its many treasures. Peter Uttley, Churchwarden during most of my research, has provided constant, kindly advice and support and has been unfailingly generous in sharing his own research and knowledge about St Mary's. His wife, Judith - our Church Secretary - has likewise been a constant source of help and encouragement as well as giving time to proof-read the drafts of my text with an unfailingly perceptive eye.

Two former Churchwardens have kindly shared their knowledge and expertise: Glenn Littlewood, gave invaluable help in mounting ladders to photograph otherwise out of reach wall plaques and windows, in addition to visiting Elland Library to photograph the ancient parish chest; Geoff Scott, whose familiarity with masons' marks, the rare sculptured head, the graveyard's monuments and the whereabouts of Thompson's mice in the St Nicholas Chapel, was second to none. The church organist, Joan Woodall, kindly furnished me with the full specification of the organ. The late Edward Gamble - sadly taken from us far too young - a trained architectural draughtsman, pointed out various features in the church from an architect's point of view. I benefited, too, from discussions with contemporaries, notably Fr Philip Chadwick, Donald Haigh and Maurice Linton, who helped to jog my early memories of St Mary's, and from Robert and June Baume, Loraine Lodge and Ian Philp for their kind assistance with material and information.

Two senior members of the Greater Elland Historical Society, Andrew Gilmour and David Glanfield very generously provided fascinating details of the church and its members, particularly during the 19th and early 20th centuries, held in their collections and kindly endorsed this project in their Foreword. My thanks go also to the staff at West Yorkshire Archive Service in Wakefield and The National Archives in Kew for their help and unfailing courtesy. Finally, I am extremely grateful to fellow members of St Mary's Parish Church Council for their support and financial help in bringing this project to the light of day. All income from sales of this book will be be passed on to church funds.

Anthony Murphy

Upper Greetland

October, 2022

GLOSSARY OF TERMS USED IN THE BOOK

Acanthus leaves.	A Mediterranean plant with thick, scallopped leaves.
Angle Volute.	A spiral used at the corners of capitals or edges of other features.
Annulet.	A ring around a circular column or shaft.
Arcade or Arcading.	A series of arches usually supported by columns used ornamentally.
Ashlar.	Squared blocks of stone cut to an even face.
Base.	The moulded foot of a column, usually rested on a plinth.
Bay.	A compartment in a church marked by columns and arcades.
Bead and reel.	Bead-like motifs alternating with cylindrical ones.
Beakhead.	An ornament like a bird's head often found on early arches.
Belfry.	The chamber in a tower where bells are hung.
Bellcote.	A small gabled or roofed housing for a bell or bells.
Boss.	A small ornamental projection, often used on ceilings.
Buttress.	A stone (or brick) structure built against a wall for support.
Capital.	The ornamental top of a column supporting the springing of an arch.
Chalice.	The cup which holds the communion wine.
Ciborium.	A cup with a cover to hold the communion bread.
Crocket, crocketted.	Ornamental hook-shaped leafy knobs on gables or capitals.
Chamfer.	A diagonal surface cut at usually 45 degrees to the other surfaces.
Chancel.	The east end of a church housing the altar, used by clergy and choir.
Corbel.	A projecting block of stone or timber to support a feature above.
Corbel table.	A row of corbels, often carved, supporting roof eaves or a parapet.
Corinthian capital.	A feature on top of a pillar with upright stylised leaves.
Cornice.	A moulded ledge, projecting horizontally upon a feature, eg a screen.
Crypt.	A vaulted chamber below a side chapel or sanctuary of a church.
Cushion capital.	Feature on top of a pillar formed by intersecting a cube and a square.
Cusps, cusped	Projecting points formed at the meeting of the foils (qv).
Depressed Arch.	Arch with a flattened head, popular from the late 15th. century on.

Diaper ornament.	Repetitive geometric decoration, usually lozenges or squares.
Double cone.	Conical mouldings placed end to end in a row.
Engaged pier	Column attached to or partly sunk into a wall or another pier.
Entablature.	Horizontal upper part of a structure supported by columns
Finial.	An ornament on top of a gable, pinnacle etc.
Floriated.	An ornamental flower-like motif.
Foil.	A curved decorative lobe: trefoil (3 cusps), quatrefoil (4 cusps) etc.
Gable.	The triangular upper part of a wall or decoration.
Gargoyle.	A carved grotesque with a spout conveying water from the roof.
Mandorla.	Round or elliptical halo framing the figure of Christ or Virgin Mary
Nave	The main body of a church where the congregation sits.
Ogee arch.	A double continuous S shaped curved arch.
Paten.	A silver plate which holds the bread to be used at the mass.
Parapet.	Low wall projecting from a roof or terrace, often with battlements.
Pediment.	A triangular upper part of a structure.
Pier.	A pillar supporting arches or a roof.
Pilaster.	A rectangular vertical column projecting from a wall.
Plinth.	A projecting stone under the base of a column.
Porch.	A covered projecting entrance.
Pyx.	A small box containing consecrated bread from the mass.
Reredos	Decorated panel above and behind the altar.
Ribs.	Arches forming part of a vault.
Rood.	The cross or crucifix usually on a beam or hung from the ceiling.
Roundel.	A circular ornamental relief.
Sanctuary.	The area immediately around the main altar of a church.
Spur.	An ornamental projection of a base, often carved.
String course.	A horizontal course projecting from a wall, often moulded.
Swag.	An ornamental drooping curve motif.
Transitional Norman.	The architectural change from rounded to Gothic pointed arches.
Triptych.	A picture or relief on three panels.
Voussoir.	Wedge-shaped stones forming an arch.

Plan of the Parish Church of St. Mary the Virgin, Elland

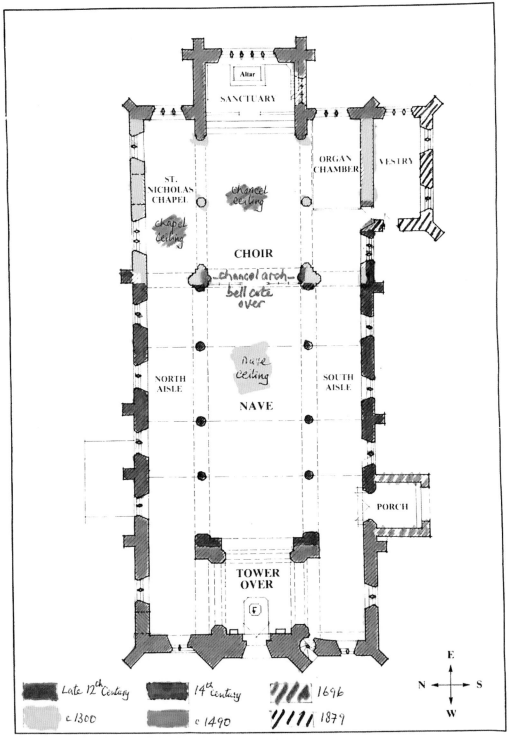

Altar

SANCTUARY

ORGAN CHAMBER

VESTRY

ST. NICHOLAS CHAPEL

chancel ceiling

chapel ceiling

CHOIR

chancel arch – bell cote over

NORTH AISLE

nave ceiling

SOUTH AISLE

NAVE

PORCH

TOWER OVER

F

Late 12ᵗʰ Century   14ᵗʰ Century   1696

c 1300   c 1490   1879

E

N   S

W

1. BEGINNINGS:

THE ELAND FAMILY AND THE FOUNDATION OF ST MARY'S CHURCH

St Mary's Church (a Grade 1 listed building) stands on a mound high above the River Calder and is situated at the convergence of four roads roughly facing the points of the compass. The route east - west was an ancient track which would have aligned with the Roman road over the Pennines at Blackstone Edge connecting York with Chester. The northern route led over the river to Halifax via Exley and the southern track led over the Ainleys (via Blackley) and on eventually towards London. During the Anglo-Saxon period the town of Dewsbury with its church (now Minster) on the eastern route became an important centre of Christianity and it is probable that itinerant missionaries including, possibly, St Paulinus of York carried the Christian message along to the tiny settlement of Elland and built a **preaching cross** on or near the mound. The stone cross no longer exists though the area still bears the name of **The Cross**. Dewsbury Minster now houses several examples of such preaching crosses from the surrounding district.

We know little of Elland until the Norman Conquest when the settlement is mentioned in the Domesday Book of 1086 under the spelling *Elant*, from the Old English *ea* ('water') and *lant* or *land*, referring to its position by the river Calder. William the Conqueror had divided up England between his senior Norman followers after his conquest of 1066. The north of England had initially resisted this domination resulting in the infamous 'Harrying of the North' (1069-70) by Norman forces which reduced what were profitable farmlands to barren wastelands. Elland's entry in the Domesday Book is thus described, along with countless others, as 'waste'.

Its pre-Conquest owner is given the name of 'Gamel', though this is misleading as the name appears several times in the Domesday Book and may well be simply a generic term for an existing Anglo-Saxon lordship. The name itself is the Latin for 'old man,' or in other words, the 'old owner'. Elland now came under the overlordship of the powerful de Laci (or 'Lacy') family, originally from Lassy in Normandy. Ilbert de Laci, head of the family, was based in Pontefract and sub-let many of his 204 manors to local leading families. It is likely that the Eland family were already prominent in the area when they became lords of the manor.

The neighbouring settlement of Halifax was situated in an area given by the king to the de Warrene family. They founded a Cluniac abbey in the outskirts of Lewes in Sussex in around 1081 and to support its endowment various parish churches were built around the country. The church of St John the Baptist in Halifax was one such foundation, built some time after 1147. Elland's increasing population would have had to make the journey north through Exley to Halifax to be baptised, married and buried so it is unsurprising that the idea of the local lord of the manor building a church for his tenants soon took shape.

There is no firm date for the foundation of St Mary's. It is highly likely that a petition by **the Eland family** - possibly Hugh de Eland or his son Richard - to their overlord, now Henry de Laci, bore fruit as the latter had recently helped Cistercian monks to acquire land in

Kirkstall to build an abbey. The abbey buildings were probably completed by the mid-1170s, though the abbey church was in use a few years before this. It is highly likely that some of the masons from Kirkstall came over to Elland to construct the church at around this time as the earliest portion of St Mary's, the transitional Norman chancel arch, contains quite distinct mouldings such as those found in the south nave aisle and south transept at Kirkstall. Although no documentary evidence for a firm dating has yet been found, the architectural style of the chancel arch and bellcote above it suggest a date around the 1170s, during the reign of the first Plantagenet king, Henry 11.

The Eland family manor house (the former Elland Hall, dismantled to make way for the Elland Bypass in 1976) was across the Calder on a rise. It was a cruck-framed timber structure

at this time, though would later be encased in stone. There are several references to members of the de Eland family in charters and lists of benefactions of Fountains Abbey, Nostell Priory, Kirkstall Abbey near Leeds, Stanlaw Abbey in Cheshire and Whalley Abbey near Burnley in Lancashire. Richard de Eland's younger son, Henry, was even buried in Kirkstall Abbey.

At some point they had intermarried with the Rachdale - or Rochdale - family and had inherited lands on the Lancashire side of the Pennines. Indeed, the Eland coat of arms - gules, two bars between eight martlets, three, two and one, argent (red background with eight silver swallows divided between two silver horizontal bars) - is very similar to that of the Rochdale family. By the twelfth century they had also acquired lands, through marriage or purchase, in Rishworth and Cliviger (near Burnley) and a descendant, Sir Hugh de Eland, would later marry in around 1290 the heiress of the Tankersley family near Barnsley and thus acquired the manor. It is evident that by the time of Elland church's foundation and thereafter the Elands were a wealthy family.

The choice of **St Mary the Virgin** as the patron saint was most likely due to the increased popularity of the mother of Christ in the 12th century and to the widespread foundation of great Cistercian houses throughout Europe, including Kirkstall, Fountains, Rievaulx and Byland in Yorkshire, all of which were dedicated to Our Lady, under the title of the Assumption, 'Queen of Heaven and Earth'. The Assumption panel in our church's medieval great east window is thus of particular significance and is especially beautiful.

The original church plan would have been an aiseless rectangular nave, roughly corresponding to the space within the current piers, with a narrower rectangular chancel, which would be widened later to conform with the width of the nave. Locally quarried millstone grit, a hard sandstone, was used in its construction. Indeed, such is the quality of the local stone that some was sent to build a granary at Kirkstall Abbey in the late 13th century. There would have been an earthen floor and no seating in these early years of St Mary's Church as was the general custom, giving rise to the well-known saying, 'the weakest to the wall'.

2. THE CHURCH BUILDING: EXTERIOR

The first impression is of a late perpendicular – that is, late 15th century - building with a square west tower of three stages with battlemented parapet and decorated by string courses. The tower, which was restored in 1859 and later in the late 1890s, is supported by west-facing diagonal buttresses. A door on the south-west buttress gives access to the tower. This is a later addition as the original entrance was from inside the church. A stairway leads to the ringing chamber, the clock chamber, the bell chamber and up to the roof (see below for further details).

To the east the low nave is embraced by aisles with windows of 14th century appearance, mostly dating from the 1856 restoration by W. H. Crossland. There are smaller buttresses at the north-west and south-west angles of the nave aisles. The eastern section of the church is more complex. Two side chapels, which extend north and south, are both supported by buttresses while the chancel itself has two pairs of buttresses to north and east and south and east. The outer pair of these are each surmounted by a projecting gargoyle at the top, and all four have a carved ogee-curved frieze a third of the way below and a further one equidistant below that. Immediately below the latter in each case is a carved incised panel. Under the 15th century east window is a door leading to a crypt which is also accessed inside the chancel by steps to the right of the altar.

A vestry, built in memory of Amy Savile of Rufford Abbey in 1879, projects from the south chapel. The main entry to the church is now through **the porch** built in 1696, which replaced one from the early 15th century. The faint traces of an early sundial can still be seen in the apex of the porch. The west door is very rarely opened these days. There is evidence of blocked-up earlier doorways in the outer stonework: in the north-west of the nave and north side chapel, for example. It is known that the latter once led into an outhouse, serving as a vestry. Above the chancel arch sits a late - and rare - 12th century bell-cote (see below).

Around the top of the side aisles below the modern guttering a corbel table with a series of decorated corbel stones adds interest to the plain stonework of the walls along with the window tracery. The aisle windows are mainly 19th century replacements though the most easterly one on the south side is an exception. The windows around the chancel and side chapel, along with the tower windows, are all authentic late 15th century, though with a certain amount of restoration and replacement stonework which is obvious to the eye.

INTERIOR

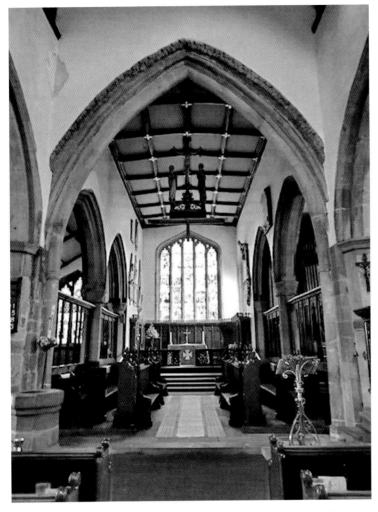

Detail of the chancel arch mouldings

Only the chancel arch remains of the original Transitional Norman church interior, apart from re-used stones in the north and south aisles and from the original west front.

The 12th century steeply pointed **chancel arch** has three orders (or rows) of voussoirs (wedge-shaped stones) with double-cone ornament, roll mouldings and simplified beakheads and was later dismantled and rebuilt around the turn of the 13th century when the chancel was widened.

This explains why the top two orders are now bonded into the north and south side walls. The arch looks symmetrical from the west but standing underneath reveals a slightly irregular alignment. It seems likely that in the rebuilding over a wooden framework the masons did not fully account for the extra width required and perhaps the mortar had not completely set, leading to some slippage. The lowest order of the arch springs from imposts with simple annulet capitals which would later be replicated in the piers of the nave.

The other surviving example of 12th century stonework, already seen on the exterior, is the **bellcote** on the roof, directly above the chancel arch. This is a rare survivor from such an early period and it is thought that only seven exist in England from Norman times. It would have housed a Sanctus bell, rung by means of a long rope by a priest's assistant or server during specific points in the Mass, notably during the Sanctus ('Holy, Holy, Holy') and at the consecration of the bread and wine. Although Mass would have been said or sung daily, most lay people attended Mass only on notable feast days in the church's calendar and the sound of the

Sanctus bell would be a brief time to stop work in the fields and town and kneel or pray or bless yourself with the sign of the cross. The bell would also have been tolled for funerals and to call people to prayer. In an age of no mechanical or electronic noise the most prominent non-human sounds of the Middle Ages would have been those made by animals, birds and the ringing of bells.

St Mary's church was in its early days a chapel of ease to Halifax Parish Church whose vicar would appoint the chaplains and priests in Elland. In addition to Elland cum Greetland, the area which it served included Rastrick cum Brighouse, Fixby, Stainland, Norland, Barkisland, Rishworth and Soyland. This remained the position until many of these areas were granted their own places of worship centuries later. The inhabitants of this wide area would have to come to Elland to be baptised, married and buried: an arduous journey given the large distances and hilly terrain.

The earliest written record of St Mary's comes in the register of the archiepiscopal see of York which refers to the 'Chapel of Ealand' in 1205. A local deed dated 1260 in Oxford University's Bodleian Library refers to one of the witnesses as 'Sir William de Eland, the chaplain of Eland.' A few years later, the York registers record that Archbishop Giffard bequeathed 3s 0d to the 'Anchoress at Ealand.' The anchoress would have lived a life of seclusion devoted to prayer, enclosed behind walls in the church, probably within sight of the altar. A further local deed of the 1280s, seen by the 18th century historian, Rev'd John Watson at Okes in Rishworth, referred to a bequest of a light to the 'Blessed Virgin Mary at Ealand' to be paid by John de Frith at Martinmas. The deed was witnessed by Hugh de Ealand, Henry de Rishworth and Thomas de Copley: all local gentlemen of good standing.

THE CHANCEL AND SIDE CHAPELS

Around the end of the 13th century or very early in the 14th when the chancel was widened two bay **arcades were constructed on the north and south sides of the chancel**. The **octagonal piers** forming these arcades are topped with large cushion capitals with spur-like additions.

The new arcades lead into two side chapels designated at that time as **chantry chapels** to the north and south of the chancel. Chantries - from the French word *chanter* (to sing) - were spaces for priests to say prayers and sing masses for the souls of the departed whose relatives had bequeathed an endowment for the purpose. The Roman Catholic belief that the soul served time in Purgatory to be cleansed of its sins on earth grew stronger throughout the later Middle Ages, particularly following the onset of the Black Death in the 1340s.

These two former chantries or **side chapels dedicated to St Nicholas** (to the north of the chancel, seen here) and to **St John the Evangelist** (to the south), continue to be used for prayer to this day, though the south chapel is now much reduced by the large organ case. Members of the Eland and Savile families were interred in the eastern parts of the church, notably the chancel and south chapel. During the installation of the present organ in 1949 a vault was discovered under the floor containing the remains of **John Dyson of Clay House** who died 2 June 1761 and **Francis** his wife who died December 1768. It seems likely that earlier remains of the Saviles and Elands lie further east though no excavations have yet taken place. The St Nicholas chapel still retains one **original square-headed north window**, the other being a later replacement.

The fine **panelled ceilings with moulded ribs** in the chancel and north chapel contain original late 15th century work, though restored in the 1850s, the chapel ceiling being canted. The rib crossings and edges each have an attractive red boss decorated with a golden four-petalled flower. The ceiling under the west tower of the same date is also ribbed but with no bosses.

The St Nicholas chapel contains **a vault,** which was long forgotten until rediscovered by workmen in April 1937 during the restoration of the chapel by the Wilson family. It houses the remains of several members of the Fixby branch of the **Thornhill** family, several of whose members are also commemorated by three wall memorials in this chapel (see below).

This crypt was constructed to contain 21 interments in separate niches each measuring 20 inches (50.8cm) high by 30 inches (76.2cm) wide and fitted with stone doors, some bearing inscriptions, in seven rows of three. Only seven of the niches contain lead coffins, the interments dating from 1754 to 1800.

The chancel once housed the two pairs of oak **miserere seats** now placed at the rear of the nave.

They are 15th century in date and allowed the clergy to perch on the raised seats during masses and lengthy prayers. 'Miserere' is Latin for 'have mercy', an ironic reference to this uncomfortable seating arrangement. Their worn appearance is a result of having been removed from the church in 1866 after the current nave pews were installed, and kept by the building contractor. For many years they languished outside in all weathers until a Mr Brook, possibly the Churchwarden John William Brook, rescued and restored them to their present condition.

THE NAVE

The very fine **nave roof** was constructed in the 13th century, replacing an earlier, simpler design. Experts from The West Yorkshire Archaeological Service have remarked that this is probably the **oldest church roof in the county** and that its structure is very similar to part of the now demolished 13th century Elland Old Hall, the family home of the Eland family.

This suggests that the family may well have employed the same carpenters and probably financed the construction. It is a typical example of the 'lowland' tradition of timberwork where each pair of rafters is linked by a collar and the framework is strengthened by a long straight brace between the collar and the lower part of the rafter. It is a simple but effective design and very pleasing to the eye giving a sense of space. It is no coincidence that the word 'nave' is derived from the Latin word *navis* meaning 'ship' as the appearance of the roof timbers resemble the hull of a ship, symbolically carrying worshippers through dangerous seas to the safety of God's presence.

The growth in population throughout the area in the 14th century, despite the setback of the plague years of the 'Black Death' in the late 1340s, led to the need for more space for worshippers. The north and south walls of the original nave were therefore pierced in around 1400 and four pairs of arcades were constructed creating bays of **six octagonal and four semi-octagonal engaged nave piers** leading into the new **north and south side aisles**. The arches are all double chamfered.

The capitals of the piers consist of two simple octangular annulets and the bases are also octagonal set upon square plinths which are mostly hidden now under floorboards. It is highly likely that the displaced masonry from the nave walls would have been reused in the outer walls of the new aisles which are still standing today. There would probably have been small, lancet (pointed) windows in the original nave but now additional light could illuminate the nave through larger windows in the new aisles. These windows themselves were replaced by nineteenth century replicas in the 'Decorated' style of the originals as seen here.

3. THE ELLAND CHARTER AND THE FALL OF THE ELAND FAMILY

A key date in the early 14th century was the granting of a **Market Charter** to the town of Elland on 24 February 1317. This followed a petition from Sir John de Eland through his overlord, now John de Warrenne, Earl of Surrey.

The king, Edward 11, granted many charters during his reign and the original Elland charter still exists in a long vellum roll containing numerous others in the National Archives in Kew (see below). The establishment of a weekly market and two annual fairs lasting six days around 11 June and 1 August in Elland would have brought profitable trade into the area, thus increasing the prestige of the town and church. The weekly market would have taken place around The Cross, as was the case in most medieval towns.

The original vellum roll opened at the Elland charter (The National Archives)

The town of Elland celebrated the 700th anniversary of the granting of the Charter in February 2017 in various ways. St Mary's Church was the venue for several events including a display arranged by the Greater Elland Historical Society, tours of the church and tower, and a talk on the history of St Mary's from its earliest days under the Eland Lords of the Manor.

The Eland family, however, would soon lose their position in the town for good. Sir John de Eland was a prosperous and influential man and served a year as Sheriff of Yorkshire and for many years locally as a Justice of the Peace. As such he represented the King's rule over a wide area and this inevitably created enmity with those who chose to break the law. Sir John had to deal with several offenders, amongst whom was a group of young men which included Adam de Beaumont, William de Quarmby and William de Lockwood whom he had to confine to York Castle and whose disreputable behaviour, once they were released - or perhaps following their escape - led to an ongoing vendetta against him.

On 29 October 1350, Sir John was returning from presiding over a law sitting in Brighouse when he was ambushed by these men and various others on his return to Elland by Cromwellbottom Woods. He was killed outright. More was to come when the same felons lay in wait for Sir John's son and heir, another Sir John, who had been attempting to have the murderers arrested, and a younger son, Thomas, as they made their way across the River Calder to Mass at St Mary's on Palm Sunday, 1351. Both men and their retainers were killed, leaving only Thomas's infant daughter, Isabel, surviving in the main line. It is often believed that all male members of the Eland family were entirely extinguished but this is not so as the older Sir John had had a son by his third wife and his two brothers also continued the line, which survives to this day. However, these younger members had been granted lands and manors elsewhere and the child Isabel was the sole inheritor of the manors of Elland and Tankersley.

The tragic events of 'The Elland Feud' would much later be written up and greatly embellished in the 16th or perhaps as late as the 17th century into a ballad and retold several times over the centuries. Much of the story was fabricated for dramatic effect and, possibly, to serve as a cautionary tale for a more recent quarrel between local gentry. However, the basic facts as described above are well documented in court rolls and legal papers in The National Archives. As the historian J. M. Kaye, who researched this subject for *The Yorkshire Archaeological Journal* in 1979, wrote: 'The official record of the Eland murders is in important respects irreconcilable with the ballad story.' Sir John de Eland seems to have been a conscientious and brave man doing his duty to bring order and justice in what was a countryside not unlike the 'wild west' of 19th century America. That policing the district was difficult is underlined by the fact that there is no documentary evidence to suggest that the murderers were ever brought to justice.

4. THE SAVILE FAMILY AND ST MARY'S CHURCH

Now that **Isobel de Eland** was a young - and wealthy - orphan she became a ward of court of the Honour of Pontefract. In 1353, shortly after her father's death, the **Savile** family, lords of the manors of Rishworth and of Golcar and Shelley, near Huddersfield, paid a considerable sum - a figure of £200 has been given in some sources (worth around £120,000 today) - for the wardship. This was closely followed by her marriage to the Savile heir **Sir John Savile**, thus uniting the manors and lands of both families.

Savile

As a Knight of the Shire, Sir John saw much military service during the Hundred Years War in France and Spain with Edward the Black Prince and his brother John of Gaunt, Duke of Lancaster and probably fought at the Battle of Poitiers in 1356. Later in life he also served three times as High Sheriff of Yorkshire. He founded by licence on 10 July 1396, a **Chantry** in the **Chapel of St John the Baptist** in St Mary's Church 'to pray for John Duke of Aquitaine and Lancaster, Sir John Sayvill and Isabella his wife and their children, Henry late Earl of Lancaster, John Sayvill and Joan his wife, the parents of the said Sir John, Thomas de Eland and Joan his wife parents of the said Isabella'.

His will was proved at York on 23 September 1399 and he was buried at his request in St Mary's Church. His widow, Isabel, swore a vow not to re-marry on 17 November 1399 in a chapel near Nostell Priory before a suffragan bishop, receiving the ring and mantle of chastity. Her eldest son Sir John Savile inherited the manors. However, this male line died out after the next generation and it was her younger son, **Henry Savile** and his descendants who would play major roles in the development of St Mary's Church. Up to this point it seems that the Saviles had based themselves at Elland Hall, the ancient seat of the Eland family, though this would soon change.

Arms of the Thornhill family

Henry Savile had made an advantageous marriage himself by marrying Elizabeth, the heiress of the wealthy **Thornhill** family in 1370.

Once again, the heiress was a child - merely two years old in Elizabeth's case - and the Saviles had to pay the Crown £126 3s 4d for the marriage rights. The manor at Thornhill, near Dewsbury, and its church dedicated to St Michael and All Angels, became the preferred seat of Henry and his elder son, Sir Thomas, who built the north chapel in Thornhill church as their family mausoleum.

His younger brother Henry, on the other hand, made another lucrative match by marrying the heiress of the **Copley** family from **Copley**

Hall, near Elland. It was this younger branch of the Saviles which continued to support St Mary's Church in Elland, notably through Henry and Elizabeth's son Thomas Savile, who married the heiress of **John Stansfield** of **Hullenedge** and then their son John Savile who settled at Hullenedge Hall, Elland. Another member of the Elland branch, Nicholas Savile, built **New Hall** in 1490. His descendants included the scholar Sir Henry Savile (1549-1622) of **Bradley Hall** (the remains of which now forms part of Bradley Golf Club) who was responsible for overseeing translations of what became known as the King James Bible (1611) from Hebrew and Greek into English. Further details of Sir Henry are given below.

The Elland branches of the Savile family left their legacy in much that we continue to admire in St Mary's church, notably in the architecture and coloured glass to which we shall now turn.

THE EXTENDED EAST END AND THE BUILDING OF THE WEST TOWER

The embellishments and extensions to Thornhill Church were followed and mirrored by those in St Mary's. Whether it was though friendly rivalry between both sides of the Savile family or perhaps a joint project, great sums of money were spent during the 15th century on enlarging and beautifying both churches. The work at St Michael and All Angels in Thornhill started under Thomas Savile in 1447 with the building of the north chapel dedicated to the Saviles. It contains numerous monuments to the family and contains some stained glass of this period. It was lengthened one bay by William Savile in 1493. A south chapel was added in 1491 and a great east window was inserted in the chancel in 1499.

At St Mary's Elland at much the same time the local Savile branch remodelled the chancel by extending its depth to provide a raised **sanctuary**, accessed by four steps, and replaced the ceiling.

New late perpendicular **four-centred** (or depressed) **windows** were inserted in the east and south sides of the chancel and in the east of both side chapels, whose ceilings were also

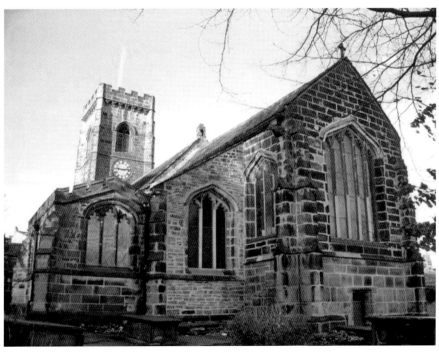

Interior late 15th century arch leading into the tower space, now a community room,

replaced. These windows were glazed at this time (see below). Both the chancel and north chapel still retain their fine late 15th century **ceilings**. External **buttresses** to both the north-east and south-east walls of the chancel were added, on which it is still possible to make out a weathered image of an **owl** from the Savile family crest. The owl remains a feature of Elland's coat of arms.

At around the same time (1490), the west wall of the nave was demolished and the church's most prominent feature, an ashlar-faced **west tower** was erected. The nave and aisles were thus extended by one bay.

The top storey of the tower contains two-light windows at each cardinal point. On the west face a large **west window** was inserted above the **west door** in the late perpendicular style which is flanked by two smaller two-light windows, now containing fragments of medieval glass (see below) along with two pairs of similar windows to north and south in the extra bay created by the tower's construction.

5. THE MEDIEVAL STAINED GLASS PROGRAMME

It is unlikely that the original 12th century church building would have contained any coloured glass, which was expensive and rarely installed in smaller churches. The first hint of any painted glass is found in a written note on the first page of the Elland Parish Church Register, 1 April 1559 stating that the window over the choir or chancel door 'was made in the yere of our Lorde 1310 as was written in the same window where the glass was broken, An. Dom. 1618'. This intriguing note suggests that a window in the eastern arm of the church contained at least one early 14th century inscription.

Windows were invariably provided by wealthy donors who could be commemorated either by inscriptions or by coats of arms of their own and their inter-married families upon the glass. The earliest evidence of a major investment in stained or painted glass in St Mary's coincides with the late 15th century building works by the Savile family. There is evidence to suggest that practically all the windows in the chancel and side chapels were glazed at this time. Today, only several panels of original glass in the great east window survive intact and we shall deal with these below.

Several antiquarians have visited the church over the years and made helpful notes on the glass. According to the historian Rev'd John Watson (who had been baptized and married at St Mary's), writing in 1775, a certain Dr Johnston had inspected the glass on 23 July 1669 and noted the coats of arms of 'private families painted in a window in the Quire' which he could not 'well make out, they were so defaced'. A century earlier, however, in his Visitation of Elland in 1584/5, the Somerset Herald Robert Glover had noted a considerable amount of heraldic glass, including the families of Savile, Quarmby, Stansfield and Golcar. One of his more intriguing notes concerned a window containing 'an old knight kneeling with his coat armour on his back. Gules, two bars between eight martlets, three, two and one argent'. This describes the arms of the Eland family which lost the manor after their murders in 1351. Glover did not state where he found this window but it would probably have been either in the chancel or a side chapel. Could this have been a memorial window to the last Sir John de Eland?

It seems very likely from written sources that most, if not all, coloured glass was concentrated in the more sacred eastern parts of the church. It was also here where members of the leading gentry were buried. There is evidence, too, that the Thornhill branch of the Saviles invested in at least one stained glass window in St Mary's which still survived, at least in part, when Rev'd John Watson recorded it in 1775. He noted that in the 'north quire' - presumably St Nicholas Chapel - an inscription invited worshippers to 'Pray for the gude prosperitie, mercy and grace of Sir John Savile Knt…and for the soul of his abovesaid wife, daughter of Sir William Vernon, for which Sir John caused this window to be made.'

The wording of this inscription is a standard form of use at this time though the couple were not from Elland, but Thornhill. This Sir John Savile (who died in 1504) married twice and a substantial carved oak memorial to his memory and his two wives, Alice née Vernon and Elizabeth née Paston (a great-granddaughter of John of Gaunt), still stands in the north chapel in Thornhill Church, near where he had also dedicated its east window. Alice, his first wife, died before 1494 so the Elland window, sadly now lost, can be securely dated to the early 1490s. We do not know if the inscription accompanied a pictorial window; it is more likely there would have been an heraldic shield in coloured glass.

The monument in Thornhill Church showing Sir John Savile between his two wives

All the evidence suggests that the glazing with stained or heraldic glass largely coincided with the enlargement or remodelling of the eastern areas of St Mary's in the 1490s. The church building as it stands now, except for the current porch and vestry, looks much as it would have done at that time. Many of the original glass and heraldic windows, however, have disappeared apart from eleven glorious panels in the Great East Window and other fragments. Some glass would have been destroyed during the Protestant Reformation under King Edward V1 (1547-53) and the English Civil War and Commonwealth (1642 - 60), when Puritans took exception to the Roman Catholic imagery. Then, from the early 19th century century up to the 1980s, industrialisation brought huge factories to Elland and West Vale, whose polluting outpourings through their dozens of tall chimneys further damaged the fragile glass.

By 1850, the church was described as a 'mutilated and dilapidated edifice' and a succession of Ministers began a thorough restoration of the church fabric. It is largely thanks to Rev'd Edward Sandford (who would acquire the Church Tithes in 1868 and became the first Rector of Elland) and his curate and successor, Rev'd Francis Musson that the church fabric and remaining medieval glass have been preserved. Sandford engaged William Wailes of Newcastle, a glazier of distinction, who had created the east window of Newcastle Cathedral and the west window in the cathedral at Gloucester, to restore and rearrange the east window in St Mary's in 1856. Wailes would also create his own ten panels for the east window and in addition created a new west window in the church and a further window in the south aisle (see below).

THE GREAT EAST WINDOW

Lucy Hamerton in her book *Olde Eland* (1901) gave helpful details about the condition of the window as she remembered it as a young girl in the 1820s. She recalled that it was then 'much delapidated' with no coloured glass at all in the lower lights. These had held mainly heraldic glass celebrating local families (largely Royalist) and would have been within easy reach of Puritan soldiers during the turbulent Civil Wars. She also noted that the best-preserved panel

was the Annunciation to Mary and that what she believed to be the coat of arms of John of Gaunt had (erroneously) a central position in the whole window.

The window consists of five lights under a **late perpendicular four-centred or 'depressed' arch** and contains twenty-one panels of pictorial glass, each one measuring 36 x 20 inches (c91.2cm x 51cm) with four canopy heads over the outer four lights. The subject of the window is of particular relevance to the church as it mainly portrays the **life of St Mary**, the mother of Jesus.

Today, only eleven of the original panels remain intact, the remaining ten being replacements installed by William Wailes which do not all follow the original iconographical programme of the originals. However, what remains is of extremely high quality, though much restored. The vivid, translucent colours and modelling of the figures suggest that the glass painting was produced by glaziers in York, a major centre of this craft. The present exceptional condition of the glass is a result of expert restoration by the York Glaziers Trust in 1997-8.

During the Second World War the precious medieval panels were dismantled and hidden in the crypt of St Nicholas Chapel for protection from possible aerial bombardments.

Sources for the Iconography of the Marian Panels

St Mary makes relatively few appearances in the Gospels and Acts of the Apostles: at her Annunciation, her Visitation to her kinswoman Elizabeth, at Jesus's Nativity and her subsequent Flight into Egypt and fleetingly thereafter at Jesus's disputation with the elders of the Temple, the marriage at Cana, His Crucifixion and - in the Acts of the Apostles - the Descent of the Holy Spirit at Pentecost.

The Christian Church sought early on to amplify the role of Mary and fill in the 'back story' of her life. This led to a number of apocryphal gospels being written in the first few centuries. These included a Gospel of Mary and, crucially, for the Elland window, the **Book of James** (also known as the **Protevangelium**). Its date and authorship are unknown though it possibly originated as early as the 2nd century. It is an infancy gospel about the miraculous birth of Mary to her elderly parents **Joachim and Anna** and her subsequent betrothal to Joseph. This early narrative became very popular during the Middle Ages and was portrayed in art through to the Renaissance. There were several events in Mary's childhood and later life described in the narrative which may well have been portrayed in the Elland window and are now missing, such as her taking her first seven steps, her dancing before the Temple altar, her spinning purple and scarlet linen for the veil of the Temple and her Coronation as Queen of Heaven, all of which were popular scenes in medieval and later art.

Reading the East Window today *(Wailes's Victorian replacement panels are also discussed).*

The panels read from the top downwards, beginning top left, if we exclude the bottom row which very likely contained heraldic coats of arms of local families and which now contain Victorian glass of key events in the life of Christ. The original Marian narrative holds good for the first row and part of the second but then the order becomes slightly confused, following the rearrangements and replacements of the 1850s restoration.

1 The Annunciation to St Anne (or Anna). *(Book of James).*

On the left St Anne in a green tunic with a blue mantle edged with fur points to a line of verse in a psalter placed on a russet gown draped over a richly decorated coffer. On the right the

Angel Gabriel extends his right hand, which is holding a green palm, towards Anne's left. He is dressed as a priest in an alb and tasselled stole and wears a floriated coronet. The Latin script below reads: *O Anna gratiosa mater matris gratiosae.* ['Gracious Anne, mother of a gracious mother'].

The Annunciation of Saint Anne (or Anna)

2 The meeting of Joachim and Anna. *(Book of James)*

'Joachim came with his flocks and Anne stood at the [Golden] Gate [in Jerusalem] and saw Joachim coming and ran and rung upon his neck'. The artist places the couple in an architectural setting of crocketed gables over arcading giving a three-dimensional effect. He has used here, as elsewhere, silver nitrate in the glass which, when fired, gives a radiant gold staining. The addition of blue-coloured acanthus leaves also adds to the lustrous effect. Joachim and his wife embrace – the former dressed as a wealthy late-fifteenth century merchant, his money-bag hanging from his belt: the Book of James describes him as 'a very rich man'. Anne is dressed in sumptuous robes edged with gold. Their facial features suggest they are past their youth. The underlying script reads: *Joachim Sancte conjux Annae.* [Saint Joachim, husband of Anne'].

The meeting of Anna and Joachim   *The betrothal of Mary and Joseph*

3 Birth of the Blessed Virgin Mary. *(Book of James).*

This very tender scene contains five figures. A serious-looking St Anne sits up in bed beneath a richly-decorated and fringed tester holding Mary, already with long golden hair, and attended by two gentlewomen, both coiffed, one holding out a cloth, the other supporting the child.

A third woman - probably the midwife - stands on the right holding what appears to be a medical instrument. The folding of the russet drapery on the bed is richly painted and the child's crib stands by the bed. The underlying script reads: *Ante colles ego parturiebar* ('Before the hills I gave birth'), recalling Proverbs viii, 25 and the fact that Nazareth is surrounded by hills.

The birth of Mary

4 Victorian glass: The anointing of Christ's feet. *(All four Gospels)*

A fair-haired woman (who has led a sinful life, according to St Luke) is seen kneeling and pouring perfume from an alabaster jar on Christ's feet, one of which is raised on a stool. The woman has no halo so is unlikely to represent the Mary of Bethany of St John's Gospel. The jar stands on the table where Jesus and three men are seated, one probably the householder, Simon a leper, and the man on the extreme right holding a money bag being Judas Iscariot. Another fair-haired figure with a halo, presumably one of the disciples, stands behind Jesus. Wailes has framed the scene with blue acanthus leaves and a simple canopy. (It is worth noting that the colours in all the Victorian glass are less vivid than those in the medieval.). The underlying script reads: *Sinite Illam at in diem sepulturae meae servet illud.* ('Let her be, so she might use it [the costly perfume] on the day of my burial' from *John* 12: 7).

5 Victorian glass: The Presentation of Christ at the Temple. *(Gospel of Luke).*

Mary, in red robe and blue tunic, with her spouse Joseph present the infant Jesus at an altar to the Jewish High Priest (here robed as a bishop, an anachronism in 1st century Palestine)) in his elaborate robes. He is depicted with a halo suggesting that this is Simeon who was often conflated with the High Priest in medieval art through to the present. The picture is framed by a low canopy and pale blue acanthus leaves. Part of the underlying script is hidden under heaving leading which may suggest that the inscription dates from the medieval period. It reads *In habitatione sancta coram ipsi ministrare* [should read *ministravi*], meaning 'I ministered before him in his holy house'. This is from *Ecclesiasticus* 24: 9-10 [from the Apocrypha], which was also used in the *Capitulum* [opening words] as part of the medieval Office of Vespers to the Blessed Virgin Mary. Fr David Burrows has commented that the whole of *Ecclesiasticus* 24 is a reflection on Holy Wisdom and the use of the text here is probably an understanding of Mary as a personification of Holy Wisdom with its specific reference to the Holy Temple. It is also just possible that Wailes used an original medieval inscription, still extant in the 1850s, which originally belonged to another panel with the Virgin Mary as its principal subject.

6 Betrothal of Mary and Joseph *(Book of James).*

The rich architectural setting of three crocketed gables and corbels supporting fan vaulting, all picked out on gold and blue, frames four figures. A mitred bishop stands between Mary and Joseph holding the marriage ring in his right hand and Mary's clasped hands in his left. Joseph looks on tenderly, his own hands also clasped, having taken off his gloves. Mary wears her traditional blue gown, here trimmed with fur, and a russet tunic. On the right stands the witness: a young man with golden hair, holding the box which had contained the ring. His right hand is raised, palm outwards as if in blessing. Unlike the other three figures he has no halo. The script reads: *Dispensatio* [should read *Disponsatio*] *tua Dei genetrix virgo.* ('Your betrothal, virgin mother of God').

7 The Assumption of the Blessed Virgin Mary.

This event is not covered in the Book of James nor is there any Biblical source for Mary's ascent into Heaven. Many early traditions sought to explain what happened to Mary and eventually the legend that she was borne up to Heaven by angels gained currency and from the 6th century onwards this was depicted in art and particularly from the 12th century in Western European art.

The Elland panel is a remarkable composition, and it is a miracle that it has survived the iconoclasm of the Protestant Reformation and Cromwell's Puritans. It is a very fine example of the genre and thanks to restoration is in excellent condition. The figure of Mary, in her blue gown as Queen of Heaven and russet tunic edged with gold, is placed in a mandorla surrounded by a glory of golden rays being borne aloft by six kneeling angels, three on either side.

Her hands are held up, palms diagonally facing outwards and her expression - beautifully etched by the unknown artist - is one of dignity and introspection. She is bareheaded with long golden tresses and with a golden nimbus. There are also traces of gold staining on the angels' hair and collars but otherwise they are etched in monochrome, thus highlighting the importance of Mary who, in contrast, is vividly portrayed.

The shadows and deep folds of the angels' drapery are painted in a sophisticated way, almost at odds with the hieratic portrayal of Mary which may suggest that a second artist was at work. The gothic script below reads: *Assumpta est Maria in coelum* ('Mary is assumed [ie raised up] into Heaven').

There have been suggestions that this panel pre-dates the others by a several years, being painted around 1475 or earlier, though there is no written evidence for this. Moreover, the panel is the same size as the others and has not been cropped to fit in. It is not dissimilar (though is superior) to an Assumption window in the Savile chapel at Thornhill Church, built in 1447. There are other fine examples of the genre in All Saints, Gresford near Wrexham (c 1500) and, in particular, East Harling in Norfolk.

The Assumption of Mary into Heaven

8 Victorian glass: Christ's entry into Jerusalem. *(All four Gospels)*

Christ in a red robe and green tunic rides a colt, here surrounded by five figures carrying palms. The modelling of the colt is rather naïve. The scene is set against the usual background of pale blue acanthus leaves and simple arcading. The underlying script reads: *Hosanna benedictus qui venit in nomine Domine.* ('Hosanna, blessed is he who comes in the name of the Lord').

9 Victorian glass: Christ in Majesty.

This is a popular subject for the apex of a window, but it is more likely that at Elland this would have depicted the Coronation of the Virgin Mary as the apotheosis of the iconographic programme. A panel on this theme is found in one of the windows of the Savile chapel, Thornhill Church. Here, Christ wears a green and purple tunic and flowing red robes, an orb in His left hand. He is surrounded by a golden glory, framed in a mauve mandorla under an ogee arch with golden decoration in what is a fine composition. There is no inscription.

10 Ascension of Christ. *(Gospel of Mark - longer ending; Gospel of Luke).*

Mary is pictured kneeling in the foreground with, probably, St John as a golden-haired young

The Ascension of
Jesus to Heaven

man, surrounded by the other disciples crowded on either side in diminishing perspective. Christ disappears above them, only the hem of his robe visible as the golden flames of a glory surround him. Mary, richly robed in russet and blue with St John in russet and gold, hold up their hands in adoration. The whole scene is again framed by this artist's typical architectural setting, with pendant bosses and three ogee canopies surmounted by crocketed gables, characteristic of late Gothic art. The script reads: *Ascendit in coelum* ('He ascended to Heaven').

11 The Resurrection *(All four Gospels).*

The risen Christ is depicted rising from the now empty tomb, a cross of resurrection in his left hand, his right hand in an attitude of benediction.

He wears only a maroon cloth, the gold of his nimbus now faded, as also have his five sacred wounds (noted by an observer in 1876). Four soldiers in full plate armour still sleep around the tomb. Here, the artist has given some depth to the scene by painting Golgotha in the background along with various figures: men being crucified, a soldier on horseback and an

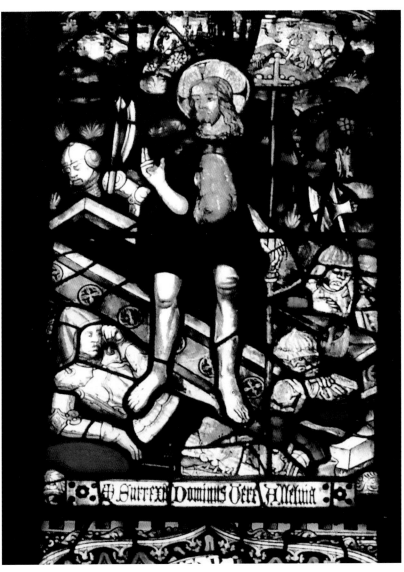

archer pulling his bow. It is a dramatic composition placed just above the crucifixion scene and below Christ's ascension into Heaven. The script reads: *Surrexit Dominus Vere Alleluia* ('The Lord is truly risen. Alleluia').

12 Victorian glass: The Crucifixion. *(All four Gospels).*

It is likely that this traditional composition replaced an original panel in the central position of the window. Christ hangs between his mother, Mary, on his right and his beloved disciple, John, on his left, carrying his Gospel. A skull, representing Adam the first man, whose eating of the forbidden fruit brought death into the world, lies beneath Christ's feet. The scene is framed by Wailes's usual pale blue acanthus leaves and a simple canopy. The underlying script reads: *Consummatum Est* ('It is accomplished' – Christ's last words).

13 Victorian glass: The Last Supper. *(All four Gospels).*

The figure of Christ is seated at table centrally between five of his disciples. St John is dressed in purple leaning on his master's left breast, whose left hand comforts him.The only figure without a halo, who must be Judas Iscariot, sits prominently on the left in profile. Christ is handing him what appears to be a coin. A chalice, an empty dish and platter of food stand on the finely painted white tablecloth. It is significant that the painter of this panel, William Wailes, has placed it directly before the priest's position as he stands in the sanctuary to consecrate the bread and wine at Holy Communion. The inscription reads: *Hoc facite in meam commemorationem* .('Do this in remembrance of me').

Victorian (William Wailes) glass: The Last Supper and The Agony in the Garden

25

14 Adoration of the Magi. *(Book of James and Gospel of Matthew).*

This is a charming scene and skilfully painted. Mary is seated, dressed in a russet gown, Jesus on her lap standing to greet the kneeling king (the magi are generally given kingly status) who is offering his gift of gold nuggets in a chalice which Jesus is already touching.

The other two Magi await their turn. The kneeling king/magus is bare-headed, his crown on the ground. Mary and Jesus are seated before a wicker enclosure representing the stable, painted in gold. An ox peers at the baby Jesus over Mary's shoulder, the ass brays skywards, looking away. Above this scene fly three angels, coloured silver, bearing a scroll with the words *Gloria in excelsis Deo et in terra pax* ('Glory to God in the highest and on earth peace'). Between blue acanthus leaves below a sun, beams of light, representing the Holy Spirit, point downwards directly to the Christ-child. The underlying script reads: *Et adorabunt omens reges* ('And all the kings worshipped him').

15 Victorian glass. Baptism of Christ. *(All four Gospels).*

A somewhat small figure of Christ, his red robe wrapped around his waist, stands in a tiny patch of blue water on the left surrounded by foliage as a tall John the Baptist above, in yellow camel skins, pours water from the River Jordan on his head. John is bearded and carries a high cross. To the left of Jesus a scroll unwinds bearing the words of God: *Meus dilectus est filius* ('This is my beloved son'). Acanthus leaves, arcades and gables, imitating the medieval frames in the rest of the east window, surround the pair. The underlying script reads: *Et baptizatus in Jordane* ('He was baptised in the Jordan').

16 Descent of the Holy Spirit at Pentecost.
(Acts of the Apostles).

Mary stands with the twelve apostles (six are almost entirely hidden behind Mary and the front six), painted largely in monochrome - apart from a flash of red on Mary's tunic - beneath a blue diapered background surmounted by a triple arcade. A dove, representing the Holy Spirit, descends from the middle arch trailing golden rays towards the apostles who are in an attitude of prayer. The script reads: *Et repleti sunt omnes Spiritu Sanctu* ('And they were all filled with the Holy Spirit'.

17 Victorian glass. Agony in the Garden.
(Gospels of Matthew, Mark, Luke and possibly John - subsumed in John 17). See larger image above in 13..

Christ kneels in prayer, a chalice before him ('Father, if thou be willing, take this cup from me'- Luke 22, 42) whilst Peter, James and John are asleep around him. There are stylised olive trees to represent the Garden of Gethsemane. The scene is framed with blue acanthus leaves and a decorated gable, a crown symbolically above Christ's head. The underlying script reads: *Non meam voluntas, sed tua fiat.* ('Not my will but thine be done').

18 Annunciation to the Virgin Mary. *(Book of James and Gospel of Luke).*

This panel parallels that of the Annunciation of St Anne (**1**) and though it differs considerably in style (a second artist seems at work) and in its treatment of the subject. Mary is kneeling at her faldstool where her open book lies on a golden cushion upon an elaborate casket, dressed as an altar. Mary holds up her hands in surprise and, perhaps, acceptance as her facial expression is one of serenity.

The kneeling Archangel Gabriel, dressed in a white priestly tunic with a golden cloak, carries a golden sceptre in his left hand, his right hand stretched towards Mary. Between them stands a bowl of lilies, the traditional symbol of Mary's purity. In the top left corner the hands of God send forth radiant beams of golden light to Mary and a small dove with a tiny flower in its beak flutters near her face. A large scroll unwinds above the two figures with the words *Ave Maria gratia plena Dms [Dominus] tecum* ('Hail Mary full of grace, the Lord is with thee'). The legend beneath continues Gabriel's message: *Benedicta in mulieribus* ('Blessed art thou among women').

The Annunciation to the Virgin Mary

19 The Visitation of Mary to Elizabeth. (Book of James and Gospel of Luke).

The two expectant mothers, Mary (on the left) and her kinswoman Elizabeth, stand face to face. Elizabeth is placing one hand over Mary's womb, which is covered by a golden sun. Mary places her own hand over Elizabeth's womb whilst she, herself, appears to raise a hand in a gesture of greeting. Both women are richly-dressed, their heads covered for modesty and have faint smiles. They stand on a chequered floor and are framed by triple canopies. The script below reads: *Et Salutavit Elizabeth* ('And she greeted Elizabeth').

The Visitation of the Virgin Mary to her kinswoman Elizabeth

20 Victorian glass: The Nativity. (Gospels of Matthew, Mark and Luke).

The baby Jesus lies on a white linen sheet and golden pillow upon a low crib. His arms are raised towards his mother, richly dressed in a blue robe and a wide red tunic fringed in silver, who kneels in prayer before him. Joseph stands behind Jesus, holding a staff. An ox and ass gaze at Jesus from their stall in adoration. The underlying script reads: *Puer nobis est natus* ('A boy is born to us')

21 Victorian glass: Christ carrying the cross. (Gospels of Matthew, Mark and Luke).

Christ, dressed in a pale blue robe and bright red tunic with golden lining, walks with the cross over his right shoulder, looking obliquely backwards. He wears the crown of thorns and has a dignified, if faraway, expression. A Roman soldier walks slightly ahead whilst his mother Mary, Simon of Cyrene, dressed in armour and a purple cloak, and St John the Beloved follow. Simon carries the cross's upright.The underlying script reads: *Posuit Dominus in eo iniquitatem omnium nostrum* ('The Lord laid on Himself all our sins' *Isaiah,* 53: 6).

FRAGMENTS OF EARLY GLASS IN SMALL WEST WINDOWS

When Rev'd Edward Sandford supervised the renovation of the church in the 1850s and 1860s his curate, Rev'd Francis Musson, gathered up the fragments of broken stained glass in a box. Some of these came from the east window, others from other windows in the chancel and side chapels and possibly also more recent glass from the nave. After Musson himself returned as Rector in 1873 he had these fragments inserted in the two pairs of west windows on either side of the west door.

The South West pair

North-west left hand window

The fragments are a jigsaw of colours and shapes and seem to be from several windows of various dates ranging from late medieval to, perhaps, as late as the late 18th and early 19th centuries. The early glass is intriguing and consists of a variety of emblems such as the heads of lions and falcons, golden-haired angels and blue acanthus leaves. Here and there parts of a Latin or English inscription are evident. It appears that much of these early pieces were of an heraldic nature and quite possibly came from the bottom row of the great east window. Others were probably from other late 15th century windows in the chancel or side chapels, financed by the Thornhill and Savile families.

The most prominent feature is a representation of **The Royal Coat of Arms** in the left- hand light of the north-west window. This depicts a shield bearing the arms of England quartered with those of France, surmounted by a coronet. The shield is encircled with the words *Honi soit qui mal y pense* ('Evil to those who think evil'), the motto of the Order of the Garter. Heavy leading obscures part of the shield though there appear to be the remains of a heraldic label, denoting the son of a monarch. Lucy Hamerton noted that this royal insignia had been wrongly placed in the centre of the window before the 1850s restoration and assumed they were the arms of **John of Gaunt**, fourth son of King Edward 111. The Saviles had been historically linked with Gaunt and Sir John Savile of the senior Thornhill branch had married his descendant Elizabeth Paston. Furthermore, John of Gaunt held Elland in his rôle of overlord as part of the Honour of Pontefract.

However, there is also the possibility that the heraldry represents a royal heir and Prince of Wales such as **Prince Arthur** the firstborn son of Henry V11, the first Tudor king. He was created Prince of Wales in 1489 and invested in

Westminster Abbey in 1490. Henry V11 ordered all churches to proclaim this event and, if possible, to represent it in art. There is also a strong local connection as the rector of Thornhill Church, Robert Frost - who donated the Jesse east window in the chancel of his church in 1499 - was Prince Arthur's Chancellor.

Among the various fragments of gothic script in Elland's west windows is an intriguing dedication at the bottom of the north-west right-hand panel. Only a part remains of what the Rev'd John Watson had noted in full in 1775.

It begins 'Pray for the gude prosperitie, mercy and grace....'. It is still possible to identify the dedication to **John Savile of Hullenedge and his wife, the daughter of Robert Hopton.** An indenture agreement between Robert Hopton of Armley Esq, and 'John Sayvell Esq' regarding Elizabeth's marriage to John still exists in the archives from Rufford Hall (the home of the later Saviles) and is dated 1484-5. It is quite possible that the window which the couple donated was indeed the great East Window. Both the royal coat of arms and the dedication point to a date of around 1490.

6. FURTHER VICTORIAN PAINTED GLASS

There is Victorian glass in several windows throughout the church, other than the ten panels in the great east window. The **chancel** houses a large window on the **south side**, erected by the **Rawson** family in 1866.

Their family seat at this time, Barkisland Hall - today an outstanding Grade 1 listed 17th century residence - lay within the parish of Elland. Made of three tall lights with traceries, the window consists of floral, geometric patterns, three of which bear sayings of Christ: 'Whoever liveth and believeth in me shall never die'. 'I am the resurrection and the life' and 'Because I live ye shall live also'. The colours - reds, blues, pinks and whites - are subdued.

The **east window of the south chapel** of St John is of plain glass set in the heavily-restored depressed arch of the 1490s rebuild and is obscured by the organ case

In the **North (St Nicholas) Chapel**, the late 15th century **east window** now contains stained glass manufactured by **John Hardman** who, along with his nephew John Hardman Powell, started making stained glass in the 1840s. As the chapel window was erected to the memory of James **Hiley**, a surgeon and his wife, who died in 1836, this would have been one of Hardman's earliest commissions.

The window consists of six panels depicting scenes from the life of Christ. All the panels frame these scenes within richly decorated architectural details picked out in silver and gold. Top left depicts **Christ healing the sick** as he is surrounded by five adults and an infant. The burnished robes of Christ and the bright blue of the reclining old man in the foreground are the dominant colours. Top centre is the highest panel and depicts the **Sermon on the Mount**. Christ sits on a hill in his red flowing robes, his right hand raised in blessing, before a single stylised tree. Numerous listeners crowd around, including several disciples who are haloed. The top right panel portrays Christ seated at table before a tablecloth and a plate of food and cutlery. He is blessing the meal. A large ewer is placed on the floor. Behind him stands a woman apparently wearing a wide bonnet though there are also

perhaps traces of a halo. Another figure across the table gestures in amazement whilst other figures look on. Christ's red robe and white tunic are dominant, though it appears that some of the colours, notably of the white glass, are fading around his face and those of some of the figures. The subject is likely to represent **Christ in Bethany** at the home of Mary, Martha and Lazarus, though the wedding feast and his first miracle of **turning water into wine** is another possibility.

On the lower register, the left-hand panel shows the young Jesus **Teaching in the Temple**. Jesus, animated, dressed in white robes stands on a raised dais on the right, books propped up at the base. Three elders and a woman listen intently, two carrying scrolls of the scriptures. Blues and reds predominate though the white glass on Jesus's face has faded. The middle scene portrays **Christ and the woman taken in adultery**. A golden-haired Christ in white tunic and red robes points to the kneeling woman at his feet as her three accusers, picked out in green and pale blue look on angrily, one clenching his fist. The final scene on the right shows **Angels ministering to Christ in the Garden of Gethsemane**. The artist depicts two angels offering sustenance to Christ before his Passion, one bearing a chalice, the other a plate of grapes and fruit. Christ, in his red robes, blesses the kneeling angel. The angels' wings are picked out in blue and auburn though, sadly, the silver of their figures and the upper part of Christ have suffered paint loss over the years.

The **North Wall of St Nicholas' Chapel wall** contains two windows. The first is of plain glass. On the right hand jamb of the second a metal plaque reads: 'To the Glory of God and memory of Sarah Hirsch Charlotte **Wilson** and William Hodgson Wilson, at one time worshippers in this Church, this Chapel of S. Nicholas was restored, and the Altar erected by members of the Family, and dedicated on the Eve of S. Nicholas, 1937.' The window itself bears the inscription 'To the glory of God and in loving memory of his Father, Mother, Brothers and Sisters. This window was dedicated by John Thwaites in 1884'. The glass was designed and painted by the **Powell Brothers of Leeds,** who initially began as church decorators. The increasing demand for painted glass from the 1870s on led to their successful move to glass painting. The window here has three lights below simple pointed heads and is divided into six scenes, three above and three below, all representing women from the Gospels. Each scene is framed within an architectural setting with blue acanthus leaves.

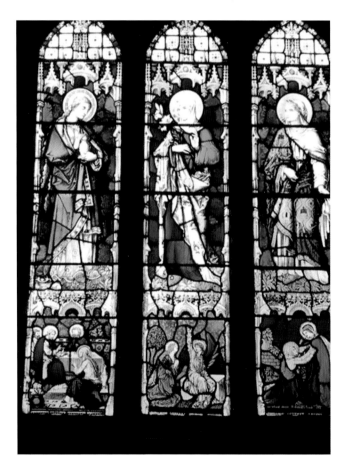

Top left portrays a **female saint holding an alabaster jar who washed Christ's feet with her tears** (Matt: 26.6f; Mark: 14. 3f; Luke: 7.37*f*; John: 11.2 - who described her as **Mary of Bethany**). Her loosened blonde hair could suggest she may be the sinner in Matthew, Mark and Luke's account, though most likely Mary of Bethany is intended, her hair loose for drying Christ's feet. She wears pink robes, edged with gold, some of it already faded. Top centre is the **Virgin Mary**, holding a long spray of lilies in her right hand, her left hand held up in a sign of blessing. Her characteristic blue mantle is partly covered by a rich, golden cloak over her right shoulder. Top right depicts a **female saint, probably Martha of Bethany**, to match her sister Mary of Bethany (top left). She wears a richly decorated green cloak over an underlying white robe. Some of the gold of her halo and white robe and face is fading.

The scenes along the bottom row are smaller by half than those above. Again, they are framed by elaborate arcading in gold and white. Bottom left portrays **Mary of Bethany,** seated at Christ's feet at supper. Two disciples, perhaps including Simon the Leper, are also seated at the table. The middle scene depicts the **Angel at the empty tomb and one of the Maries -**

perhaps Mary Magdalene. The angel points heavenward with his right arm. Mary in pink robes and loose blonde hair, kneels, her hands clasped. A stylised tree stands on the left. The right panel portrays two female saints, one kneeling before the other with arms outstretched. The standing figure embraces and comforts her. It seems likely that the upright figure represents **The Virgin Mary**, dressed in her blue mantle, though the white paint of her face and halo have faded. The kneeling figure in a russet gown could be her kinsman, **Elizabeth at the Visitation.** Part of a wall and an urn containing flowers (perhaps lilies, suggestive of Mary) in the background places the meeting in a garden.

The third and fourth windows along the north wall contain plain glass. The fifth window is dedicated 'In affectionate memory of Abraham **Hirst** of Hullen Edge Esqre by his Nephews and Nieces A.D. 1866'. The subject of the two-light window is the parable of **The Good Samaritan**. The battered and bruised traveller is seated half naked on the left, his blue and white cloak over his knees.

The good Samaritan, bearded and dressed in a bright red gown leans over him holding him up and cleaning his upper body with a cloth. He has already bandaged his head. The Samaritan's horse looks on in the background, beside a tree and green bush. The scene is framed by two slim pillars and an arch. The tracery above is painted with red, white and blue patterns. The right hand light shows the Samaritan with the innkeeper, dressed in a blue tunic, pointing to the traveller who is slumped on the ground, bandaged and half-dressed. The upper tracery is similar to that of the left hand panel.

The sixth window - the last one on the north side - is dedicated 'To the Glory of God and in memory of **Francis Musson** Priest for 21 years Rector of Elland, who died Feb. 20th 1892. Aged 66 years. This window was erected by Parishioners & Friends'. The cost was £70. It is singularly appropriate that such a fine window was dedicated to the Rev'd Musson who, it may be recalled, did much to preserve the ancient fragments of glass from, chiefly, the eastern part of the church and had them inserted in the two pairs of windows in the west wall. It is also significant that the parishioners and friends chose to place the glazing and painting with the eminent designer and leading stained glass studios of **Charles Eamer Kempe** (1837-1907). Examples of his work are found in dozens of churches and cathedrals throughout Britain and the window in St Mary's is a fine example of his exceptional figurative work and translucent use of colour and white glass.

The subject of the window is the parentage of **St John the Baptist: Zacharias** or **Zechariah and Elizabeth**. Zacharias stands on the left, richly dressed as a priest of the order of Abia (or Abijah) in the Temple (Luke: 1. 5*f*). He is dressed in long white robes and a high turban with a red band and is barefoot (which usually signifies a saint in religious art). A red nimbus surrounds his head also denoting his saintliness. In his left hand he holds the golden chains of a thurible (censer) which he has filled with incense using a golden spoon. His face is finely painted, as indeed is the elaborate background of flowers, leaves and patterns and the colourful borders. A scroll above his head announces: *Zacharias pater divi Johannis Baptistae* ('Zacharias father of St John the Baptist').

Elizabeth on the right is equally beautifully painted, her face - clearly that of an older woman - is finely etched as she looks down at her young son. She is wearing a white cloak edged with a black and silver pattern, with a similarly white tunic over a red dress. Her halo is blue. Her son is already wearing the yellow camel skin of his years in the wilderness and he carries his symbol, the long cross and banner. He carries a scroll with the words: *Ecce agnus Dei* ('Behold the lamb of God'), in reference to Jesus. Mother and son are surrounded by a similar rich background and borders to those framing Zacharias. Above Elizabeth's head hangs another scroll: *Elizabetha mater divi Johannis* ('Elizabeth mother of St John').

The seventh window along the north is within the tower space and has plain glass. The two pairs of medieval glass fragments at the west end have already been discussed. **The West Window** high up in the tower is not clearly visible from the church's main interior owing to the recent additional inner ceiling of the community room and can be seen only from the sanctuary or from inside the first floor of the tower. For several decades it was even further obscured by the construction of a gallery in the 18th century. Indeed the *Halifax Guardian*, writing of its installation in 1851 was appalled by this situation as we shall see later.

The window's fine late 15th century stonework may well have encased coloured glass at its inception but sadly no record of such early glass has as yet been found, though it is possible that some of the fragments in the lower windows may have been part of the original scheme. The 1851 glass was created by William Wailes of Newcastle who, of course, also restored the east window. It was given by the parishioners in memory of two ministers of Elland, Rev'd Christopher Atkinson, who served the church from 1800 to 1843, when he was succeeded by his son William, minister up to 1849.

The window consists of three lights divided into six scenes with six traceries above. Top left we see **The Presentation at the Temple**, with the child Jesus, arms outstretched, being held by his mother, who wears a long blue dress covered by a green mantle. Joseph stands behind, in a red gown. Simeon, in white and red robes, holds out his hands to receive the child. Another figure in white is partially visible on the extreme right. The figures are set against a blue background and framed by a high arcade surmounted by crocketed and richly decorated red and gold architectural features. Above this is a diamond pattern of white and silver glass. The borders are also richly painted with floral motifs.

The middle scene depicts **The Baptism of Christ.** Christ in the centre, partly naked though with a russet gown from the waist down stands in the River Jordan - here

Photo courtesy of Glenn Littlewood

a small patch of blue - as John the Baptist, on a small green rise above, pours water over Christ's head. He is dressed in brown and carries a staff with a pennant. This scene differs from Wailes's painting in the east window (which may have copied the remains of the original medieval panel) by adding four figures on the extreme left. The architectural frame above is practically identical to the left hand window with the addition of a dove, symbolising the Holy Spirit, over a scroll with the words of God: 'This is my beloved Son'.

The top right-hand scene shows Christ holding a child to his breast, his right hand raised in blessing. This is perhaps referring to his words **'Suffer little children to come unto me'** (Matthew: 19. 13-15; Luke: 18. 15-17). Christ, in a white robe and red mantle, is attended by three standing male figures on the right and three kneeling women, one holding a child, on the left. The architectural framework and background is identical to the first window.

The three lower panels are much smaller and each depicts a figure within a quadrilobe, with floral borders against a decorated leaded diamond background. All three figures are angels with large wings of blue, white, green and gold. The angel on the left in a white robe and green cloak faces right. He holds a scroll with the words, 'His name was called Jesus'.The angel in the centre in a blue mantle over a white tunic looks outwards with a scroll which reads: 'The same is He which baptizeth with the Holy Ghost'. The angel on the right, dressed in green and white, faces left holding a scroll with the legend 'Suffer little children to come unto me.' This is a well-preserved window with vibrant colours which still retain their lustre and shows William Wailes' work at its best.

The South Aisle of the nave contains five windows, all part of the restoration in the 1850s. This wall of the church had been subject to structural alterations in the early 18th century when the first of three galleries was built around the church to accommodate the growing population. There is stained glass in the first three windows, looking from east to west.

The **first window** (which is actually in **St John's Chapel**) is extremely fine and was beautifully designed and painted by the firm of **John Hardman**, which began manufacturing stained glass in 1848, having been encouraged by the great Victorian church artist and architect, Augustus Pugin. It bears the inscription 'To the Glory of God this window is placed in the Church of St Mary Elland by William Irvine **Holdsworth**, Greenroyd, Halifax' and portrays **The Transfiguration of Christ:** Matthew17: 1-8; Mark 9: 2-8; Luke 9: 28-36 and mentioned in 2 Peter 1: 16 – 18. It is undated but is thought to have been inserted in 1876.

This square-headed window contains three lights, each with cinquefoil tracery divided horizontally into two scenes with figures. The figures are set against an architectural background of white and gold pinnacles and crocketed gables. Top left shows **Moses** in a blue tunic covered by white robes with decorated gold edging. He holds a staff in his extended right hand and the tablet containing the Ten Commandments in his left. He faces slightly to his left to the central image of Christ and he bears two short horns on his head. This part of his iconography is traditional but for some time now has been recognised as being based on a mistranslation of a passage in Exodus 34: 29-30, 35 where the Hebrew word *qeren* can mean both 'horn' and 'shining' (rather like a horn). Moses has thus been portrayed with horns for centuries (even, famously, by Michelangelo).

The central top panel depicts the transfigured **Christ**, facing outwards with arms aloft in a white robe with gold patterns. He is set against a background of bright red swirls of drapery on which are superimposed twelve roundels of haloed heads, perhaps representing the heavenly host. He is standing on a slight rise, representing Mount Tabor.

The figure in the top right panel shows the prophet **Elijah**, bearded and facing to his right, his arms stretched out towards Christ. He is robed in white with a vivid blue tunic over his arms and shoulders. Set against a red background, he - like Moses in the left hand panel - is embraced by an outer hemicircle of white light and a similar but wider band of the same which is intended to envelop Christ and represents the brilliant shining light of Transfiguration.

The lower order of panels, slightly smaller with no painted pinnacles or gables above their background of three-dimensional triptychs, depict the three disciples, **Peter, James and John**, who accompanied Jesus up the mountain. On the left, in a blue tunic and embroidered russet robe one of the older disciples - either Peter or James - kneels to his left, drowsy with sleep as he holds his head with his left hand. In the centre, the other older disciple props himself up with his left side, gazing outwards sleepily, his left hand on top of his head, one of his naked feet stretched out. He is dressed in a pale blue tunic and maroon robe and behind him golden rays fan out from below the Christ figure above. The youngest disciple, John, on the right, beardless with fair hair and robed entirely in red, kneels to his right in an attitude of prayer. Behind him are placed stylised green boughs and leaves of trees. Below each apostle is an architectural motif in white and gold bearing the window's dedication.

The **second window** along the south wall was designed and painted by the Leeds firm of **Powell Brothers** (as in second window in the north aisle). It bears the dedication 'To the Glory of God in loving memory of John **Wilkinson** of Beech Grove. This window is dedicated by his widow Sarah Wilkinson in 1885'. The window consists of two lights each with trefoil tracery with a small amount of coloured glass above. Both lights illustrate a composite scene with **two angels** on the left, the nearer one kneeling, the second one standing and both facing to their left, their arms outstretched towards **Christ** in the right hand light. He leans towards them, his right arm outstretched, his left hand over his right breast. **Two further angels** stand behind and to his right, one holding Christ's left elbow, the one on his right holding his right arm and gazing across at him. The angels in the left hand panel wear long cream robes with pink tints, the nearer angel with an olive-green tunic, the other in bright red. The white and yellow feathers of their open wings are iridescent and finely drawn.

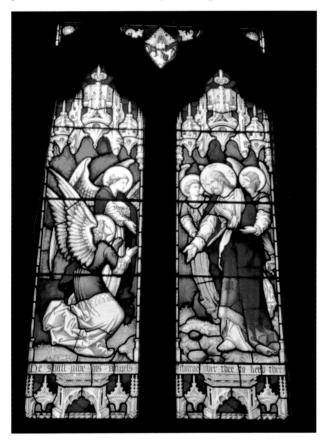

In the right-hand panel the nearer angel mostly hidden behind Christ wears a mixture of white, pink and blue; the second angel is robed in light green and white. Christ Himself wears a white tunic with yellow tints and a bright red cloak. The drapery of all five figures is delicately painted and the colours are striking. As indeed are those of the background architectural settings with red and amber gables above, and bright blue diapered glass behind the figures who stand on pale green vegetation. On the bottom left, drawn outlines of buildings represent the holy city. The gothic script beneath the scenes, itself standing above further three-dimensional architectural features, reads 'He shall give his angels charge over thee to keep thee' from Psalm 91:11 – words of comfort to the bereaved donor and her late husband.

The third window down this aisle is yet another designed by **William Wailes** and bears the dedication: 'Erected by **A. Pitchforth** in affectionate memory of his late family. June 1869.' The architectural frame of a square-headed, two light window with trefoils and a small amount of coloured glass above the two cusps are similar in arrangement to the previous window. The scene in the left panel depicts **The laying out of Christ - the Pietà** - following his crucifixion. Christ, in white grave cloths lies on a richly-decorated bier.

His beloved disciple, St John dressed in purple, is leaning over him, adjusting the cloths. His mother, in bright green, leans over John, her right hand clutching her throat whilst Mary Magdalen kneels with bowed head in the foreground caressing Christ's right hand. Her long blond tresses and her alabaster jar, pictured bottom left, clearly identify her and also reference the 'Mary' who anointed Christ before the Last Supper.

Two bearded men are also portrayed: on the extreme left an older man, wearing a green cloak and russet cap. On the extreme right, a younger man in orange with a mauve cap grasps the cloth with both hands. One of these - presumably the younger man - is assuredly Joseph of Arimathea, who arranged Christ's burial in his own tomb; the older man perhaps represents Nicodemus who assisted Joseph in anointing the body with spices. Neither man is given a halo here, though they are traditionally regarded as saints in the Orthodox, Roman Catholic and Anglican Churches. The background to the scene is of pale blue glass in addition to pastel green, mauve and pink vegetation. The three crosses of Calvary stand in stark contrast on a green hill.

The right-hand panel shows **Christ Resurrected**, standing erect in robes of bright red, green and white. He holds up his hands, the cross of resurrection in his left hand. Below him lie two sleeping soldiers in vivid blue, green and russet robes. Leafy vegetation grows around Christ's feet as he stands against a bright blue background. On the extreme right is a representation of the now discarded grave cloth and an upright stone column of the empty tomb. Below both panels are small frames of angels in red and white with outstretched wings of gold, purple and green and bearing a scroll. The left one reads: 'Blessed are the dead'. The right one completes the sentence: 'which die in the Lord'.

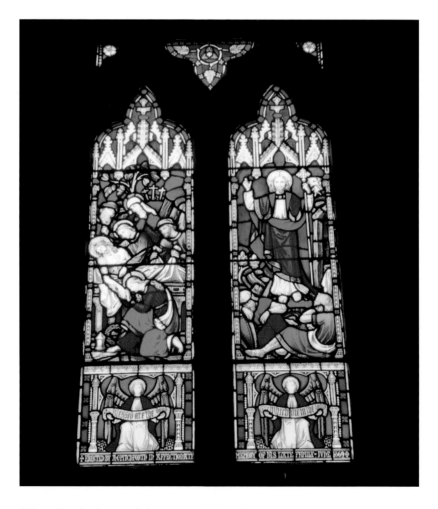

The third and fourth windows of the south aisle (the last one being in the tower space) are of plain glass.

7. INTERIOR BURIALS AND MEMORIAL TABLETS

Some years before the restoration of St Mary's in the 1850s/60s there still existed - probably in the north chapel - remains of several sculpted memorials which had been recorded by the antiquarian the Rev'd John Watson in 1775. According to drawings reproduced in his book *The History and Antiquities of the Parish of Halifax in Yorkshire*, these represented members of the Savile and Thornhill families and dated from the sixteenth and seventeenth centuries. Lucy Hamerton, a long-serving member of the church, recalled in her book *Olde Eland* (1901) that her family had seen them early in the 1800s. Sadly, these memorials have all disappeared without trace. However, today, the church contains several more recent commemorative plaques attached to its walls.

The Chancel has always been considered the most important part of the church where high status parishioners were buried and commemorated. Over the years, along with the side chapels, it was the burial place as we have seen of the Eland, Savile, Thornhill and, later, Clay families as well as some members of the clergy. The Rev'd John Watson, writing in 1775, recorded several high status burials in the chancel, from a list produced by the antiquarian and genealogist, James Torre (1649-1699). In addition to Saviles and Thornhills one gravestone had a Latin inscription to Peter Ashton, Priest, who died 30 October, 1698 aged 65. A note by Dr Johnston dated 23 July, 1669 revealed that two members of the Clay family of Clayhouse, Greetland had also been interred in the chancel: John Clay, gent., who died 18 June, 1616 and his grandson, Captain John Clay. The latter, a Royalist soldier, had in fact died of his wounds on 13 September 1643 several weeks after the battle of Adwalton Moor (near Batley), in which the Parliamentarian army had been decisively beaten.

From the eighteenth century onwards, the Saviles having moved to Rufford Abbey, the Thornhills to Riddlesworth Hall in Norfolk and the main Clay male line being extinct, other local families were in the ascendancy and some were memorialised by stone or marble tablets in the eastern arm of the church.

Alongside the window on the **south wall of the chancel** a large wall tablet erected by the **Rawson family,** surmounted by a coat of arms and white marble bust records that 'Thomas **Horton** Esquire, of Howroyde' died in 1829 and that his widow, Lady Mary Horton died in 1852. Above the altar rail a monument records that 'near this place below lies the body of William Horton of Howroyde who died aged 64 in 1715'. This also refers to the death of Mrs Mary Horton who died in 1750. There is a further monument to the Hortons further west on this wall. A small, white marble tablet on a black base with triangular cornice high up between the two arcades commemorates 'Thomas Horton, Esquire' and his widow, Lady Mary Horton, both of Howroyde. This fine Grade 1 listed Manor House, originally built by the Horton family in 1642, still stands in the village of Barkisland which was, until the nineteenth century, within the parish of Elland.

Five memorial tablets decorate the **north wall of the chancel**. The lower three are larger and consist of rectangular tablets surmounted by a tall, black triangular pediments and small additions below. The one nearest the east window records the life of Jeremiah **Dyson** of Willow Hall in Skircoat, who died in 1791. He was a 'merchant resident many years in LISBON and a Member of the British Factory there.' His wife Elizabeth and son Thomas are likewise remembered.

The central tablet was erected in memory of Benjamin **Walker** 'late of Bay Hall near Huddersfield' who died aged 88 in 1808. His niece, Mary, had married Daniel **Rushforth** of Elland who are also both commemorated, Daniel being described in glowing terms: 'He was thro' Life a pious & faithful Observer of religious and moral Duties'. The name of their grandson Richard Walker Rushforth (died 1875), was added in the hemicircle below the main plaque.

The left-hand slightly smaller tablet commemorates Thomas **Horton** of Barkisland Hall who married Everilde **Thornhill**, 'daughter of John Thornhill, Esquire by whom he had six Sons and five Daughters of whom the only Survivors' were Susanna, Elizabeth and Anne, the latter being interred in 1750. Barkisland Hall, still today a magnificent structure, had been built by John Gledhill who married Sarah, a daughter of the Horton family, and bears their initials with the date of its completion in 1638.

A further tablet on the upper north wall of the chancel, a simple white marble plaque with a raised apex, records the death in 1808 of Elizabeth **Rushforth**, daughter of Richard **Collingwood** of Elland. Her husband died in 1841 whilst his second wife, Mrs Mary Ann Rushforth, daughter of Richard Collingwood of Elland died in 1856.

On its right, the final tablet high on the north wall is composed of a raised shield of white marble on a larger plaque and records two members of the **Haigh** family: John the father, who died at the advanced age of 91 and his son, also John, who died in 1808 aged 70. The widow of the younger Haigh is also recorded as Susannah, daughter of John **Walker** of Feathers Green in Sowerby who died in May 1818, aged 75. Beneath the shield is a small crest of the Haigh family.

The **North Chapel**, as explained earlier, was from the onset built as a resting place for members of the **Thornhill family**. In addition to the niches in the crypt in this chapel, described above, there are two fine memorial plaques to members of the family on the north wall and one on the south. It may be recalled that the heiress of the Thornhills had married into the Saviles in the 15th century. The younger Thornhill branch which were buried in Elland had inherited Fixby Hall, within St Mary's ancient parish, and indeed there was a further union with the Saviles when the two families later intermarried.

The impressive marble wall memorial at the entrance to the north chapel is one of the earliest in the church, dating from the reign of King Charles 11 and may be compared with the Grantham monument (see below). It incorporates a rectangular plaque of marble surrounded by a wreathed border made of rare blue john semi-precious stone, both materials mined only in parts of Derbyshire. The monument is supported by a brown plinth blazoned with the (now fading) crest of the **Wentworth** family and a tall brown column with Corinthian capitals, probably made of cockleshell marble, on either side. The use of two types of stone from Derbyshire may be a homage to John Thornhill's first wife. Additional plinths on each column support brown-coloured figures with right arms upraised. They probably held some device at one time. Above the plaque in the centre, slightly leaning forward, a further wreathed device incorporates a composite coat of arms of Thornhill and Wentworth. The head of another figure stands on a helmet (signifying knighthood) and mantling at the apex. The whole monument is supported by two floriated corbels.

The inscription on the plaque reads: 'IN MEMORY of John Thornhill of Fixby Esq who died on the 21st Day Octr 1669, in the 54th Year of Age, He was twice married: for his first Wife

he had Dorothy Collinbell Daughter & Heiress of George Collinbell Esqr in Derbyshire, From this happy Wedlock, he had but one Daughter named Ann, who died within ye compass of two Years. He afterwards married Everilde, eldest Daughter & Coheiress of Sir George Wentworth Knight of Wooley [*sic*], in the County of York, Sept 17th: 1650, by whom he had 3 Sons & 3 Daughters, Viz: Everilde, Elizabeth, John, George, Frances & Thos' [*Thomas*]. Elizabeth & John died young. He lies interred near this Place. FAREWELL. *RESQUIESCAT IN PACE QUI PACIFICE VIXIT. [May he rest in peace, he who lived in peace].*

Woolley Hall, between Wakefield and Barnsley, was the seat of the Wentworth family for generations up to the 20th century. The most celebrated member was Thomas, 1st Earl of Strafford (1593-1641), statesman and supporter of King Charles 1. Woolley Hall, near Wakefield, came into the Wentworth family in the mid 16th century. It is a Grade 11* listed building.

The second north wall memorial to the Thornhills, further east, is also a fine composition. It is dedicated to six members of the family including George Thornhill of Fixby (died 1687), who is also commemorated by a plaque on the opposite wall (see below). The marble plaque also lists his four sons: Brian (died 1701, aged 24), Thomas (died 1751, aged 73), John (died 1756, aged 77), George (died 1754, aged 73) and the latter's wife Sarah (died 1758, aged 52). It is highly likely that all these members, along with those on the previous plaque are interred in the Thornhill vault: indeed, several are recognised by inscriptions on the niches. Fixby Hall, now the home of Huddersfield Golf Club, is a fine Grade 11 listed building.

The construction of the wall tablet is not dissimilar to the previous monument. The marble tablet is surmounted on a floral rectangular marble plinth and framed by two pillars (with foliated capitals) possibly made of cockleshell marble from Derbyshire behind which are plain pilasters. These all stand on decorated corbels with swags. Below the tablet is a curved panel with a foliated device. At the top of the monument a broken pediment frames a shield bearing the Thornhill coat of arms flanked by a further two floral swags. It is likely, given its style, that this monument was erected on the death of Brian Thornhill in 1701, with space for his family to be added later. These two monuments on the chapel's north wall were subject to restoration and cleaning by Elliott Ryder Conservation in around 2012.

The last monument in the north chapel is squeezed into a space high up on the **south wall** between the eastern wall and the easternmost arch of the chancel. As mentioned above, this was erected 'IN MEMORY of George Thornhill who married the Daughter of THOMAS WIVELL, Esqr: by her had Eight Sons and Three Daughters, he died in the 32nd Year of his Age in the Year of our Lord, 1687'. Beneath a scrolled pattern, the inscription continues, 'Whose Body now rests in Peace waiting the Resurrection of the Just'. This black marble plaque is enclosed in a lighter marble frame. It stands between two black pillars with Corinthian capitals. The pediment above contains a cartouche with the coloured arms of Thornhill and Wivell conjoined.

Moving on to the **South Wall of the Nave Aisle,** this contains one monument between the first two windows. The white marble plaque on a dark grey marble base is dedicated to Mary and Ely **Wilkinson,** Esquire of Broad Carr. Mary died in April 1840 aged 67, John in September 1847 aged 70. Their son Ely, who died in January 1853 aged 40, is also recorded. At the apex of the dedication is a carving of a dove, symbolising the Holy Spirit. The plaque is supported by two corbels with foliated designs.

The North Wall of the Nave Aisle at the western end contains an early, impressive monument to Thomas **Grantham** and family. It has also received attention from the Elliott Ryder Conservation team. From the top down it consists of a central decorated shield with surrounding mantling, surrounded by a helm which itself has a carved head above. The shield, which bears the arms of the Grantham family, is also flanked by two further undecorated shields. A moulded entablature sits above a tall course of carved stiff leaf foliage and a plain rectangular panel. A moulded course of bead and reel decoration runs vertically below on both sides, returning on itself and ending in spiral volutes. The material in these elements seem to be alabaster and are finely carved. They frame a rectangular black inscription panel of carboniferous limestone which is surrounded by two thin, decorated timber elements. Below the inscription panel and volutes is a plain base with a central carved rosette. The whole monument is supported by five corbels, the central one being in the form of a grotesque head.

The inscription reads: 'This Monument Likewise preserves the Memory of Thos Grantham Esqr of Mure in the County of York, Son of Thos Grantham Esqr: late of Goltho in the County of Lincoln; He married Frances, second Daughter of Sir George Wentworth of Wooley, and departed this life at Fixby, April 1st: 1668, in the 35th: Year of his Age. John Grantham, youngest Son of the said Thos: Grantham Esq: of Goltho, died at Fixby March 7th : 1667, in the 17th: Year of his Age. Frances Grantham, Wife of the abovesaid Thos: Grantham Esqr: of Mure, died March 12th: 1692 & lies in her Husband's Grave, Beside them, lies Vincent Grantham their only Son, who died when he was twelve Years of Age. Whose Bodies now rest in Peace waiting the Resurrection of the just.'

It is clear that the Grantham and the early Thornhill monument in the North Chapel can be considered a pair as they relate to the same extended families and were produced and erected at around the same time: the 1660s. The opening word 'Likewise' in the Grantham inscription strongly suggests that it may originally have been placed alongside, or at least close to, the Thornhill memorial. The quality of both compositions and inscriptions are of a high order.

The Tower space (now the community room at the west of the church) contains four wall monuments. On the south side, close to the west wall, hangs a memorial in white and black marble dedicated to the **Drake** family. It is similar in style to the lower memorials on the chancel north wall. At the top, a tall triangular pediment in black marble contains a white urn with two handles. Below this a smaller white marble raised pediment surmounts an entablature set upon two pillars with simple capitals standing on a flat panel above a curved extension containing an inscription. The pillars and entablature frame a white marble panel leaning inwards containing an inscription to Thomas Drake 'late of Ashday Hall in this parish who departed this life at Walworth in the parish of St Mary Newington in the County of Surrey on the 6th June 1819 in the 77th year of his age. His remains are deposited in the above parish of St Mary Newington with those of his late wife'. The roundel below the main section of the monument adds the inscription: 'This monument was erected by his nephew Thomas Drake as an intended tribute of gratitude and of esteem for one universally esteemed and lamented'. Ashday Hall, Thomas Drakes' original residence, is an impressive Grade 11 listed early 18th century Manor House in the village of Southowram, though the history of the manor goes back several more centuries.

To the right of the previous monument high up on the west wall hang memorials to Mary, wife of John **Crowther**, 'Surgeon of Elland', died 16 June 1819 aged 30 and to John **Hirst** and his wife Delia. The two seem to be connected, the Crowther monument perching above the other, its lower part - a circular striated section receding to a small knob - just touching the much larger Hirst memorial. The inscription tablets of both are similar, trapezoidal in shape, in white marble on a black base. The Crowther section is surmounted by a reversed version in black of the tablet's shape with a semi-circular disc at its centre. The Hirst tablet has a decorated pediment of two spiral motifs meeting at the centre of a flat pediment. Below the tablet a further white marble base is decorated with two swags above a central oval disc partly surrounded by a floral wreath on a semi-circular disc. The lower tablet describes 'John Hirst Esquire of Bradley Mills, near Halifax' who died in 1837 and was 'erected by her who best knew his worth, His deeply deploring widow'. His widow, Delia, died six years later in 1843, aged 49 according to the additional inscription.

To the right of the central west door is a large, imposing monument squeezed in between a large stone pier and a pair of windows containing the medieval glass discussed earlier. Indeed, this memorial is practically now above the kitchen area of the community room. This is hardly ideal, as the Elliott Ryder Conservationist observed in his notes. However, its size and position just above eye level does make it easier to read than others around the church.

It is dedicated to **Northend Nichols** and members of his extended family. Northend Nichols, as well as rejoicing in an unusual Christian name, was something of a character, as we shall see later. The monument itself is impressive. It consists of a plain dark- grey background panel surmounted by a white marble carved female figure leaning on a large urn. To the right of the scene is a cross and palm tree, presumably representing the Holy Land. The white marble inscription panel is surmounted by a moulded entablature and stiff leaf course and flanked by foliate pilasters. It sits on two ornately carved corbels on either side of a small shield which appears to be blank.

The inscription reveals that 'Northend Nichols, Esqr,…having formerly served as Captain in His Majesty's 37th Regiment of Foot, in which he distinguished himself, during the long and arduous campaign in North America, as well as in other parts of the Globe, at last sought retirement from public life, at Elland, the place of his nativity, where he died on the 27th day of July, 1818, aged 81 years'. His army service in North America would clearly have been during the American War of Independence in the 1770s.

His only sister Sarah **Wood** 'of Staups-House in Northowram' who had pre-deceased him in 1807, is listed next. The remains of both were interred 'in the family vault in this church'. Her only son, 'Samuel Wood Esqre who had died even earlier, is then recorded. He, 'after a residence of several years in the East Indies, died on his passage from thence to his native country, the 17th day of July, 1798, aged 32 years. His remains were interred in the island of Tranquebar'. The label 'East Indies' at that time referred to those areas of south-east Asia - now India, Pakistan, Sri Lanka, Bangladesh and Myanmar (Burma) - where the British were trading and later colonising. 'Tranquebar' is not actually an island but an historic coastal town in Tamil Nadu, southern India, now called Tharangambadi, meaning 'land of the swinging waves'.

The daughter of Sarah Wood, Martha **Hoyle**, wife of the Revd E. Hoyle, who died in 1824, aged 53 is next recorded. She was 'in life respected and beloved and in death lamented'. It concludes with the following inscription: 'This monument is erected by a near surviving Relative, from the tenderest motives of Gratitude and Affection.' However, further names are added below: Phoebe, widow of 'John **Greenwood** Esqre of Cross Hill Halifax, and Daughter of the above Sarah Wood', who died in 1829, aged 68. Finally the 'Revd Charles John Wood **Barton**, B.A. grandson of the above E. and Martha Hoyle and son of the Revd Chas. Barton, who died at Canton in China, Septr 2nd. 1851 aged 25 Years'.

The final wall monument is mounted on the south wall of the tower space (currently the kitchen area) close to the angle with the west wall. It is dedicated to Rebecca and William **Wilkinson.** Backed by a black panel with a raised point at the apex, the tablet consists of a simple rectangle of white marble surmounted by a decorated pediment standing on a wide plinth with two decorated corbels. The main decoration is within the triangular space above the pediment and consists of a folded shroud draped over a decorated urn, all in white marble against the black background. Within the inscription panel Rebecca is described as being of Brow House in Greetland and the daughter of Samuel and Mary **Walker** of 'Holy Well Green'. She was born in Stainland in 1792 and died in June in 1852, aged 60. Her husband, William Wilkinson, is recorded as dying in May 1855, aged 64.

In addition to those high status interments in the chancel mentioned earlier, there were also many other burials within the church walls. The earliest of these were most probably unrecorded by gravestones, which came into use only from the sixteenth century onwards for the wealthy and from the eighteenth century for others. Under the present floorboards and seating lie dozens of parishioners whose gravestones paved the church up to the restoration of the 1850s. The earliest of these refers to a member of the family which would found the **Brooksbank** School (known later for a time as Elland Grammar) in 1712: 'Here lies the remains of Nicholas **Brooksbank** of Elland whose soul returned to God that gave it, the [*illegible*] day of January 1670.'

Many of the family graves recorded in the main body of the church (including under the tower space) contain surnames still found in the area: **Wilkinson, Radcliffe, Bottomley, Holroyd, Ramsden, Schofield, Hodgson** and **Woodhead.** Some families were also interred in the chancel: **Rushforth, Outram, Burnett, Denbigh** and **Dyson.** The last interment in the church was that of Martha **Rushworth** who died 7 March, 1853, aged 75 years. Following the church's restoration no further burials took place within the church walls.

WAR MEMORIALS

A bronze tablet is attached to the north pier of the tower leading into the community room recording the 62 parishioners who lost their lives in the Great War of 1914-1918. They were members of St Mary's, All Saints and St Michael's churches. The last-named church was first established in a conservatory in the Lower Edge area of the parish by the Rev'd Christopher Atkinson in 1843 but it took over fifty years before church and school buildings were completed. St Michael's eventually closed as a place of worship in 1954 though the schoolroom remained open and The Eucharist continued to be offered until 1979 when it, too, was closed, to be demolished shortly after.

Below the Great War memorial a smaller bronze tablet records the names of the six parishioners who lost their lives in the Second World War of 1939-1945. One of the young men listed on the Great War memorial is also remembered by a brass plaque on the back row of the south (*decani*) choir stalls. Killed in the battle of the Somme on 27 August, 1916 aged 22, Rifleman Leonard Sutcliffe of the King's Royal Regiment had been a member of the church choir.

A further metal plaque, beneath the main war memorials, is connected with the Second World War. Awarded by the Ministry of Aircraft Production in 1941, shortly after the Battle of Britain when many aircraft had been lost, it recognises the contribution of the people of Elland and District who 'earned the gratitude of the British Nations sustaining the valour of the Royal Air Force and fortifying the cause of freedom by the gift of **Spitfire Aircraft**.' The churches and townspeople had collected valuable funds in the war effort.

FURTHER INTERIOR MEMORIALS

Contributions towards the funding of the new glass in the west window, in memory of the **Reverend Atkinsons**, father Christopher and son William, who were ministers between 1802 and 1849, exceeded the cost and a lectern-cum-reading desk was purchased with the surplus. A brass plaque on the rear of the desk, used by the assistant priest on the north (*cantoris*) side of the chancel, bears a brass commemorative plaque with an inscription in gothic lettering: 'This reading desk and lectern erected with the residue of the funds subscribed for the memorial window at the west end of this church, placed there in memory of the **Revd. Christopher Atkinson, M.A.,** who died May XVth MDCCCLIII [1853] aged LXX [70] years, also of his son the **Revd. William Atkinson, M.A.,** who died April XI MDCCCL [1850] aged XXXVII [37] years, successively incumbents of Elland. Their remains were deposited in the family vault at St Paul's Church, Leeds.'

Two small brass plaques are also attached to the priests' seats on either side of the chancel, both with the simple inscription: 'In Memory of William **Robison** died April 11th 1913.'

The restoration of the church from the mid 1850s onwards is commemorated by a dark grey plaque with a raised gold inscription in gothic lettering above the war memorials which registers the completion of the work in 1866. The names of the incumbent, Edward **Sandford** and the two churchwardens, Thomas Wallis **Townsend** and John Gilbert **Robinson** are inscribed. The name of a more recent long-serving churchwarden, Miles Twisleton **Prestwich**, who died in office in 1986, is recorded on an elegant stone plaque on the westernmost pier of the nave.

On the west side of the organ case plaques have been affixed to record the faithful service of church organists (see below).

8. THE INTERIOR FABRIC

Baptismal Font.

The original medieval font in which generations of infants had been baptised was thrown out in 1651, early during the rule of the Puritan Commonwealth under Oliver Cromwell to be replaced by a simple basin. Following the return of the Monarchy under King Charles II the present font, made of local millstone grit, was erected in 1662.

The large basin and slightly smaller trunk are octagonal, standing on a wider, octagonal plinth. The Churchwardens' Accounts reveal that the body and top of the new font with leading, staples and lock - along with ale for the workmen - cost £6 17s. It was transported to the church by Mr John Clay of Clayhouse, who was paid 5s 6d. Later, in 1850, it was replaced by

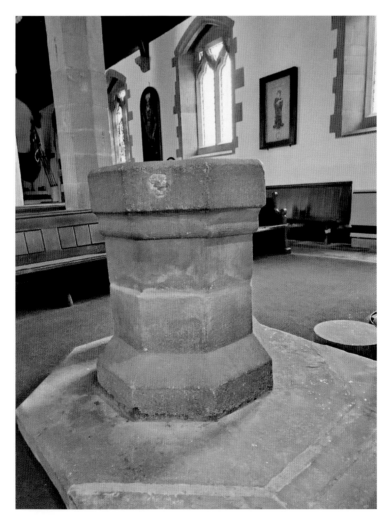

a newer version but this proved unpopular and the 1662 font was returned in 1856 during the church restoration. A font was originally placed at the south-west of the nave near the porch entrance symbolising a new beginning in the church of Christ. This was the case at St Mary's until 1928 when it was moved to the back of the tower space before the west door. In recent years it has been moved once more to, this time to the front of the nave, before the north side of the chancel arch, as a witness to the congregation.

Church Seating.

When the church was first built and for many years during the medieval period the people had no seating and simply stood, or knelt, on the bare earth. Occasional benches along the walls for the elderly and infirm would have provided the only relief. The church would have been later paved with local stone though, as we have seen, it was also used for burials, a practice which continued up to the mid 19th century. The chancel was initially reserved for leading families and even by 1648 the cost of a burial in the chancel at 6s 8d was double that of in the nave (3s 4d).

After the Reformation and the establishment of the Church of England, individual seats and benches were gradually introduced at their own expense by the wealthier members of the congregation for themselves, their tenants and retainers. Inevitably they chose to position them in and around the chancel. Others followed, filling up the nave. Gradually 'rental fees' were introduced, a practice which continued for generations. These arrangements often led to arguments. The Churchwardens' Accounts include several references to these events; one such, dated 2 April 1583, gives a very detailed list of the proposed seating 'for the avoyding of troble and contention that hath beene and doth Dayly arise amongst sundry Inhabitants of the same parish'. At times arguments led to threats. During the early 1800s when some of the seating was being replaced by pews made of deal (rented at two shillings per family), Capt. Northend Nichols, a retired army officer whose monument has already been discussed, would often stand by his original oak family pew with its brass plaque and, sword drawn, deter others from using or replacing it!

The restoration of the church in the 1850s/60s brought an end to these contentious arrangements. The eastern arm was laid with black and red Minton tiles, with floorboards and stone flags covering the nave gravestones. Fine, new oak pews with decorated finials at each end were installed in the nave and remain in use to this day, providing seating for around 250 people.

Altar/Communion Table and liturgies

The original chancel altar would have been made of stone and, in accordance with Roman Catholic practice, would most likely have contained a holy relic, related to the patron saint, St Mary. During the course of the Reformation from the reign of King Edward VI onwards, church altars were replaced by wooden tables. At St Mary's the new communion table was railed in 1671 and in 1693 silk covers were added to the rails. Around ten years later the communion table cloth was repaired at a cost of 12s 4p. In 1878 the table was considered to be unsafe and was replaced by the present one. It would later be restored by Mr Brook (the craftsman who restored the *miserere* seats) and in 1904 was given to the newly opened, though as yet incomplete, All Saints' Church in Elland, where it is currently in use as a bookstall. It contains fine examples of 16th century carving.

The altar has traditionally been placed against the east wall of the chancel though at times during its more recent history it has been moved to the chancel entrance or to the front of the nave. It is currently restored to its original position in front of the east wall. There is also an altar at the east end of the St Nicholas Chapel (see below) and a small communion table at the entrance of the much reduced Chapel of St John the Evangelist, where much of the space now contains the organ chamber and console.

Mass would have been said or sung at any or all of these altars during the Middle Ages on a daily basis. With the introduction of the Book of Common Prayer in the sixteenth century the service of Holy Communion generally took place weekly. The offering of Holy Communion was reduced considerably during the Commonwealth (1649-1660) and even after the restoration of the monarchy communion services were restricted to one a month (as recorded in 1695). The fact that most parishioners received holy communion at Easter is underlined by an entry in the Accounts stating that it was celebrated on three days over Easter in 1665. The bread and wine over the weekend cost £2 1s 7d. A later entry in 1688 notes that the bill for the Easter and preceding three celebrations, stretched over six months came to £4 7s 3d.

The introduction of the Revised Book of Common Prayer in 1662 is recorded in St Mary's Accounts when 11s 6d was spent on a copy (or copies) in that year. Two years earlier following the restoration of the monarchy under King Charles 11 a copy (or copies) had already been purchased at a cost of 8s. Doubtless this would have been the earlier book, banned under the Commonwealth. A further interesting note in the Accounts for 1688 refers to a payment to 'Francis Bentley for binding the Great Bible, 10s.' In the same year there is a note of contributions amounting to £1 14s 5d from parishioners towards the cost of '6 Communions for the poor'.

During the eighteenth and nineteenth centuries Matins, the Litany, a weekly sermon together with Evensong were the principal forms of worship. However, under the influence of the Evangelical Revival and the Oxford Movement weekly communion services were gradually restored, along with a revival of traditional vestments. St Mary's was, in fact, associated with an early phase of the evangelical revival when in 1767 the Rev'd Henry Venn, Vicar of Huddersfield, gathered together a group of clergy for mutual fellowship and support, subsequently known as the Elland Society. This Society, which still exists to support evangelical ordinands and clergy in the Province of York, met regularly in Elland until the mid nineteenth century.

The Pulpit

It is likely that a temporary, moveable preaching pulpit would be used during the medieval period. Preaching was not the dominant feature of worship at this time when the liturgy of the Latin Mass took precedence. Readings from the scriptures used the Latin Vulgate of St Jerome, the 5th century theologian. Early translations into English of the Holy Bible arrived in parish churches only in the first decades of the sixteenth century, when the 'Great Bible' was often chained to the lectern. With the establishment of the Church of England during this period preaching took on greater prominence, particularly under the influence of Puritanism.

The first reference to a pulpit by name at St Mary's was in 1662, when it is recorded that the pulpit cushion was repaired. In 1668 the Churchwardens' Accounts noted that 'The Reading Place was mended'. A few years later in 1683 the pulpit was raised and a reading seat was added. Further repairs and expenses continued into the next century with cloth hangings and 'fringes' now adorning the pulpit-cum-lectern, attesting to its increasing importance. By 1826 it had been adapted or perhaps replaced by a 'three-decker' construction with a sounding board above, under which was a wooden dove with outstretched wings. The lowest of the

three 'decks' was occupied by the parish clerk, the middle section contained the priest's reading desk, whilst he delivered his sermons from the top section. Long sermons were increasingly in fashion and the purchase of hour glasses, recorded in the Accounts, are an indication of this: they tended to last a full hour.

The present pulpit was installed at the front of the nave on the south side in 1853, during the major restoration of the fabric.

It is beautifully carved in oak in the High Church style and rests on an octagonal stone plinth carved in the shape of a chalice.A brass plaque on the south chancel pillar reads: 'This pulpit was erected in October 1853 in memory of the Reverend David Meredith who as incumbent of Elland cum Greetland for nearly three years preached the gospel faithfully and affectionately in this church. He died on the Twenty-eighth day of January MDCCCLIII. [1853]'.

The Lectern

The beautiful brass lectern with decorative shaft and base is also in the traditional High Church style first introduced by Augustine Pugin in the mid 19th century. The reading surface itself is engraved with four circular motifs of the letter 'M' signifying 'Mary'. It was probably installed in St Mary's during the incumbency of Canon Ernest Winter or shortly after.

9. FORMER GALLERIES, ORGANS AND ORGANISTS, CHURCH CHOIR, BELLS AND CLOCKS

With the increase in population in the Elland area throughout the 18th and 19th centuries the church's accommodation proved inadequate and a number of galleries were constructed to meet the demand for seating. The first reference to these in the Churchwardens' Accounts came in 1725/6 with a further note in 1732.

The work, particularly in the latter year, involved drastic alterations to the south side of the church where the aisle wall and windows were partly removed and an outer stone gable was built with transom windows to admit daylight. The work involved large payments to a stonemason, a carpenter, a glazier, a plasterer and a blacksmith. A painting dated around 1840 gives a vivid impression of this southern extension.

An early painting showing the gable on the south side

In addition to the extra seating on the south side, a gallery was also erected in the west of the church under the tower. New pews and benches were also installed under the gallery. In 1802, a further gallery was built along the western part of the north side of the church to join up with that in the west. It was accessed by an outside staircase at the west end of the north wall. There is visible evidence for this former doorway on the exterior wall in the use of bricks which now block the entrance. The north gallery measured 53 feet (16.15 m) long and 11 feet 6 ins (3.5m) wide. A rough drawing of this gallery giving the occupants' names in 1808 is found in the Churchwardens' Accounts.

Finally, in 1805, a faculty was granted to allow the erection of a gallery over the chancel, measuring 17 feet (5.18m) long and 12 feet (3.65m) wide and which stood 13 feet (3.96m) above ground level. Access to this was through a small door in the south chapel leading to a staircase and it is likely that it accommodated a choir and possibly instrumentalists who would support congregational singing. Hanging in front of the chancel gallery was the royal coat of arms between the crests of the Thornhill and Rawson families. It is highly unlikely that the ancient chancel arch would have been visible beneath this construction and its adornments.

The priority accorded to the coats of arms of the monarch and local prominent families over religious symbols is an interesting comment on earlier times. In fact, the display of royal coats of arms had a long history in the English Church. Having proclaimed himself Head of the English Church, King Henry VIII had ordered that the Royal Arms should be displayed on the chancel (or choir) screen of every church in the land. In St Mary's the Church Accounts note that at the onset of the Commonwealth the Royal Arms were defaced on the orders of Oliver Cromwell in 1651. A year later the Commonwealth Arms were set up at a cost of 16s 6d. When the monarchy was restored in 1660, Luke Dobson was paid 13s 6d for 'mending the Royal Arms with new boards and rehanging them'.

Seating in the galleries was free and mostly used by poorer people, with specific areas allocated to members of the local workhouse. They were all removed in the church's great restoration of the 1850s/60s. By then many non-conformist churches, particularly along the hills and valleys of Elland's far-flung parish, and the growth of new Anglican churches in Stainland, Greetland and Rastrick, had attracted congregations away from St Mary's. Further, the Evangelical revival within the Church of England and the influence of the Oxford Movement led to a renewal of ritual liturgical worship and the reintroduction of beauty into Anglican churches. The galleries were now seen as an eyesore and regularly criticised by parishioners and in the local newspapers. They had outlived their purpose.

The Organ

The first written reference to an organ in St Mary's refers to a newly-built instrument erected on the chancel gallery in 1805. Constructed by an organ builder called Garrard, it was officially 'opened' in 1806 by one Stopford, a well-known local musician. It was operated by bellows and pumped by hand by men from the local workhouse: in 1835 one of the leading organ blowers, George Allum, died after 29 years' service. His immediate successor, Thomas Garside, in an effort to add more glamour to the role, succeeded in persuading the Churchwardens to supply him with a suitable uniform. On 17 January 1836 he appeared on the chancel gallery resplendent in scarlet waistcoat, breeches and topcoat and wearing a three-cornered hat.

Following the dismantling of the galleries in 1853, a new organ was possibly erected on the site of the former wooden vestry in the south chapel, though a former churchwarden has suggested that it may have been placed in the tower space at the west end of the church.

GREAT ORGAN

1 Violone 16ft.   2 Open Diapason 1 8ft. 3 Open Diapason 2 8ft.   4 Clarabella 8ft

5 Salicional 8ft.   6 Octave Diapason 4ft. 7 Flute 4ft.   8 Twelfth 2 2/3ft

9 Fifteenth 2ft.   10 Mixture 3 ranks. 11 Tromba 8ft.

SWELL ORGAN

1 Giegen Diapason 8ft. 2 Hohl Flute 8ft. 3 Echo Gamba 8ft. 4 Celeste 8ft.

5 Giegen Principal 4ft. 6 Wald Flute 4ft. 7 Mixture 3 ranks. 8 Contre Posaune 16ft

9 Posaune 8ft (from 8). 10 Oboe 8ft. 11 Clarion 4 ft (from 8) 12 Tremolant

CHOIR ORGAN

1 Rohr Bourdon 16ft. 2 Open Diapason 8ft 3 Rohr Gedackt 4ft (from 1).

4 Dulciana 8ft. 5 Viol D'Orchestre 8ft 6 Quint 5 1/3ft 7 Gemshorn 4ft

8 Rohr Flute 4ft (from 1) 9 Dulcet 4ft (from 4) 10 Tweflth 2 2/3ft (from 6)

11 Fifteenth 2ft (from 4) 12 Piccolo 2ft (from 1). 13 Nineteenth 1 1/3ft (from 6).

14 Tromba 8ft (from Great) 15 Clarinet 16 Tremulant

PEDAL ORGAN

1 Sub Bass 32ft. 2 Open Wood 16ft 3 Bourdon 16ft. 4 Violone 16ft

5 Rohr Bourdon 16ft (from Choir). 6 Violincello 8ft (from 4) 7 Bass Flute 8ft

8 Viola 4ft (from 4). 9 Contra Posaune 16ft (from Swell). 10 Posaune 8ft (from 9)

11 Clarion 4ft (from 9)

COUPLERS

1 Swell to Great. 2 Swell to Great Octave. 3 Swell to Great Sub Octave

4 Swell to Choir 5 Choir to Great. 6 Swell Octave. 7 Swell Sub Octave.

8 Choir Octave 9 Choir Sub Octave. 10 Great to Pedal. 11 Swell to Pedal 8ft.

12 Swell to Pedal 4ft 13 Choir to Pedal

ACCESSORIES

1 Balanced Swell Pedal. Balanced Choir Pedal.

5 Thumb Pistons to Great and Pedal Organ 5 Thumb Pistons to Swell Organ

10 Toe Pistons duplicating the above. 5 Thumb Pistons to Choir organ.

1 Reversible Thumb and Toe Piston to Great and Pedal.

1 Reversible Thumb Piston to Swell and Great.

Whatever the case, with the arrival of electricity the foundations of the present organ were installed in the south (St John's) Chapel during the incumbency of the Rev'd Francis Musson (1872-1893) by Alexander Young of Manchester. Finance had been raised by public subscription and the funds allowed also for the purchase of a new lectern. The new organ was overhauled and improved in 1917 but would be rebuilt with additional pipes in 1949 by Messrs. Binns, Fitton and Haley of Leeds. A detached console was included and an electro-pneumatic action installed. It was re-dedicated by the Rev'd Bernard C Pawley, Rector of Elland on 30 September in that year.

In 1987 minor additions and alterations were carried out by John Clough of Bradford: the Great tromba stop was duplicated on the Choir, a stop was deleted and a 4 ft flute was added to the Great, replacing a 4 ft Principal. The present full **specification of the organ** is as follows, with all the organ stops on each of the three keyboards plus pedals. The lengths of each pipe as well as the couplers (which combine the stops) are given, along with other accessories. It will be clear that a pipe organ is a complicated affair - as is, indeed, playing it. St Mary's organ is considered to be one of the finest in the area and attracts guest soloists to the church's annual organ recital as part of the Patronal Festival.

Church Organists.

It is recorded in a diary kept by William Wooler (born 1776 died c1845) that he was first organist at St Mary's and held office from 1806-1811. He would later become landlord of The Fleece inn. He was succeeded by Richard Ramsden, who received one bottle of wine a month by way of payment. William Wooley returned in 1831 though his second tenure was short-lived as he resigned on 5 May 1832 to be replaced by Abraham Hanson for two years. Eli Dyson or 'Dayson' succeeded him but died only two years later. John Dyson/ Dayson, perhaps a relative, next took on the role in January 1845. Wooler noted wryly in his diary that he 'had a good finger guilty of running but [he's] no bouby [*sic*] with time and perseverance will make a good player'.

Portrait of William Wooler, the first organist.
(Courtesy: The Greater Elland Historical Society)

Joseph Garsed took on the role in the 1860s until 1870 when his brother Jabez Garsed held the post until 1906. A member of the firm David Garsed and Sons of Spa Field Mills, Elland, he was described as a 'gentleman' who saw organ playing 'more a recreation than a task' in his obituary in the Halifax Courier and Guardian. A brass plaque to his memory is attached to the organ case, which adds that "the organ was restored by members of the congregation and the stop 'viol d'orchestre' was added by his widow and family. A.D. 1914".

He had been succeeded in 1906 by two men whose service was short-lived: Mr Burns, the Rector's brother-in-law and Mr Thomas, who left the parish. Jabez Garsed had returned to help out but his ill-health caused him to retire. He was then succeeded by Herbert Bramley, LRAM, ARCM, who played for many years until his sudden death on 6 November 1932. His brass plaque was dedicated by his widow and daughter in 1934. Following a period of temporary organists, Ernest Haigh took on the role in 1940. He had previously been a member of the choir since 1912. As the brass plaque to his memory following his death on 8 July 1980 attests, he was 'organist and choir member in this parish for 68 years': a remarkable achievement. His son, Donald Haigh, who was previously a choir member, had already taken on the role of organist in 1964. He remained in post for an astonishing 56 years until his retirement in 2020, an achievement already recognised by an invitation to a garden party at Buckingham Palace in the presence of HM Queen Elizabeth II in May 2016. His brass plaque sits next to that of his father and those other long-standing organists. At the present time the role is filled by Joan Woodall, ARSM, another experienced musician and the church's first full-time lady organist.

Church Choir

There has been a robed choir at St Mary's since at least the late 19th century, introduced by Rev'd Winter. Prior to this, a non-robed mixed choir had led the services. Initially the Rev'd Winter's choir consisted of men and boys but by the mid 20th century ladies were introduced and shortly afterwards girls joined the boys. The choir early on became affiliated to the Royal School of Church Music and was trained by the organist. It accompanied worship for the services of Matins, Sung Eucharist and Evensong, performing settings of the Canticles and Holy Communion, often including an anthem.

Shortly after Donald Haigh took on the post of organist, his wife Joyce, a professional musician who had studied at the Royal College of Music, took over the supervision and training of the choir. At the present time with younger singers leaving for university, older members retiring and fewer singers available, the choir now assembles only for special services. Joyce Haigh, though herself now officially retired after many years' faithful service, continues to direct the choir on those occasions.

Church Bells

The late 12th century bellcote above the chancel arch testifies to the use of a single Sanctus bell, now long gone. This would probably have been replaced from time to time. It is extremely unlikely that additional bells would have been installed in the church until the completion of the west tower in the 1490s. The earliest written reference to any bell comes as late as 1506 when Miles Woodhead bequeathed 40 shillings for the purchase of a bell. Six years later, Nicholas Woodhead – possibly a relative – left '8d [pence] to the bell at Eland'.

The ringing chamber in the west tower was accessed from inside the church by a winding ascent of thirty-three stone steps just two feet wide. Nowadays, the only access is through an outer door to the south of the central west door which leads to the same steps.

Further bells were added in the tower, as the Churchwardens' Accounts refer to a 'fourth' bell in 1649, on the eve of the Republican Commonwealth. The bells are frequently mentioned in the Accounts and were well cared for with ongoing repairs over the years. They were re-hung in 1714 at a cost of £19 16s and four years later needed to be re-cast in York, so were clearly in regular use. These original bells rang for the last time on 13 January 1826 and were finally replaced that year and moved to one of the towers in Methley Hall, by then the principal home of the Savile family (elevated to the Earldom of Mexborough in 1765).

A new set was cast for St Mary's by William Dobson of Downham Market in Norfolk. The cost of £552 12s suggests that they would have been the full octave which are still occasionally in use today. A report in The Halifax Guardian in 1893 noted that the tenor bell carried the inscription 'Fixby 1825' along with the name of Churchwarden Crowther. The peal of bells was soon recognised as being particularly tuneful. Indeed, a local Directory noted in 1845 that the peal of eight bells was 'noted for (its) sweetness'.Their introduction on 13 March 1826 led to great rejoicing in the town when seven teams of ringers took part in their dedication.

Further work was required some years later when no fewer than eleven teams of ringers participated in the re-dedication. During the restoration of the church from 1850 the belfry floor was raised, along with the dismantling of the west gallery, thus allowing the west window to be seen from the church interior. In 1894 the bells were supplied with new headstocks by Mears & Stainbank of Whitechapel, London - a famous bell foundry - and the current bells remain intact today from the time they left the Norfolk foundry in the 1820s. They are tuned to the diatonic key of F major as follows:

Tenor	16 cwt [hundredweight]	F
VII.	12 cwt	G
VI	9.5 cwt	A
V	8.5 cwt	B flat
IV	7 cwt	C
III	6.5 cwt	D
II	5.5 cwt	E
Treble	5.25 cwt	F

Quite apart from their use in announcing church services - sadly, a rare occurrence these days as fewer ringers are available - and at weddings, church bells have long played an important role in spreading news, particularly before the onset of mass communication. Events of national importance were broadcast by peals of bells, such as the death or coronation of a monarch, the threat of invasion or for marking an anniversary. Throughout the 17th century they were rung in Elland every 5 November, including throughout the Commonwealth, celebrating the arrest of the Gunpowder Plot conspirators and the survival of the monarch and Parliament. The bell-ringers were usually paid 10s.

In recent times church bells rang out throughout the country when peace was restored at the end of the two world wars of the 20th century and also at Queen Elizabeth II's coronation on 2 June 1953. On a more local note, church records show that in 1650, during the Commonwealth, a bell at St Mary's was rung at 5 am on most days to rouse the people to work, a practice which continued for many years.

Occasionally today teams of bell-ringers choose St Mary's to execute complicated peals on what are considered some of the finest bells in the area. A relatively recent event was recorded on a board in the ringing room.

There are records of many Elland teams winning prizes and competitions going back to 1833.

A view of some of the bells and wheels today.
(Courtesy of Peter Uttley)

The Tower Clock

The clock room lies above the bell-ringing chamber in the west tower and reached by a wooden staircase from that chamber, the bells themselves being yet higher up in a space accessed by a somewhat daunting perpendicular 'Jacob's Ladder'.

The first reference to a clock came in 1648 when the Churchwardens' Accounts recorded that the current one needed repairing. In 1671 a new one was made by John Ballard. This was later replaced by a new instrument costing £5 10s by Sam Ogden of Halifax, the old one being sold to St Bartholomew's Church, Ripponden. This was possibly the eight- day clock referred to in an article published in The Halifax Guardian which had been replaced in 1859 during Rev'd Edward Sandford's time as Rector. At that time the dial was sent to a Mr Royston of Manchester. This dial was the first to be illuminated and had been fitted in 1844 at a cost of £200, raised by public subscription. There had so much delay in its installation that it became a huge done of contention and described as 'a disgrace' in the local Press.

There was panic when, on 31 March1867 during a sermon by Rev'd John Irvine, one of the clock weights weighing 26 cwt (around 1321 kilos) crashed through the floor of the clock chamber into the west end of the church. Men, women and children screamed and ran for the exit, leaving coats and hats behind.

The present clock by Smith of Derby was installed in 1911 and is housed in a glass-fronted case against the north wall of the clock chamber and has four dial faces, around the west tower. It rings the quarters on bells II, III, IV and VII and the hours are struck on the tenor bell.

10. THE VESTRIES, SCULPTURED HEAD, MASONS' AND APOTROPAIC MARKS, 19th and 20th CENTURY RESTORATIONS AND ADDITIONS

Vestries

It is unlikely that a separate vestry, or priests' robing room, existed in the medieval church. When the extension to the chancel was built in around 1490 a large underground space, accessed by steps, was created on the south side of the altar (now known as the 'Bone Hole' or 'Bone House', following its later use as an ossuary). There is the remains of a small canted window, now blocked, part way up the steps. This early vestry most probably served its purpose until a lean-to building was built in the north-east angle of the north (St Nicholas) chapel. Evidence of the now blocked entrance is plainly evident on the outside of the church.

This outbuilding was demolished in the early 19th century when a small wooden vestry was installed in the south chapel. Once the chancel gallery was removed during the church's restoration in the 1850s and a new organ installed in the south chapel, this temporary vestry had to be removed. It was then that the underground vestry in the sanctuary became once more in use. This all changed when the present stone purpose-built vestry was added to the south-east of the church. Built in memory of Amy Savile, widow of Henry Savile of Rufford Hall in 1879, it is accessed from St John's Chapel by a door, above which is a late 15th century four-centred arch, similar in style to the windows added to the eastern arm of the church by the Savile family in the 1490s. It is possible that there was originally a window above this door.

Sculptured Stone Head

To the right (west) of the vestry door is a corbel stone below the springing of the arch separating the south aisle from St John's Chapel.

The figure is bearded with wavy hair parted in the centre. Whilst several of the corbels inside and outside the church have decorative motifs, this is the only example of sculptured figurative art. It must date from the building of the side aisle in around 1400. By that time the Savile family were lords of the manor - it may be recalled that Sir John Savile had established the south chantry in 1396 - and, whilst no written records exist, it may not be too fanciful to suggest that a leading member of the Savile family may be represented here, perhaps Sir John Savile himself.

Masons' and Apotropaic Marks

There are a number of masons' marks on pillars throughout the church, particularly under the west tower. They are not easy to spot and tend to be fairly simple with straight lines, often intersecting or creating an angle and are cleanly carved with sharp instruments by skilled craftsmen. Medieval masons belonged to guilds which trained them through apprenticeships and supervised their work. There are several reasons for these marks. They could mark the assemblage of specific stones - sometimes this was done even as they were quarried - and, importantly, mark specific work done by individual craftsmen, who were paid accordingly.

These masons' marks are often confused with apotropaic, or protective, marks found in early churches (and, indeed, in private homes). Although medieval churches were built in an age of all-embracing Roman Catholic faith, most people generally experienced a greater sense of the numinous and also clung on to ancient superstitions than in later, so-called post-Enlightenment times. The presence of evil perpetrated by the devil and his agents was seen as a tangible threat and church-goers believed that their church had to be protected from malevolent forces.

One way of deflecting these malign influences was thought to be the use of protective marks in strategic places. A clear example of this in St Mary's can be found on a south pier in the chancel (built around 1300). The two interlocking Vs, rather like a W, represent the Latin phrase *Virgo Virginum* ('Virgin of Virgins'), an obvious invocation to the Blessed Virgin Mary.

This sign is fairly common in medieval churches and is especially relevant in one dedicated to Christ's mother. The one in St Mary's has been outlined with chalk for visitors to see.

The Restorations of the Church: 19th and 20th centuries.

By 1850 the state of the church was described in one local newspaper report as 'a mutilated and delapidated edifice'. The minister, Rev'd William Atkinson, was already making the first strides towards improving its condition. The galleries, as described above, were removed and the belfry floor was raised to allow in light from the west window. However, Rev'd Atkinson died in office during the course of this work and his successor, Rev'd David Meredith continued the improvements despite the opposition of some diehard church members. He, too, died in office in 1853 and it was his successor, Rev'd Edward Sandford who took matters in hand and went on to complete the full restoration of the church. He was able to engage the parishioners with his vision and funds were raised for a comprehensive restoration of the building which would eventually cost £1500 - around £180,000 today - though it must be borne in mind that labour and materials were much cheaper at that time.

The Nave and Aisles

The appearance of the present church is thanks largely to the efforts and imagination of Edward Sandford and his architect, William Henry Crossland of Leeds (1835 - 1908), a pupil of the renowned Sir Gilbert Scott. Still only in his twenties, he had an office in Halifax at the time and so was close to hand and had a growing reputation: amongst his other future projects was the highly impressive Rochdale Town Hall. The large stone gable with its transom windows disfiguring the south aisle in St Mary's was removed and the original wall replaced in his restoration of the 1850s/60s. The 14th century decorated windows had already been removed on this side in the construction of the gallery and those along the north side had largely been disturbed by its own gallery and were also in a state of decay. The local stonemason firm of Hanson Bros. was engaged to replace all but three of the side windows with copies of the originals. New aisle roofs were also constructed of oak, resting on carved corbels. At the east end of each aisle two fine timber supports in late medieval style also rest on decorated corbels. A local joiner, Henry Hawkyard, was engaged in the general restoration.

Crossland's removal of the chancel gallery allowed the wonderful 12th century chancel arch to be seen for the first time in centuries. The original 13th century roof timbers which had been totally covered by a plaster ceiling for generations were also now visible again. Lucy Hamerton, a regular worshipper throughout her long life, gave a fulsome description of the effects of the restoration in her book *Olde Eland* (1901). She estimated that the new oak pews in the nave along with the choir arrangements in the chancel was 'calculated to accommodate nearly eight hundred persons, the whole being free seats'. This was a rather generous calculation. According to the *Halifax Guardian*, 'Considerable annoyance arose considering the sittings in the new pews and James Luty the sexton was assaulted trying to sort out the sittings'. Seating arrangements, as we have seen in earlier times, continued to be a matter of dispute.

In spite of these teething problems the church, which had been closed for the building works, was re-opened with great rejoicing by the Bishop of Ripon in July 1866. The 'Royal Standard' was hoisted on the tower and the church bells peeled shortly before 11 o'clock. As the Halifax Guardian reported, 'the whole neighbourhood hurried to the church where in one common cause and for one common purpose no distinctions may exist beyond those of virtue and goodness alone'.

Two old paintings

The two old framed paintings of **Moses and Aaron** are currently displayed on either side of the body of the church. Originally hung on either side of the east window, leading to the local saying that couples were married 'between Moses and Aaron', they gradually became rather shabby in appearance and the Churchwardens of the day decided to restore them. However, the estimate was so large that an appeal to other local Anglican churches to share the cost was made. This assistance was refused, leading to litigation and they were taken down and kept in the former rectory for several years until their restoration.

Aaron, the elder brother of Moses, is depicted as the High Priest of the Israelites, which was part of the Law given to Moses on Mount Sinai. He is dressed as described in detail in Exodus 28 with a breastplate bearing twelve stones secured by gold chains and worn over an ephod. He wears a turban and is holding a thurible (incense holder) on a long chain. Moses is portrayed in flowing robes, carrying a rod or staff in his right hand, with reference to Exodus 17:1-7, when he struck the rock at Horeb in the wilderness to bring forth water for his people.

Restoration of The Chancel

Lucy Hamerton in *Olde Eland* recalled that in 1826 there was a painted reredos in the sanctuary depicting the lamb of God, above which was a cross. She describes also seeing a

board bearing the Ten Commandments in two sections, the Lord's Prayer and the Apostles' Creed. It is clear that these early arrangements were taken into account in the later restoration. She also noted the pictures of Aaron and Moses, described above.

Much care and attention to detail were taken in the restoration of the sanctuary and chancel in the 1850s/60s when an expert craftsman, J. A. Carey of Durham was engaged to design the beautiful oak **reredos**, **sidescreens** (or parcloses) and **communion rails**. He entrusted the work to J. Moody, also of Durham, whose skills are particularly evident in the reredos. This is divided into arched compartments with fine tracery and surmounted by richly carved strawberry leaf moulding.

Each compartment is inscribed with raised letters containing the Ten Commandments, the Lord's Prayer and the Apostles' Creed. A fine oak door with a copy of late Perpendicular arch gives access to the old vestry stairs on the south-east corner, whilst on its right are recessed seats - or *sedilia* - for clergy and for communion vessels. During the Middle Ages these would probably have been stone insertions in the south wall.

The oak communion railing is supported by stiles, divided by an exquisite perforated tracery of cusped circles. The oak side screens, too, are finely carved with tracery along the top of the rectangular openings with discreet colouring in reds, blues and gold.

There is also very fine workmanship in the choir stalls, particularly the front ones on either side, where tall floral finials rise at the ends of each stall and incised panelling with trefoils decorate each of the four upright backs. Small pillars are carved beneath the seats of the end stalls.

A processional cross is generally attached to the easternmost *cantoris* choir stall. It was given in memory of **Captain William George Graham** of the Northumberland Fusiliers, who lost his life on the Western Front on 24 June 1915 during the First World War. He was buried in St Quentin Cabaret Cemetery in Belgium.

A more recent processional cross can be found at the entrance to St Nicholas Chapel.

It was designed by the church architect **George Pace** (1915 - 1975). Although a modernist in style he respected traditional artistic values and this is a very fine example of his work. The cross was given in memory of Mr Victor McClay.

Mention has already been made of the restoration of the east window and the ceilings in the chancel and side chapels. It seems relevant here to draw attention to both the later rood screen and the rood itself which are prominent features of the present church.

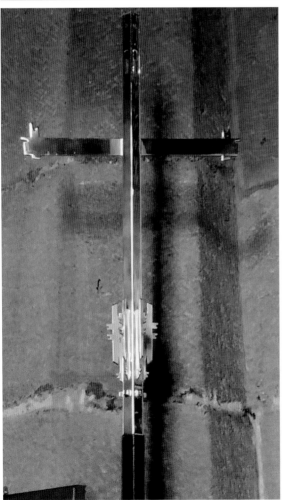

(top picture)
The Captain Graham
processional cross

(bottom picture)
George Pace's
processional cross

Rood Screen and Rood

There would undoubtedly have been a representation of the crucifixion of Christ - the Holy Rood - at the entrance to the chancel in the medieval building which would have rested on a crossbeam fixed to the chancel walls. In larger churches, monastic and cathedral buildings there was often a stairwell which gave access to a gallery on top of the rood, known as the rood loft from where Biblical readings or choral singing took place. The word 'rood' is of Anglo-Saxon origin though also has connections with Scandinavian languages and refers to the representation of Christ on the cross.

The Edwardian Reformation of 1547- 53 led to the destruction of many rood screens as they were regarded by Puritans as a form of idolatry, along with representation of saints and the Virgin Mary. Even though several were replaced under the Roman Catholic Queen Mary (1553 - 58), they were again gradually removed under the growing Protestant settlements of Queen Elizabeth I (1558 - 1603).

With the renewal of traditional liturgy in the 19th century under the influence of the Oxford Movement, and the growing revival of gothic architectural forms under Augustine Pugin and the Arts and Crafts movement, there was a return to pre-Reformation imagery.

At St Mary's church there was also an early 20th century revival of this traditional form. The **Rood or Choir Screen** until recently divided the nave from the chancel with two central doors but is currently situated at the back of the nave pews.

It was erected, along with the Rood, in 1920 in memory of **Canon Ernest Winter**, Rector of Elland from 1893 to his death, following Evensong in St Mary's Church, in 1917 (see below). A brass plaque on the south pillar of the chancel contains a dedication 'to the glory of Almighty God and in gratitude for the loved memory and noble example of Ernest Winter'.

The Rood, showing the crucified figure of Christ with the Virgin Mary on his left and his beloved disciple St John on his right, once rested upon the screen but now hangs suspended above the chancel. Both the screen and rood are beautiful examples of high church Gothic Revival art and are the work of the renowned artist and architect **George Halford Fellowes Prynne** (1853 - 1927), a close friend of Canon Winter, and whose brother, Edward, was also a celebrated artist and stained glass designer. The screen is divided into six compartments, the centre two being the heavy carved doors. The carpentry with its combination of semicircular arches, surmounted by decorative circles containing filigree gothic motifs is exquisite, whilst there is further intricate detail along the overlying wide crossbeam, itself surmounted by a delicate line of patterned figures.

As for the **Rood** itself, the figures of Christ, Mary and St John are beautifully carved.

Jesus is raised above the others arms outstretched upon the cross, the ends of whose beams are decorated with golden diamond motifs. Mary in her blue robes as Queen of Heaven is praying, her hands together, whilst St John raises his open left hand to Jesus, his right hand clasping his blue and white robes to his breast. Christ stands on a further golden diamond motif, the summit of a richly carved upward sweeping rise, representing Calvary, in the centre of which is carved a representation of the bread and wine of the Holy Eucharist. It is altogether a powerful and potentially transformative image.

The Restoration of St Nicholas Chapel

The chapel was entirely restored in 1937, thanks to a bequest from the Wilson family, the memorial plaque to whom has already been described above. The Chapel and altar were dedicated on the eve of St Nicholas Day, which falls on 6 December. They commissioned the renowned furniture maker **Robert Thompson of Kilburn** (1876 - 1955) in North Yorkshire, whose trademark carved mouse was carved into almost all of his work. He was part of the 1920s revival of the Arts and Crafts movement which had been led earlier by William Morris, Thomas Carlisle and John Ruskin in the second half of the 19th century.

It is said that his use of a mouse as a trademark had its origins in a conversation Thompson had with one of his carvers about being 'as poor as a church mouse'. Whether true or not, there are several examples of his mouse on the reredos, the altar and other furniture in St Mary's St Nicholas Chapel. This delightful example is intricately carved on the oak reredos (behind the altar) and shows a mouse perched within a sunflower.

Detail from the reredos in the Chapel

11. THE PARISH CHEST, HOPE CHEST, PARISH REGISTERS AND CHURCHWARDENS' ACCOUNTS AND WANDS, COMMUNION PLATE, GRAVEYARD BURIALS.

Former Parish Chest

For centuries a large **Parish Chest** was kept in St Mary's for storing important documents, such as the Parish Registers, Churchwardens' Accounts, wills and other legal papers, as well as the church's silver Communion Plate. It is also likely that it once contained the Lord of the Manor's copy of the 1317 Elland Charter. At some point - possibly shortly after the restoration of the church in the late 19th century - it was moved to the local Elland Board Office, renamed the Elland and District Council Offices on Southgate, at the reorganisation of local government in 1894.

Following further local government reorganisation in 1973 the chest was given a new home in Clay House, Greetland, once the family home of the Clay family but, after several later owners and tenants, was now in the care of Calderdale Council. This remained the situation until 2021 when the Council decided that it could no longer maintain Clay House, whose future now became unclear. The chest is currently upstairs in Elland Library in the Edith Pretty Room, where it can be viewed by appointment.

Photo courtesy of Glenn Littlewood

Made of solid oak with two compartments, it had three heavy metal bolts requiring padlocks on the main section (one is now missing) and one on the smaller, though these seem to have replaced earlier, simpler key locks, now only the key holes with escutcheon plate now remain (see also the section on **Church Registers** below). Although it is now in a somewhat worn condition, the chest still retains its sturdiness and solidity. It is secured by seven iron bars on the two lids and further strengthened by bars underneath and at both ends and it stands on a later base. Its age is uncertain though its appearance and style suggest that it could date from as early as the mid 16th century though an early 17th century build is also equally possible. It is almost certain that it was made for St Mary's as a strongbox some time after the compilation of Parish Registers became obligatory. As we shall see below, St Mary's records date from 1559.

Hope Chest

Today a more recent oak chest is housed in the church. The **Hope Chest** is so called as it is part of a tradition in which young ladies carved a chest before marriage. This particular version was carved by Miss Beatrice Lumb in 1911, prior to her own marriage and was later given to the church in her memory. It is a beautifully-carved piece of work with floral designs above scrolls along the front and back and diamond and circular designs on the shorter sides. It is currently placed behind the back pews on the north side and used for housing furnishings and vestments.

Church Registers and Churchwardens' Accounts

In the early years of the English Reformation, King Henry V111 ordered his chief minister, **Thomas Cromwell**, to introduce the keeping of **church baptism, marriage and burial registers** in places of worship. Before that time these rites of passage were often hardly ever recorded by priests, apart from in occasional notes about leading families.

The royal mandate was issued in **1538**, enforcing the vicar or curate to keep a list of the details and to provide 'a sure coffer' (a sturdy chest) with at least two locks: one key for the clergy, the others for Churchwardens. The entries were to be made each Sunday under a penalty of 3s 6d (to go towards church repairs). Unfortunately, many - if not most - churches made these notes on individual sheets of paper which often went astray.

In **1558**, Queen Elizabeth 1 passed a second mandate strengthening the decree of her late father and this proved more effective. The first entries in **St Mary's parish registers began in 1559.** Some early records are not easy to read, are written in Latin and give only limited information, such as just the father's name at his son's baptism or merely the name of the deceased. Once again, the requirement of a parish chest was emphasised in the new decree as these were increasingly used to contain such important legal documents as removal orders, bastardised bonds, overseers of the poor records, tithe awards, maps, enclosure details and, of course, Churchwardens' Accounts.

In **1597** an order was issued that required all paper copies of the church records to be copied on parchment in books. St Mary's records were thus written up retrospectively on vellum parchment in book form. The requirements for a safe parish church chest were further increased in **1603** when three locks had to be installed, and the chest opened only when all three key-holders were present. It may be the case that St Mary's old parish chest was made at this time. All St Mary's early original Births, Marriages and Burials Registers along with those Churchwardens' Accounts which survive are now held at the West Yorkshire Archives in Wakefield.

The first page of St Mary's Parish Registers from 1559
(Courtesy of West Yorkshire Archives)

An early list of Churchwardens of Elland Parish from 1603
(Courtesy of West Yorkshire Archives)

The Parish Registers have also been transcribed from 1559 up to 1850 and copies are available in local Reference Libraries and on a DVD, made by Calderdale Family History Society. The first registered baptism was on 4 April 1559; the first marriage on 16 April 1559 and the first burial on 1 April 1559. There are over 10,000 entries in the registers of parishioners from Ripponden (including Soyland), Sowerby Bridge (including Norland), Rastrick, Fixby, Stainland, Barkisland and, of course, Elland cum Greetland.

The earliest of St Mary's **Churchwardens' Accounts** which survive in a handwritten book date from 1648 to 1757, though some retrospective notes going back to the mid-16th century are included. The role of the Churchwardens has changed in several ways over the centuries though in certain matters remain similar. They are lay members of the church who are responsible for the provision of requirements for divine service, the allocation of seats and the keeping of order during services. They are legal guardians of the church's moveable goods, such as furniture, plates and ornaments and are required to keep an inventory of these. However, the responsibility for the maintenance of the church fabric with the financial obligations involved was transferred to parochial councils (the Parish Church Council, or PCC) in 1921.

For centuries - the origin of the role dates from the 14th century - churchwardens had far more extensive responsibilities as, in an age of almost universal church attendance and prior to local government reorganisation in the late 19th century, the church parish - certainly from Tudor times - was the main unit of local administration. Churchwardens held important positions in the community at large. Elected (as today) by the laity and unpaid they were charged with collecting and administering parish funds and thus keeping detailed financial accounts of parish business: hence the origin of the name 'Churchwardens' Accounts'.

For many years there were six (and sometimes eight) churchwardens in St Mary's Church, elected by the townships of Elland cum Greetland, Stainland, Barkisland, Rishworth with Norland, Soyland with Fixby and Rastrick with Brighouse. A complete list of the churchwardens' names from 1603 to 1734 exists in the Accounts. After this date, only Elland's representatives are listed. As daughter churches and nonconformist churches were built in the outlying townships during the 18th and 19th centuries this number was reduced to just two, both from Elland cum Greetland.

Amongst their responsibilities until 1868 concerned the oversight of collecting the church rates, needed for the upkeep of the church. This was levied on parishioners owning property or land; those who did not contribute could be prosecuted in the church courts and it was the Churchwardens' duty to oversee this. In 1601, a Poor Law Act gave authority to Churchwardens

to raise local taxes, supported by overseers, to support the poor of the parish. Early account books reveal that they were also responsible for the relief of itinerant poor, in addition to dealing with vagrants from other parishes who had to be removed. In 1644 it is recorded that they had to pay 8s. 6d. for the repair of Elland Bridge. The upkeep of local roads also fell within their remit at this time, as indeed was the extermination of vermin. The work of Churchwardens was a time-consuming and often a thankless task, though as pillars of the community their role was essential and inevitably influential. Today their involvement with society at large may have disappeared but their duties within the church community still remain extensive.

Churchwardens' Wands.

The importance given to the status of Churchwardens was at one time exemplified in their dress, particularly in the 18th and early 19th centuries. The three-cornered hats and decorated dress coats have long gone but the ceremonial staves, or wands remain, if now reserved for special occasions.

St Mary's church retains two Wardens' Wands dated 1838, beautifully painted with the royal coat of arms and the arms of Savile/Elland and surmounted by golden crowns. An elegant pair of more recent examples, possibly dating from the 1920s, are topped with a brass cross within a mandorla (an almond shape). The carrying of a wand or staff reflects a time when it reflected a person's standing. Its origin also remind us that keeping the peace in the parish was an early responsibility of the Churchwardens who had the authority to stop rowdiness and misbehaviour when a staff came in handy. On a rather less extreme note, another use of their wand was to lightly tap those churchgoers who - shame on them! – fell asleep during those hour-long sermons.

Today, the Churchwardens at St Mary's use their wands only on ceremonial occasions, such as at the arrival of a Bishop or a civic dignitary, when they may be carried in procession.

Communion Plate

In the early years, the Mass was said or sung every day but only the clergy would have taken the consecrated bread and wine with any regularity. Indeed, it was not uncommon for the laity to receive Mass only at Easter. For them the chalice or cup, in which the consecrated wine becomes through transubstantiation the blood of Christ, took on an almost mystical significance.

Generally, only precious metals such as silver or, in richer churches, gold were used for the making of the chalice, though pewter was also not uncommon. Other vessels such as a paten which covered the chalice, and a ciborium and a pyx, in which consecrated bread was kept, were also often part of the communion plate, along with silver candlesticks for both practical and symbolic use.

With the establishment of the English Church at the Reformation, Holy Communion was offered regularly to the laity and there was an upsurge in the manufacture of communion plate. Sadly, very little of these early pieces survive today. During the English Civil Wars of the 1640s, which involved large forces on both the Royalist and Commonwealth sides, there was an urgent need for money. Silverware was melted down and sent to various mints around the country to produce coinage and churches were pillaged for their collections.

Following the restoration of the monarchy in 1660 and the revision of the Book of Common Prayer in 1662 there was a renewed growth in communion plate. St Mary's is fortunate in having purchased some silverware from this period, the earliest being a silver chalice and cover from 1650, a rare item from the Commonwealth period, mentioned in the Accounts as costing Elias Wilson and the Churchwardens £5. John Whittell and his fellow wardens bought another silver chalice and paten in 1669; a further chalice was acquired and embossed 'for the use and service of y(e) Church at Eland', in 1678. All this silverware was assayed in London, as were two pairs of candlesticks from the same period. These items are still in existence though kept in a secure place and very rarely brought into church for services today.

More recent pieces include several given by parishioners. The Holroyds of Stainland donated a fine silver-gilt flagon, once owned by Miss Tomazia Holroyd. An alms plate and various chalices, patens and crosses are still in regular use as is a silver oyster shell used for baptisms. There is an obvious sense of the continuity of worship in St Mary's in receiving communion from a chalice used by many generations of worshippers, including, perhaps, even direct ancestors.

The Churchyard and Burials

The church building is surrounded by burials on all four sides, the more extensive area lying to the east. Indeed, this part of the churchyard once extended beyond the walls and across what is now the Halifax - Huddersfield road. When this was built in 1812/13 several human bones had to be removed and placed in the eastern crypt of the church.

Given the antiquity of the church, thousands of burials from what was an extensive parish have taken place both inside and around the church. The vast majority of these would, throughout the Middle Ages, have been unmarked. Only members of leading families could afford a memorial, often within the church walls. Following the Reformation in the first part of the 16th century, gravestones began to appear for other parishioners who could afford them. The earliest example at St Mary's dates from 1599, recording the life of John Hanson, who married Agnes Savile of New Hall, and who died aged 82.

A stone near the vestry door, though difficult to read now, records the life of a former curate: 'here sleepeth the Bodie of Edward Sunderland Mr of Artes and Preacher of God's word at AEland almost 32 yeres, whose soule departed to God that gave it Januarie 29th 1632.' Some of his children are also inscribed.

Much easier to read as the inscription is deeply - and expertly - incised and also near the vestry door lies the grave of Thomas Lawson, 'sonne of William Lawson of Woburne in Bedfordshire whose soule returned to God that gave it in Norland, June 13 Anno Domini ['in the year of our Lord] 1648'. A later burial is further recorded on the same stone.

The population of Elland cum Greetland almost tripled between 1763 and 1845 to 6,465. Even before then accommodation in the churchyard was proving inadequate. In 1805 the leading landowner, Richard Lumley Savile with other freeholders gave half an acre of land to the east of the church for further burials. Entrance to the churchyard has been from that time onwards through two gates and (formerly) stiles, situated to the north-east and to the south-west, the latter leading to the Cross where the weekly market took place. Even then townspeople used the path between the two gates as a thoroughfare and, according to the

Churchwardens' Accounts, did much damage by leaving rubbish and breaking gravestones, a problem which unfortunately is still with us today.

The Accounts refer to a 'chamber' built over the south-west gate and every year from 1648 onwards a rental was paid - initially 3s 4d rising to 5s - for its use. It is possible that this was a schoolroom, as another reference states that in 1663 the sum of 3s was paid for repairs to the 'Schoolroom' floor. It is therefore apparent that St Mary's was already providing - or at least facilitating - some form of education to local children. This has continued over the years up to the present with the Church of England Junior, Infants and Nursery School in Westgate.

According to even earlier references concerning the local Savile family from the 16th century, it transpires that two of their sons were prepared for entering Brasenose College, Oxford University by the curate at St Mary's, who would probably have provided tuition in the classical languages of Latin and Greek. They were the two sons of Henry Savile and his wife Elizabeth (née Ramsden) of Bradley Hall. The elder boy, John (1545 - 1607) following a legal career, would go on to serve in Government as Baron of the Exchequer (1598 - 1606). He was knighted by King James 1 and later sat as MP for Aldborough and served as Sheriff of York. His brother Henry (1549 - 1621) had an exemplary academic career. Having matriculated at Oxford aged only 12, he excelled in Latin, mathematics and astronomy and as a Fellow and later Warden of Merton College, became tutor to Queen Elizabeth I. He travelled abroad widely and published pioneering works on astronomy, mathematics and theology (publishing translations of the complete works of St John Chrysostom). Knighted by King James 1, he led teams of translators preparing the King James Bible (1611) and founded two professorial chairs at Oxford. He is commemorated by a fine monument in Merton College Chapel at Oxford.

The two boys would probably have been tutored by St Mary's church's then Curate, Hugh Gledhill. It is more likely that he would have travelled to Bradley Hall to teach them than in the church, though one cannot discount a schoolroom existing near the church and that he had other pupils.

There used to be another building in the churchyard, known as 'The Castle' which stood in the south-east corner near the present main road. It was a large building with pointed gables, a tall wooden cross over the entrance and boasted beautiful plasterwork and stained glass windows. It is unclear whether it was a clergy house or had some other ecclesiastical purpose. In its latter years it was said to be haunted and ended up being transformed into a public house known as, appropriately, the 'Ring o' Bells'. It was finally demolished in 1835 when the graveyard was extended, thanks to a gift of land in that year by John Savile, 3rd Earl of Mexborough.

A further building still standing today opposite the tower though empty for many years was formerly the 'Rose and Crown' inn. Built in 1682 on the thoroughfare then known as 'Watergate', it may well have started life as a a clergy house and it is on record that, when it opened as a public house, the Churchwardens would hold their meetings there and adjourn for a drink after the services.

Opposite the south-west gate once stood the Glebe House used as a clergy house from 1807 until what would become the Rectory was built in 1852, at the bottom of Westgate. In 1830 the south side of the churchyard (now along Church Street) was fenced off at a cost of £56; the fence along the shorter west boundary cost £26. The eastern boundary was eventually fenced in 1843 at a cost of £56. This arrangement lasted until the restoration of the church from 1855-66, when iron railings were erected on all three sides. Most of these would be removed at the onset of the Second World War, ostensibly for the war effort, as indeed were countless other iron artefacts around the country.

It often surprises visitors to find that several graves in the churchyard are owned by people seemingly unconnected with their occupants. It was often the case that certain wealthier people bought up burial plots to rent out to those who could not afford one. For a few pence they were able to bury their families though the grave plot could be re-used by others with whom they had little or no connection. This arrangement fell into disuse once most people were able to at least afford a burial if not a commemorative grave slab or upright.

One of Elland's more celebrated burials was that of Lucy Hamerton (mentioned frequently in this book) whose tomb with its tall upright cross to the south-east of the chancel is still well-maintained. It records that she died on 7 May 1915, aged 91. Her sister, Emma, rests alongside her.

Another gravestone of interest in the north-east of the churchyard records what must be one of the earliest casualties of the railways: 'In memory of Joseph Park of Elland who departed this life on the 2nd day of January 1847 aged 32 years.

> No tyrant's persecution could his spirit bend
>
> To freedom's cause he struggled to the end.
>
> At last in prime of life, like many it was his lot,
>
> To fall a victim to the Railway Juggernaut.'

He was accidentally killed around midnight at Dewsbury Station by an engine. One wonders whether he was indeed militating against those steam 'juggernauts' spreading rapidly along the valleys. With the building of Huddersfield Road below St Mary's Church there was no further expansion of the churchyard possible and burials eventually ceased in 1861. From now on they would take place in the new cemetery in Exley Lane, above the town to the north.

12. CANON WINTER AND THE FOUNDING OF ALL SAINTS, ELLAND

Canon Ernest Winter

Ernest Winter was born in Newhaven, Sussex on 1 August 1860, the eldest child of William, a master mariner - probably fishing off the Sussex coast - and Mary Ann. He was baptised over thirty miles further east down the coast in the church of St Mary in the Castle, Hastings on 1 November in the same year. This now former church (until recently an arts centre) was situated not far from the beach where fishing vessels are still hauled ashore with their catch. It is tempting to think that he arrived there in his father's boat. He would later give his birthplace as Hastings, perhaps regarding his baptism as the key event in his spiritual life.

After local schooling he found employment as an assistant in an architectural practice in Lewes, the county town of Sussex. During these few years he made acquaintance with a future lifelong friend, the architect and church designer, **George Halford Fellowes Prynne** who was part of the High Church school of Gothic Revival Architecture. Prynne had spent time in North America before finding work back in London working for the architect George Edmund Street. Ernest Winter soon found himself drawn inexorably towards not only the architecture but also the practice and liturgy

The imposing classical façade of the former church of St Mary in the Castle, Hastings

of High Church Anglican worship and realised that his calling was to the priesthood.

At first he went with an older friend up to Oxford to read for Holy Orders but his friend, realising that he could not afford the time required, left for Lincoln Theological College. Ernest decided to join him and there he came under the spiritual guidance of Bishop Edward King. Following his formation Ernest Winter was made Deacon by Bishop Walsham How at Wakefield Cathedral in 1888. His first appointment was to assist the Rev'd (later Archdeacon) Joshua Ingham Brooke at the church of St Michael and All Angels, Thornhill, a church with strong historical links through the Savile family to St Mary's, Elland, though Rev'd Winter may not have been aware of this at the time. He had not yet been priested when he moved with Ingham Brooke to Halifax Parish Church, where he remained four years. During this

All Saints' Church from the north-east. (photo by Tim Green, Wikipedia Commons)

time he served as priest-in-charge at the recently founded St Michael and All Angels' Mission Church at Southowram on the hills above Halifax. On the death of Rev'd Francis Musson at St Mary's Elland, Archdeacon Ingham Brooke chose Ernest Winter to succeed him as Rector. He was inducted on 7 April 1893. At his first sermon The Halifax Guardian reported that 'so crowded was the building that to accommodate the worshippers forms had to be placed in the aisles.'

His administrative and management skills along with his remarkable energy immediately made an impact. He soon made many improvements to the fabric of St Mary's, particularly the west tower. He also threw his energy into developing the National School in Elland and in the opening of a Church Institute. He introduced a Missionary Association and formed the Church Lads' Brigade. Above all he made prayer and the sacraments central to worship and in his preaching made a huge impression on the congregation.Towards the end of the 1890s the church was packed on Sundays. Indeed, the Sunday School children could fill the church themselves. Further, many worshippers, unable to find suitable accommodation in St Mary's were seen drifting down to the church in West Vale. It was clear that with the natural expansion of the population (Elland's population in 1901 was 10,412) coupled with the efforts of Rev'd Winter that a second Anglican church was needed in Elland.

A site was chosen for the daughter church to the south-west of St Mary's in what were then open fields which were kindly gifted by Lord John Lumley Savile. Rev'd Winter's wish was for an Anglo-Catholic church built on High Church principles. Indeed, he already had an architect in mind: his old friend George Fellowes Prynne who by now had a well-established practice. Funds had to be raised and the Rector launched an appeal for £5,000 addressed to all the 2,400 homes in Elland, which brought in nearly half the amount, mainly in promises, He helped Lucy Hamerton publish her book *Olde Eland*, writing the Preface with receipts from the sales going towards the Appeal.

Plans for the new church, to be called **All Saints**, were drawn up by 1897 by Prynne and the foundation stone was laid in 1900. The chancel, transepts and the first three bays of the nave were completed in time for the dedication on 4 November 1903, at which the architect himself led the procession, carrying the cross he had designed as a gift to the new church. Owing to difficulties with ongoing funding for such a vast project the church was not consecrated until 30 April 1912, when the project was declared 'debt-free'.

Ernest Winter - now an honorary Canon of Wakefield Cathedral - set about raising more funds to complete the nave with two further bays, building a baptistery, cloister and an adjacent hall. A generous gift of £7,000 from a friend of Canon Winter enabled the additional work. These final sections of the church were dedicated on 23 September 1917. The original plan had included an entry through the west end into the baptistery but the First World War interrupted any further work. Following Canon Winter's death in January1917, Prynne added a bronze corpus (the figure of Christ) to his original processional cross and later designed the magnificent reredos and high altar, completed before his own death in 1927. Canon Winter had once described his friend Prynne 'as good a churchman as he is an architect.'

Canon Winter died in the vestry of St Mary's on Sunday 14 January 1917, having collapsed after preaching a sermon during Evensong. He was just 57 and was buried in Exley cemetery. His friend George Fellowes Prynne designed the cross made of Cornish granite which

Canon Ernest Winter
(photo courtesy of Canon David Burrows)

stands 10 feet 9 inches tall above his grave, erected in 1918. As mentioned earlier, the rood and choir screens in St Mary's, also designed by Prynne, were dedicated to his memory. The church of All Saints is in itself is a fine monument (now Grade 2* listed) and testament to his life. The refurbishment of the latter church's Lower Vestry into the **Canon Winter Centre**, dedicated by Bishop Stephen Platten on 30 October 2011, was a further fitting tribute to the vision and energy of this remarkable priest.

13. LIST OF CHAPLAINS, CANTARISTS, CURATES, AND RECTORS OF ST MARY'S.

For centuries after St Mary's was built it was considered a Chapel of Ease in the Archdiocese of York whose incumbents were (and still are) appointed by the Vicar of Halifax. This situation was confirmed following the Reformation. There were times when there was no resident cleric in Elland and other times when the nominated minister lived elsewhere and appointed a priest to act on his behalf. Occasionally these substitutes were not even in holy orders and were inevitably unpopular.

The following list is remarkably complete from the early 14th century with just one known incumbent prior to this. A **chaplain** was the term used for **priests** who served St Mary's in its status as a Chapel of Ease to Halifax Parish Church. A **cantarist** was responsible for singing the mass for the departed in one of the chantry chapels. A **curate**, as used in the list, usually stands in for the incumbent priest. Four Elland ministers became Vicars of Halifax Parish Church.

The list does not include assistant priests or deacons who have also served in the parish. The attribution 'Dom', an abbreviation for 'Dominus' ['Lord'], was used as a term of respect towards a priest but could also refer to a knight ('Sir') and anyone with a master's degree from Oxford or Cambridge. It is retained here where it appears in the records. The first incumbent to be styled **rector** was Edward Sandford in 1868. A few details about each incumbent are added where these are known.

1260. Sir William de Ealand	Chaplain
1399. John Disford	Chaplain
1402. Thomas Cross. He is mentioned in the foundation of St John's Chantry	Cantarist
1402. Dom John de Broughton	Cantarist
1411. Dom Ralph Pillay	Cantarist
1418. Dom Thomas Bogher or Bower	Cantarist
1450. Dom John Lister	Cantarist
1459. Thomas Strenger	Chaplain
1481. Robert Gledhill	Chaplain

1483. Dom Richard Stoke... Cantarist

1506. John Bottomley .... Chaplain

1517. John Brooksbank... Curate

1520. Dom John Halywell .... Chaplain

1520. John Greenwood .... Curate

1534. John Brook ....Priest

1535. Sir John Helliwell.

He was commissioned 'to sequester all and singular, the goods and cattals ('chattels')
of John Savile late of Hullynedge, generosus [gentleman], Chap[lain]' .... Cantarist

1540. Thomas Ovington. The first incumbent of the Reformation. His status is not clear.

1541. John Bentley..Priest

1542. John Scisson. (There was clearly a rapid succession of clergy during these early
       years of the Reformation) .... Cantarist

1546. Richard Northend..Priest

1547. Paul Mayson..Priest

1547. Hugh Gledhill..Curate

1561. Michael Savile ....Curate

1565. Robert Milnes (buried at St Mary's) ....Curate

1566. (?) .... Skolefield. (Status not known)

1575-76. Roger Walker ....Curate

1577. John Leigh. His daughter Elizabeth was baptised 25 December 1577 ....Curate

1588. Richard Worrell..Curate

1592. Adam Wright

1593. Costan Mawde. Died 17 November 1600; buried at St Mary's..........................Curate

1596. Joshua Smith. He was appointed before the death of his predecessor.

1601. Edward Sunderland (buried in St Mary's churchyard) ....Curate

1633. John Thompson...Curate

In the Halifax Register: 'I, John Thompson MA was elected and appointed Curate of Ealand by Henry Ramsden, Vicar of Halifax, by whom I was allowed and authorised to receive surplice fees at buryals, marriages and christenings etc…on condition that the rest of the inhabitants that usually resorted to divine service at Ealand would make up the aforesaid sum to forty pounds by the year or thereabouts so as there might be convenient maintenance for an able and ingenious minister'. *Signed*….J. Thompson.   Henry Ramsden

1650. Robert Towne.

A controversial incumbent at this difficult time of the Puritan Commonwealth. He was described as an 'Antinomian' - someone who held strongly to the doctrine of the guidance of the elect by the Holy Spirit which is above conventional and moral law. He was considered a fine scholar but was ejected from Elland in 1660 at the Restoration of the monarchy. Other ministers also served St Mary's during the Commonwealth:

1651-3. Robert Holdsworth

1652   (?) Abbott

1656. R. Walker.

Oliver Heywood, the 17th century non-conformist minister and diarist, described him as promising 'fair, yet proved a pleasing temporiser at the change of times. He went north: is dead'.

1657. William Tomlinson.. Minister

1663. Josiah Broadhead. (Later Vicar of Batley).

1667. Peter Ashton.

He was buried in the Chancel, 1698. The inscription described him as 'a divine of orthodox faith and sound doctrine: an example of primeval piety and lover of peace.'

1699. Richard Petty. Formerly of Knaresborough he was Peter Ashton's son-in-law. Curate

1700. Jeremiah Bairstow.

Buried in the churchyard, his gravestone describes him as 'a truly venerable man, if the science of letters, probity of manners and sanctity of life have any claim to that character during a term of more than 30 years'.

1731. George Smith.

On his death a petition was sent to the Archbishop of York requesting that the stipend allowed him of £70 p.a could be supplemented by 'Bounty Money' so that 'a worthy successor' could be found.

1734. Thomas Anderson MA.

Appointed on condition he lived in Elland as many of his predecessors did not. However, it appears that he failed to do so, engaging low paid curates, two of whom were not ordained priests. He neglected the parsonage and refused to come to Elland when one of his curates, Mr Schofield was ill. Instead he appointed a young schoolmaster with no university education to the curacy. The parishioners begged the archbishop to intervene.

1736. Benjamin Bayley .... Minister

1737. William Twisleton .... Minister

1746. Abraham Schofield .... Curate

1746. William Stackhouse .... Curate

1758. John Harrison MA (Signed the Churchwardens' Accounts)

1761. Robert Ogden.

1761. Samuel Ogden

1768. George Burnett MA .... Minister

Burnett was the curate of the evangelical Vicar of Huddersfield, Henry Venn (see above) and came to Elland when Venn moved south, bringing many of Venn's congregation to St Mary's. In the Accounts is found an agreement from 1772 when the sum of £40, donated by Thomas Thornhill of Fixby towards the minister's stipend 'for reading prayers in the church' at £8 pa over 5 years, was gifted by Burnett towards 'the Charity School in Eland'. This arrangement was to paid by the Thornhill family for 'as long as the money remains in my lands'. This payment remained part of the incumbent's stipend until recent years.

1782. Mr Houghton assisted George Burnett and lived at Great House, now the Fleece Inn.

1793. Thomas Watson.

1802. Christopher Atkinson .... Minister

He seems to have been an irascible man. A contemporary wrote of him in his diary: 'a bad-tempered man, fond of contradiction, plays off a good deal of authority which is indecent and unbecoming'. When two newly-elected MPs were welcomed to church with a peal of bells he turned the ringers out and locked them in the chamber. In 1835 he annoyed his flock by moving the church clock forward by twenty minutes.

1843. William Atkinson (son of his predecessor) .... Minister

The glass in the west window of the tower was dedicated to his memory and to that of his father, along with a lectern and reading desk (see above).

1849. David Meredith .... Minister

He sold the old parsonage - or Glebe House - and founded the Rectory at 40 Westgate. The current pulpit was erected to his memory (see above).

1853 Edward Sandford .... Rector

He was responsible for the important restoration of the church from 1855 onwards (see above). Following this in 1868 he availed himself of the District Church Tithes Act of 1865 and purchased Batty's Tithes and annexed them permanently to the living. A church tithe has origins in the Anglo-Saxon period in England and refers to a tenth of the income raised by taxation or rents.

1873. Francis Musson .... Rector

Formerly the Rev'd Sandford's curate. It was he who collected up the various pieces of stained glass not used in the restoration of the east window and had them inserted in the two pairs of lower west windows. The stained glass window by Charles Kempe in the north wall is dedicated to his memory.

1893. Canon Ernest Winter .... Rector

Honorary Canon of Wakefield Cathedral. An exceptional man with vision and organisational abilities who made improvements to the church and its surroundings. An Anglo-Catholic, he was the driving force behind the building of the daughter church, All Saints (see above). He died after Evensong at St Mary's on 14 January 1917. The rood and rood screen in St Mary's are dedicated to his memory. See above for fuller details of his life and work. He was the first Rector of Elland as incumbent of both churches.

1917. Canon Morris Arthur Maddocks .... Rector

Honorary Canon of Wakefield Cathedral. The Parish Hall was built during his long ministry and many improvements were made to the church and school. On leaving Elland he became Vicar of Kirkburton and retired in 1953, sadly dying later that year.

1941 Wilfred Lewis Howlden .... Rector

He remained only eighteen months during the difficult period of the Second World War. He then moved to Kent as Vicar of Yalding, near Maidstone.

1945. Bernard Clinton Pawley .... Rector

He served as an army chaplain in the Second World War prior to which he was curate of Leeds Parish Church. He suggested the first book on the history of St Mary's undertaken by D and A Greenwood, which took five years in the research and writing, and wrote the wide-ranging Foreword. He left Elland to be Canon Residentiary at Ely Cathedral, followed by a similar role in St Paul's Cathedral, before his appointment as Archdeacon of Canterbury in 1972. A noted commentator on Vatican affairs, he established the Anglican Centre in Rome in 1966. He was a delegate to the World Council of Churches in 1968 and 1975. He died in 1984, aged 70.

1955. Harry Eastwood .... Rector

He trained for the ministry at St Aidan's Theological College, Birkenhead. He arrived in Elland from St John's, Cleckheaton where he was Vicar. Whilst Rector of Elland he introduced Stewardship ('Planned Giving') to help subsidise the parish costs. Upon leaving Elland he became Vicar of Middleton-in-the-Wolds and was later Vicar of Goathland, serving also as Chaplain at RAF Fylingdales, near Pickering. In his retirement he assisted at services in Filey.

1963. Jack Raymond Howarth .... Rector

He gained a Science degree before being called to the ministry and trained at Mirfield College of the Resurrection, being ordained in 1936. He first served as Curate of St Columba's, Anfield before a further Curacy in Illingworth. During World War 2 he was a Chaplain in the RAF Voluntary Reserve. He came to Elland after some years as Vicar of Manningham. After he left Elland he served as Vicar of St John's Cragg Vale until his retirement from full-time ministry in 1978 with further honorary posts in Haydock and Edinburgh.

1975. Canon John Charles Gore .... Rector

He also trained at Mirfield, taking his degree at Leeds University, and was ordained in 1954. After five years as a Curate in Middlesbrough he served several years as a missionary in Africa, becoming a Canon of Lusaka Cathedral. Whilst Rector of Elland he oversaw the production of the fine coloured booklet commemorating the 800th anniversary of St Mary's. He later became Vicar of St Augustine's, Wembley Park, before returning north in semi-retirement as Priest-in-charge at Heptonstall up to 1999.

1986. Peter Thornton Hirst.. Rector

He trained for the ministry at Ely Theological College and awarded a BA from Leeds University. Ordained in 1962, he served in Lichfield, Wednesfield and Salford before becoming Team Rector at St Aidan's, Bellingham prior to his arrival in Elland. He later served in St Stephen's, Kirkstall.

1991. Canon Nicholas Martin Wood..Rector

He trained for the ministry at St Augustine's College, Canterbury and is an Associate of King's College, London (AKC). Ordained in 1976, he first served as Curate of East Ham with Upton Park and Forest Gate, later being appointed as Vicar of St Luke's, Leyton and came to Elland after a spell as Chaplain of Barking Technical College. Appointed an Honorary Canon of Wakefield Cathedral he later achieved a Master of Theology degree at Lampeter, University of Wales. After leaving Elland he took on administrative roles near Chelmsford in Essex, was appointed an Honorary Canon of Chelmsford Cathedral and as Honorary Curate of St Martin's, Basildon in Essex.

2005. Canon David Burrows SSC ....Rector

He trained for the ministry at Lincoln Theological College, achieving the degree of BA and, later, a MA degree at the University of Leeds. Ordained in 1989, he served as a Curate in Atherton Bywater (Ripon) and Manston (Leeds) and was appointed Vicar of St Anne's, Southowram in 1995. He was Team Rector in Elland until the Team Parish of St Mary's and All Saints' churches was disbanded in 2011 following a consultation which he launched concerning its legal status, there being only one full-time stipendiary priest. As a result, each church was henceforth governed under its own separate church council. At the time of writing Fr David remains the one stipendiary priest in what is a Joint Benefice. He was appointed an Honorary Canon of Wakefield Cathedral in 2010 and served as Rural Dean of Brighouse and Elland 2008-2015.

SELECTED LIST OF SOURCES AND BOOKS CONSULTED

Bilson, John, 'Elland Church Chancel Arch', *Yorkshire Archaeological Journal (YAJ),* vol.26, 1922

Blackburn, Alan D., *Towards the Century and Beyond: the History of All Saints Church Elland, 1949-2017*, CJW Printers, Elland, 2018

Butler, L.A.S (ed.), 'The Yorkshire Church Notes of Sir Stephen Glynne (1825-1874), *Yorkshire Archaeological Society Record Series,* 159, Woodbridge, 2007

Clay, C.T.. 'The Family of Eland', *YAJ*, Vol.27, 1924

Clay, C.T., 'The Family of Thornhill', *YAJ*, Vol 29, 1929

Clay, J.W. (among others), 'The Antiquities of Elland', *Halifax Antiquarian Society*, 1902

Clay, J.W., 'The Savile Family, *YAJ*, vol.25, 1920

Crockford's Clerical Directory, various editions.

Crossley, E.W., 'A Note on Elland Church', *YAJ*, vol. 25, 1920

Elliott Ryder Conservation, 'Conservation Report on Three Church Monuments in the Church of St Mary the Virgin Elland West Yorkshire', 2012

Gore, John, *Parish Church of St Mary the Virgin, 1180-1980*, Pilling Printers, Elland, 1980

Greenwood, D and A, *A History of Elland Church*, Advertiser Press, Huddersfield, 1954

Halifax Courier and Guardian.

Halifax Guardian, notably articles written by 'Yellender' (Edwin Kidd) in the 1890s. Copies held by the Greater Elland Historical Society.

Hamerton, Lucy, *Olde Eland, Being Reminiscences of Elland*, W H Gledhill, Elland, 1901

Hargreaves, John A., *Halifax: A History*, Lancaster, 1999, 2020

Harman, Ruth, Pevsner, Nikolaus, *Yorkshire West Riding: Sheffield and the South (The Buildings of England)*, Harmondsworth, 2017

Kaye, J. M., 'The Eland Murders 1350-1: a study in the legend of the Eland feud', *Yorkshire Archaeological Society Journal,* vol 51, 1979

Murphy, Anthony, 'The Medieval Glazing of St Mary's Church, Elland', *Transactions of the Halifax Antiquarian Society,* ed. J.A.Hargreaves, vol 24 new series, 2016

Rinder, Albert, *A History of Elland*, CJW Printers, Elland, undated (1980s)

Ryder, P., *Medieval Churches of West Yorkshire*, West Yorkshire Archaeology Service, 1994

Thurlby, Malcolm, 'Some Design Aspects of Kirkstall Abbey', *Yorkshire Monasticism: Archaeology, Art and Architecture* (ed. Lawrence R. Hoey), The British Archaeological Association, 1995

Watson, John, *The History and Antiquities of the Parish of Halifax in Yorkshire*, London, 1775

West Yorkshire Archives, Wakefield, Parish Records and Churchwardens' Accounts of St Mary the Virgin Elland. Ref. D79

Wood, Rita, St Mary the Virgin, Elland, Yorkshire, West Riding. A report on the 12th century chancel arch, on a visit made 1 Feb 2011 for The Corpus of Romanesque Sculpture in Britain & Ireland. Report available online.

Woodland, Adam, *History of the Savile Family to 1504*, undated pamphlet.

Wooler, William, diary from the 1830s onwards. Typescripts held by Greater Elland Historical Society.

World Wide Web: essential these days, particularly Wikipedia and Malcolm Bull's encyclopaedic Calderdale Companion, *www.calderdalecompanion.co.uk*

THE AUTHOR

Photograph by Alex von Koettlitz

Anthony (Tony) Murphy was educated at Elland Grammar (now Brooksbank) School and St John's College York, and took master's degrees at Brasenose College Oxford and the University of York's Centre for Medieval Studies. He held various senior posts in secondary schools mainly in the south-east and returned to the Elland area in 2005, rejoining St Mary's Church. He has published widely on the arts and history, including an acclaimed biography, *Banks of Green Willow* (Great Malvern, 2012, 2nd ed. 2016) of the English composer George Butterworth, who lost his life in the 1916 Battle of the Somme. His book inspired a full-length documentary film and DVD, *All My Life's Buried Here* (2019) in which he appeared. He was elected a Fellow of the Royal Society of Arts in 2013 and is a member of both the Halifax Antiquarian and the Greater Elland Historical Societies.